Promise and Presence

An Exploration of Sacramental Theology

'Not just the splendid Protestant text book on the sacraments that we have needed for many years, but also a profound reflection on the doctrine of God, on grace and on revelation. Only on this kind of basis can we ever develop sensible visions of Church and ecumenism.'

Philip Endean SJ, University of Oxford, and editor of *The Way*, a journal of Christian spirituality published by the British Jesuits

'John Colwell's book is a remarkable achievement, exploring a sacramental theology which is both evangelical and thoroughly catholic. Firmly rooted in the Baptist way of being the church, he succeeds in offering a vision of a true catholicity that might be owned by those in every Christian tradition, and which therefore presents an effective ecumenical challenge. Basing his approach in a careful doctrine of the Trinity, he argues cogently that God communicates the divine presence and promises in a 'mediated immediacy' which does not bypass the created order. (In wisely declining to insist on an absolute difference between 'sacrament' and 'sacramentality', the author makes his discussion widely accessible and persuasive.) This is a lively, pungent, sometimes provocative account which is grounded in pastoral and personal experience and draws on a deeply scholarly grasp of both historical and modern theology. The author gives us an example of practical theology as it should be done, achieving its primary aim of speaking about God, while showing the centrality of sacrament to the whole of Christian thought, and offering guidelines for Christian practice without underestimating the freedom of God's Spirit.'

Paul S. Fiddes, Professor of Systematic Theology, University of Oxford, and Principal of Regent's Park College, Oxford

'We live in strange ecclesial times. Who could have anticipated a wonderful book on sacraments by a Baptist theologian? But John Colwell has done nothing less than write an extraordinary constructive account of sacramentality that anchors the sacraments in the very nature of God. He is well aware he has entered controversial ecumenical waters. But he traverses those controversies with great theological erudition and judgment. This book is destined to be controversial, but it will be so in the best sense just to the extent the questions raised by Colwell will help us all better think about these extremely important issues surrounding the sacraments. *Promise and Presence* is highly recommended for Catholic and Baptist alike.'

Stanley Hauerwas, Gilbert T. Rowe Professor of Theological Ethics, Duke Divinity School, Durham, North Carolina

'John Colwell undertakes to derive the mediated character of God's work *ad extra* from the triune shape of God's own being, and the comprehensively sacramental character of the church's life from the necessity of mediation. It is a remarkable effort, and would be even if it failed. As it is, it is carried through with wide scholarly range, conceptual sophistication, and wit. Perhaps it is also worth noting that the work, besides its intrinsic worth, may be read as a mature example of the theology cultivated at King's College London under the leadership of the late Colin Gunton.'

Robert Jenson, formerly Senior Scholar for Research at the Center for Theological Inquiry, Princeton, Professor Emeritus of Religion, St Olaf College, Minnesota

Promise and Presence

An Exploration of Sacramental Theology

John E. Colwell

Paternoster is an imprint of Authentic Media
9 Holdom Avenue, Bletchley, Milton Keynes, MK1 1QR, UK
and
PO Box 1047, Waynesboro, GA 30830–2047, USA

11 10 09 08 07 06 05   7 6 5 4 3 2 1

British Library Cataloguing in Publication Data
A catalogue record for this book is available from the British Library

ISBN 1–84227–414-7

Typeset by A.R. Cross
Printed and bound in Great Britain
for Paternoster
by Bell & Bain Ltd, Glasgow

For
Rosemary
with gratitude and deepest affection

Contents

Preface

I suspect that some may view this work as an inexcusably long letter of
resignation: it is uncommon—to say the least—for any Protestant, less still
a non-conforming Baptist, to attempt what I am sure some will interpret to
be a defence of the seven sacraments as recognised by the Roman
Catholic communion.[1] For those identified in that communion it will be
tempting to dismiss this work as trivial and uninformed simply on the
basis of the identity and ecclesiology of its author. I must confess from
the outset that such dismissal would not be without justification—it is not
possible to be comprehensive,[2] and, not inhabiting a High-Church
tradition, I am only too aware that there may be perceptive and formative
sources that I have entirely ignored. Conversely, for those sharing my
own Free Church tradition, the temptation rather will be to dismiss the
author on the basis of the work: to attempt such a work, by definition, is
to be perceived as having abandoned a tradition.

Of course, were I to be unduly concerned by such dismissals I would
not have embarked on this project in the first place. While I hope I will
always be eager to learn from constructive criticism, a thick skin is a
precondition for writing. But I hope, nonetheless, that both sets of critics
might remain with me beyond the contents' page. In the first place, as the
following introductory chapter clarifies (and contrary to any impression
given by the table of contents), this book is not primarily a defence or
interpretation of the sacraments, it is rather an exploration of
sacramentality; an identification of issues inherent in a Christian doctrine
of God that have consequences, not just for our understanding of the
sacraments, but more fundamentally for our understanding of the entirety
of God's relatedness to the world. As such it is my modest hope that this
may constitute some small contribution to ecumenical debate, not by
seeking to identify common ground or bases for compromise, but by
unwrapping more basic theological issues too often ignored or taken for
granted (in my experience) within ecumenical debate.

But I would be deceiving myself and others were I to pretend that what
follows represents a detached and objective investigation of theological

---

[1]   Some may recall a similar confession of idiosyncrasy at the beginning of the
Preface to P. T. Forsyth's lectures on Church and sacraments: '[m]y position is neither
current Anglican nor popular Protestant. I write from the Free Church camp, but not from
any recognised Free Church position...' P. T. Forsyth, *The Church and the Sacraments*
(London: Independent Press, 2nd edn, 1947), p. xv.

[2]   I remain indebted to Prof. Colin Gunton, my friend and former doctoral
supervisor, for reassuring me on this point at the beginning of my serious academic
studies.

themes. The pretence to such objectivity, of course, is always delusory, but here it is not even being attempted. In the first place, I write not just as a student of theology but as a Christian pastor deeply disturbed by the spiritual and emotional damage wrought by the rival claims to immediacy (in the sense of the unmediated) and agency of which this book is a sustained rebuttal. In the second place, I write in conscious reflection on a personal spiritual pilgrimage marred at various points through the beguiling temptation to those rival claims, but marked more formatively (I trust) by an unpresuming confidence in the promise of a mediated presence that lies at the root of a truly sacramental theology and spirituality. As I confess elsewhere in this book, I write as one who has wrestled with recurring depression for most of my adult life; I write as one for whom felt-experience is frequently elusive; I write as one for whom spiritual and emotional darkness have become common companions; I write as one for whom promise and mediated presence have therefore become increasingly precious.

And, since this is the case, alongside and preceding the more usual expressions of gratitude to mentors, conversation partners, colleagues, and editors, my deepest thankfulness is reserved for those who have continued with me through the times of darkness and have served as living sacraments, as mediations of a promised presence. My deepest gratitude is to Rosemary who has borne with my angst-ridden life with unfailing patience and affection. This is my third book to be published and the first to bear a dedication. It is dedicated to Rosemary, not out of polite convention but because she represents to me so much of that with which this book is concerned. I am grateful to those churches of which I have been a part, that have endured my failures and loved me through my failings. I am grateful to generations of students who have participated in my seminars on Church, Ministry, and Sacraments and who together constitute the crucible in which every theme of this work has been tested. I am grateful to colleagues who have brought perceptive criticism to this text (though any remaining dross is entirely my own responsibility), but who more profoundly have brought the loyal friendship of fellow pilgrims. My thanks are due especially to Colin Gunton for his unfailing encouragement and his godly impatience with my self-doubts. Colin, who supervised my doctoral studies over twenty years ago, died suddenly while I was writing this book. I miss him more than I can begin to express: he was a loyal friend and confidant; virtually every academic thought I have had has, in some respects, been a response to him and to his theological perception; the first section of this book in particular is dependent upon his insights. Increasingly since Colin's death I am grateful to Steve Holmes for his friendship, the sharpness of his perception and his astonishing and encyclopaedic familiarity with the tradition. I am grateful to Ian Randall, a true 'soul-friend' and goad. And finally I am grateful to Tim and Sarah for their many conversations on these themes and for providing, together with Philip, Emily, Lucy, and Rosemary, the most precious and supportive family life.

I am grateful to my publishers, Paternoster, for their willingness to tackle a project of this length and detail, and especially to Robin Parry for his unfailing graciousness and encouragement and to Anthony R. Cross for his painstaking efforts with this manuscript. The extraordinary length of this book is largely an outcome of the number (and detail) of the footnotes—and perhaps it is appropriate to explain the footnote 'strategy' adopted here. Footnotes are intended to serve two quite different purposes for two quite different readers: some footnotes offer brief explanations or biographical portraits to those readers for whom some terms and persons are unfamiliar; the majority of footnotes, conversely (and as is fitting in any academic work), offer further references, citations, or arguments in support of the discussion of the text. I trust that the text of the book can be read profitably with no reference to footnotes whatsoever, but I hope that the footnotes included provide that which is satsifying to both groups of readers.

Finally, and in some contradistinction to the opening paragraph of this preface, I am grateful to Baptists of previous generations who have witnessed to a real and mediated presence: to C. H. Spurgeon for his deeply moving series of sermons at Communion;[3] to Michael Walker for his outstanding study of Baptist attitudes to the Lord's Table[4] and for a series of sermons on the 'I am' sayings in John's Gospel that had a deep and lasting effect on a newly ordained Baptist minister; and to George Beasley-Murray, not just for his magisterial and definitive writing on the subject,[5] but for his insistence to his students that there was a great deal more to baptism than mere witness—would that he had been better heeded by more of us.

John E. Colwell.
Easter 2005

---

[3] C. H. Spurgeon, *Till He Come: Communion Meditations and Addresses* (London: Passmore & Alabaster, 1896).

[4] Michael J. Walker, *Baptists at the Table: The Theology of the Lord's Supper amongst English Baptists in the Nineteenth Century* (Didcot: Baptist Historical Society, 1992).

[5] G. R. Beasley-Murray, *Baptism in the New Testament* (London: Macmillan, 1962); see also *Baptism Today and Tomorrow* (London: Macmillan/New York: St Martin's Press, 1966).

Abbreviations

ANF	*Ante-Nicene Fathers of the Christian Church*, 10 vols., eds. Alexander Roberts and James Donaldson (Edinburgh: T & T Clark/Grand Rapids, MI: Eerdmans, 1993–97 [1885–96])
CCC	*Catechism of the Catholic Church* (London: Geoffrey Chapman, 1994)
CD	Karl Barth, *Church Dogmatics*, vols. I–IV, ET eds. G.W. Bromiley and T.F. Torrance (Edinburgh: T & T Clark, 1956–75)
ES	Henricus Denzinger, *Enchiridion Symbolorum: Definitionum et Declarationum de Rebus Fidei et Morum* (Barcelona: Herder, 24th edn, 1946)
IJTS	*International Journal of Systematic Theology*
Institutes	John Calvin, *Institutes of the Christian Religion*, ed. J.T. McNeill, trans. F.L. Battles (Philadelphia, PA: Westminster Press, 1960)
LG	*Lumen Gentium* or *The Dogmatic Constitution of the Church* (Vatican II, 21 November 1964) in *Vatican Council II: The Conciliar and Post Conciliar Documents*, ed. Austin Flannery (Dublin: Dominican Publications, 1975), pp. 350-426
LW	Martin Luther, *Luther's Works* vols. 1–55, gen. ed. (vols. 1–30) Jaroslav Pelikan, gen. ed. (vols. 31–55) Helmut T. Lehmann (Philadelphia, PA: Muhlenberg Press, 1955–75)
*NPNF*1	*The Nicene and Post-Nicene Fathers of the Christian Church*, First Series, 14 vols., ed. Philip Schaff *et al.* (Edinburgh: T & T Clark/Grand Rapids, MI: Eerdmans, 1991–98 [1887–94])
*NPNF*2	*The Nicene and Post-Nicene Fathers of the Christian Church*, Second Series, 14 vols., ed. Philip Schaff *et al.* (Edinburgh: T & T Clark/Grand Rapids, MI: Eerdmans, 1994–98 [1887–94])
PG	*Patrologia graeca*, 162 vols., ed. J.-P. Migne (Paris: Petit-Montrouge, 1857–86)
PL	*Patrologia latina*, 217 vols., ed. J.-P. Migne (Paris: Petit-Montrouge, 1844–64)
ST	St Thomas Aquinas, *Summa Theologica*, trans. by Fathers of the English Dominican Province (Westminster, MD: Christian Classics, 1981)
SJT	*Scottish Journal of Theology*
YE	*The Works of Jonathan Edwards*, gen. ed. (vols. 1–2) Perry Miller, gen. ed. (vols. 3–9) John E. Smith, gen. ed. (vols. 10–22) Harry S. Stout (New Haven, CT: Yale University Press, 1957–)

Introduction

In essence there are only two theological questions: 'what kind of God' and 'so what'. At the beginning of their theological studies, often daunted by the prospect of biblical languages, of hermeneutics and exegesis, of church history, of systematics, of pastoralia and social studies, I offer this observation as encouragement to my students. Of course, some might dismiss the saying as trite but I affirm it with all seriousness and gladly defend it. There really are but two theological questions. If a question is truly a theological question it is, at root, a question concerning the nature of God. Certainly it may present itself in some other form—as a question of hermeneutics, of ecclesiology, of eschatology—but all such questions, as theological questions, are essentially questions about God. And this, then, is the manner in which they ought to be addressed, not as discrete issues to be resolved independently of each other, but as authentically theological questions, as out-workings of a doctrine of God, as responses to a series of 'so what' questions deriving from some understanding of God's nature. Theology, throughout all its various sub-disciplines, remains theology; and theology is simply the study of God.

Recent years have witnessed the rise of 'Applied Theology' as a distinct sub-discipline—indeed, my first full academic job was to establish such a course—yet I remain uneasy with the approach for two reasons. In the first place, and most fundamentally, to reserve the term 'Applied Theology' for any single sub-discipline seems to imply that other sub-disciplines of theology are 'un-applied'. Now simply as a response to the bookish and esoteric manner in which theological study has so often been pursued this reaction may appear to have some validity—but surely it is that to which it is reacting that should be exposed as invalid. The two theological questions to which I reduce all theological questions for the sake of my students are inseparable, or perhaps more accurately, they are two aspects of a single question. I haven't addressed the 'what kind of God' question in an adequate or valid way unless I have also addressed the 'so what' question. Or, to state the matter with greater theological precision: I have misconstrued the significance of the word 'God' if I fail to recognise that any statement about God necessarily has significance for all reality; I cannot consider God in academic detachment without misconstruing the significance of the word 'God'. All valid theology, then, is 'applied' theology; by definition it must address a series of 'so what' questions. As a student of *Christian* theology I could express the matter more succinctly: the discipline of Christian theology is pursued through discipleship *and in no other valid way*; there can be no valid 'un-applied' theology; Christian theology, properly understood, is inseparable from Christian discipleship and spirituality.

But it is my second source of unease with this fashionable sub-discipline which is more pertinent in this context—an unease related to the manner in which such courses may be pursued in practice rather than any unease with the principles upon which the sub-discipline is founded. Generally (and at risk of some over-simplification) applied theology proceeds by engaging in theological reflection upon some aspect of Christian life or ministry; rather than taking its starting point in Scripture or in the development of the Christian tradition, it begins anecdotally with some event, experience, practice, or dilemma, and then, having isolated key issues implicit within that situation, it attempts to reflect upon those issues theologically and to formulate theological responses. Or at least that's the theory. Having now marked scores of essays and dissertations of this nature I remain troubled by the untheological nature of so much supposed theological reflection. It may be, of course, that a bookish and detached approach to theology at undergraduate level inhibits our subsequent ability to make the most basic of connections. Whether or not this may be the case, it remains comparatively rare for a student on such a course to acknowledge explicitly that questions of liturgy, church architecture, cohabitation, social action, discrimination, mission, church government, etc., are all at root questions of the nature of God. Of course, connections are made, and they are theological at least derivatively (or no-one would have passed), but they often fail to move beyond the recognition that some particular question of church government raises issues of ecclesiology, or that questions of cohabitation raise issues about a theology of marriage, or that the evils of discrimination offend a doctrine of humanity—all these are theological responses but they are not theological enough, or rather, they are insufficiently focused on the centre, on the nature of God.

This book is not intended primarily as a discussion of the sacraments of the Church since this would be precisely to fall into the trap I have just outlined and illustrated. Within ecumenical encounter issues of sacraments and ministry are generally the most contentious but all too often they have been debated in terms of biblical semantics, liturgical development, and Aristotelian philosophy. I am not pretending for a moment that such issues are irrelevant or unimportant—but I am suggesting that they are secondary. As with any other theological issue, questions of the nature of the Church, of its ministry, and of its sacraments, are primarily and foundationally questions of the nature of God. This is the chief contention of this book; this is the significance of its title; and this is the reasoning underlying its structure.

It would have been possible and valid, of course, to approach this theme in the manner of applied theology by examining various understandings of ministry and sacrament with the intention of exposing their underlying theological assumptions—but this would have issued in a rather negative and disparate book. I attempt rather to begin more traditionally with Scripture and the development of Christian doctrine with the aim of identifying key themes in a Christian understanding of God that should inform, not just our understanding of ministry and sacrament, but more fundamentally our understanding of God and of God's relatedness to the world. To anticipate and to summarise, I maintain that God as narrated in the gospel story is one who promises to mediate his presence to us, albeit here and now in a provisional rather than ultimate manner. Or, to put the matter negatively, God as narrated in the gospel cannot be presumed upon, manipulated, or encountered in any unmediated or ultimate way in this present age.

The implications of these inferences for an understanding of the sacraments should be fairly obvious but I spend the greater proportion of this book reviewing various debates concerning the sacraments in the light of these foundational observations. But before that, intervening between discussion of a general theology of sacramentality and a more specific discussion of the sacraments, I discuss the sacramentality of the Church and the Word, not as sacraments themselves (though there may be a case for so defining them), but rather as sacramental entities that confer context, definition, and validity on all other ecclesial sacramental action and event. The book is therefore divided into three unequal sections: the third and longest (seven chapters) being dependent upon the second and the first (two chapters apiece); the second being dependent upon the first and forming a general introduction to the third.

The tentative (and perhaps non-sustainable) distinction between the sacraments and the sacramental will recur throughout this book as a means of avoiding unnecessary and unhelpful semantic squabbles. Generally within the Western Catholic tradition the term 'sacrament' has been reserved for those seven ecclesial rites identified by the chapter headings of the final section of this book. Occasionally within this tradition the Church and the Word have also been termed 'sacraments' though usually with the recognition that both are so in a distinct and perhaps more fundamental sense. For the sake of conformity to this convention therefore I refer to the Church and the Word as sacramental rather than sacraments—any more compelling theological basis for such a distinction will be discussed in the appropriate chapters. My own Protestant tradition, of course, if it has retained the term sacrament at all (and some have preferred to abandon it for reasons to be discussed later), has tended to restrict the term to the two gospel ordinances of baptism and the Lord's Supper with the possible addition of penance (as with the early Luther)[1] and ordination (as perhaps with Calvin). It would certainly have been easier for me—not to say less offensive to many of my friends and colleagues—had I complied with this Protestant convention, referring to ordination, marriage, etc., as sacramental rather than as sacraments. That I choose not to do so is not merely an outcome of natural mischievousness (though I would have to plead guilty to the charge) but more basically because increasingly I find the distinction unsustainable. In the first place an argument can be made—and will be made in subsequent chapters—for the implicit (if not always explicit) ordaining by Jesus of each of these ecclesial rites (though some qualification will be suggested in some instances). In the second place I shall also argue that each of these rites is related essentially, rather than merely tangentially, to the gospel promise and dynamic. But thirdly and most basically I find it thoroughly unhelpful to define sacraments with reference to dominical ordinance rather than with reference to an underlying dynamic—not least when both Catholic and Protestant writers generally tend to refer in practice to this underlying sacramental dynamic before any reference to dominical ordinance.[2] Having stated the case, and though I shall reinforce the case in the final chapters of this book, I do not want to overstate the case or risk jeopardising an argument for the sake of semantics. Ultimately I really do not care too much whether we refer to something as a sacrament or as a sacramental act. I am far more concerned to recognise and to affirm an underlying dynamic as it is rooted in the nature of God and of God's relatedness to the world. It is this that constitutes the focus and purpose of this book.

It is generally assumed that Tertullian was the first to translate the Greek word μυστήριον with the Latin word *sacramentum*,[3] referring firstly to the mystery of God's plan of salvation and secondly to those symbols of that mystery within the life of the Church.[4] In general use the

---

[1]   *'To begin with, I must deny that there are seven sacraments, and for the present maintain that there are but three: baptism, penance, and the bread.'* Martin Luther, *The Babylonian Captivity of the Church* (1520), in *LW* vol. 36, pp. 3-126 (p. 18).

[2]   I hope that it is already clear that I use the term 'Catholic' as an abbreviated means of referring to the Roman Catholic Church, whereas I will use the term 'catholic' as referring to the Church's continuity and connectedness.

[3]   Tertullian was probably born in Carthage, North Africa, in the mid- to late-second century. His writings date approximately from between AD 196–212. He was certainly one of the first major Christian thinkers to write in Latin. Trained as a lawyer, he is remembered chiefly for his writings on the person of Christ and the doctrine of the Trinity, as an apologist, and for his association with the Montanist sect.

[4]   For the development of the term 'sacrament' see, for instance, F. W. Dillistone, *Christianity and Symbolism* (London: Collins, 1955). While Dillistone's preference for the term symbol is understandable, and while he makes an excellent case for the importance and inevitability of such symbolism, it is certainly my purpose in this book to affirm the sacramental as more than symbol.

Latin term referred both to a sum deposited by the parties involved in a lawsuit and also to a military oath of allegiance. It is possible that, as a lawyer himself, Tertullian had both these meanings in mind when offering this translation though it is the second to which he draws attention, emphasising the commitment implicit in a Christian's participation in these mysteries.[5] However, though at the Reformation some Anabaptist writers (in reaction to Ulrich Zwingli's covenantal view of baptism and in response to his memorialist view of the Lord's Supper[6]) make much of this second significance of the term, emphasising what we do within a sacramental rite virtually to the exclusion of anything that God does, it is surely unwarranted to read such one-sided significance back into Tertullian: he introduces the term as a translation for a Greek word meaning 'mystery' after all; he uses the term in the first place of this 'mystery' of God's purposes within the world.

In the writings of Augustine of Hippo it could be questioned whether a sacrament is even defined by an underlying dynamic, less still a dominical ordinance;[7] a sacrament here is merely a sign, a sign that pertains to divine things,[8] a sign that resembles the thing signified,[9] a visible word.[10] Augustine's understanding of the sacraments is scattered throughout his writings and never attains systematic formulation (itself not insignificant for an understanding of the development of Christian thought on the theme). Consequent upon this lack of more rigorous definition Augustine identifies many such 'visible words' within the Old Testament and New Testament Scriptures.

---

[5]   Tertullian, *On Baptism*, in *ANF*, vol. 3, pp. 669-679.

[6]   'The cornerstone of Zwingli's thinking on the sacraments was that the Spirit had no need of "vehicles" by which to impart grace: the sacraments do not give grace but testify that grace has been given.' B. A. Gerrish, *Grace and Gratitude: The Eucharistic Theology of John Calvin* (Edinburgh: T & T Clark, 1993), p. 142. Ulrich Zwingli (1484–1531) was born at Wildhaus, was ordained priest in 1506, and moved to Zurich in 1519 where he introduced Reformation. His works *On Baptism* and *On the Lord's Supper*, dispute the identification of the sign and the thing signified while affirming that Christ, though bodily at the Father's right hand, can be perceived by faith.

[7]   Aurelius Augustine (354–430) was born in Thagaste, North Africa, became a Christian while serving as a public orator in Milan, and after returning to North Africa was consecrated bishop of Hippo in 395. Though much of his writing is occasional and less than systematic he is the most prolific writer of the Patristic period and is generally considered to be the principal Father of Western Christianity.

[8]   Augustine, *Letter to Marcellinus* 7 (Letter 138), in *NPNF* 1, vol. 1, p. 483.

[9]   Augustine, *Letter to Boniface* 9 (Letter 98), in *NPNF* 1, vol. 1, p. 410.

[10]   'The word is added to the element, and there results the Sacrament, as if itself also a kind of visible word'. Augustine, *Homilies on the Gospel of John* (Tr. 80 3), in *NPNF* 1, vol. 7, pp. 7-529 (p. 344).

In the twelfth century, firstly Hugh of St. Victor (1096–1141),[11] and then Peter Lombard (c.1095–1161),[12] formulated explicitly dynamic definitions of the sacraments which limited their number by specifying them to be signs communicating grace. Hence Hugh first limits Augustine's definition by the recognition that '[n]ot every sign of a sacred thing can properly be called a sacrament', and then offers the following positive definition:

> a sacrament is a physical or material element set before the external senses, representing by likeness, signifying by its institution, and containing by sanctification, some invisible and spiritual grace.[13]

The phrase 'containing *by sanctification*' (my emphasis) would seem to preserve Hugh's definition from any static interpretation: something occurs within the sign that causes this grace to be present. By omitting Hugh's reference to 'a physical or material element' Peter Lombard was able to include penance among the sacraments and to identify specifically the seven rites that had already generally become recognised by this time. The term 'sacramentals' was then applied to those rites, such as the use of holy water for sprinkling, which were deemed to have less specific sacramental effect. For Peter Lombard,

> Something can properly be called a sacrament if it is a sign of the grace of God and a form of invisible grace, so that it bears its image and exists as its cause. Sacraments were therefore instituted for the sake of sanctifying, as well as of signifying...[14]

---

[11]   In 1114 Hugh joined the community of Augustinian Canons (founded at St. Victor by William of Champeaux a few years previously) and remained there, chiefly leading its school, until his death.

[12]   Encouraged by Bernard of Clairvaux, Peter Lombard studied theology first in Rheims and then in Paris (where he may have been Hugh's pupil). He became a canon of Notre Dame in 1145 and was consecrated bishop of Paris in 1161.

[13]   Hugh of St. Victor, *de sacramentis* IX, 2; in *PL* 176.317C-318B, quoted (and translated) in Alister E. McGrath (ed.), *The Christian Theology Reader*, second edition (Oxford: Blackwell, 2001), p. 531.

[14]   Peter Lombard, *Senentiarum libtri quatuor* IV.i.4, in *Sententiae in IV Libris Distinctae* (Rome: Editiones Collegii S. Bonaventuri, 1981), vol. 2, 233.9-20, quoted (and translated) in McGrath (ed.), *The Christian Theology Reader*, p. 532. Marcia L. Colish comments that, for Peter Lombard '[s]acraments contain and convey grace objectively when administered in the appropriate way, by the appropriate minister, with the appropriate intention. The ability of the recipient to receive and make fruitful use of the grace mediated by sacraments depends, in turn, on the faith and intention he brings to their reception. Lacking the correct faith and intention, he receives the sacramental medium alone, the *sacramentum tantum*, but not its spiritual content, the *res sacramenti*.' Marcia L. Colish, 'Peter Lombard', in *The Medieval Theologians*, ed. G. R. Evans (Oxford: Blackwell, 2001), pp. 168-183 (p. 178).

It is in the writings of Thomas Aquinas that we encounter a thoroughly systematic treatment of the sacraments that develops and refines the sense in which a sacrament conveys grace with reference to Aristotle's analysis of causality.[15] Initially Thomas accepts Augustine's explicit view that 'every sign of a sacred thing is a sacrament',[16] but Thomas also infers from Augustine (rightly or wrongly) that a sacrament is no empty or vain sign, it is a *cause* of grace, a *means* of grace.[17] Aristotle had distinguished four types of causality: efficient cause, final cause, material cause, and formal cause.[18] This perceptive and helpful classification of causality is employed extensively by Thomas[19] and later by John Calvin.[20] The first and dominant significance of Thomas' application of this classification is his careful distinguishing of first and secondary cause, then principal and instrumental cause.[21] But the pertinence of these distinctions for this discussion is his subsequent identification of the sacrament itself, and the

---

[15]   Thomas (1224/5–74) was born in the castle of Roccasecca near Aquino. He was schooled at the Benedictine Abbey of Monte Cassino and, after studying at the University of Naples, became a Dominican Friar in 1244. In 1246 he became a pupil of Albert the Great in Paris and began his own teaching career with lectures on Peter Lombard's *Sentences* in 1254, being appointed 'Master' at Paris University in 1256. He is generally recognised as the most significant and influential of the Medieval theologians with extensive lectures on Scripture and a series of theological disputations besides his two greatest works, the *Summa contra Gentiles* and the unfinished *Summa Theologica*. Seeking to respond to Aristotelian philosophy (newly rediscovered through contact with Islam) Thomas was considered insufficiently Aristotelian by Averroists and overly Aristotelian by Franciscans.

[16]   *ST* III 60 2.

[17]   *ST* III 62 1: 'Augustine says...that the baptismal water *touches the body and cleanses the heart*. But the heart is not cleansed save through grace. Therefore it causes grace: and for like reason so do the other sacraments of the Church'.

[18]   Aristotle, *Physics* ii 3, 7; *Metaphysics* I iii. For an outline of Aristotle's categories see Antony Flew, *An Introduction to Western Philosophy: Ideas and Argument from Plato to Popper* (London: Thames and Hudson, 2nd edn, 1989), p. 159; or Bertrand Russell, *History of Western Philosophy and its Connection with Political and Social Circumstances from the Earliest Times to the Present Day* (London: Unwin, 2nd edn, 1979), p. 181.

[19]   *ST* I 19 8.

[20]   John Calvin (1509–64) was born at Noyon, France, studied at Paris and Orléans, became convinced by Reformation teaching and after spending time in Strasbourg and Basle, joined Guillaume Farel in Geneva where both were invited to implement Reformation teaching. Though, in dispute with the city council, both were forced to leave Geneva, Calvin subsequently returned in 1541 and remained until his death (despite continuing tensions with the city council that opposed certain aspects of his reforming programme).

[21]   Thomas Aquinas, *Commentary V Metaphysics*, lecture 2; cited in Thomas Aquinas, *Philosophical Texts*, selected and trans. Thomas Gilby (Oxford: Oxford University Press, 1951), 111, pp. 43-44.

minister of that sacrament, as *instrumental* causes of grace; his refusal to identify the sacrament or the human minister of that sacrament as *efficient* causes of grace; his insistence that God and God alone is the *efficient* or *first* cause of grace in any sacrament.[22]

The significance of this distinction cannot be overstated. It could be argued that the Reformed notion of 'limited atonement'—the idea that Christ died only for the elect rather than for all men and women—arose at least in part as a consequence of some later representatives of the Reformed tradition referring to the blood of Christ as if it were the *efficient* rather than *material* cause of salvation (a distinction that Calvin himself was careful to maintain).[23] Similarly, any popular drift to view the action of the priest, rather than the action of God, as the *efficient* cause of grace within the sacrament represents a move from sacramentalism to sacerdotalism,[24] a move from confident expectation to assured assumption, a move from prayerful instrumentality to assumed agency, a move from dependence to manipulation.

Of course, the use of the term 'grace' here, by Thomas and by most representatives of the Medieval Western tradition, lends itself to similar distortion. In the next chapter of this book reference will be made to the tendency within the Western tradition, following Augustine, to depersonalise the Spirit, to refer to the Spirit as a something rather than a

---

[22]   '[T]he instrumental cause works not by the power of its form, but only by the motion whereby it is moved by the principal agent: so that the effect is not likened to the instrument but to the principal agent... [I]t is thus that the sacraments of the New Law cause grace: for they are instituted by God to be employed for the purpose of conferring grace.' *ST* III 62 1; cf. 64 1-2. Note that, at various points in the *Institutes*, Calvin cites Christian preaching, the Holy Spirit, and the rise of faith in the believer, as instrumental causes of salvation: *Institutes* III xiv 17 and 21.

[23]   So for instance John Owen comments: 'If the death and oblation of Jesus Christ (as a sacrifice to his Father) doth sanctify all them for whom it was a sacrifice; doth purge away their sin; redeem them from wrath, curse, and guilt; work for them peace and reconciliation with God; procure for them life and immortality; bearing their iniquities and healing all their diseases;—then died he only for those that are in the event sanctified, purged, redeemed, justified, freed from wrath and death, quickened, saved, etc.; but that all are not thus sanctified, freed, etc., is most apparent: and, therefore, they cannot be said to be the proper object of the death of Christ.' John Owen, *The Death of Death in the Death of Christ*, in *The Works of John Owen*, ed. W.H. Goold (London: Banner of Truth, 1967), vol. 10, pp. 140-421 (p. 214); or more recently, 'Christ did not win a hypothetical salvation for hypothetical believers, a mere possibility of salvation for any who might possibly believe, but a real salvation for his own chosen people. His precious blood really does "save us all"; the intended effects of his self-offering do in fact follow, just because the cross was what it was.' J. I. Packer, *Among God's Giants: Aspects of Puritan Christianity* (Eastbourne: Kingsway, 1991), p. 174.

[24]   Sacerdotalism is generally defined as 'priestcraft', an undue stress on the authority and status of a priestly order or class.

someone. A someone is a free agent, a something is not. A something may be considered to be at our disposal in a manner that a someone may not (or ought not) to be so considered. It is at least possible that Thomas' tendency to use the word 'grace' (a tendency common to most Medieval Western theologians) where John Calvin (not to mention the Eastern Fathers of the Church) would refer to the presence and action of the Spirit is an outcome of this depersonalising trend. As again will be argued in the next chapter of this book, while the word 'grace' may rightly be used with reference to that which God freely does within us, it ought firstly to be acknowledged as a reference to an essential perfection of God's nature, to that which God is freely, gratuitously. The notion of grace, then, as an automatic event, as a something at our disposal, as an outcome that can be presumed, is a fatal theological distortion.[25]

Throughout this book I intend to affirm Thomas as wholly innocent of this distortion: his insistence that God alone is the efficient cause of grace in the sacrament preserves him from this failing by maintaining the freedom of God within the sacrament, by maintaining grace as grace. Nonetheless it was this tendency to perceive grace as at our disposal, this rise of sacerdotalism, this move to view the sacraments under the rubric of *ex opere operato* without explicit reference to the gracious freedom of God, against which the Reformation was at least partly a reaction.

A further recurring theme of this book will be the comparison of Thomas Aquinas and John Calvin: like others, I am increasingly more impressed by the similarities than by the dissimilarities of their thought.[26] Both crucially maintain this distinction between the efficient and the instrumental. Both crucially maintain the distinction between the

---

[25]   So, for instance, Colin Gunton's comment on Thomas' division of uncreated grace and created grace: '[t]hat is another form of the dualism that separates divine and human action rather than integrating them. According to the alternative being suggested here, uncreated grace is to be understood as the eternal gracious freedom of the love in which Father, Son and Spirit are from and for each other in eternity. God's being is eternally gracious because that is a way of characterizing the reciprocal love of persons. This grace takes temporal form in the gracious ways towards us of the triune God, in the economy of creation and redemption mediated by the Son and the Spirit. "Created grace" is correspondingly not a substance poured into us or in some way bringing about effects in our action, nor is it only a form of divine aid, but consists in forms of gracious action that are realized in the free human response to the gracious Spirit.' Colin E. Gunton, 'God, Grace and Freedom', in *God and Freedom: Essays in Historical and Systematic Theology*, ed. Colin E. Gunton (Edinburgh: T & T Clark, 1995), pp. 119-133 (p. 133).

[26]   See for instance Arvin Vos, *Aquinas, Calvin, and Contemporary Protestant Thought: A Critique of Protestant Views on the Thought of Thomas Aquinas* (Grand Rapids, MI: Eerdmans, 1985); also Gerrish, *Grace and Gratitude*. Though note also that this seems to have been Calvin's own understanding: '...in 1543 he [Calvin] could write: "On the beginning of justification there is no quarrel between us and the sounder Schoolmen".' Gerrish, *Grace and Gratitude*, p. 97; cf. *Institutes* (1559) III xiv 11.

immediate and the mediate. Both acknowledge God's freedom as the freedom of his covenant love. Both therefore can affirm an assurance of faith without this degenerating into an arrogant presumption.

For Calvin perhaps the chief means by which this gracious freedom of God is maintained in relation to the sacraments is that of promise. Having (like Thomas before him) accepted Augustine's definition of a sacrament as a 'visible sign of a sacred thing', Calvin offers his own fuller definition:

> It seems to me that a simple and proper definition would be to say that it is an outward sign by which the Lord seals on our consciences the promises of his good will toward us in order to sustain the weakness of our faith; and we in turn attest our piety toward him in the presence of the Lord and of his angels and before men. Here is another briefer definition: one may call it a testimony of divine grace toward us, confirmed by an outward sign, with mutual attestation of our piety toward him.[27]

For Calvin, then, a sacrament is a sign both of God's gracious promise to us and of our responding promise to God. But for Calvin, again like Thomas, this is no empty sign, it is a sign through which God, by his Spirit, accomplishes that which is signified:

> the sacraments properly fulfill their office only when the Spirit, that inward teacher, comes to them, by whose power alone hearts are penetrated and affections moved and our souls opened for the sacraments to enter in. If the Spirit be lacking, the sacraments can accomplish nothing more in our minds than the splendor of the sun shining upon blind eyes, or a voice sounding in deaf ears. Therefore, I make such a division between Spirit and sacraments that the power to act rests with the former, and the ministry alone is left to the latter—a ministry empty and trifling, apart from the action of the Spirit, but charged with great effect when the Spirit works within and manifests his power.[28]

The point to note here is that Calvin, like Thomas, defines a sacrament primarily with respect to this dynamic of God's action. Certainly he acknowledges the breadth of this definition; it 'embraces generally all those signs which God has ever enjoined upon men to render them more certain and confident of the truth of his promises'.[29] Certainly Calvin subsequently focuses his discussion on the 'ordinary' (*ordinaria*)

---

[27]   *Institutes* IV xiv 1.

[28]   *Institutes* IV xiv 9. Clearly a comparison can be drawn here with the Eastern orthodox practice of epiklesis (ἐπίκλησις), the calling down of the Spirit upon the elements at the Eucharist. But note also the comparison with Peter Lombard's distinction between the *sacramentum tantum* and the *res sacramenti*, though here the distinction is rooted explicitly in the operation of the Spirit rather than in the faith of the recipient (a faith that Calvin would have recognised as an outcome of the Spirit's operation).

[29]   *Institutes* IV xiv 18.

sacraments of the Church,[30] that is to say on those ceremonies specifically ordained by Christ.[31] Certainly he then limits his discussion to baptism and the Lord's Supper, concluding that these two ceremonies alone are properly termed sacraments (though see further discussion of this in subsequent chapters of this book).[32] But none of this gainsays the essentially dynamic definition of sacramentality with which Calvin begins his discussion.

To summarise, what we have then, at the root of both the Catholic and the Reformed tradition, is an understanding of a sacrament, not as an empty sign, but as a sign through and in which God freely accomplishes that which is signified, not in a manner that can be presumed upon or manipulated, but in a manner that is truly gracious. It is this understanding of sacramentality that is assumed within this book; it is this understanding of sacramentality that I shall attempt, in the next chapter, to root in an understanding of the nature of God; but this understanding of sacramentality is hardly the context in which this book is written.

As I acknowledge within this book's preface, most of that which is presented here was honed and tested in a series of seminars on the themes of Church, Ministry, and Sacraments at the College in which I teach. I am inexpressibly grateful to generations of students for their comments, their criticisms, their appreciation, and their reactions. And I really cannot overstate the surprised—if not shocked—reaction of some students that someone teaching in this particular College can hold the views that I hold. Most students I teach come from a context in which baptism is a human witness to something that has already occurred, Communion is a memorial service celebrated once a month (and certainly not perceived as central to Christian worship and life), marriage is a covenant (at best) and a contract (at worst), ordination is merely the Church's recognition of personal vocation, while confirmation, penance, and last unction are expressions of serious theological error. I find this context both regrettable and depressing but recognise that it reflects broader assumptions not limited to Baptists, or even to Evangelicals, but rooted in Enlightenment and post-Enlightenment thought.

One outcome of the Enlightenment's focus on the sufficiency of individual perception was a prioritising of the unmediated, of private rationality, of felt experience. And this individualistic emphasis on the

---

[30] '*Verum praesentis instituti est, de his Sacramentis peculiariter disserere quae Dominus ordinaria esse volui in sua Ecclesia*', *Institutes* IV xiv 19: Battles translation of *ordinaria* as 'ordinary' is both lame and misleading at this point; surely 'ordered' or 'regular' would be more appropriate.

[31] *Institutes* IV xiv 19.

[32] 'Apart from these two, no other sacrament has been instituted by God, so the church of believers ought to recognize no other; for erecting and establishing new sacraments is not a matter of human choice.' *Institutes* IV xviii 19.

unmediated is ubiquitous. At risk of over-simplification, it lies at the root of the thought of Fredrick Schleiermacher[33] and of Rudolf Otto,[34] of John Wesley,[35] and of John Wimber.[36] I shall argue later in this book that, notwithstanding his formative protests against the Liberal Protestantism of the nineteenth century, it vitiates the work of Karl Barth.[37] It is no coincidence, I suspect, that Tractarianism's[38] renewal of sacramental theology within Anglicanism occurred within the context of the Romantic Movement's reaction to Enlightenment rationalism and empiricism. Unfortunately (and I can only comment as a distant observer), like so many reactions, the Tractarian Movement's reaffirmation of the *ex opere operato* principle, itself lacking the caution implicit in Peter Lombard, Thomas Aquinas, and John Calvin, at least ran the risk of reasserting empiricism in new guise. A grace perceived to be at our disposal is no grace at all.

Evangelicalism also can be understood, at least in part, as a reaction to the Enlightenment, but this reaction too tended only to perpetuate the assumptions against which it was a reaction: at one extreme it issued in the strident rationalism of the biblical inerrancy movement;[39] at the other extreme it issued through 'conversionism', Pentecostalism, and the

---

[33]   Friedrich Schleiermacher (1768–1834) was born in Breslau (Silesia). He taught at Halle and then at Berlin and is generally viewed as the father of modern theology. Though critical of his pietistic (Moravian) upbringing Schleiermacher's mature thought is rooted in the religious life

[34]   Rudolf Otto (1869–1937) was born in Peine, Germany, to pietistic Lutheran parents. He taught at Göttingen, Breslau and Marburg and was principally concerned to maintain the integrity of religious experience.

[35]   John Wesley (1703–91) was born in Epworth, Lincolnshire, studied at Oxford and was ordained in 1725. He became involved with the early 'Methodists' and, after an evangelical 'conversion' in 1738 became the effective leader of that movement in England.

[36]   John Wimber (1934–97) taught church growth at Fuller Theological Seminary, Pasadena, was senior pastor of the Anaheim Vineyard from 1977–94, and founded the Association of Vineyard churches.

[37]   Karl Barth (1886–1968) was born in Basle, Switzerland, and, following pastorates in Geneva and Safenwil, marked his rejection of Liberal Protestantism with the publication of a commentary on the letter to the Romans. He taught at Göttingen, Münster, and Bonn before, having refused to take the oath of loyalty to Hitler, he was dismissed from his professorial chair and returned to Basle where he lived and taught beyond retirement until his death.

[38]   The Tractarian (or Oxford) movement began in the mid-nineteenth century and brought fresh impetus to a High-Church tradition within the Church of England. Its leading thinkers included John Keble (1792–1866), Edward Bouverie Pusey (1800–82), Richard Hurrell Froude (1803–36), and John Henry Newman (1801–90).

[39]   Perceptively Harriet Harris dubs this 'biblical foundationalism'. Harriet Anne Harris, *Fundamentalism and Evangelicals* (Oxford: Clarendon Press, 1998).

Charismatic Movement, in even greater focus on felt experience—an emphasis and expectation greatly compounded by the consumerism that is a characteristic of our present post-modern context.[40] It is this latter emphasis that I hold to be the more dangerous since, unlike Tractarianism, it is so widespread, influential, and (supposedly) 'successful'.

As should be apparent from this (admittedly cavalier) analysis of contemporary spiritualities, I consider the notions of 'disposable grace' and 'unmediated grace' to be but two forms of a single error—and I hope to establish, primarily in the next two chapters, but also throughout this book, that it really is a *theological* error. And I contend that only through the Church confronting and repudiating this error in its twofold form can we have hope of sustained credibility in a generation that is all too weary of exaggerated claims, unfulfilled promises, and idealistic hopes. Perhaps a renewed focus on the promise of God's mediated presence and action in both Word and sacrament may provide some corrective to a consumerist obsession with unmediated felt experience and may also serve as a means through which a theological account of the instrumentality of Christian ministry can be re-asserted.

---

[40]   For a discussion of the origins and shape of Evangelicalism see D. W. Bebbington, *Evangelicalism in Modern Britain: A History from the 1730s to the 1980s* (London: Unwin Hyman, 1989).

PART ONE

CHAPTER 1

Sacramentality and the Doctrine of God

At that time Jesus came from Nazareth in Galilee and was baptised by John in
the Jordan. As Jesus was coming up out of the water, he saw heaven being
torn open and the Spirit descending on him like a dove. And a voice came from
heaven: 'You are my Son, whom I love; with you I am well pleased.' (Mark
1.9-11)

As it has often been expressed,[1] the doctrine of the Trinity presents
Christians with a grammar for speaking about God appropriately in the
light of the gospel story. The doctrine of the Trinity ought not to be seen
as itself a problem but rather as the Church's response to a problem — or
rather as the Church's response to its defining story.[2] In faithful response
to the gospel story the Church is compelled to speak of God as God is
named in that story, as Father, Son, and Spirit. I am aware of course of the
contemporary difficulties of such language — of the desirability for
gender inclusive language and of the more serious theological error of
conceiving God in male terms — but the gospel story confronts us and
imposes upon us parameters of language which we cannot avoid or evade
without infidelity.[3]

---

[1]   So for instance see Thomas F. Torrance, *The Ground and Grammar of Theology*
(Belfast: Christian Journals, 1980); Robert W. Jenson, *Systematic Theology*, vol. 1, *The
Triune God* (Oxford and New York: Oxford University Press, 1997), pp. 18ff, referring to
George Lindbeck, *The Nature of Doctrine* (Philadelphia, PA: Westminster, 1984); Rowan
Williams, *On Christian Theology* (Oxford: Blackwell, 1999).

[2]   'The problem of the Trinity has met us in the question put to the Bible about
revelation. When we ask: Who is the self-revealing God? the Bible answers in such a way
that we have to reflect on the triunity of God. The two other questions: What does this
God do and what does He effect? are also answered primarily, as we have seen, by new
answers to the first question: Who is He? The problem of the three answers to these
questions—answers which are like and yet different, different and yet like—is the problem
of the doctrine of the Trinity.' *CD* I/1, p. 303.

[3]   So, for instance, the following from Gavin D'Costa: '...I have argued that in
Christianity there should not be a "man God" nor a "woman God", for both constitute
idolatry. At the same time, the representation of the trinity cannot escape sexuate
symbolization, such that the church must remain ever vigilant against a double closure:
either making God male or female or denying that both male and female might equally,
but differently, represent God's redeeming activity in history. If the church turns its signs

At one level, and for the more radical wing of theological feminism, a rejection of traditional Trinitarian language is an outcome of Feuerbach's proposition that all religious language is merely a projection of our own culture, feelings, and assumptions.[4] If this is truly the nature of religious language then it is entirely reasonable and valid to substitute alternative projected language, language (for instance) deriving from women's experience, from felt spiritualities. If religious language is projected language then really any language will do; no language can be deemed to be invalid; no language, for that matter, can claim any primacy of validity. But where no language can be declared invalid nothing is meaningful. If Feuerbach is right then religious language is grammar-less and, thereby, meaning-less; any form of language serves; nothing is significant. If Feuerbach is right then Christianity is an a-historical myth; just another instance of projected language; just another way of affecting to speak of God when in reality (as Karl Barth memorably put it) we are merely speaking of ourselves.[5] Foundational to the claims of Christian theology is that its language is the language of witness, not projected language but language seeking to be faithful to its defining story. It may, of course, lapse into unfaithfulness; its witness may become distorted by its context, by patriarchy, by euro-centrism, by self-interest. But its redemption lies by way of greater faithfulness; by a more careful listening to the gospel; by an ever-deeper concern to be shaped by its story rather than by the attempt, consciously or unconsciously, to shape it.

Less dismissively, Trinitarian language can be challenged, not by its rejection as mere projected language, but by reinterpretation through reclassification. If Trinitarian language is metaphorical (and surely all language is metaphorical in a broad sense), then metaphors more appropriate to a contemporary culture might validly be substituted; it is the reality expressed within the metaphors, rather than the metaphors

---

into fixed essences, an ahistorical idolatry follows.' Gavin D'Costa, *Sexing the Trinity: Gender, Culture and the Divine* (London: SCM Press, 2000), p. 202

[4]   Ludwig Feuerbach (1804–72) studied theology at Heidelberg and at Berlin under Hegel. Having rejected theism he taught briefly at Erlangen and continued academic work in a private capacity. For a feminist example of this assumption, see for instance Carol P. Christ, *Laughter of Aphrodite: Reflections on a Journey to the Goddess* (San Franscisco, CA: Harper, 1987).

[5]   'For this theology, to think about God meant to think in a scarcely veiled fashion about man, more exactly about the religious, the Christian religious man. To speak about God meant to speak in an exalted tone but once again and more than ever about this man—his revelations and wonders, his faith and his works.' Karl Barth, *The Humanity of God*, trans. John Newton Thomas and Thomas Wieser, Fontana Library of Theology and Philosophy (London and Glasgow: Collins, 1961), pp. 35-36.

themselves, to which the Church is called to witness.[6] This form of argument is deeply persuasive. How can language about God be anything other than metaphorical? God, in essence, is utterly unknowable to us. Does not Calvin speak of God accommodating himself to our language?[7] The language of revelation is the language of accommodated expression; it is not the language of limitation or encapsulation. Throughout Scripture, especially throughout the Old Testament, the metaphorical nature of language about God is explicit: God is like a father; God is like a mother; God is like a king; God is like a rock; God is like a fortress. In such a context it would be perverse to treat the metaphor of 'father' (or 'mother' for that matter) as more direct or literal (whatever 'literal' might mean in relation to God) than the metaphor of 'rock' or 'fortress'. But such precisely is *not* the context of Trinitarian language. On the lips of Jesus the term 'Father' is not a metaphor but a form of address, a name. As Robert Jenson has argued, we are allowed to eavesdrop a conversation on earth that re-presents a conversation in eternity: we do not understand the reference of this language; we do not understand its structure or syntax; we therefore are not at liberty to change it or improve it; we may only listen to it and witness to it.[8] To employ the language of Father, Son, and Spirit is not to apply gender to God,[9] it is simply to name God, or better it is to witness to the way in

---

[6]   For a much fuller response to this form of argument see Colin E. Gunton, 'Proteus and Procrustes: A Study in the Dialectic of Language in Disagreement with Sallie McFague', in Alvin F. Kimel, Jr. (ed.), *Speaking the Christian God: The Holy Trinity and the Challenge of Feminism* (Grand Rapids, MI: Eerdmans, 1992), pp. 65-80.

[7]   '[B]ecause our weakness does not attain to his exalted state, the description of him that is given to us must be accommodated to our capacity so that we may understand it. Now the mode of accommodation is for him to represent himself to us not as he is in himself, but as he seems to us.' *Institutes*. I xvii 13.

[8]   'How do we know what God's name is? Only if he lets us overhear the conversation of heaven, across the border of our own non-being and new being. And *why* he and his saints let us overhear one name instead of another we may think equally suited, we do not know at all.' Robert W. Jenson, 'What is the Point of Trinitarian Theology?', in Christoph Schwöbel (ed.), *Trinitarian Theology Today: Essays on Divine Being and Act* (Edinburgh: T & T Clark, 1995), pp. 31–43 (p. 36); cf. 'That God is unknowable must not be construed to mean that he is but vaguely glimpsed through clouds of metaphysical distance, so that we are compelled—and at liberty—to devise namings and metaphors guided by our religious needs. It means on the contrary that we are stuck with the names and descriptions the biblical narrative contingently enforces, which seem designed always to offend somebody; it means that their syntax is hidden from us, so that we cannot identify synonyms or make translations. It means that we have no standpoint from which to relativize them and project more soothing visions.' Robert W. Jenson, 'The Hidden and Triune God', *IJTS* 2 (2000), pp. 5-12 (pp. 6-7).

[9]   '[W]e need to use both "fathering" and "mothering" images while at the same time transcending them both: "The God/ess who is both male and female, and neither

which God is named in the gospel story. For Christians, Father, Son, and Spirit is the name of God.[10]

Stories such as the baptism of Jesus, therefore, are determinative for Christian speaking about God. God is to be named within Christian theology as God has named himself within the gospel story.[11] God is named in the story through one called Father sending one called Spirit on one called Son. God is named through one called Son offering his life as a sacrifice through one called Spirit to one called Father (Hebrews 9.14). God is named through one called Father raising one called Son from the dead through one called Spirit (Romans 1.4). God is named through one called Spirit being received from one called Father by one called Son and being poured out upon the Church (Acts 2.33). In this gospel story God is named as Father, Son, and Spirit, and the doctrine of the Trinity is the Church's response to this naming of God in the attempt to be faithful both to the plurality and the unity implicit in that naming. For God to be named as Father, Son, and Spirit defines and specifies, rather than denies or threatens, God's unity and simplicity. It is precisely as the one who is named as Father, Son, and Spirit that he is both one and simple.[12]

---

male nor female, points us to an unrealised new humanity," the "messianic humanity" of Galatians 3.28.' Sarah Coakley, '"Femininity" and the Holy Spirit', in *Mirror to the Church: Reflections on Sexism*, ed. Monica Furlong (London: SPCK, 1988), pp. 124-135 (p. 132), referring to Rosemary Radford Ruether, 'The Female Nature of God: A Problem in Contemporary Religious Life', in J. B. Metz and E. Schillebeeckx (eds.), *'God as Father?': Concilium* 143 (New York: Seabury Press/Edinburgh: T & T Clark, 1981), pp. 61-66 (pp. 65-66): 'God(ess) must be seen as beyond maleness and femaleness. Encompassing the full humanity of both men and women... God(ess) restores both men and women to full humanity... The God(ess) who is both male and female, and neither male or female, points us to an unrealised new humanity' (p. 66).

[10]   'Thus the phrase "Father, Son, and Holy Spirit" is simultaneously a very compressed telling of the total narrative by which Scripture identifies God and a personal name for the God so specified; in it, name and narrative description not only appear together, as at the beginning of the Ten Commandments, but are identical. By virtue of this logic, the triune phrase offers itself as the unique name for the Christian God, and is then dogmatically mandated for that function by its constitutive place in the rite that establishes Christian identity. The church is the community and a Christian is someone who, when the identity of God is important, names him "Father, Son, and Holy Spirit." Those who do not or will not belong to some other community.' Jenson, *Systematic Theology*, vol. 1, p. 46.

[11]   While I am not entirely persuaded by the arguments of Robert Jenson in his essay 'The Father, he...', in Kimel, Jr. (ed.), *Speaking the Christian God*, pp. 95-109, and while I am content to use the word 'God' as a pronoun (as in the phrase 'God-self', for instance) I do find the expression awkward and artificial. Nonetheless, I trust that I do enough throughout this book to clarify that in following the tradition by using the male third-person pronoun with reference to God I am certainly not implying that God is male.

[12]   As my friend and colleague Steve Holmes indicates, the doctrine of the Trinity is the expression of the simplicity of this God rather than the denial of that simplicity.

And it is hardly surprising that the Church struggled and struggles to express a faithful response to this narrative naming. This is advanced grammar, not first-year Latin. Tensions in how to express this unity in plurality and plurality in unity issued in the great schism between the Eastern and Western traditions. That distinction, essentially a distinction between the thought of Augustine and the thought of those collectively known as the Cappadocian Fathers,[13] will be crucial for the argument in the latter part of this chapter. But initially it is sufficient to engage with what unites rather than what divides those traditions—with the simple affirmation of plurality within unity—without engaging too specifically with the manner in which such plurality and unity may be properly expressed.

As will be noted again later in this chapter, when Augustine deduces a Trinity from the statement 'God is love' he initiates a series of unhelpful moves. For God to be love, argues Augustine, implies a lover, a beloved, and love itself.[14] Which may sound quite persuasive until one realises that what has been deduced is a duality or 'binity' rather than a Trinity; there are but two 'persons' here; the Spirit, as love, has been depersonalised. And in this implicit depersonalisation of the Spirit, one suspects, lies the root of much that has proved problematic in Western theology. To depersonalise the Spirit is to reduce the Spirit to an object, all too easily perceived to be at our disposal. To depersonalise the Spirit, therefore, is to invite all the distortions of manipulation that have beset the Western Church, not just in interpretations of sacramental theology, but also in interpretations of spiritual experience in terms of impersonal and indeterminate power rather than personal and transforming presence. Moreover—as also will be argued later—any minimising of the rôle of the Spirit will issue in a tendency towards the unmediated rather than the mediated.

But all this is to anticipate the second and subsidiary theme of this chapter. Augustine's fundamental mistake here, surely, is the direction (or form) of his logic, his unexpected move to deduce rather than to infer. I say 'unexpected' since, until this point in *De Trinitate*, Augustine's dominant concern has been to reflect prayerfully upon the gospel story: he may not always achieve this persuasively, but this (at least for the most part) is the direction and form of his argument, inferring theological conclusions from the narrative of Scripture. Then abruptly,

---

Stephen R. Holmes, '"Something Much Too Plain to Say": Towards a Defence of the Doctrine of Divine Simplicity', in *Listening to the Past: The Place of Tradition in Theology* (Carlisle: Paternoster Press, 2002), pp. 50- 67; cf. *ST* I 3 1-8.

[13]   This gender exclusive title itself ignores the influence of Macrina on the thought of her brothers Basil and Gregory (see below).

[14]   'There, then, also are three things: he that loves, and that which is loved, and love.' Augustine, *On the Holy Trinity*, in *NPNF* 1, vol. 3, VIII x 14, pp. 17-228 (p. 124).

after a brief interlude in which he notes the Cappadocians' rather different treatment of the matter, he changes direction in the attempt to deduce a Trinity from a theological proposition. Why?[15] Surely Scripture itself infers God's nature as love from the gospel story in its Trinitarian form:

> This is how God showed his love among us: He sent his one and only Son into the world that we might live through him. This is love: not that we loved God, but that he loved us and sent his Son as an atoning sacrifice for our sins. (1 John 4.9-10)

It is not, then, that a doctrine of the Trinity is a deduction from the theological proposition that God is love; it is rather that the proposition that God is love is an inference (indeed, a scriptural inference) from the Trinitarian shape of the gospel story. Indeed, if Augustine can validly be criticised—as he has been criticised—for conceiving arbitrary will, rather than loving will, as essential to God, this may in part be an outcome of the insufficient grounding of his affirmation of God's lovingness in the gospel narrative and its Trinitarian shape.[16] And if Western theology more generally can validly be criticised—as it has been criticised—for a tendency to focus upon divine arbitrariness rather than divine lovingness, this may be an outcome of a residual monarchianism,[17] a tendency to resolve a doctrine of the Trinity in the implicitly unitarian direction of a single and inscrutable divine sovereignty.[18]

---

[15]   In response to this question we might note that the book was a very long time in the writing and its final publication seems to have been prompted by an unrevised section of it having been made public without Augustine's consent.

[16]   This tendency in Augustine is especially pronounced in his later anti-Pelagian writings: Augustine, *Anti-Pelagian Writings*, in *NPNF* 1, vol. 5.

[17]   Monarchianism was a term coined by Tertullian (and others) to refer to two quite different evasions of a doctrine of the Trinity, both emphasising the single rulership of the one God: Tertullian, *Against Praxeas* in *ANF*, vol. 3, pp. 597-627.

[18]   'At the fountainhead of the Western treatment of creation is Augustine's subtly altered account of the matter... [I]n his theology, the mediation by Christ and the Spirit, as well as the teleological directedness of the creation, play too limited a role, a first effect is that the link, so beautifully maintained in Irenaeus between creation and redemption, becomes weakened to the point of disappearing, so that it is rarely adequately treated in Western theology after this time. And second it comes to be that the theme of love becomes subordinate to that of will. If not in Augustine, certainly in those who learned from him, creation becomes very much the product of pure, unmotivated and therefore arbitrary will, a will that operates equally arbitrarily in the theology of double predestination that became after him so much a mark of the Western tradition.' Colin E. Gunton, *The One, The Three and the Many: God, Creation and the Culture of Modernity*, The Bampton Lectures 1992 (Cambridge: Cambridge University Press, 1993), pp. 120-121.

The doctrine of the Trinity is the Church's reflection upon the naming of God in the gospel story as Father, Son, and Spirit; it is the Church's faithful acknowledgement that God is in eternity as he is named here; it is the affirmation that this threeness in oneness and oneness in threeness is the truth of God eternally; it is the confession that eternally in God there is intimacy, relationship, covenant love. Or, to reverse the direction of Augustine's deduction: only because God is affirmed as Triune in response to the gospel story can God be affirmed as eternally loving.

Now I realise that this final proposition is signally politically incorrect; it is deeply offensive to Judaism, to Islam, to Jehovah's Witnesses—but it is the truth inversely consequent upon Augustine's deduction or, more accurately, it is the manner in which the Church's confession of God's lovingness occurs. The scriptural confession that 'God is love' (1 John 4.8 and 16) is stark and unqualified—philosophically we must recognise the impossibility of affirming that God *is* anything—Augustine, therefore, is entirely justified in focusing on the significance of the confession (would that the tradition had focused upon it more consistently), and even if his deduction may be an inappropriate and ineffective means of deriving a doctrine of the Trinity, it is nonetheless valid albeit negatively: to affirm God as loving without at the same time affirming some form of plurality in God is simply incoherent (and it is incumbent upon 'monistic' faiths to explain how, within the bounds of monism, such incoherence may be overcome).

If God is God then every form of dualism is excluded; God is God alone; there is no other eternal reality; all other reality is contingent; the doctrine of creation out of nothing (which will be explored in the next chapter) is an inevitable consequence of the simple affirmation that God is God. But if God is love, as Augustine rightly observes, this implies a dynamic of loving; it implies both a subject and an object; it implies plurality. Therefore if God is truly God and if God is truly love this can only imply some plurality in God. This may be an invalid means of deriving a doctrine of the Trinity—as we have seen, it doesn't even necessarily issue in a *Tri*nity; a doctrine of the Trinity is only properly derived through reflection on the gospel—but it is nonetheless a valid deduction with respect to what it excludes.

The urge to ignore this negative deduction is, of course, overwhelming. Especially in our more recent and sanitised context, the notion of God as sheer arbitrary will is highly unattractive if not repulsive: God so conceived—as sadly God has too often been conceived within the Western tradition—is indistinguishable from a capricious omnipotent tyrant. Consequently, in our contemporary context, the assumption of God's lovingness is generally accepted and rarely disputed. But all too easily God's lovingness is affirmed without explicit reference to his Triunity and at the expense of God's 'Godness', or, rather, God's lovingness is affirmed by some implicit qualification or redefinition of the word 'God'. That is to say, all too often God's lovingness is affirmed by assuming creation to be in some sense necessary to God. This strategy takes a variety of forms and poses under a variety of names, but whether it is the notion of God's becoming as expressed within the process theology of Charles Hartshorne,[19] or the all too common and glib refutation of divine impassability in the misguided attempt to render God's lovingness in terms of an all too transient affectation and responsiveness,[20] its implication is the same: God's lovingness is conceived in terms of God's relatedness to creation; and creation therefore is conceived as in some way necessary to God for God to be defined as loving.

But, in the first place, if creation has been rendered necessary to God for God to be defined as loving, then God as loving is no longer God alone without creation; if God is eternally loving then creation must participate in God's eternity; God is no longer 'God'. Moreover, in the second place, if God's love for creation is necessary for God to be defined as loving, then God's love for creation is 'unfree', and love that is unfree or necessitated surely isn't authentic love. That is to say, this strategy of conceiving God as loving in relation to creation does not merely threaten the 'Godness' of God, it also threatens the lovingness of God's love; it, in fact, undermines the very thing it was devised to affirm. The point is made with great effect in Thomas Weinandy's masterly response to affirmations of divine passability: the misguided (not to say misinformed) urge to conceive of God as affected by creation, as suffering and changing in response to creation, actually issues in a conception of God as less loving than the 'impassable' God of the Christian tradition; the 'impassable' God of the Christian tradition was already perfectly loving in himself as Father, Son, and Spirit.[21] Only if God, as truly God, is truly loving in himself, without reference to creation, can God's love for that which is not himself be conceived as truly loving, as free, as unnecessitated, as grace. The point was made previously by Karl Barth in rejection of universalism (the notion that all men and

---

[19]   See for instance, Charles Hartshorne, *Man's Vision of God and the Logic of Theism* (New York: Harper, 1941), or *A Natural Theology for our Time* (La Salle: Open Court, 1967).

[20]   So for instance, '[t]he God of theism is poor. He cannot love nor can he suffer.' Jürgen Moltmann, *The Crucified God: The Cross of Christ as the Foundation and Criticism of Christian Theology*, trans. R. A. Wilson, and J. Bowden (London: SCM Press, 1974), p. 253; cf. Paul S. Fiddes, *The Creative Suffering of God* (Oxford: Clarendon Press, 1988); and the more recent 'open-theism' movement represented by Clark H. Pinnock, *Most Moved Mover: A Theology of God's Openness* (Carlisle: Paternoster Press, 2001).

[21]   Thomas G. Weinandy, *Does God Suffer?* (Edinburgh: T & T Clark, 2000).

women will necessarily be saved or restored): to infer ultimate salvation as a necessary consequence of God's love is to render God's love as dependent upon ultimate salvation (i.e., if all men and women are not ultimately saved then God is not truly loving); but love which is necessitated is not love; love which is necessitated is not grace; only if God does not have to love can his love be seen as free, as gratuitous. And precisely because God is love in himself, in the perfect intimacy and communion of Father, Son, and Spirit, God's love for us takes the form of grace, it is unnecessitated, it is free.[22]

This recognition of divine freedom, of course, underlies the entirety of Barth's theological thought. That God is the one who reveals himself as Lord is, as Colin Gunton rightly recognises, simply what Barth means in his prolegomena by the word God.[23] God is *Gegenstand* not *Objekt*; he is irreducibly the subject of every encounter, never the object; he stands over against us and confronts us; he never submits himself to our scrutiny; he never falls into our hands; he reveals himself to us precisely in his hiddenness; he reveals himself to us but never in such a way that renders him at our disposal; he gives himself to us but he never gives himself away.[24] It is within this context that Barth discusses the threefold form of the Word of God: the Word of God in Scripture and in Christian preaching similarly is never at our disposal; the Word of God is God himself in his revelation; the Word of God is being given, it is never simply given.[25]

Barth's stress upon the freedom of God in revelation is rightly recognised as continuous with his earlier emphases in, for instance,

---

[22]   'If we are to respect the freedom of divine grace, we cannot venture the statement that it must and will finally be coincident with the world of man as such (as in the doctrine of the so-called *apokatastasis*). No such right or necessity can legitimately be deduced. Just as the gracious God does not need to elect or call any single man, so He does not need to elect or call all mankind.' *CD* II/2, p. 417.

[23]   'An exposition of Barth's arguments in his development of the doctrine of the Trinity will reveal that his phrase "God reveals himself as the Lord" performs for him the same function that "that than which no greater can be conceived" performed for Anselm: it provides him with reasons for using the word *God* in rational discourse.' Colin E. Gunton, *Becoming and Being: The Doctrine of God in Charles Hartshorne and Karl Barth* (Oxford: Oxford University Press, 1978), p. 125.

[24]   'The speech of God is and remains a mystery to the extent that its totality as such, and hence with all the weight and seriousness of God's Word, is always manifest to us only on one side and always remains hidden on the other side.' *CD* I/1, p. 174

[25]   'If in respect of the event of hearing God's Word we do not point to a datum in man's existence, nor to the limit of all the data of human existence, nor finally to the possibility of a contingent experience, but only to faith, and that means to the Holy Spirit, we are simply confirming what was said at the beginning...namely, that the question "What is the Word of God?" can be answered only by indicating the How of God's Word in an interpretation of its threefold form.' *CD* I/1, p. 186.

Romans[26] and *The Word of God and the Word of Man.*[27] Here as there, the emphasis seems to fall on what cannot and must not be said; an emphasis more on the divine 'No' than the divine 'Yes'; the freedom of God as the Lord; the freedom of God from any form of external necessity or constraint. It is important to recognise therefore, that when he comes to his discussion of the doctrine of God, Barth seems almost to make yet another fresh beginning, commencing his discussion again with God's 'knowability' and, most pertinently, offering a fresh definition of God—whereas for volume one of the *Church Dogmatics* God is 'the One who reveals Himself as Lord', in volume two and thereafter the God of the gospel is 'the One who Loves in Freedom'.[28]

In this definition we encounter the 'Yes' of the gospel that was to dominate and to give shape to the remainder of Barth's theological work. It is a 'Yes' that could not be uttered without previously uttering the 'No'; without previously affirming God's 'Godness'; without previously affirming God's freedom from every form of external necessity or constraint; without previously repudiating every form of human religion that seeks to define, confine or control. But it is a 'Yes' that enfolds and totally overwhelms the 'No'. God as narrated in the gospel story is the free Lord; he is unnecessitated and unconstrained; he is truly 'God'—but he is not capricious or arbitrary; his freedom is not indeterminate; his freedom is the freedom of his love; his freedom is *his* freedom, the freedom of the Father, the Son, and the Spirit, the freedom of the one who is eternally perfectly loving in this communion and intimacy. God's aseity and simplicity as Father, Son, and Spirit is the aseity and simplicity of perfect love. God does not need that which is other than himself to love in order to be perfectly loving, he is already and eternally perfectly loving in the communion of Father, Son, and Spirit without that which is other than himself. But that God does love that which is other than himself, that through the Son and the Spirit he creates and redeems, is not arbitrary or capricious, it is entirely consistent and not inconsistent with God's eternal nature; it is unnecessitated but it is not incoherent; it is a free and gracious reiteration of God's love within himself for that which is other than himself.[29]

---

[26]   Karl Barth, *The Epistle to the Romans*, trans. Edwyn C. Hoskyns from 6th edition (London, Oxford and New York: Oxford University Press, 1933).

[27]   Karl Barth, *The Word of God and the Word of Man*, trans. Douglas Horton (London: Hodder & Stoughton, 1928).

[28]   'God is who He is in the act of His revelation. God seeks and creates fellowship between Himself and us, and therefore He loves us. But He is this loving God without us as Father, Son and Holy Spirit, in the freedom of the Lord, who has His life from Himself.' *CD* II/1, p. 257.

[29]   'God's loving is necessary, for it is the being, essence and the nature of God. But for this very reason it is also free from every necessity in respect of its object. God

Now I realise that all this is not easy to follow, it is simple, but it is not easy for us to grasp (though this says more about us than about the gospel). In a culture of modernity we have come to associate freedom with arbitrary choice (though modernity's assumption may itself be a response to a Western tradition that had already embraced a pagan notion of divine arbitrariness).[30] The notion of a determinate freedom appears incoherent to us, yet, as I have argued elsewhere and has been argued far more effectively by others, it is in fact the notion of indeterminate freedom that is incoherent.[31] For a choice to be mine and owned as mine

---

loves us, and loves the world, in accordance with His revelation. But He loves us and the world as He who would still be One who loves without us and without the world; as He, therefore, who needs no other to form the prior ground of His existence as the One who loves and as God.' *CD* II/1, p. 280; cf. John E. Colwell, *Actuality and Provisionality: Eternity and Election in the Theology of Karl Barth* (Edinburgh: Rutherford House, 1989), p. 199: 'this happening of God is not haphazard or arbitrary: actuality implies possibility; who God is in His revelation He is previously in Himself; His relatedness to us in love is the reiteration of His relatedness to Himself in love'; cf. also Eberhard Jüngel's comment that '[t]his correspondence signifies that God's being as self-relatedness is a being in becoming, which possesses the peculiarity of being able to *reiterate itself*'. Eberhard Jüngel, *The Doctrine of the Trinity: God's Being is in Becoming*, trans. Horton Harris (Edinburgh and London: Scottish Academic Press, 1976), p. 103.

[30]   I am hesitant to affirm or to identify too closely with the contemporary theological movement termed 'radical orthodoxy' — I am especially suspicious of any 'orthodoxy' that has so little to say of Jesus and the gospel story and so much (relatively) to say of Plato — but the movement is not alone in recognising that something went drastically wrong for the Western tradition in the nominalism of John Duns Scotus (c.1266–1308) and William of Ockham (c.1285–c.1349). My only hesitation with respect to a notion of divine arbitrariness is that the Western tradition may have already gone wrong, at least seminally, in the thought of the very writers this movement seeks to affirm. See for instance Catherine Pickstock, *After Writing: On the Liturgical Consummation of Philosophy* (Oxford: Blackwell, 1998), and John Milbank *et al* (eds.), *Radical Orthodoxy: A New Theology* (London: Routledge, 1999). For this criticism of Milbank in particular see Gunton, *The One, the Three and the Many*, p. 55, fn. 20

[31]   '[T]he very aspects of our experience that seem to support the idea of self-agency, freedom, and responsibility are paradoxically impossible if man is an indeterminate cause. The indeterminist must deny that a man's action can be explained wholly in terms of his will, motives, desires, or character, for to do so would imply that man is not entirely a free agent. But if acts are completely spontaneous (having no sufficient condition), then how are we to attribute responsibility to anyone?... [N]ot only does free will not contradict determinism, it is inconceivable without it.' Stanley Hauerwas, *Character and the Christian Life: A Study in Theological Ethics* (Notre Dame and London: University of Notre Dame Press, 1994 [1975]), pp. 19-20; cf. my discussion in John E. Colwell, *Living the Christian Story: The Distinctiveness of Christian Ethics* (Edinburgh and New York: T & T Clark, 2001), pp. 175-176. The classic discussion of

implies that such choice springs from my history, my preferences, my values. For such choice to be truly my *choice* it must be free from all external determining factors; for such choice to be truly *my* choice it must be determined, at least in some respect, by my own nature. It is the notion of indeterminate choice, then, that is incoherent. God defined in the gospel isn't arbitrary will: he is Father, Son, and Spirit; he is perfect intimate communion; he is perfect love. He is utterly free but his freedom is not indeterminate; he is utterly free as himself, he is not free to be other than himself; his freedom is the freedom of his love, it is not a freedom incoherent with his eternal identity and nature. That God loves that which is other than himself is unnecessitated, it is utterly free, but it is not indeterminate or arbitrary; it is grace; it is the love of the one who loves in freedom.

The purpose of this admittedly complex exposition of Trinitarian theology is simply to identify the theological significance of the word 'grace'. Such definition could, of course, have been attempted by a less circuitous route, by reference to dictionaries, by reference to the use of the word within the theological tradition, but the outcome of such a strategy would have proved less stable and, ultimately, misleading and unpersuasive. I am aware, of course, that this word 'grace' has been used in theological discourse (legitimately and perhaps sometimes illegitimately) with a wide range of signification: distinction has been made between uncreated grace and created grace; between irresistible grace and resistible grace; between common grace and special, particular or saving grace; there are doctrines of infused grace; there are doctrines of prevenient grace. But without prejudice (for the moment) to the legitimacy or otherwise of such distinctions, grace primarily and essentially is a theological concept and its significance must therefore be rooted in an understanding of God. I have tried to demonstrate that grace, as God's free or gratuitous love, is properly conceived with reference to God's Triunity—and improperly conceived otherwise. Precisely because God is named as Father, Son, and Spirit in the gospel story his love for that which is other than himself is free, it is gratuitous, it is grace. Were God not to be so named his love for that which is other than himself would either be arbitrary (not a reiteration of his eternal nature) or 'unfree' (a necessary prerequisite for the definition of God as loving). But God is named as Father, Son, and Spirit; he is perfect love eternally in himself. His love for that which is other than himself therefore is not arbitrary. His love for that which is other than himself therefore is not necessitated. His love for that which is other than himself therefore is grace.

---

this occurs in Jonathan Edwards, *Freedom of the Will*, in *YE* vol. 1, ed. Paul Ramsey, pp. 135-439.

As was noted in the introduction, the most basic definition of sacramentality, assumed and accepted both by Thomas Aquinas and John Calvin, is that a sacrament is a means of grace. This definition of sacramentality, therefore, is itself dependent upon definitions of these two dynamics, the dynamic of mediation (means) and the dynamic of presence and transformation (grace). And grace—at least as I have tried to define it Trinitarianly—is a dynamic; it is not a something. That which is mediated sacramentally is the presence and action of this one who loves in freedom; it is gratuitous; it is grace. It is not a 'something' at our disposal; it is not a 'something' we can manipulate—such notions do not merely misunderstand sacramentality, they misunderstand and offend a doctrine of God. It is God's presence and action that is communicated sacramentally and God cannot be manipulated; he is never at our disposal; he is not capricious, but neither is he subject to necessity; a sacrament may be the means of his presence, but it is never his prison; he is freely and graciously here, but he is not confined or controllable here or anywhere else.[32] If grace might rightly be used with reference to a gift then this one who loves in freedom remains the free Lord of the being-givenness of that gift; God may give himself but he never gives himself away; he never becomes our possession or property—as Thomas Aquinas rightly maintains, God and God alone is the efficient cause of grace in a sacrament.

The legitimacy or otherwise of the various uses of this word 'grace' then ought properly to be determined with reference to this essentially theological definition: whatever other tests of legitimacy may be applied, it is only ever valid to speak of grace—of prevenient grace, of infused grace, of common grace, etc.—if the reference is genuinely to 'grace', to that which is gracious, to that which is freely given, to that which is never at our disposal, to that which is beyond manipulation.

John Calvin's reference to 'promise' offers the same safeguard but is liable to the same distortion as Thomas' reference to instrumental cause. If a Catholic tradition has proved itself liable to an objectifying of grace, implying God's presence, action, and gift to be at our disposal and manipulable, then a Reformed tradition is similarly liable to a presumption upon promise. The notion of promise is helpful in a number of respects: it is implicitly personal rather than impersonal; it should exclude the capricious or the arbitrary (although, in practice, this was not always the case); it makes explicit the relationship of the sacrament to the Word (a relationship similarly crucial for Thomas Aquinas and to be

---

[32]   The point is conceded, albeit rather negatively, at the very beginning of Paul Haffner's account of the sacraments: 'Although God is not bound by these efficacious sacred signs instituted by His Son, in general they are the privileged channels where He touches the lives of His faithful.' Paul Haffner, *The Sacramental Mystery* (Leominster: Gracewing, 1999). p. 1.

explored in chapter four); it signifies that which is freely given; it is more suggestive of a future hope than of a present realisation. But, extracted from a focus upon the irreducible freedom of God's love, covenant becomes mistaken for contract; promise becomes the ground for presumption; assurance is misconstrued as insurance, as a 'guarantee of the guarantee' (as Barth put it so aptly),[33] as something in our possession, as something binding God to necessity. But God's promise never becomes God's prison; he who was free in the giving of the promise remains free in its fulfilment; we may confidently hope for the fulfilment of that promise but we can never presume upon it; it never becomes our possession, 'right', or due.

Whether then we seek to understand the sacramental in terms of grace or in terms of promise we are directed to the one who, as eternal love in Triune communion, loves in freedom and who remains free in every expression of that love to that which is other than himself. As Karl Barth himself owns, it is this tendency towards the manipulative and presumptuous that, at least in part, contributed to his eventual abandonment of a sacramental theology in any recognisable traditional form: too easily mystery is reduced to magic, promise becomes possession.[34]

But I suspect there may be a far more compelling source for this final rejection, a source pervading the entirety of Barth's theological thought.

For all its usefulness in identifying the essential freedom of God's love, it ought not to escape notice that Barth's definition of God as 'the One who Loves in Freedom' fails in precisely the same manner as was earlier noted of Augustine's deduction: it falls short of a doctrine of the Trinity. For God to be one who loves in freedom implies (as Augustine recognises) a lover and a beloved—but that is all: it need not imply that this lover and beloved are the Father and the Son identified in the gospel story; it certainly does not imply that the love between this lover and beloved is personal, is the Spirit. Earlier, within his prolegomena and with breathtaking openness, Barth affirms this less than personal account of the Spirit:

> even if the Father and the Son might be called 'person' (in the modern sense of the term), the Holy Spirit could not possibly be regarded as the third 'person.' In a particularly clear way the Holy Spirit is what the Father and the Son also are. He is not a third spiritual Subject, a third I, a third Lord side by side with two others. He is

---

[33]   'We are not grasping at more but at less, and ultimately at nothing at all, if in addition to the guarantee which is identical with God Himself we think we must grasp at an unequivocal experience, at a guarantee of the guarantee so to speak, in order that we may then decide for certainty of faith, as though a certainty for which we must first decide could be the certainty of faith.' CD I/1, p. 465.

[34]   CD IV/4, pp. 108-109.

a third mode of being of the one divine Subject or Lord... He is the common element, or, better, the fellowship, the act of communion, of the Father and the Son.[35]

This blatant depersonalising of the Spirit and persistent preference for the term 'mode of being' with reference to God's threeness is startling,[36] not for its innovation, but for its candour. The tendency to speak of the threeness of God as subsistent relations rather than as subsistencies (or persons) in relationship merely locates Barth in the Western tradition of Augustine and Thomas.[37] Barth's rejection of the individualistic definition of the word person as expressed by Boethius,[38] together with his unease concerning contemporary connotations of personality,[39] are commendable, but surely a more appropriate response would issue from a more theological definition of the term, a definition of person arising from a careful listening to the gospel narrative.[40]

As Barth rightly acknowledges, the term 'person' (*persona*), like the term 'Trinity' (*Trinitas*), was used by Tertullian in response to the error usually termed 'Sabellianism', the error of conceiving Father, Son, and Spirit to be merely temporary modes of the reality of God assumed in the context of God's relatedness to creation.[41] Barth, therefore, can justly

---

[35] *CD* I/1, pp. 469-470.

[36] 'The concept of the revealed unity of the revealed God, then, does not exclude but rather includes a distinction (*distinctio* or *discretio*) or order (*dispositio* or *oeconomia*) in the essence of God. This distinction or order is the distinction or order of the three "persons," or, as we prefer to say, the three "modes (or ways) of being" in God.' *CD* I/1, p. 355.

[37] For a recent and robust defence of this approach, see Paul Fiddes, *Participating in God: A Pastoral Doctrine of the Trinity* (London: Darton Longman and Todd, 2000).

[38] Boethius (c. 480–524), in *The Consolation of Philosophy*, trans. W. V. Cooper (London: Dent, 1902), defined 'person' as 'an individual substance of a rational nature' (*persona est naturae rationabilis individua substantia*).

[39] 'It is as well to note at this early stage that what we to-day call the "personality" of God belongs to the one unique essence of God which the doctrine of the Trinity does not seek to triple but rather to recognize in its simplicity... "Person" as used in the Church doctrine of the Trinity bears no direct relation to personality. The meaning of the doctrine is not, then, that there are three personalities in God'. *CD* I/1, pp. 350-351.

[40] 'Barth's proposal to use mode of being...as the equivalent for "person", rather than as a way of referring to the way in which persons are who they particularly are, not only makes it impossible to redeem the concept of person from its modern individualistic usage, but also replicates the Western tendency to make the Trinity practically redundant by depriving the persons of distinctive forms of agency.' Gunton, *The One, the Three and the Many*, p. 191, fn. 11.

[41] 'The word *persona*, πρόσωπον, like *trinitas*, which is supposed to have been used first by Tertullian, originates with the controversy against the Sabellian heresy and is thus designed to denote the being in and for themselves of Father, Son and Spirit respectively.' *CD* I/1, p. 355. It should be acknowledged that Sabellius himself (a

claim to be avoiding this Sabellian error by his insistence that these subsisting modes of being are eternal, that God is eternally who he is within revelation.[42] But it is difficult to avoid the impression that Barth's expression of the doctrine of the Trinity in terms of the dynamic of revelation—a Trinity of 'Revealer', 'Revelation', and 'Revealedness'— alongside his preference for this term 'mode of being' undermines his own defence besides explicitly depersonalising the Spirit.

The ambiguity of the term *persona* as used by Tertullian, as also of its Greek equivalent (πρόσωπον), only served to compound and prolong the problem of modalism: both terms could signify persons in the sense of subjects; both terms could signify temporary identities or characters adopted dramatically (both words could refer to masks used in a play). Maybe then it was partly to avoid such ambiguity that Basil of Caesarea,[43] perhaps following Origen (c.185–254), preferred to speak of Father, Son, and Spirit as three subsistencies (τρεῖς ὑπόστασεις) sharing one essence (μία οὐσία) or nature (φύσις):[44] the single and indivisible essence

---

contemporary of Tertullian's) proposed a sophisticated form of modalism that avoided the notion of God (the Father) suffering (patripassianism) through the suggestion that Father and Son were rent apart at the Crucifixion and that the Father brought forth the Spirit in order to bind the Son back to him in absolute unity.

[42]   'What we have here are God's specific, different, and always very distinctive modes of being. This means that God's modes of being are not to be exchanged or confounded. In all three modes of being God is the one God both in Himself and in relation to the world and man. But this one God is God three times in different ways, so different that it is only in this threefold difference that He is God...'. *CD* I/1, p. 360.

[43]   Basil of Caesarea (c.329–79), was brother to Macrina (d.379) and to Gregory of Nyssa (c.330–c.395). These two brothers, together with Basil's friend Gregory of Nazianzus (c.329–90), are usually referred to collectively as the Cappadocian Fathers. Though initially accepting of the compromise formula proposed by Eusebius of Caesarea (c.265–339)—that Christ was of 'similar' substance (ὁμοιούσιον) to the Father—Basil became persuaded by the ὁμοούσιον ('of one substance') of Nicene orthodoxy through the influence of Athanasius (c.297–373) and, together with Nyssa and Nazianzus, was influential in bringing about the triumph of Trinitarian orthodoxy at the Council of Constantinople in 381, a council chaired by Nazianzus who had become Bishop of Constantinople. Adopting a phrase previously used by Basil the Great, the council affirmed the deity of the Spirit by adding the following clause to the creed agreed at Nicea: 'We believe in the Holy Spirit, the Lord, the giver of life, who proceeds from the Father. With the Father and the Son he is worshipped and glorified. He has spoken through the Prophets.' Nazianzus resigned at the conclusion of the council, disappointed that it had stopped short of affirming the Spirit as of one substance (ὁμοούσιον) with the Father and the Son.

[44]   'The distinction between οὐσία and ὑπόστασις is the same as that between the general and the particular; as, for instance, between the animal and the particular man. Wherefore, in the case of the Godhead, we confess one essence or substance so as not to give a variant definition of existence, but we confess a particular hypostasis, in order that our conception of Father, Son and Holy Spirit may be without confusion and clear. If we

(οὐσία) of God subsists in the Father, the Son, and the Spirit; these three subsistencies (ὑπόστασεις) are distinguished by the distinctiveness of their inter-relations (ἰδιότης). For Basil, then, relatedness is ontological: it defines the subsistence of the Father, the Son, and the Spirit. For Gregory Nazianzus also, 'Father' is the name of the 'relation' (σχέσις) the Father has with the Son; the Father is distinguished through 'unbegottenness' (ἀγεννησία), the Son through 'begottenness' (γέννησις), the Spirit through 'procession' (ἐκπόρευσις).[45] Gregory of Nyssa similarly affirms the unity of the three hypostases (τρεῖς ὑπόστασεις) with the recognition that every external act of God is common to all three persons though in a manner distinct to each person: every external act of God has its origin in the Father, proceeds through the Son, and is perfected through the Spirit.[46]

It is this notion of relationship as ontological, as defining of persons, that seems to have eluded most Western thinkers and that has potential for

---

have no distinct perception of the separate characteristics, namely, fatherhood, sonship, and sanctification, but form our conception of God from the general idea of existence, we cannot possibly give a sound account of our faith. We must, therefore, confess the faith by adding the particular to the common. The Godhead is common; the fatherhood particular.' Saint Basil the Great, *Letter to Amphilochius* (Letter 236 6), in *NPNF* 2, vol. 8, p. 278. It seems that not until Calvin was the significance of this distinction in Greek expressed and understood in Latin: '"Person," therefore, I call a "subsistence" in God's essence, which, while related to the others, is distinguished by an incommunicable quality. By the term "subsistence" we would understand something different from "essence".' (*Personam igitur voco subsistentiam in Dei essentia, quae ad alios relata, proprietate incommunicabili distinguitur. Subsistentiae nomine aliud quiddam intelligi volumus quam essentiam*) *Institutes*. I xiii 6.

45   'This is what we mean by Father and Son and Holy Ghost. The Father is the Begetter and the Emitter; without passion of course, and without reference to time, and not in a corporeal manner. The Son is the Begotten, and the Holy Ghost the Emission; for I know not how this could be expressed in terms altogether excluding visible things... Therefore let us confine ourselves within our limits, and speak of the Unbegotten and the Begotten and That which proceeds from the Father...' St. Gregory Nazianzen, *The Third Theological Oration on the Son* (Oration 29 2), in *NPNF* 2, vol. 7, pp. 301-309.

46   'But in the case of the Divine nature we do not similarly learn that the Father does anything by Himself in which the Son does not work conjointly, or again that the Son has any special operation apart from the Holy Spirit; but every operation which extends from God to the Creation, and is named according to our variable conceptions of it, has its origin from the Father, and proceeds through the Son, and is perfected in the Holy Spirit. For this reason the name derived from the operation is not divided with regard to the number of those who fulfil it, because the action of each concerning anything is not separate and peculiar, but whatever comes to pass, in reference either to the acts of His providence for us, or to the government and constitution of the universe, comes to pass by the action of the Three, yet what does come to pass is not three things.' St. Gregory of Nyssa, *Dogmatic Treatise on 'Not Three Gods' to Ablabius*, *NPNF* 2, vol. 5, pp. 331-336 (p. 334).

repudiating individualistic understandings of personhood that have blighted Western theology and Western society.[47] It is this notion of relationship as ontological that seems to elude Augustine in particular when he acknowledges the difficulty of distinguishing between generation and procession,[48] and when he insists on declaring the Spirit to proceed from both the Father and the Son.[49] This double procession of the Spirit—that the Spirit proceeds from the Father *and the Son* (*qui ex Patre Filioque procedit*)—was affirmed as an addition to the Nicene/Constantinople Creed at the Council of Toledo in 589, was officially adopted in Rome in 1014, and issued in the eventual schism of Eastern and Western traditions in 1054.

While again I acknowledge that this all too brief résumé may appear complex, the issue itself is simple: if the Father, the Son, and the Spirit are distinguished by their mutual relationships, then to suggest that the Spirit proceeds both from the Father and the Son is to imply confusion in those relationships and therefore in those identities. If that which distinguishes and defines the Father is his relationship to the Son and the Spirit, and if that which distinguishes and defines the Son is his relationship to the Father and the Spirit, then to suggest that the Spirit's relationship to the Father is identical to the Spirit's relationship with the Son (which is how the Eastern tradition interpreted the West's insertion of the *filioque* clause), is to jeopardise the distinct identities of the Trinity.

Perhaps I need to clarify that this is not intended as an apology for the Eastern tradition,[50] nor even as an insistence upon the use of the term 'person' with reference to the Father, the Son, and the Spirit. The issue is not whether Father, Son, and Spirit are referred to as persons, as subsistencies, or as identities. The issue is rather the manner in which Father, Son, and Spirit are identified and distinguished.

And the matter is not easily resolved. Once the *filioque* clause has been introduced it is difficult to deny it without implying the non-relatedness

---

[47]   For a sustained account of this argument see, for instance, John Zizioulas, *Being as Communion: Studies in Personhood and the Church* (London: Darton Longman and Todd, 1985), and Gunton, *The One, The Three and the Many*.

[48]   '[I]t is most difficult to distinguish generation from procession in that co-eternal, and equal, and incorporeal, and ineffably unchangeable and indivisible Trinity...'. Augustine, *On the Holy Trinity*, XV xxvii 48.

[49]   'Further, in that Highest Trinity which is God, there are no intervals of time, by which it could be shown, or at least inquired, whether the Son was born of the Father first, and then afterwards the Holy Spirit proceeded from both; since Holy Scripture calls Him the Spirit of both.' Augustine, *On the Holy Trinity*, XV xxvi 45.

[50]   As Robert Jenson and others observe, the distinction introduced by Gregory Palamas (1296–1359) between the essence of God and the divine 'energies' reintroduces a form of monarchianism, an unknown God behind and beyond the persons of the Father, the Son and the Spirit. Jenson, *Systematic Theology*, vol. 1, pp. 152-153.

of the Spirit to the Son (with quite disastrous consequences). Remove the *filioque* clause from the Creed and the only references to the relatedness of the Spirit and the Son are the references to the Son's incarnation ('by the power of the Holy Spirit he became incarnate of the Virgin Mary, and was made man')[51] and to the worship and glory appropriately offered to Father, Son, and Spirit ('with the Father and the Son he is worshipped and glorified').[52] Remove the *filioque* clause from the Creed and there is no explicit reference to the Spirit's relatedness to the Son in eternity. Remove the *filioque* clause from the Creed and there is no implicit reference to the relatedness of the Son to the Spirit in the latter's rôle as 'the Lord, the giver of life'; that is to say, there is silence concerning the relatedness of the work of the Spirit and the Son in creation if not, in some respects, in redemption. But if the Spirit is not explicitly related to the Son in the work of creation and redemption then the Son, as the goal of creation, might be knowable without reference to the Spirit; the rationality of creation might be independently perceivable. And if the Spirit is not explicitly related to the Son in the work of creation and redemption then the Spirit, as God's presence within creation and within the creature, might be comprehended without reference to the Son; the presence and action of the Spirit within creation and within the creature might be indeterminate. That the Western tradition, notwithstanding its inclusion of the *filioque* clause, has been blighted by a dualistic division between nature and grace and by indeterminate claims to spiritual experience may suggest that the inclusion of the *filioque* clause, of itself, is an inadequate (or inappropriate) defence against such misconstruction.

Of course, there have been various formulas suggested as possible bases for accommodation between the Eastern and Western traditions. The most common suggestion is that the phrase 'who proceeds from the Father *through* the Son' might prove acceptable to both traditions and might more appropriately express the relatedness of the Spirit to the Father and the Son. Alternatively Jürgen Moltmann, in his book *The Trinity and the Kingdom of God*, proposed that we should speak of '[t]he Holy Spirit, who proceeds from the Father of the Son, and who receives his form from the Father and the Son'.[53] Tom Smail commends the substitution of the word 'through' but opines that such limited amendment would be inadequate: it might be an appropriate expression of the mediate nature of the Spirit's eternal proceeding from the Father, but surely a complementary clause is needed making explicit the mediate

---

51 *'et incarnatus est de Spiritu Sancto ex Maria Virgine, et homo factus est'.*

52 *'cum Patre et Filio adorandum et conglorificandum'.*

53 Jürgen Moltmann, *The Trinity and the Kingdom of God: The Doctrine of God*, trans. Margaret Kohl (London: SCM Press, 1981), p. 187.

nature of the Son's eternal generation (rather than just the mediate nature of the Son's incarnation).[54]

I suspect that Tom Smail is essentially right,[55] but I also suspect that such amendments will never prove acceptable: in days when the Church is so tragically divided it is difficult to conceive of a truly ecumenical council being convened, less still agreeing—and only a truly ecumenical council would have authority to approve an alteration to the Creed (precisely the basis for the East's offence at the unilateral decisions of Toledo and Rome). Nonetheless such suggestions, particularly Tom Smail's more comprehensive proposal, draw attention to an implication of Trinitarian theology that is often overlooked and is less than explicit in the Creed as presently recited (in East or West).

As noted already, neither Augustine's formula nor Barth's necessarily imply a Trinity of persons (or identities): for God to be loving even for God to be the one who loves in freedom, may imply the person of the lover and the person of the beloved but it does not imply the *person* of love.[56] Generally in the context of the Western tradition the Spirit is

---

54   'If, then, we are to be true to the total New Testament witness on this matter, we must say not only that the Spirit comes from the Father through the Son, but also that the Son comes from the Father through the Spirit. There is not just a one-sided dependence of the Spirit on the Son, as the West has taught, but a mutual dependence of the two upon each other. Both have their source in the Father, but each does what he does and is who he is in relation to and dependence upon the other. Their relationship is described better as a co-ordination of the two than as a subordination of the one to the other.' Tom Smail, *The Giving Gift: The Holy Spirit in Person* (London: Hodder and Stoughton, 1988), p. 141.

55   Note that in a later work, Jürgen Moltmann seems to arrive at a similar conclusion: 'if instead we note the experience of the Spirit out of which Christ himself comes and acts, and ask about the trinitarian structure which can be detected in that, we discover that the Spirit proceeds from the Father and determines the Son, rests on the Son and shines through him. The roles of Son and Spirit are then exchanged. The Son proceeds from the Father and has the impress of the Spirit. We might say that Christ comes *a patre spirituque*, from the Father and the Spirit—though in fact it is better to avoid any undifferentiating "and" in the trinitarian structure altogether.' Jürgen Moltmann, *The Spirit of Life: A Universal Affirmation*, trans. Margaret Kohl (London: SCM Press, 1992), p. 71.

56   Note Jürgen Moltmann's criticism of Barth's account of the Trinity as being an expression of Hegel's notion of the Absolute Subject rather than an intent listening to the gospel narrative. One may not want to affirm every aspect of Moltmann's alternative but this criticism, particularly in relation to the earliest parts of the *Church Dogmatics*, is difficult to counter persuasively. Moltmann, *The Trinity and the Kingdom of God*, pp. 139ff.: 'The reason for the difficulties Barth gets into here with his acceptance of the Idealistic reflection Trinity of the divine subject, is that he puts the divine lordship before the Trinity and uses the "doctrine of the Trinity" to secure and interpret the divine subjectivity in that lordship. That is why Barth presents the "doctrine of the Trinity" as Christian monotheism and argues polemically against a "tritheism" which has never

conceived as the bond of love between the Father and the Son or, more recently, as the 'openness' of the love of the Father and the Son to that which is other than God. The problem with the first view is that it depersonalises the Spirit; the problem with the second view is that it again seems to imply that what is other than God is somehow necessary to God for God to be fully God. But what if we take seriously Tom Smail's proposal that the Father's relatedness to the Son (and the Son's relatedness to the Father) is mediated by the Spirit and that the Father's relatedness to the Spirit (and the Spirit's relatedness to the Father) is mediated by the Son?

If we listen more intently to the gospel story and to the manner in which it narrates this Triune relatedness we cannot fail to observe, as Jürgen Moltmann has noted, that the gospel story itself has a Trinitarian structure;[57] that which is narrated here is not just the story of Jesus, but rather the story of his relatedness to the Father through the Spirit and of the Father's relatedness to the Son through that same Spirit.[58] The words and actions of the Son are the words and actions of the Father mediated by the Spirit. There is no action within the narrative that is not an action of the undivided Trinity. There is no action within the narrative that is not an action mediated by the Spirit. The Father's love and calling to the Son is mediated by the Spirit at Jesus' baptism. The ministry of Jesus is a demonstration of the Father's kingdom in the power of the Spirit. The sacrifice of the Son is mediated to the Father by the Spirit. The Father's raising of the Son from the dead is mediated by the Spirit. At every point the Spirit is the agent of mediation between Father and Son.

John Owen, the seventeenth-century Puritan theologian,[59] in the course of his magisterial account of the work of the Spirit, similarly concludes that since '...there is no...division in the external operations of God...' and since '[t]he Holy Ghost...is the *immediate, peculiar, efficient cause* of all external divine operations...' then '[t]he Holy Spirit is...the

---

existed. That is why he uses a non-trinitarian concept of the unity of the one God—that is to say, the concept of the identical subject' (pp. 143-144).

[57]   'The history in which Jesus is manifested as 'the Son' is not consummated and fulfilled by a single subject. The history of Christ is already related in trinitarian terms in the New Testament itself'. Moltmann, *The Trinity and the Kingdom of God*, p. 64.

[58]   As will become clear in the next chapter (though implicitly at the conclusion of this chapter) I cannot endorse Moltmann's Trinitarian analysis in its entirety.

[59]   John Owen (1616–83) was appointed chaplain to Oliver Cromwell and subsequently became Dean of Christ Church, Oxford, and then Vice-Chancellor of the University (forfeiting such offices on the restoration of the monarchy). A leading participant in the Westminster Assembly, Owen was instrumental in the drafting of the Savoy Declaration of Independency—a 'Declaration of Faith and Order Owned and Practised in the Congregational Church in England' (1658).

immediate operator of all divine acts of the Son...'.[60] Owen then proceeds
to list ten instances of the work of the Spirit in and upon the Son
(together with a further indirect work of the Spirit towards the Son);[61] he
cites each as an immediate work of the Spirit but one must add that each,
as an immediate work of the Spirit is itself a mediation of the love and
action of the Father. Similarly Richard Sibbes (1572–1635), another
Puritan pastor and theologian, writes of every immediate work of the
Spirit as a mediated work of Father and Son.[62]

In every respect and in every instance the relatedness of the Father to
the Son and the relatedness of the Son to the Father as narrated in the

---

[60]   John Owen, *A Discourse concerning the Holy Spirit* (1674), in *The Works of
John Owen*, vol. 3, pp. 161-162.

[61]   Accordingly, Owen, *A Discourse concerning the Holy Spirit*, p. 162, the
'*framing, forming, and miraculous conception of the body of Christ in the womb of the
blessed Virgin* was the peculiar and especial work of the Holy Ghost'; the 'human nature
of Christ being thus formed in the womb by a *creation act* of the Holy Spirit was in the
instant of its conception *sanctified*, and filled with grace according to the measure of its
receptivity' (p. 168); the 'Spirit *carried on that work whose foundation he had thus laid*'
(p. 169); the 'Holy Spirit, in a peculiar manner, anointed him with all those
extraordinary powers and gifts which were necessary for the exercise and discharging of
his office on the earth' (p. 171); it 'was in an especial manner by the power of the Holy
Spirit he wrought those great and *miraculous works* whereby his ministry was attested and
confirmed' (p. 174); by the Spirit 'was he *guided, directed, comforted, supported*, in the
whole course of his ministry, temptations, obedience, and sufferings' (p. 174); Jesus
'*offered himself up unto God through the eternal Spirit*' (p. 176); there 'was a peculiar
work of the Holy Spirit towards the Lord Christ whilst he was in the *state of the dead*...the
union of his person, his soul in its separate state was in an especial manner under the
care, protection, and power of the Father, preserved in his love until the hour came
wherein he showed him again the path of life' (p. 180); there 'was a peculiar work of the
Holy Spirit in his *resurrection*' (p. 181); it 'was the Holy Spirit that *glorified* the human
nature [of Christ], and made it every meet for its eternal residence at the right hand of God,
and a pattern for the glorification of the bodies of them that believe on him' (p. 183); and
'[t]here is yet another work of the Holy Spirit, not immediately in and upon the person of
the Lord Christ, but *towards him*... [H]is witness-bearing unto the Lord Christ, — namely,
that he was the Son of God, the true Messiah, and that the work which he performed in the
world was committed unto him by God the Father to accomplish' (pp. 183-184).

[62]   '...Christ's nature must not only be sanctified and ordained by the Spirit; but he
must receive the Spirit to enrich it, for whatsoever is wrought in the creature is by the
Spirit. Whatsoever Christ did as man, he did by the Spirit. Christ's human nature,
therefore, must be sanctified, and have the Spirit put upon it. God the Father, the first
person in Trinity, and God the Son, the second, they work not immediately, but by the
Holy Ghost, the third person. Therefore, whatsoever is wrought upon the creature, it
comes from the Holy Ghost immediately. So Christ received the Holy Ghost as sent from
the Father and the Son'. Richard Sibbes, *A Description of Christ* (1639), in *Works of
Richard Sibbes*, vol. 1, ed. Alexander B. Grosart (Edinburgh: Banner of Truth, 1973), pp.
1-31 (p. 17).

gospel story is a mediated relatedness; it is never unmediated.[63] And if that which is narrated in the gospel story is a reiteration of the form and manner of the love between Father and Son in eternity, if revelation is truly revelation, if God is in eternity who he is in this narrative, then even in eternity the love between the Father and the Son is mediated and never unmediated.

It is not sufficient, then, to refer to the Spirit as the (impersonal) love uniting Father and Son; he is rather the (personal) mediator of that love; he is the one who mediates the love of the Father to the Son and the love of the Son to the Father. This is the form and manner of the mutual love of Father and Son narrated in the gospel story. Moreover, since the love and self-giving of the Father to the Son and of the Son to the Father is absolute, since the persons of the Trinity mutually and fully indwell each other (the insight expressed in both Eastern and Western traditions by the doctrine of perichoresis),[64] it is only because this absolute love and self-giving is mediated, rather than unmediated, that the persons of the Trinity remain distinct, that the Trinity does not collapse into an indistinct monad.[65] This is not a speculative attempt to define the utterly unknowable and indefinable essence of God.[66] This is simply to listen trustfully to the narration of the gospel story, believing that this is truly revelation, that this is true and not untrue or misleading. The absolute and self-giving nature of the love of this Lover for this Beloved is such that, were it not a mediated love, the distinction between Lover and Beloved

---

[63]   One could add a similar and complementary statement concerning the Spirit: the Father gives the Spirit through the Son to the Church; the Spirit offers the worship, prayer and service of the Church through the Son to the Father—but this is to anticipate the next chapter.

[64]   Perichoresis ($\pi\epsilon\rho\iota\chi\omega\rho\eta\sigma\iota\varsigma$) or *circumincessio* refers to the mutual indwelling or interpenetration of the persons of the Trinity. The Latin term appears to have been used first by Maximus the Confessor (c.580–662) in relation to the divine and human natures of Christ. The term was applied to the persons of the Trinity by John of Damascus (c.665–749) though the root idea occurs much earlier in Irenaeus (c.130–c.200), Athanasius (c.296–373) and the Cappadocians.

[65]   I am immensely grateful to Tom Smail for his friendship and for several lunches and long walks during which we have debated Trinitarian and sacramental theology. I am particularly grateful for a conversation in a restaurant in Westerham where Tom shared this insight that the Spirit's mediation maintains the distinctness of the Father and the Son.

[66]   The Cappadocians' efforts to speak of the divine subsistencies was not in any respect a denial of the unknowability of the divine essence. For a discussion of this with respect to Gregory of Nyssa, see Sarah Coakley, *Powers and Submissions: Spirituality, Philosophy and Gender* (Oxford: Blackwell, 2002), pp. 109-129.

would collapse (as indeed it seems effectively to have collapsed all too often in the Western tradition).[67]

And neither then is it sufficient to speak of God as the one who loves in freedom, he is rather the one who mediates his love in freedom. If Barth has increasing difficulty in affirming the sacramentality of the sacraments, this may be an outcome of resistance to notions of manipulation or 'magic', but it is surely more fundamentally an outcome of his analysis of the Trinity, of his explicit depersonalising of the Spirit, of his tendency to subsume the work of the Spirit into the work of the Son, of his all pervading tendency (noted more than once by Colin Gunton) to affirm the unmediated immediate rather than the mediated immediate.[68] This tendency is unmistakable in Barth's discussion of the relation between baptism with the Holy Spirit and baptism with water in the final 'fragment' of the *Church Dogmatics*, but it is similarly represented by the implicit distinction between the ontological and the ontic within his discussion of the doctrine of election,[69] and represented again (and even earlier) in his discussion of the threefold form of the Word of God—as I have opined elsewhere, even to speak of a *three*fold form of the Word implies that the Word can be spoken in some

---

[67]   So Colin Gunton notes that the 'Spirit is that which, far from abolishing, rather maintains and even strengthens particularity. It is not a spirit of merging or assimilation—of homogenization—but of relation in otherness, relation which does not subvert but establishes the other in its true reality.' Gunton, *The One, the Three and the Many*, p. 182; cf. Wolfhart Pannenberg, *Systematic Theology*, vol. 2, trans. Geoffrey W. Bromiley (Edinburgh: T & T Clark, 1994), p. 197. Richard St. Victor (d.1173), a pupil of Hugh, comes to a similar conclusion concerning the personhood of the Spirit in his *De Trinitate*, the goodness and love of God, the *summum bonum*, must be shared with the other, and that other also must share the love (*caritas*) received. Richard St. Victor, *De Trinitate* 3 2 and 3 11). But while this avoids the inherent individualism of Augustine and Boethius, it nonetheless, as with Augustine, rests upon a deduction from the statement that God is love rather than upon a reflection on the narration of Father, Son and Spirit in the gospel story.

[68]   See for instance, Colin E. Gunton, *The Triune Creator: A Historical and Systematic Study* (Edinburgh: Edinburgh University Press, 1998), pp. 162ff., or his 'Salvation', in John Webster (ed.) *The Cambridge Companion to Karl Barth* (Cambridge: Cambridge University Press, 2000), pp. 143-158. This phrase, 'mediated immediacy', appears to have been introduced by John Baillie: '[c]learly, then, the immediacy of God's presence to our souls is a mediated immediacy.' John Baillie, *Our Knowledge of God* (London: Oxford University Press, 1939), p. 181.

[69]   Barth speaks of the work of the Spirit in the calling of the elect as the 'objective difference' (*die objektive Unterscheidung*) which 'corresponds objectively' (*entspricht objektiv*) to the distinction between elect and 'other men'. CD II/2, p. 345, cf. Karl Barth, *Die Kirchliche Dogmatik* II: *Die Lehre von Gott*, 2 (Zürich: Evangelischer Verlag, 1942), p. 380; cf. my discussion of this in *Actuality and Provisionality*, pp. 283ff.

unmediated manner, can be spoken other than through the mediation of preaching or Scripture.[70]

My concern here is not so much to question immediacy (though, as I shall argue in the next chapter, any notion of immediacy requires clear and careful qualification) as to deny the unmediated. The relatedness of Father and Son is mediated by the Spirit. Every action of the Father toward the Son and of the Son toward the Father is mediated by the Spirit. And, since the Spirit's rôle within the Trinity is to mediate the love and action of Father and Son, then every work of the Spirit finds its source and goal in the Father and the Son—there can be no indeterminate, un-sourced or un-goaled work of the Spirit; he is the mediator of love and action; he is neither the source nor the goal of that love and action; his person, subsistence, and identity is as the mediator of divine love and action, not as the source or goal of divine love and action.

What I have sought to establish in this first and foundational chapter is that grace and mediation are truths of the very nature of God and are defined decisively within God's Triune self-relatedness. The Trinitarian grammar of Christian theology gives structure and definition to the language of grace and mediation. The purpose of the next chapter is to explore the significance of grace and mediation, thus defined, for an understanding of God's relatedness to that which is other than God, to the world, to us. Simply put, I want to argue that he relates to us as the one that he is, as the one who loves freely (gratuitously), as the one who freely mediates that gratuitous love.

---

[70]   Colwell, *Living the Christian Story*, p. 150, fn. 10; cf. *CD* I/1, pp. 88ff. and *CD* IV/3, pp. 114ff. Note in this respect the distinction in Barth's thought, apparently commended by John Webster, between the (unmediated) Word of Christ and any word mediated through the Church (*CD* IV/3, p. 836). But how then is this Word of Christ spoken and heard if not through the Church, through Scripture, or through the world? Cf. John Webster, *Barth's Moral Theology: Human Action in Barth's Thought* (Edinburgh: T & T Clark, 1998), pp. 142ff.

CHAPTER 2

Sacramentality and the Doctrine of Creation

Jesus said to them, 'My Father is always at his work to this very day, and I, too, am working.'...

'I tell you the truth, the Son can do nothing by himself; he can only do what he sees his Father doing, because whatever the Father does the Son also does. For the Father loves the Son and shows him all he does. Yes, to your amazement he will show even greater things than these.' (John 5.17 and 19-20)

It is surely no coincidence that two of the earliest Christian thinkers to clarify a doctrine of the Trinity were also responsible for developing a distinctively Christian understanding of the relatedness of God and the world.[1] In his Treatise against Hermogenes,[2] Tertullian considers that there are but three ways in which God's relatedness to the material universe could be conceived: either the material universe emanated from God (an idea dismissed by both Hermogenes and Tertullian); or the matter out of which God formed the universe exists eternally as God exists eternally (which is what Hermogenes himself had argued, which was assumed by various gnostic groups, and which was a form of dualism generally held in the Hellenistic world);[3] or the material universe was

---

[1]   'We shall understand the distinctiveness of the Christian theology of creation only if we realise that these three themes—creation as an article of the creed; creation out of nothing; and creation as the work of the whole Trinity, Father, Son and Holy Spirit—are in some way bound up with each other, both historically and systematically.' Gunton, *The Triune Creator*, p. 9

[2]   Tertullian, *Against Hermogenes*, in *ANF* vol. 3, pp. 477-502.

[3]   Tertullian outlines Hermogenes' views thus: 'He...concludes that He [God] made nothing out of Himself, since He never passed into such a condition as made it possible for Him to make anything out of Himself. In like manner, he contends that He could not have made all things out of nothing—thus: He defines the Lord as a being who is good, nay, very good, who must will to make things as good and excellent as He is Himself; indeed it were impossible for Him either to will or to make anything which was not good, nay, very good itself. Therefore all things ought to have been made good and excellent by Him, after His own condition. Experience shows, however, that things which are even evil were made by Him: not, of course, of His own will and pleasure, He would be sure to have made nothing unfittingly or unworthy of Himself. That, therefore, which He made not of His own will must be understood to have been made from the fault of something, and that is from Matter, without a doubt.' Tertullian, *Against Hermogenes*, ch. 2.

created by God out of nothing. For the first to be the case would be to imply that creation shared the divine nature, would be to imply that creation was effectively itself divine, and would therefore be to jeopardise any ultimate distinction between Creator and creation.[4] For the second to be the case would imply that God was not God alone,[5] would imply that there were two sources for all reality, would validate the common notion of a dualism between spirit and matter, and would thereby forfeit the notion of the essential goodness of creation. Tertullian concludes that only the third option—that God creates the universe out of nothing—preserves the 'Godness' of God in relation to creation. One could add that only this doctrine of creation out of nothing does justice to the biblical witness by maintaining both creation's distinction from God and creation's continuing and absolute dependence upon God.

The development of this doctrine of creation out of nothing was as much an 'innovation' as was the development of the doctrine of the Trinity: both doctrines derive from the Church's reflection on the gospel story,[6] and, though Tertullian never develops the idea, one could argue that something very much like a doctrine of the Trinity is necessary to maintain these truths of creation's distinctness and creation's dependence (not to mention God's freedom to be present within creation) without contradiction. Tertullian certainly does affirm that God creates through his Wisdom and his Word, but he undermines the insight both by seemingly identifying Word and Wisdom and also by assuming that both Word and Wisdom are begotten in time and therefore do not participate in God's eternity.[7]

---

[4]   Thus Tertullian states (apparently repeating Hermogenes' own view): '[e]verything, however, both which was made and which He made must be accounted imperfect, because it was made of a part, and He made it of a part; or if, again, it was a whole which He made, who is whole Himself, He must in that case have been at once both a whole, and yet not a whole; because it behoved Him to be a whole, that He might produce Himself, and yet not a whole, that He might be produced out of Himself. But this is a most difficult position. For if He were in existence, He could not be made, for He was in existence already; if, however, he were not in existence, He could not make, because He was a nonentity...moreover, that He who always exists, does not *come into* existence, but exists for ever and ever. He accordingly concludes that He made nothing out of Himself, since He never passed into such a condition.' Tertullian, *Against Hermogenes*, ch. 2.

[5]   'Hermogenes, therefore, introduces two gods: he introduces Matter as God's equal. God, however, must be One...'. Tertullian, *Against Hermogenes*, ch. 4.

[6]   The innovative nature of this doctrine of *creatio ex nihilo* is discussed by Frances Young in her article '"Creatio ex Nihilo": A context for the emergence of the Christian Doctrine of Creation', *SJT* 44 (1991), pp. 139-151.

[7]   Tertullian, *Against Hermogenes*, ch. 18. Indeed, the non-eternity of the Son had earlier been one of Tertullian's arguments against Hermogenes' view of the eternity of matter. Tertullian, *Against Hermogenes*, ch. 3.

A similar yet more promising reflection on God's relatedness to creation is proposed by Irenaeus of Lyons (c.130–c.202), a contemporary of Tertullian's who, like Tertullian, developed his thinking in response to the challenges of gnostic dualism, in this case those challenges posed by a particular and complex form of gnosticism associated with Valentinus (belief in a hierarchy of powers under God, the material creation being the work of a 'Demiurge' rather than God himself). Since Irenaeus claims to have heard Polycarp preach, it is commonly assumed that he originated from the Smyrnan region of Asia Minor (modern day Turkey). He accompanied Pothinus (an evangelist sent by Polycarp to Gaul) and, after the martyrdom of Pothinus in 177, Irenaeus succeeded him as bishop of Lyons (Irenaeus himself may have died a martyr's death in 202).

The first book of Irenaeus' major work, usually referred to as *Against Heresies*,[8] is chiefly a description of this form of gnosticism propounded by Valentinus and of its predecessors (though Irenaeus devotes some space to highlight the internal inconsistencies of these gnostic teachings). He begins his second book with a clear affirmation of the one God as the only creator, 'commanding all things into existence',[9] and uses this foundational statement to refute Valentinus and to expose his teachings as deriving from pagan notions, including the assumption that creation was formed 'out of previously existing matter'.[10] But even in the course of this refutation, before Irenaeus has come to a positive exposition of a doctrine of creation according to the catholic tradition, he affirms that this one and only God made all things *through* the agency of the Son and the Spirit.[11] And this insight remains one of Irenaeus' two 'big ideas' throughout the remainder of these five books: the Son and the Spirit, God's Word and God's Wisdom, are the agents or mediators of the Father's creative work; all that God does in respect of that which is other than himself is done through the agency of the Son and the Spirit:

---

[8]   Irenaeus, *Against Heresies*, in *ANF* vol. 1, pp. 315-567.

[9]   'It is proper, then, that I should begin with the first and most important head, that is, God the creator, who made the heaven and the earth, and all things that are therein...and to demonstrate that there is nothing either above Him or after Him; nor that, influenced by any one, but of his own free will, He created all things, since He is the only God, the only Lord, the only Creator, the only Father, alone containing all things, and Himself commanding all things into existence.' Irenaeus, *Against Heresies*, II i 1.

[10]   Irenaeus, *Against Heresies*, II xiv 4.

[11]   'But there is one only God, the Creator—He who is above every Principality, and Power, and Dominion, and Virtue: He is Father, He is God, He the Founder, He the Maker, He the Creator, who made those things by Himself, that is, through His Word and Wisdom...'. Irenaeus, *Against Heresies*, II xxx 9

> For with Him were always present the Word and Wisdom, the Son and the Spirit, by whom and in whom, freely and spontaneously, He made all things...the Son, was always with the Father; and that Wisdom also, which is the Spirit, was present with Him, anterior to all creation...[12]

Here there would seem to be no equivocation concerning the eternity of the Son and the Spirit, together with the Father before all creation. Here there is certainly no equivocation concerning the uniqueness of God and the non-eternity of creation. But most crucially for the theme of this book, here there is the clearest acknowledgement of the mediate nature of God's presence and action towards all that is other than himself—a mediation not confined to the initial act of creation but characterising the entirety of God's relatedness to creation.[13]

And this recognition of the mediate-ness of the entirety of God's relatedness to creation leads on to Irenaeus' other 'big idea' and other key response to the dualism represented by Valentinus, namely the continuity of creation and redemption, a continuity rooted in the recognition that both creation and redemption are the work of the one God and that both creation and redemption are mediated by the Son and the Spirit. It is in this context that Irenaeus writes of redemption as a recapitulation ($\overset{'}{\alpha}\nu\alpha\kappa\epsilon\phi\alpha\lambda\alpha\acute{\iota}\omega\sigma\iota\varsigma$) of creation, not simply or merely as a return to an original perfection, but rather and more profoundly as a restoration that brings about the fulfilment of that originally intended perfection.[14] For Irenaeus it is not just that the eternal Son assumes the frail and fallen flesh of Adam (though he certainly does),[15] it is also and

---

[12]   Irenaeus, *Against Heresies*, IV xx 1.

[13]   'He has come within reach of human knowledge (knowledge, however, not with regard to His greatness, or with regard to His essence—for that has no man measured or handled—but after this sort: that we should know that He who made, and formed, and breathed in them the breath of life, and nourishes us by means of the creation, establishing all things by His Word, and binding them together by His Wisdom—this is He who is the only true God)...'. Irenaeus, *Against Heresies*, III xxiv 2.

[14]   'For it behoved Him who was to destroy sin, and redeem man under the power of death, that He should Himself be made that very same thing which he was, that is, man; who had been drawn by sin into bondage, but was held by death, so that sin should be destroyed by man, and man should go forth from death... God recapitulated in Himself the ancient formation of man, that He might kill sin, deprive death of its power, and vivify man...'. Irenaeus, *Against Heresies*, III xviii 7. 'The idea that Irenaeus cannot decide about the fall, or whether Christ comes to move us forwards or backwards, thus appears to be entirely misguided. Recapitulation involves a reversal that takes us ahead again.' Douglas Farrow, 'St. Irenaeus of Lyons: The Church and the World', *Pro Ecclesia* 4.3 (1995), pp. 333-355 (p. 349).

[15]   'There is therefore...one God the Father, and one Christ Jesus, who...gathered together all things in Himself. But in every respect, too, He is man, the formation of God; and thus He took up man into Himself, the invisible becoming visible, the

primarily that Adam is created in the image of the eternal Son with the goal of being perfected in that image.[16] Consequently for Irenaeus, in contrast to Tertullian, creation has an eschatological directedness; it has a τέλος; it has a goal:

> For Tertullian, the fate of the creation is eventually to come to nothing: that which comes from nothing will eventually return there. For Irenaeus, that which comes from nothing is destined to become something, and it is perhaps the notion of creation as that which is directed to an eschatological perfection which is one of the most neglected features of Irenaeus' thought.[17]

Colin Gunton has made much of this distinctive understanding of creation, its eschatological orientation, and its mediate-ness. He has made much also of the consequences of the abandonment of this more ancient tradition, and it is difficult to avoid the conclusion that he is correct. To conceive of the material creation as the shadow of eternal realities rather than as the foreshadowing of an eschatological future is to deprive creation of its eschatological goal and to reduce it to the static. And to conceive of the material creation as mediated through eternal forms rather than through the agency of the Son and the Spirit is to depersonalise the mediate-ness of creation.[18]

---

incomprehensible being made comprehensible, the impassable becoming capable of suffering, and the Word being made man, thus summing up all things in Himself: so that as in super-celestial, spiritual, and invisible things, the Word of God is supreme, so also in things visible and corporeal He might possess the supremacy and, taking to Himself the pre-eminence, as well as constituting Himself Head of the church, He might draw all things to Himself at the proper time.' Irenaeus, *Against Heresies*, III xvi 6

[16]   '[I]t was said that man was created after the image of God, but it was not [actually] shown; for the Word was as yet invisible, after whose image man was created.' Irenaeus, *Against Heresies*, V xvi 2. A similar understanding of the provisionality and eschatological directedness of Adam can be found in the work of Edward Irving: 'Adam, then, is presented as perfect, but incomplete. Creation cannot have been created perfect in light of both its subsequent demise and the appearance of Christ. Irving argues, "if the creation had been perfect and sufficient while yet the Christ was unconstituted, then why should there be a Christ at all? There cannot be two perfections, there cannot be two unchangeables, otherwise there were two gods."' Graham McFarlane, *Christ and the Spirit: The Doctrine of the Incarnation According to Edward Irving* (Carlisle: Paternoster Press, 1996), pp. 98-99. quoting from *The Collected Writings of Edward Irving in Five Volumes*, vol. 5, ed. G. Carlyle (London: Alexander Strahan, 1864), p. 98.

[17]   Gunton, *The Triune Creator*, p. 55.

[18]   '[T]he doctrine of the superior status of the heavens and the inferiority of the material world were contaminations of the doctrine of creation which had been adopted into the tradition. They derived from its "Babylonian captivity" to a non-trinitarian theology in which God the Son and God the Spirit were crowded out by a pagan ontology, so that God the Father was transmogrified into a monistically conceived deity owing much to Greek negative theology. Philo's introduction of the forms into the mind of God,

The quotation from John's Gospel at the beginning of this chapter similarly implies a continuity of creation and redemption, a goal to which the Father is working through the Son, a mediated continuity of God's action. And it is with this mediate-ness of creation through the personal agency of the Son and the Spirit that this chapter is chiefly concerned.

In the first place the eternal Son, the λόγος of God, is the rationality of creation; he is creation's source, mediation, centre, and goal.[19] The rationality of creation, then, is not impersonal or purposeless; the rationality of creation consists in its being sourced from and directed towards participation in the eternal Son's relatedness to the eternal Father. And, as was argued in the previous chapter, the Son's relatedness to the Father and the Father's relatedness to the Son is itself mediated by the Spirit; it is the Spirit, as the mediator of the relatedness of Father and Son, who preserves the distinct identities of Father and Son within this intimate communion of absolute love. Accordingly then (and in the second place), it is the Spirit who mediates the relatedness of the particulars of creation to their source, centre, and goal in the Son, thus preserving their contingent particularity. It is through the Spirit that the contingent particularity of creation is maintained in the context of its absolute source, centre, and goal; it is through the Spirit that the orientation of creation to its source, centre, and goal is maintained in the context of its genuine and contingent particularity. That is to say, just as the Spirit, as the mediator of the love of Father and Son, maintains the distinct identities of Father and Son within the absolute intimacy of their eternal communion, so also the Spirit, as the mediator of creation's relatedness to the Son before the Father, maintains the distinctness and particularity of creation in the context of its divine orientation:

> The Spirit, by thus relating the world to the Father through the Son...enables an omnipresence which is not the homogeneous presence of a container but the

---

adopted by Origen and reinforced by the doctrines of the eternity of heavenly bodies, generated a hierarchical view of being which, by minimising the importance of the material world, took attention away from that world within whose very structures the Son of God condescended to live, in a body shaped for him by the Spirit of God the Father. More than that, the platonic forms effectively displaced the eternal and incarnate Son as the means by which God the Father was related to the world. The outcome was that God was conceived to be related to the world by an immaterial structure rather than by the one who became flesh. The effective exclusion of the doctrine of the Trinity from the structuring of the Christian doctrine of creation is therefore at the root of its Babylonian captivity and of the apparent mutual exclusion of theology and science.' Gunton, *The Triune Creator*, p. 116.

[19]   'For by him all things were created: things in heaven and on earth, visible and invisible, whether thrones or powers or rulers or authorities; all things were created by him and for him. He is before all things, and in him all things hold together.' Colossians 1.16-17.

presence of one enabling the world to be and become truly itself... When God the Son is the (personal) principle of the world's unity and coherence, the Holy Spirit, through that same Son, becomes the focus of the particularity of things; their becoming 'perfect'—complete—as distinctly themselves.[20]

There is, therefore, no unmediated presence or action of God within or toward creation; the relatedness of God to creation is mediated in the Son and through the Spirit. Or, to put the matter more *theo*logically: God relates to creation as the One that he is, as the Father, the Son, and the Spirit, as the One whose free, loving relatedness is itself mediated. And herein, I believe, lies the possibility for a proper understanding of a sacramental dynamic and of sacramental particulars.

But, before proceeding with this theme, it may be appropriate to pause briefly and to underline the distinctness of this explicitly Trinitarian and dynamic account of God's relatedness to creation (together with its sacramental possibilities) in relation to more common contemporary accounts of God's relatedness to creation—proposals which would appear to owe more to the alternatives rejected by Tertullian and Irenaeus.

In the first place a Trinitarian account of God's relatedness to creation is a repudiation of any mechanistic account of the universe that effectively evacuates the universe of God's dynamic presence. Inherently deistic accounts of God's relatedness to creation that arose during the Enlightenment and that are implicit in the thought of Isaac Newton[21] and William Paley[22] may not posit a Platonic notion of the eternity of matter but, by effectively restricting God's creative activity to the zero point of creation, and by considering the dynamics of the universe as determined by 'natural law', such accounts imply a *created* and *contingent* dualism that empties the world of God's dynamic presence just as thoroughly. Here the rationality of the universe is assumed to be independent of the identity of the eternal Son, the divine λόγος, and, as such, the rationality of the universe is assumed to be perceivable and comprehensible without reference to the eternal Son (its source and goal) and without the mediation of the Spirit. Here, then, the relatedness of God to creation is conceived monistically rather than Trinitarianly. If not explicitly a unitarian rejection of the doctrine of the Trinity, this typically Enlightenment account at very least constitutes a rejection of any Trinitarian understanding of creation, thus limiting the pertinence of Trinitarian theology to a doctrine of redemption and, as a consequence, reinforcing that disjunction between creation and redemption which

---

20   Gunton, *The Triune Creator*, p. 143.

21   Isaac Newton, *Philosophiae Naturalis Principia Mathematica* (1687), trans. I. B. Cohen and A. Whitman (Los Angeles, CA: University of California Press, 1997).

22   William Paley, *Natural Theology, or Evidences of the Existence and Attributes of the Deity Collected from the Appearances of Nature* (London: R. Faulder, 1802).

Irenaeus was at such pains to deny. All too easily Catholic notions of the distinction between nature and grace and Evangelical notions of miracles as divine interventions serve to reinforce the assumptions of this second order dualism through which the universe, once created, continues to exist in effective independence. To contrast nature and grace is to imply an 'un-graced' nature; is to imply the independence of nature from any active and continuous mediation through the Son and the Spirit. Similarly to speak of divine interventions is to imply a contrasting divine absence and inactivity as the 'normal' or 'natural' state of the cosmos. A doctrine of the Trinity is irrelevant and unnecessary for such conceptions of God's relatedness to creation.

But the common reaction to this mechanistic account represents no real advance, at least in Trinitarian terms. Panentheistic affirmations of creation as God's 'body',[23] while reaffirming the continuity of God's presence within creation (and creation's consequent livingness) do so at the expense of any genuine distinctness of God and creation. God thus conceived may not be contained or enclosed within creation, God thus conceived may vastly exceed creation, but creation has no distinct identity in relation to God, and God's identity—as inclusive of creation—is no longer authentically free in relation to creation. If creation's identity is in any sense included in God's identity, then the distinctness and particularity of creation is forfeited. If God's identity is in any sense dependent upon creation's identity (and it is difficult to see how such a conclusion could be avoided), then God is rendered unfree and God's relatedness to creation is no longer truly and continually gratuitous. The difficulty with panentheistic accounts, as with the mechanistic accounts against which they are a reaction, is that God again is conceived monistically rather than Trinitarianly—or rather, God is conceived other than as defined in the gospel story.[24] Once again the rationality of creation is conceived other than Christologically. Once again the Spirit, as the mediator of divine presence and action, is rendered redundant. Monism in the context of a mechanistic conception of the universe issues in a creation vacated of God's presence and action. Monism in the context of a panentheistic conception of the universe issues in an

---

[23] See, for instance, Sally MacFague, *The Body of God: An Ecological Theology* (London: SCM Press, 1993).

[24] That this way of thinking renders a doctrine of the Trinity redundant is illustrated by the tendency in such contexts to speak of creation in terms traditionally reserved for Christ: '...in apparent response to dualistic thinking, imputed to traditional theology, some feminist theologians describe the relation of God and the world not in terms of transcendence and absoluteness but in terms of immanence and interdependence. In so doing, they ascribe to the world attributes traditionally reserved for the Incarnate Word.' David A. Scott, 'Creation as Christ: A Problematic Theme in Some Feminist Theology', in Kimel, Jr. (ed.), *Speaking the Christian God*, pp. 237-257 (pp. 239-240).

unmediated, indistinct, and therefore indeterminate notion of divine presence.

Writing towards the beginning of the Enlightenment era (and specifically in response to the empiricism of John Locke), Jonathan Edwards' notion of God's preserving of creation as 'perfectly equivalent to a *continued creation*' certainly repudiates any mechanistic notion of the universe.[25] As Robert Jenson has noted:

> ...Edwards clearly saw that Christianity could not long coexist with a mechanist worldview. Nor did he think Christianity needed to, since mechanism was, he judged, a mere conceptual blunder, an anachronism that resulted from reading the antique conceptuality of substance onto terms in the formulas of modern science... [H]e shares the position of David Hume: a cause is any event that appears in the protasis of a true proposition of the form 'If...happens, then...will happen.' A cause does not 'make' its effect happen; nor need there be any other occult connection between them.[26]

In this respect, it is difficult to comprehend the common objections to Edwards' view.[27] If God created the universe in such a manner that it

---

[25]   'It will certainly follow...that God's *preserving* created things in being is perfectly equivalent to a *continued creation*, or to his creating those things out of nothing at *each moment* of their existence. If the continued existence of created things be wholly dependent on God's preservation, then those things would drop into nothing, upon the ceasing of the present moment, without a new exertion of the divine power to cause them to exist in the following moment... It will follow...that God's upholding created substance, or causing its existence in each successive moment, is altogether equivalent to an *immediate production out of nothing*, at each moment, because its existence at this moment is not merely in part from God, but wholly from him; and not in any part, or degree, from its antecedent existence.' Jonathan Edwards, *Original Sin*, in *YE* vol. 3, pp. 401-402.

Jonathan Edwards was born in East Windsor, Connecticut, on 5 October 1703. He studied at Yale and, after a brief period as tutor, he joined his maternal grandfather, Solomon Stoddard, in the pastorate at Northampton, Massachusetts, remaining as sole pastor after Stoddard's death in 1729. Dismissed from the pastorate in 1750 over a dispute concerning church membership and communion, Edwards was appointed pastor of a 'mission' church in Stockbridge (perhaps his most significant period of writing) before being invited to become President of Princeton College and dying in March 1758 as the result of a reaction to a smallpox inoculation. For an excellent account of Edwards' theological contribution see Stephen R. Holmes, *God of Grace and God of Glory: An Account of the Theology of Jonathan Edwards* (Edinburgh: T & T Clark, 2000).

[26]   Robert W. Jenson, *Systematic Theology*, vol. 2, *The Works of God* (Oxford and New York: Oxford University Press, 1999), pp. 39-40. For a fuller account of Edwards' views in these respects see Robert W. Jenson, *America's Theologian: A Recommendation of Jonathan Edwards* (Oxford and New York: Oxford University Press, 1988).

[27]   'A distinction between creation and "preservation" or between initial and "continuing" creation has been rightly used to warrant that there was a first existence at a

could continue to exist and function mechanistically and independently then such a universe would have no need of God's preserving action; it would appropriately be void of his presence. But if God created the universe in such a manner that it remains continually dependent upon his presence and action, then only that divine presence and action preserves the universe from collapse into nothingness.[28]

However, taken together with Edwards' conviction that all reality is grounded in God's perception,[29] one can begin to understand the fear that here again the distinctness and particularity of creation is jeopardised.[30] If creation has no reality or continuity other than as perceived by God then in what meaningful sense can creation be distinguished from God?[31]

The first difficulty here is with the word 'perception' itself. For us to perceive something is a passive occurrence rather than an active and creative occurrence; we may choose to look at something or not to look at something, but our seeing of that something is 'given' to us; we are recipients (or, perhaps, participants). And our seeing of something is certainly not the cause of the existence of that something. It was in this

---

zero point of time. But such distinctions can have no other metaphysical or religious significance. The world is no less dependent on God's creating word in any moment of its existence than it was at the beginning.' Jenson, *Systematic Theology*, vol. 2, p. 9

[28] 'To what purpose can it be, to talk of God's preserving things in being, when there is no need of his preserving them? Or to talk of their being dependent on God for continued existence, when they would of themselves continue to exist, without his help...'. Jonathan Edwards, *Original Sin*, p. 402.

[29] 'Though we suppose that the existence of the whole material universe is absolutely dependent on idea, yet we may speak in the old way, and as properly and truly as ever: God in the beginning created such a certain numbers of atoms, of such a determinate bulk and figure, which they maintain and always will; and gave them such a motion, of such a direction, and of such a degree of velocity; from whence arise all the natural changes in the universe forever in a continued series. Yet perhaps all this does not exist anywhere perfectly but in the divine mind. But then, if it be inquired what exists in the divine mind, and how these things exist there, I answer: there is his determination, his care and his design that ideas shall be united forever, just so and in such a manner as is agreeable to such a series... God supposes its existence; that is, he causes all changes to arise as if all these things had actually existed in such a series in some created mind, and as if created minds had comprehended all things perfectly. And although created minds do not, yet the divine mind doth, and he orders all things according to his mind, and his ideas.' Jonathan Edwards, 'The Mind', in *Scientific and Philosophical Writings*, in *YE* vol. 6, pp. 332-393 (p. 354).

[30] For such objections see for instance Paul Helm, *Faith and Understanding* (Edinburgh: Edinburgh University Press, 1997), pp. 152-176.

[31] The parallels here with the views of George Berkeley are impressive though no clear link between the two authors has yet been established. Arguably Berkeley's account would benefit even more from Trinitarian revision.

respect that George Berkeley was (and is) greatly misunderstood:[32] it is not our perception but God's perception that constitutes the being of anything. For Jonathan Edwards (as also for George Berkeley) divine perception is both active and creative. Indeed, how could it be otherwise: God is 'simple'; his being is identical with his understanding which is identical with his will. For God to perceive an entity is for God to will that entity is for God to create that entity.

But the key issue is that for Edwards (if not explicitly for Berkeley) this creative perception is a Trinitarian act: God perceives the universe as the one he truly is; as Father, Son, and Spirit.[33] I am not suggesting that Edwards' Trinitarian account of reality and of our knowledge of it is adequate—it still assumes a predominately Augustinian, rather than Cappadocian, account of the Trinity—but I am suggesting that it is indicative of the manner in which Berkeley's account can be 'corrected'. Since God perceives the universe as the one he truly is—as Father, Son, and Spirit—his perceiving of the universe is a mediated perception. And in the implicit mediate-ness of that creating perception the distinct contingency of the universe is preserved. Edwards' account of the relatedness of God to creation, in all its dynamic radicality, remains committedly Trinitarian and never collapses into the monadic. Here, at least potentially, the mediating agency of the Son and the Spirit maintain the distinctness of the particulars of creation in relation to the Father; the contingent remains truly and dynamically contingent.

The sheer dynamism, continuity, and livingness of this account is the first reason for introducing the work of Jonathan Edwards at this point. At the beginnings of the Enlightenment and in radical response to its mechanistic notions of the universe Edwards asserts the continuing and total dependence of creation upon God. The coherence of apparent causality within the universe is simply an outcome of divine constancy.

---

[32]   George Berkeley (1685–1753) was born near Kilkenny in Ireland, graduated from Trinity College, Dublin, in 1704 and was made a fellow in 1707. In 1724 he became Dean of Derry and in 1734 was consecrated Bishop of Cloyne. His key philosophical ideas, reflected in his early notebooks as much as in his later, mature, works, are principally responses to the ideas of Locke and Newton.

[33]   'As to God's excellence, it is evident it consists in the love of himself. For he was as excellent before he created the universe as he is now. But if the excellence of spirits consists in their disposition and action, God could be excellent no other way at that time, for all the exertions of himself were towards himself. But he exerts himself towards himself no other way than in infinitely loving and delighting in himself, in the mutual love of the Father and the Son. This makes the third, the personal Holy Spirit or the holiness of God, which is his infinite beauty, and this is God's infinite consent to being in general. And his love to the creature is his excellence, or the communication of himself, his complacency in them, according as they partake of more or less of excellence and beauty; that is, of holiness, which consists in love; that is, according as he communicates more or less of his Holy Spirit.' Edwards, 'The Mind', p. 364.

There is no 'un-graced' nature.[34] All reality is the immediate (though implicitly mediated) issue of divine causality.[35]

Moreover, this conception of divine perception underlies Edwards' distinctive notion of human perception—and this is the second reason for introducing his ideas at this point:

> Our perceptions, or ideas that we passively receive by our bodies, are communicated to us immediately by God...[36]

Edwards, like Berkeley, understands human perception as a gift, but Edwards' more thoroughly Trinitarian account permits him to conceive of that gift as a participation. Our perception, then, is a mediated perception; it is an immediate action of the Spirit whereby we are brought to participate in God's perception. There is no unmediated or independent perception; all perception is a mediated immediacy; all perception is a mediated participation in God's Triune perception.[37] And since for Edwards there can be no perception without affectedness, all human perception is consequently a participation in divine affection. This rebuttal of the classical distinction between perception and affectedness is the other key strand of Edwards' epistemology and underlies his writings both on the theme of revival (to know God by the Spirit is for our affections to be changed) and on the theme of sin (sin is distorted affection). To perceive any particular of creation, then, is to participate through the Spirit in God's perception of that particular and in God's affection for that particular. Were it not for the distortion of human sinfulness, all perception would be an impression of the beauty and harmony of particulars and, thereby, an impression of the absolute beauty

---

[34]　In this respect note that John Milbank draws attention to the 'integralism' of Vatican Two (i.e., the integral unity of nature and grace), to the French version of this integralism (represented by Maurice Blondel) that 'supernaturalizes the natural', and to the German version (represented by Karl Rahner) that 'naturalizes the supernatural'. John Milbank, *Theology and Social Theory* (Oxford: Blackwell, 1990), pp. 206-207.

[35]　'At his most youthfully speculative, Edwards could identify space, the field of physical phenomena, with the field of God's consciousness: God thinks movements and resistances in universally mutual harmony, and that is the "substance" of the physical world—if, as Edwards says, we "must needs" use that word.' Jenson, *Systematic Theology*, vol. 2, pp. 40-41.

[36]　Edwards, 'The Mind', p. 339.

[37]　So also Colin Gunton: 'If Christ is the mediator of creation, then he is the basis of created rationality and therefore of human knowledge, wherever and whatever; we might say, of all human culture. But that point must be developed pneumatologically also, so that all rationality, truth and beauty are seen to be realised through the perfecting agency of God the Spirit, who enables things to be known by human minds and made by human hands.' Colin E. Gunton, *A Brief Theology of Revelation* (Edinburgh: T & T Clark, 1995), pp. 124-125.

and harmony of the Triune God as their source and goal; all perception would be revelatory.

It must be emphasised that this is not Edwards' version of a 'natural' theology in the sense of any independently accessible knowledge of God: there is no independently accessible knowledge of anything; all knowledge is a gift; all knowledge is a mediation. This is rather Edwards' attempt at a genuine 'general' revelation: all knowledge is mediated and therefore, at least potentially, all knowledge may be a mediation of the knowledge of God. But if the knowledge of anything at all is a gift then the knowledge of the one who mediates the knowledge of anything at all is similarly a gift. Truly to know any particular is to know that particular in relation to the Son as its source and goal, is to know that particular as that which is loved in the Son by the Father. But such knowledge, indeed all knowledge, is mediated by the Spirit and the Spirit is the free Lord—there is nothing necessary or automatic here. Moreover, such knowledge is mediated by the Spirit in the context of human sinfulness and distortion: we do not yet know as we are given to know nor do we yet love as we are given to love.

With Edwards then, as with Irenaeus before him, lies the possibility of a truly dynamic and Trinitarian account of God's relatedness to creation that avoids mechanistic notions of a creation evacuated of divine presence on the one hand and, on the other hand, avoids any implicit divinisation of creation that blurs the distinction between creation and Creator. Both pitfalls are the outcome of a monism that excludes the possibility of the mediation of created reality and of the perception of that reality. Both pitfalls are overcome by a Trinitarian account of the mediation of created reality and of the perception of that reality. Here God remains truly God: neither absent from created reality even in true distinctness from that reality, nor simply identified with created reality even in constant mediation of that reality. And consequently here creation remains truly creation: neither independent of God even in its true distinctness from God, nor simply identified with God even in its constant dependence upon God. Or, as Jeremy Begbie expresses it:

> ...God's loyalty is a respectful loyalty. He gives his world a measure of independence and autonomy, allowing it 'room' to be itself. For his love achieves its ends by respecting the 'otherness of the other'. This should make us wary of attempts to interpret the New Testament 'cosmic Christ' passages as suggesting a 'sacramental universe', impregnated with divine causes, as if Christ could in some sense be 'read off' the face of nature. A more judicious approach to Biblical language about the relation between Christ and creation should properly remind us that God's love for creation entails him honouring its integrity as something distinct from himself. The created world may indeed be regarded as the area for Christ's ceaseless activity, but this does not alter its finite, contingent createdness: its deepest secret lies outside its own reality. Indeed, as is often pointed out, a

proper stress on the contingency of the created order has proved crucial to the momentum of contemporary science. Moreover, to speak of this divine respect in terms of God's 'self-limitation', as some are keen to do, is arguably unnecessary and potentially misleading. It may be appropriate to use such language in certain contexts, but God's refusal to violate the created order is better construed as an expression of his unswerving faithfulness to it, not as a sign of a retreat into some kind of self-imposed impotence.[38]

As Begbie rightly observes, this account of God's relatedness to creation does not imply a 'sacramental universe', not just because (as Begbie states and as has been argued above) Christ cannot simply be 'read off' created reality, but rather because a sacrament is a 'sign': not merely the mediation of a particular but the mediation of God's presence and action through that mediated particular. To conceive of creation as God's body (as has already been noted) is to ascribe to creation as a whole that which properly is ascribed uniquely to Christ and is therefore to deny Christ's distinctiveness. Similarly, to presume the sacramentality of all creation is to undermine the sacramentality of specific signs within creation. When all is deemed to signify nothing remains significant. Pan-sacramentalism emasculates sacramentality.[39] William Cavanaugh makes a similar comment with respect to the work of Leonardo Boff:

> In Leonardo Boff's book on the sacraments, one finds chapters entitled 'Our Family Mug as Sacrament' and 'My Father's Cigarette Butt as Sacrament.' Although Boff considers the Eucharist to be one of the 'special' sacraments, he contends that anything on earth can be a sacrament for a particular individual, provided she look through the object itself and see the presence of God. God is always present in everything, he argues, but the person of faith must learn to read the deeper meaning behind the signs. This attempt to re-enchant the secular world, however, only leaves the world more bereft of God. If God always stands 'behind' signs, then signs become interchangeable, and God never truly saturates any particular sign. This approach easily flip-flops into the modern post-Kantian suspicion of all representation as unable to reveal the transcendent.[40]

The recognition of the Trinitarian mediation of creation and of our perception of creation, therefore, need not imply the sacramentality of all particulars—it rather identifies the general context and dynamic whereby

---

[38] Jeremy Begbie, *Voicing Creation's Praise: Towards a Theology of the Arts* (Edinburgh: T & T Clark, 1991), pp. 171-172.

[39] While Alexander Schmemann offers us a beautiful walk through the Orthodox Liturgy it is difficult to avoid the conclusion that this is but another form of 'pan-sacramentalism'. Alexander Schmemann, *The World as Sacrament* (London: Darton, Longman and Todd, 1965). And perhaps a similar tendency occurs in William Temple, *Nature, Man and God* (London: Macmillan, 1940), pp. 473ff.

[40] William T. Cavanaugh, *Torture and Eucharist: Theology, Politics, and the Body of Christ* (Oxford: Blackwell, 1998), p. 13.

any single particular may be sacramental. It affirms the Spirit as the mediator of every particular of creation and of our perception of those particulars. It affirms Christ as the source, goal, and therefore the ultimate significance of every particular of creation. But it does not imply any necessary mediation of the immediate presence and action of Christ in every particular of creation. That God once encounters Moses through a burning bush (Exodus 3.2ff.) does not imply that all bushes are sacramental, even though our perception of any bush, not to mention the existence of any bush, is actively mediated by the Spirit.

Nonetheless, even a cursory reading of Scripture identifies God's apparent predilection, not just for bushes, but for physical, material means of mediating his presence and action.[41] God parts the Red Sea when Moses raises his staff. God leads Israel through the wilderness by a pillar of cloud and of fire. God gives water to his people when Moses (again with his staff) strikes the rock. God delivers Israel from deadly venom when they gaze at a bronze serpent set up by Moses. And throughout this narrative it is through Moses that God speaks to his people, just as subsequently he will lead them through judges and kings and will speak to them through prophets. Having established a material universe God tends not to bypass it. He mediates his presence by the Spirit through the physical particulars of creation that themselves are mediated by the Son and the Spirit. Nothing could be further from the supposed dualistic division of spirit and matter beloved of gnostics and not a few contemporary 'charismatics'. Even the Spirit takes form as a dove, as wind, as fire. And ultimately the Word becomes flesh and dwells among us.[42] For Christian theology, of course, the central and defining significance of the Incarnation cannot be overstated: God is revealed to us ultimately, not in some unmediated epiphany, but in and through the flesh of a Nazarene carpenter. In the defining core of the Christian story there is no unmediated divine presence; all that God is and does here is done by the mediation of the Spirit through the flesh assumed by the Son. Here centrally and definitively God does not bypass the materiality of the universe he has created.[43]

---

[41]   The point is made effectively in an article by Brian Horne, 'The Sacramental Use of Material Things', in Martin Dudley and Geoffrey Rowell (eds.), *The Oil of Gladness: Anointing in the Christian Tradition* (London: SPCK, 1993), pp. 7-18.

[42]   'I am not suggesting that God has a body in the same way that we are embodied, but that God commits God's own self to body—or rather, to bodies—as a meeting place with us.' Fiddes, *Participating in God*, p. 279.

[43]   'Christ is the Sacrament of the Father, the One who is sent by the Father, and who makes Him visible, in the power of the Holy Spirit. In this sense, the sacramental mystery is rooted in the mystery of the Most Holy Trinity. However, it is a gratuitous gift, for God was never bound from external or internal necessity to create, and never bound to reveal Himself, and never bound to share His Life and Love.' Haffner, *The*

But although God mediates his presence to Moses through the burning bush he never promises that the bush will be a continuing sign through which he mediates his presence. In this respect it is probably unhelpful and imprecise to think of the bush in sacramental terms: God mediates his presence through the bush; in this respect the bush is utilised as a 'means of grace'; but it is never constituted as such through a promise of God. God could mediate his presence through any bush; God could declare any ground to be holy ground; but he has not promised to do so, and a sacramental sign is constituted as such through a promise of God: the sacramental is *res promissa* (a matter of promise).[44] For both Luther[45] and Calvin a sacrament is preceded by a promise; Calvin speaks of a sacrament as that through which a promise of God is sealed and ratified to us.[46] This episode of the burning bush, then, should be contrasted with what is promised to Israel, for instance, with respect of the Tabernacle and the Temple:

> Place the cover on top of the ark and put in the ark the Testimony, which I will give you. There, above the cover between the two cherubim that are over the ark of the Testimony, I will meet with you and give you all my commands for the Israelites. (Exodus 25.21-22).

The Exodus narrative concludes with the 'glory of the LORD' filling the Tabernacle (Exodus 40.34)—in this culminating instance the promise was perceptibly fulfilled—but this would not always be the case. The Tabernacle, and later the Temple, stood in Israel as visible signs of God's

---

Sacramental Mystery, p. 2. For this notion of Christ as the primordial Sacrament see also O. C. Quick, *The Christian Sacraments* (London: Nisbet, 2nd edn, 1932), p. 105; Edward Schillebeeckx, *Christ the Sacrament* (London: Sheed and Ward, 1963), pp. 13ff.; and John Macquarrie, *A Guide to the Sacraments* (London: SCM Press, 1997), pp. 35-36.

44   Robert Jenson identifies promise as 'the decisive maxim of all the Reformation's theology: God's gifts are *res promissa*, "the stuff of promise."' Jenson, *Systematic Theology*, vol. 1, p. 14

45   'For God does not deal, nor has he ever dealt, with man otherwise than through a word of promise...'. Martin Luther, *The Babylonian Captivity of the Church* (1520), in *LW* vol. 36, pp. 3-126 (p. 42).

46   '[A] sacrament is never without a preceding promise but is joined to it as a sort of appendix, with the purpose of confirming and sealing the promise itself, and of making it more evident to us and in a sense ratifying it.' *Institutes* IV xiv 3; cf. Gerrish, *Grace and Gratitude*, p. 104. This notion of a sacrament as the seal of a promise will be revisited later in this book. The language of appendage, however, would seem to be less than helpful, conveying the impression of a mere supplementary and extraneous addition rather than (as Calvin surely intends) the appointed means through which a promise is mediated.

mediated presence,[47] constituted as such by God's promise. That which is given by the Spirit for us to perceive is the sacramental sign, a material particular established as a sign through a divine promise. That which is not necessarily given by the Spirit for us to perceive is the immediate fulfilment of that sacramental sign: the immediate presence and action of God by the Spirit is received through faith on the basis of promise.

But it is the promise, rather than the faith, that constitutes the sacramental sign. Faith is not constitutive. Faith simply is a trustful resting on a given promise. The other problem with Boff's account of the sacramental as identified in the above quotation is the assumption that the sacramental is constituted by a human ability (and responsibility) to perceive: God simply is present in everything, it is down to us to discern God's presence, and when we do so then that particular through which God's presence is discerned becomes sacramental to us. But this is to reverse and therefore to misconstrue (and forfeit) the sacramental dynamic. That which constitutes any single particular as a sign of God's presence and action is not our ability to discern (or to believe) that presence and action but rather God's promise that such a single particular will be such a sign without prejudice to our ability to discern that presence and action. A sacrament is the promise of presence and action *whether that presence and action are discerned or not.*[48] A sacrament is a 'mystery' (μυστήριον): it is never dependent simply upon our ability to discern; it never falls under our control.[49]

> He was in the world, and though the world was made through him, the world did not recognise him. He came to that which was his own, but his own did not receive him. Yet to all who received him, to those who believed in his name, he gave the right to become children of God—children born not of natural descent, nor of human decision or a husband's will, but born of God. (John 1.10-13).

'The Word became flesh'. The Word's becoming flesh was not dependent upon human recognition. Indeed, his appearance 'in a body'

---

[47]   Note how phrases such as 'the glory of the LORD', 'the angel of the LORD', 'the name of the LORD' serve to preserve the mediateness of this divine presence.

[48]   'Sacraments, in the classic formulation, "*contain* the grace they signify": the event of a sacrament defines a place, and at that place is the divine reality that the sacrament communicates to the world. Precisely so, the place from which God comes is throughout Scripture a sacramental reality: it is neither a delineable region of created space, related spatially to another such region, earth, nor is it therefore unlocatable by earthlings.' Jenson, *Systematic Theology*, vol. 2, p. 123. emphasis added.

[49]   Though the manner in which Barth uses the following definition will later be questioned, the definition remains valid: '[i]n the New Testament μυστήριον denotes an event in the world of time and space which is directly initiated and brought to pass by God alone, so that in distinction from all other events it is basically a mystery to human cognition in respect of its origin and possibility.' *CD* IV/4, p. 108.

is itself identified as 'mystery' (μυστήριον).[50] There would be one occasion when Jesus' face would shine 'like the sun' (Matthew 17.1ff.). There would be more than one occasion when the Father would speak, identifying Jesus as the Son. But generally Jesus was surrounded by no visible halo. All that was generally given to human perception was a human body. But those who received this mystery were transformed by it—it is not just the mystery of faith; it is the 'mystery of godliness'.[51]

As with all sacramental signs, the Tabernacle and the Temple were visible and material acts of prayer in the light of God's specific promise to be present and active within these sacramental signs. This prayer-like character of a sacramental sign is especially clear in Solomon's prayer at the dedication of the Temple (1 Kings 8.22-23). There is no sense here that the Temple is constituted as a sacramental sign through Solomon's prayer (or through the subsequent prayers of God's people): the Temple is constituted as a sacramental sign through the promise of God (v.29); Solomon can restate that promise; the promise can subsequently be restated by the people as they pray; but the restatement of the promise does not constitute the promise; the restatement of the promise is itself a prayer, not an incantation.[52] There is certainly no sense here that the Temple in some way contains or restricts God: even the heavens cannot contain God (v.27); God is never confined or imprisoned in a sacramental sign; he remains free to mediate his presence and action elsewhere; he remains free even in the fulfilment of his promise—there is nothing presumptuous in Solomon's prayer. And neither, therefore, is there any sense here of an immediacy of fulfilment that can be assumed. At this dedication, the Temple (like the Tabernacle before it) is filled with the 'glory of the LORD' (vv.10-11), but there is no implicit expectation within Solomon's prayer that this will always be the case, that there will always be a perceptible immediacy of God's mediated presence. On the contrary, the entire prayer takes the form of a humble petition and is couched within the eschatological framework of God's ultimate purposes for Israel; that which this sacramental sign ultimately signifies—the immediate presence of God on earth (v.27)—is fulfilled eschatologically.

All this, of course, was the theory. It quickly fell apart in practice. Just as the bronze snake set up by Moses became an object of idolatrous worship (2 Kings 18.4) so also the Temple became a basis for presumption (Jeremiah 7.4). But God will not be presumed upon:

---

[50]   1 Timothy 3.16.

[51]   Greek, εὐσεβείας, 1 Timothy 3.16.

[52]   'When the word accompanies the sacrament, it must retain its essential character as proclamation; it is not a magical formula empowered to consecrate the elements even if mumbled in Latin. The sacramental word is not an incantation, but a promise.' Gerrish, *Grace and Gratitude*, p. 139.

...I will reject Jerusalem, the city I chose, and this temple, about which I said, 'There shall my Name be.' (2 Kings 23.27)

All too easily we confuse instrumentality and agency. All too easily we confuse the sacramental sign with the reality signified. All too easily we confuse an instrumental cause with an efficient cause. All too easily we assume an unmediated immediacy and lose sight of the mediate. That which Thomas Aquinas and John Calvin have in common is a recognition of the mediateness of sacramentality: a sacrament is a 'means' of grace; only God is the efficient cause of grace within a sacrament. It was perhaps the loss of this stress on the mediate in the years intervening between Thomas and Calvin that provided a basis for the sacramental presumption against which the Reformation was a protest.[53] G. C. Berkouwer helpfully notes the manner in which the sacramental dynamic can commonly be misunderstood in one of two ways:

> The efficacy of the sacraments has often been misinterpreted, either by objectivizing them, or by making them dependent upon the subject. The mystery of the sacrament can be understood, however, only if both of these concepts are rejected. For God's acting differs from the objectivity of things in this world, and faith is something other than a subjective disposition which can be investigated as to its presence or absence.[54]

The purpose of the first chapter of this book was to identify God's grace as his truly gratuitous and mediated love to that which is other than God—and to do so through a rehearsal of an understanding of God's Triune relatedness. The purpose of this second chapter has been to identify the truly gratuitous and mediated manner of God's relatedness to creation and, thereby, the truly gratuitous and mediated nature of God's presence and action through sacramental signs within creation. The Son and the Spirit are the mediating agents of creation—thereby preserving creation's true contingency, its continual dependence upon God and its genuine distinctness from God. And only the Son and the Spirit are truly agents of God's presence and action within creation, all else is instrumental, even human agents can be no more than instruments of

---

[53]   Note the tendency of the Franciscan movement after Duns Scotus to abandon the notion of secondary or instrumental causality, seeing God as the sole and simple cause of grace. I suspect that it would be inappropriate (historically and philosophically) to link this with the rise of the notion of *ex opere operato*—it nonetheless indicates an undermining of the prominence in Thomas of the notion of instrumentality: '[w]hereas for Thomas a sacrament was an instrumental cause by which God, the principal cause or agent, imparted grace to the soul, Scotus could only understand a sacrament as a sure sign that, by a concomitant divine act, grace was simultaneously being imparted.' Gerrish, *Grace and Gratitude*, p. 168.

[54]   G. C. Berkouwer, *The Sacraments* (Grand Rapids, MI: Eerdmans, 1969), p. 89.

God's presence and action. But such we can be: through the mediation of the Spirit we can participate in the Son's communion with the Father; through the mediation of the Spirit we can be instrumental means through which creation itself is moved towards its eschatological goal in the Son.[55]

And such too are sacramental signs: established by a promise of God to mediate his presence and action through the agency of the Spirit in and through these distinct material particulars of creation, sacramental signs, for all their present potency, are eschatologically orientated to a fulfilment in the agency of the Son before the Father:

> Just as the Holy Spirit makes the sacramental elements into the vehicles at once of the praise of God and of the creation of human community, so the human calling is to enable through that same Spirit all the creation to praise its maker. That calling or enabling is, like the sacraments, eschatological in its orientation. Creation...has an end: that all things may be offered, perfected and transformed, to their creator. The primary offering, just like the primary realisation of human community, is made in worship.[56]

---

[55]   'I am suggesting, then—albeit in a very compressed outline—that human creativity is supremely about sharing through the Spirit in the creative purpose of the Father as he draws all things to himself through his Son.' Begbie, *Voicing Creation's Praise*, p. 179

[56]   Colin Gunton, *Christ and Creation: The Didsbury Lectures 1990* (Carlisle: Paternoster Press/Grand Rapids, MI: Eerdmans, 1992), p. 115.

PART TWO

PART TWO

CHAPTER 3

The Sacramentality of the Church

Now I rejoice in what was suffered for you, and I fill up in my flesh what is still lacking in regard to Christ's afflictions, for the sake of his body, which is the church. I have become its servant by the commission God gave me to present to you the word of God in its fulness—the mystery that has been kept hidden for ages and generations, but is now disclosed to the saints. To them God has chosen to make known among the Gentiles the glorious riches of this mystery, which is Christ in you, the hope of glory. (Colossians 1.24-27)

By the time Karl Barth reached the fourth volume of his *Church Dogmatics*, possibly becoming aware that this project would never be completed, he must have realised that his chosen structure had committed him to include a broad range of significant theological themes under the single heading of a doctrine of reconciliation. Besides an ethics of reconciliation (which itself remained unfinished at his death),[1] he needed here to reflect upon the person of Christ, the work of Christ, the nature of sin, the nature of salvation, the doctrine of the Church, and the nature of Christian life (and to engage with a doctrine of the Spirit in relation to each of these themes, and explicitly in relation to the Church and the Christian). Notwithstanding the significant (and perhaps inevitable) defects of this approach (the details of which are not the immediate concern of this study),[2] Barth's achievement here is considerable and impressive, not least in his systematic relating of the themes of sin, Church, and Christian life, explicitly to the person and work of Christ. Here possibly we encounter the pinnacle of the *Dogmatics*, Barth at the height of his mature understanding (though, for this reader at least, his

---

[1]   *CD* IV/4; cf. Karl Barth, *The Christian Life: Church Dogmatics IV.4 Lecture Fragments*, trans. Geoffrey W. Bromiley (Edinburgh: T & T Clark, 1981).

[2]   For instance (and perhaps most notably) Barth has often been criticised for the division between the deity and humanity of Christ to which his chosen structure commits him. Though his dealing with these themes in narrative form is original and brilliant, his treatment of Christ's priesthood as an aspect of his deity, and not also his humanity, is potentially calamitous. For a perceptive outline of this difficulty together with its inherent dualistic roots and implications see T. F. Torrance, *Karl Barth: Biblical and Evangelical Theologian* (Edinburgh: T & T Clark, 1990), pp. 133ff.

treatment of the doctrine of God in the first part of the second volume remains his most perceptive and radically innovative contribution).

Within this systematic architecture, then, Barth reflects upon the Holy Spirit's gathering of the Church[3] in relation to the obedience of Christ as Son of God,[4] human sin as pride,[5] salvation as justification,[6] and the Holy Spirit's gift of faith;[7] he reflects upon the Holy Spirit's upbuilding of the Church[8] in relation to the exaltation of Christ as Son of Man,[9] human sin as sloth,[10] salvation as sanctification,[11] and the Holy Spirit's gift of love;[12] and he reflects upon the Holy Spirit's sending of the Church[13] in relation to glory of Christ as the Mediator,[14] human sin as falsehood,[15] salvation as vocation,[16] and the Holy Spirit's gift of hope.[17] All this, as already stated, is insightful and helpful—not least to someone (like me) from a contemporary Baptist or Free Church background—for here the Church is defined and described dynamically in relation to the Spirit and not at all in institutional or ritual terms: the Church consists of those who are gathered by the Spirit in faith, upbuilt by the Spirit in love, and called by the Spirit in hope. Indeed (and problematically), here there are surprisingly few references to baptism or Eucharist (though these were intended as major themes for the fourth part of the volume on an ethics of reconciliation).[18]

This notion of the 'gathered' church was a key distinctive for most (though not all) sixteenth-century Anabaptists and remains determinative for the ecclesiology of the Baptist Union of Great Britain and for most baptistic churches and connections. In reality a notion of believer's baptism and a notion of a gathered church are mutually defining—it is possible to hold the latter without the former (as has been true of most streams of Congregationalism) but it would be difficult to hold rigidly to the former without, at the same time holding to the latter—if the church is

---

3   *CD* IV/1, pp. 643-739.
4   *CD* IV/1, pp. 157-357.
5   *CD* IV/1, pp. 358-513.
6   *CD* IV/1, pp. 514-642.
7   *CD* IV/1, pp. 643-779.
8   *CD* IV/2, pp. 614-726.
9   *CD* IV/2, pp. 3–377.
10   *CD* IV/2, pp. 378-498.
11   *CD* IV/2, pp. 499-613.
12   *CD* IV/2, pp. 727-840.
13   *CD* IV/3, pp. 681-901.
14   *CD* IV/3, pp. 3-367.
15   *CD* IV/3, pp. 368-478.
16   *CD* IV/3, pp. 481-680.
17   *CD* IV/3, pp. 902-942.
18   Barth's rejection of any form of sacramentalism, particularly in relation to his discussion of baptism, will be considered in ch. 5 of this book.

defined by baptism, and if baptism is for those who profess faith, then the church is a gathering of believers. The notion of the church as 'gathered', then, alongside the notion of believer's baptism, was developed in the sixteenth century (and has continued thereafter) in reaction to the notion (or at least the practice) of a 'sacral society' — the blurring of the boundary between the Church and the world that was characteristic of the Church in Medieval Europe and that was implicitly perpetuated by the Magisterial Reformers.[19]

But this defining of the Church as 'gathered' is not without its difficulties. In the first place and most simply (as is demonstrated by the difficulty in the previous paragraph of knowing when to speak of 'Church' and when to speak of 'church') a notion of the Church as gathered is inherently local; it is difficult (though maybe not impossible) to speak of the 'Church' as gathered — and Baptists generally have not been noted for their understanding of the universal Church in its catholicity — affirmations of connectedness, even the strongest such affirmations, fall short of a confession of catholicity (a connectedness across the ages of the Church rather than merely a connectedness of contemporary churches). But related to this difficulty, and even more problematically, the notion of the Church as 'gathered' has tended in practice both toward sectarianism and various forms of perfectionism.

The definitive Anabaptist confession of the nature of the Church was formulated at a meeting at Schleitheim in 1527 and was probably drafted by a young Anabaptist leader named Michael Sattler (formerly a Benedictine) who was executed a few months later.[20] The Schleitheim Confession consists of seven articles: an affirmation of believer's baptism (infant baptism is depicted as 'the greatest and first abomination of the Pope'); an affirmation of the 'ban' as an instrument of church discipline; an affirmation of the Lord's Supper for those united to the church through baptism (and not 'banned'); a call for 'godly separation' from 'evil and the wickedness which the devil has planted in the world'; an affirmation of the pastoral ministry of the 'shepherd'; an absolute denial of 'the sword' or of magistracy (as being 'outside the perfection of Christ'); and an absolute denial of the taking of oaths.[21] Here then, in

---

[19]   The term 'sacral society' to describe this phenomenon was coined by Leonard Verduin, in his book on the development of Anabaptism: *The Reformers and their Stepchildren* (Grand Rapids, MI: Eerdmans, 1964).

[20]   Given the breadth and diversity of those groups labelled 'Anabaptist', there is some dispute concerning the degree to which this confession can validly be taken as definitive. Nonetheless, if the notion of a mainstream of Anabaptist life and confession is meaningful this confession is representative of such.

[21]   The full confession can be found in J. H. Yoder (trans. and ed.), *The Legacy of Michael Sattler* (Scottdale, PA: Herald Press, 1973), pp. 34-43. For a full comment on the

what was taken at least by Zwingli[22] and Calvin[23] as a definitive Anabaptist confession, is an explicitly and radically separatist understanding of the Church: the Church is separated from the world through baptism as a mark of the faith of those baptised; the Church is further marked by an active and radical separation from everything that is characteristic of the world (taken here to be inherently and radically evil); the Church, therefore, is separated from the structures and commitments of the world as represented by the magistracy, the 'sword', and the taking of oaths; and the Church is separated through a rigorous process of church discipline from those who previously have professed faith but have fallen into sin.[24] While Martin Luther's understanding of the relationship between Church and State was expressed in terms of two radically distinct kingdoms, he nonetheless increasingly held the Christian to be obliged to live responsibly and obediently within the kingdom of this world despite being a citizen of the kingdom of heaven.[25] Contrastingly, the Schleitheim Confession assumes these two kingdoms to be opposed, rather than overlapping, and the Christian to be utterly separated from the one in order to be genuinely a part of the other.[26]

---

text see C. A. Snyder, *The Life and Thought of Michael Sattler* (Scottdale, PA: Herald Press, 1984).

[22]   Ulrich Zwingli, *Refutation of the Tricks of the Baptists (In catabaptistarum strophas elenchus*: 1527), in *Selected Works*, ed. Samuel Macauley Jackson (Philadelphia, PA: University of Pennsylvannia, 1972), pp. 123-258.

[23]   John Calvin, *Brief Instruction for Arming All the Good Faithful Against the Errors of the Common Sect of the Anabaptists* (1544), in Benjamin Wirt Farley (ed. and trans.), *Treatises against the Anabaptists and against the Libertines* (Grand Rapids, MI: Baker Book House, 1982), pp. 36-158.

[24]   Interpretations of the 'ban' were to be a source of division amongst Dutch Anabaptists as represented by Menno Simons and Dietrich Philips and similarly amongst the Swiss Brethren (with Pilgram Marpeck urging a less harsh interpretation)—though in fairness to the Anabaptists the strictness of the 'ban' should perhaps be set in the wider context of the execution of those excommunicated within 'sacral' societies. As I have argued elsewhere, for the Anabaptists there was a 'world' (distinct from the Church) into which the offender could be excommunicated. John E. Colwell, 'A Radical Church? A reappraisal of Anabaptist Ecclesiology' (Tyndale Historical Theology Lecture, 1986), *Tyndale Bulletin*, 38 (1987), pp. 119-141 (pp. 136ff.); cf. Walter Klaassen (ed.), *Anabaptism in Outline: Selected Primary Sources* (Scottdale, PA: Herald Press, 1981), pp. 211ff.

[25]   This understanding of the relationship between Church and State as the relationship between two kingdoms, an understanding that underlies his writings in response to the Peasants' Revolt, is expressed most fully in Luther's treatise on 'Temporal Authority' of 1523, Martin Luther, 'Temporal Authority: To What Extent it Should be Obeyed' (1523), trans. W. A. Lambert, revised Walther I. Brandt, in *LW* vol. 45, pp. 81-129.

[26]   While John Calvin also uses the language of two kingdoms he does so more hesitantly and this must be comprehended within his understanding of the relatedness of

Some years ago I found myself in dispute with a theological friend over the question of whether or not it was possible to affirm a notion of a 'gathered' Church without at the same time assuming a notion of a 'pure' Church. In actuality, of course, there have been 'gathered' churches where the notion of the Church's purity has at least been muted (and this constituted my rather weak line of defence at the time), but the Schleitheim Confession provides significant weight for my friend's accusation. Here the Church's gatheredness is established by the Church's separateness, and here the entire emphasis falls upon that from which, rather than that to which, the Church is separated. The Church is separated from evil which, according to the articles of Schleitheim, necessitates an absolute separation from the world and its structures. Moreover, since the true Church is marked by godly separation it must separate itself from everything named 'church' that is not thus separated. Here at least the notion of a gathered Church explicitly issues in the notion of a pure Church which, in turn, implies a schismatic Church (though, of course, the authors of the Confession would refute the latter charge simply by denying that the entities from which they were separating themselves were 'Church' at all). Concede these assumptions and the ever increasing multiplication of Christian denominations is inevitable. Within such a context any affirmation of the Church's catholicity and connectedness is rendered a meaningless pretence: the invisibility of the Church (in stark contrast to the visibility of the churches) is stressed to the point of effective ecclesial docetism. Indeed, most sixteenth-century Anabaptist groups (as appears to be the case with some of their present Restorationist counterparts) held a doctrine of the fallenness of the Church: the Holy Spirit was making a radical new beginning.[27]

Moreover, this manner of conceiving the Church as gathered presumes a competency in assessing the faith and the separateness of its adherents. If baptism is exclusively for believers then surely the Church is obliged to assess the authenticity of that belief.[28] If the Church's gatheredness is constituted by the separateness of its adherents then the Church is obliged to assess the authenticity of that separateness. Historically this assumed competency in assessing the validity of faith and practice becomes even

---

law and grace within a single covenant—God has but one word of gracious command to both Church and world: *Institutes* III xix 15.

[27]   For example, the following statement from the Bern Colloquy: '...the true church came to an end some time, and we have made a new beginning upon the rule from which others had departed.' *Bern Colloquy* (1538), quoted in Klaassen (ed.), *Anabaptism in Outline*, p. 111.

[28]   The relationship between baptism and faith will, of course, be discussed more fully in ch. 5 of this book.

more pronounced where the significance of baptism is qualified:[29] authentic participation in the Church is not then primarily defined sacramentally but rather by the perceived genuineness of an individual's belief and behaviour. I remain bemused by contemporary expressions of this gathered Church principle that seek to give priority to 'belonging' over 'believing' and 'behaving' but without any clear sacramental theology or commitment which alone (as I shall argue below) renders such coherent.

It is not my purpose here to refute this notion of the Church as 'gathered'—indeed in a post-Christendom context, where even the outward trappings of a sacral society are under some threat, only a notion of the Church as 'gathered' has any meaningfulness—it is rather my purpose to reaffirm that the Church is defined primarily by its being 'gathered to' rather than (as seems to be the case for the Schleitheim Confession) by its being 'gathered from'. This, after all, should be the outcome of Barth's structure in his treatment of the doctrine of reconciliation (though, as I shall argue later, he rather jeopardises this by his 'ethical' treatment of baptism). The Church is not defined primarily by its ethical separation from the world—though this is to be an expected outcome if its being gathered by the Spirit is a reality—it is defined primarily by its being gathered by the Spirit to Christ; it is defined by its witness to Christ's identity and its participation in his life, death, and resurrection; it is defined by its sharing in the justification, sanctification, and vocation that are identified in his person and are the outcome of what he has accomplished; and only as a consequence of its being defined in relation to Christ is the Church then defined by its faith, its love, and its hope (which are, in reality, a participation in his faith, his love, and his hope).

Now I expect that there may be some who will object that the root meaning of the Greek word ἐκκλησία, the word translated by the word 'church', refers to being called 'out' (ἐκ κλῆσις). There is insufficient space here for a long excursus on hermeneutics, suffice it to say that etymology (the study of the derivation of words) can be dangerously misleading.[30] Words are slippery: as they are used within communities their significance develops and changes. Words rarely 'mean' that which their root derivation might suggest—and this is especially true of words

---

[29]   See for instance the discussion in John Bunyan, 'Differences in Judgment about Water Baptism, no Bar to Communion', in *The Whole Works of John Bunyan*, ed. George Offor (London: Blackie & Son, 1862), vol. 2, pp. 616-642; cf. 'A Confession of my faith', in *Works,* vol. 2, pp. 593-616, and 'Peaceable Principles and True', in *Works,* vol. 2, pp. 648-657.

[30]   For this argument in detail see James Barr, *The Semantics of Biblical Language* (Oxford: Oxford University Press, 1961), or, more recently, Peter Cotterell and Max Turner, *Linguistics and Biblical Interpretation* (London: SPCK, 1989).

that acquire specialised significance within a particular community (words such as ἐκκλησία). This word is only used twice in the Gospels, in Matthew 16.18 (a passage to which we shall return) in the context of Peter's confession of Christ, and in Matthew 18.17 specifically in the context of dealing with one who sins but more generally in the context of gathering in the name of Christ. When Paul writes to the 'church of God in Corinth' he parallels this term of address with their identification as 'those sanctified in Christ Jesus and called to be holy' (1 Corinthians 1.2).[31] Similarly he identifies those who are the church at Thessalonica as those 'in God the Father and the Lord Jesus Christ (1 Thessalonians 1.1; cf. 2 Thessalonians 1.1).[32] It must be admitted, of course, that the significance of the word ἐκκλησία is developing within the New Testament rather than already 'developed'—but within this development the word is used overwhelmingly in relation to Jesus Christ as the one to whom the Church is gathered rather than in relation to that from which the Church is being gathered.

This gathering of the Church to Christ by the Spirit is clearly attested by the manner in which Barth has organised this fourth volume of his *Dogmatics*—but what is less than clear here is that this gathering of the Church to Christ by the Spirit occurs sacramentally, in a mediated and immediate rather than in an unmediated and immediate manner. Certainly Barth emphasises that this gathering, upbuilding, and sending of the Church is something done to and in the Church by the Holy Spirit, just as the awakening of the Christian to faith, love, and hope is similarly an awakening by the Spirit—this is not something that the Church or the individual Christian can accomplish independently; it is something done within us and through us rather than simply something done by us. But what is more muted here is that this immediate action of the Spirit is itself mediated and not unmediated; that the Spirit gathers, upbuilds, and sends the Church precisely through its sacramental life and worship; that the Spirit awakens the individual Christian to faith, love, and hope precisely through the Christian's participation in the sacramental life and worship of the Church. Indeed, as has already been mentioned, Barth's increasing concern to define baptism ethically rather than sacramentally—as that which we do in response to that which God has done rather than that through which God does what he does—forfeits the possibility of any sacramental understanding of the Church's gathering, upbuilding, or sending.

And this here, as elsewhere, is a fatal flaw. If the Church is defined by some unmediated immediate act of the Spirit then docetic notions of the

---

[31]   τῇ ἐκκλησίᾳ τοῦ θεοῦ τῇ οὔσῃ ἐν Κορίνθῳ, ἡγιασμένοις ἐν Χριστῷ Ἰησοῦ, κλητοῖς ἁγίοις.

[32]   τῇ ἐκκλησίᾳ Θεσσαλονικέων ἐν θεῷ πατρὶ καὶ κυρίῳ Ἰησοῦ Χριστῷ.

Church's invisibility are the inevitable outcome. An unmediated act of the Spirit is, by definition, invisible, and indeterminate. A Church constituted by such an unmediated act would consequently be invisible and indeterminate. Similarly, if the identity of an individual Christian as a Christian is defined by some unmediated immediate act of the Spirit then individual Christian identity is intangible, imperceptible, and imprecise; an assurance of Christian identity, then, could only be grounded in the vagaries of felt experience or the presumption of supposed ethical outcomes.

In distinction, then, to Barth's unmediated notion of the Church's existence, the Church is to be defined in the first place (in every sense) in and through baptism; it is through the means of baptism that the Holy Spirit primarily gathers, shapes, and commissions the Church.[33] Through baptism the Church is gathered to Christ and in Christ before the Father. Through baptism the Church is shaped by the Spirit in conformity with Christ. Through baptism the Church participates in the Son's mission to the world as commissioned by the Father. The significance of baptism will be more fully discussed in chapter 5 of this book (and the relationship between baptism and confirmation will be discussed in chapter 6 of this book): suffice it for now to affirm baptism, not as a merely human ethical response to God's grace in Christ (as if any truly ethical response could ever be merely human), but as a means through which God has promised to mediate that grace in Christ to us by his Spirit. It is the promise of God (and nothing else) that establishes baptism as the primary defining sacrament of the Church. In and through baptism the Church shares in the baptism of Jesus and thereby comes to participate in his life, death, and resurrection; to participate through the mediation of the Spirit in the Son's relatedness to the Father.[34] Baptism defines the Church and the individual Christian as being 'in Christ'.

---

[33]   Deliberately here, and from here onwards, I am preferring to speak of the 'shaping' of the Church than, with Barth, of the 'upbuilding' (*die Erbauung*) of the Church, and of the 'commissioning' of the Church than, with Barth, of the 'sending' (*die Sendung*) of the Church.

[34]   Tom Smail cites Heribert Mühlen as proposing this identification of the Church with Christ's baptism as an alternative to identifying the Church with Christ's incarnation (a distinction that will be developed later in this chapter): 'Against this Heribert Mühlen proposes that the Church should be understood rather as an extension of the baptism of Jesus. The Church's relationship to Christ, he argues, is quite different from the relationship of Godhead and manhood in the incarnation. There God and man are united in the single person of the incarnate Son. In himself the Son is a single person who is both God and man and not a relationship between two persons.' Tom Smail, *The Giving Gift: The Holy Spirit in Person* (Darton, Longman & Todd, London, 2nd edn, 1994), p. 186, referring to Heribert Mühlen, *Una Mystica Persona: die Kirche als das Mysterium der Identität des Heiligen Geistes in Christus und den Christen—eine Person in vielen Personen* (München: F. Schöning, 1964), ch. 7.

Baptism, therefore, defines the Church; the Church consists simply of those who are baptised.[35]

Moreover, baptism, as defining of the Church, is neither a charade nor an empty ritual simply because God has promised to act by his Spirit in and through baptism and that action of God is a reality. But this action of God in baptism is eschatologically orientated: our ultimate participation in Christ and in his resurrection lies in the future rather than the present. This eschatological orientation of baptism does not undermine baptism's true ethical significance—the one baptised is even now a new creation in Christ by the Spirit through the divine promise—but it does determine that ethical significance as provisional and therefore to be anticipated humbly. Or, to put the matter otherwise, the eschatological orientation of baptism undermines any assumption of the Church's present purity or perfectedness—the perfection of the Church lies in its Christ-enclosed future rather than in its Christ-witnessing present.

And to understand the Church as defined and identified through baptism enables an understanding of the Church's universal 'being-gatheredness' in correspondence to its local 'being-gatheredness'. Those added to any local church through baptism are, by means of that rite, incorporated into Christ and thereby added to the one universal and catholic Church. And correspondingly, to be a member of Christ and of his Church is validly to be fully a member of any local Church—unless, of course, one insists upon defining a local 'church' other than by its 'in-Christness'. The contemporary and not uncommon Baptist practice of making a distinction between baptism and local church membership is therefore an intolerable incoherence.[36] Moreover, this intolerable incoherence is compounded by the multiplication of church membership 'courses' that append all manner of supposedly covenantal commitments as 'conditions' of local church membership. I find it difficult to think of a word for such practices other than 'apostasy': it is simply a departure from Christ (and it derives, I suspect, from an oxymoronic belittling of the significance of baptism within baptistic connections of churches). Contrary to all such confusions, to be baptised is to be included in the Church and to be included in the Church is to be baptised. Baptism, and only baptism in this primary sense, defines the Church.

But secondarily the Church is defined by Communion.[37] Through participation in the Lord's Supper, as previously through baptism, the

---

[35]   The difficulties of this 'simple' definition for the penitent thief (Luke 23.43) together with non-sacramental communities such as the Quakers or the Salvation Army will again be discussed in ch. 5 of this book.

[36]   The supposed justifications for this distinction will also be discussed in chs 5 and 6 of this book.

[37]   See in particular Jean-Marie Roger Tillard, OP, *Église d'églises: L'ecclésiologie de communion* (Paris: Cerf, 1987); also Zizioulas, *Being as Communion*, pp. 15ff.

Holy Spirit gathers, shapes, and commissions the Church in relation to Christ before the Father. Through the Lord's Supper the Church is gathered to Christ and in Christ before the Father. Through the Lord's Supper the Church is shaped by the Spirit in conformity with Christ. Through the Lord's Supper the Church is renewed in its participation in the Son's mission to the world. The significance of the Lord's Supper will be more fully discussed in chapter 7 of this book: suffice it for now to affirm the Eucharist as not merely a human remembering of God's grace in Christ, but as a means through which God has promised to mediate that grace in Christ to us by his Spirit. And, as with baptism, it is the promise of God that establishes the Lord's Supper as a means through which such grace is mediated. In and through its sharing in this supper the Church, by the Spirit, participates in the life, death, and resurrection of Christ. In and through its sharing in this Supper the Church, by the Spirit, participates in the relatedness of the Son to the Father, it participates in the Son's priestly ministry of worship and intercession. And through its participation through the Spirit in the Son, the Church is renewed by the Spirit in the life of the Son.

Moreover, as with baptism, the Lord's Supper is eschatologically orientated. Just as the Lord's Supper, through the mediation of the Spirit, is a participation in that inaugurating supper in the upper room and in the once and for all event of the Cross, so also, through the mediation of the Spirit, the Lord's Supper is a participation in the eschatological feast that represents our final and ultimate communion with the Father, in the Son, and through the Spirit. As with baptism, the Lord's Supper is a making present and visible by the Spirit, albeit provisionally, of that which is future and beyond our sight. The Church's ultimate communion with God is represented and anticipated here through the mediating action of the Spirit.

The Church, then, is defined by the Lord's Supper just as it is defined primarily by baptism. The Church consists of those who are gathered by the Spirit to this Supper; those who are gathered by the Spirit to this Supper are the Church. Or, to put the matter more directly, the communion which is the Church is defined by the Communion in which it gathers. Since it is defining of the Church, as will be reinforced in a later chapter, the Lord's Supper is the irreducible centre of the Church's life and worship. Where the Lord's Supper is marginalised the definition of the Church is jeopardised if not forfeited.

And, as with baptism, there is a correspondence between the local gathering of a church at the Lord's Supper and the Church's universal and catholic identity. The Lord's Supper, by representing and defining the Church's unity with Christ, represents and identifies the Church's catholic and universal unity. In the Lord's Supper, certainly and sadly, we are confronted with the scandal of the Church's present divisions, schisms, and disunity. But in the Lord's Supper thus understood, far more certainly, we are confronted by the true essence and source of the Church's unity in which those present divisions, schisms, and disunities, are overcome and negated. The Church's unity is not established through human agreement and association; the Church's unity is established in the Church's Communion; the Church's unity consists in its unity in Christ, through the Spirit, before the Father. To participate in the Lord's Supper is to be united through the Spirit in Christ, and to participate in the Lord's Supper, then, is to be united through the Spirit with all those who are so united in Christ—whether we like it, recognise it, and discern it, or not. By being united with Christ through the Lord's Supper we are united with all who are united with Christ, with all who have gathered, are gathering, or will gather to him, eucharistically. To be gathered to Christ at the Lord's Supper is to be gathered to the whole Church catholic and universal, and the Lord's Supper, thereby, defines the Church in its catholicity and universality.

It would be tempting for a Baptist Protestant, of course, to restrict this sacramental definition of the Church to the rites of baptism and the Lord's Supper—but, in the light of subsequent chapters of this book, this would be incoherent as well as inappropriate. In relation to the Church's sacramental definition something also needs to be said with respect to penance and ministry—and, of the two, it is the former that represents the greater 'challenge'.

As has already been noted, the Schleitheim Confession, principally (though not exclusively) through its promotion of the 'ban', witnesses to a pronounced concern for the purity of the Church and, consequently, for the rigorous practice of church discipline. And though (again as already noted) there was considerable dispute, both amongst Dutch Anabaptists and amongst the Swiss Brethren, concerning the strictness of the 'ban', Anabaptist groups generally were marked by an active concern for church discipline to the degree that it would be no exaggeration to claim that they held the practice of church discipline to be among the marks of the true Church.[38] Now it must be admitted that amongst these early Anabaptists this concern for church discipline—a concern shared by early Baptist groups in Britain—took a predominantly negative form. The 'ban' was a means of excluding individuals from the fellowship of the local church (an exclusion derived from a rather negative reading of Matthew 18.15ff. and of 1 Corinthians 5.1ff.) and the differing views of the strictness of the 'ban' related chiefly to the strictness with which such excluded members should be 'shunned'. The 'ban', therefore, was a

---

[38]   For general introductions to the Anabaptists of the Sixteenth Century see W. R. Estep, *The Anabaptist Story* (Grand Rapids, MI: Eerdmans, 1975); Verduin, *The Reformers and their Stepchildren*; or G. H. Williams, *The Radical Reformation* (Philadelphia, PA: Westminster Press, 1962).

form of penalty for perceived sin—it may have had a positive and reformative purpose, but its focus in practice was largely negative and penal.[39]

This emphasis upon church discipline amongst early Anabaptists and Baptists was, of course, a response to a perceived lack of discipline amongst the churches from which they were separating themselves. Anabaptists viewed the Lutheran and Reformed churches, and Baptists also viewed the Church of England, as largely unreformed in matters of active Christian discipleship and practical holiness. The Magisterial Reformation was perceived to remain content with that blurring of the boundaries between Church and world that had been characteristic of the Catholic Church: a doctrinal reformation might have occurred, but a reformation of discipleship was still lacking. However, though this perception was not without foundation it ought not to be overstated: the protracted conflict between Calvin and the Genevan city council was largely focused on the claimed competency of the latter in matters of church discipline—and Calvin could hardly be accused of promoting moral laxity. But more pertinently, the continuing practice of the sacrament of penance within the Catholic Church was a form of response—and arguably a more positive form of response—to the issues of discipline and discipleship.

A sustained discussion of the sacrament of penance (or better, a sacrament of cleansing or restoration), as with baptism and the Lord's Supper, must be postponed until a later chapter of this book. I am aware, of course, that of all sacramental issues this is probably the most challenging for a Baptist Protestant to discuss. I am aware that Martin Luther held the practice of penance to militate against penitence.[40] I am also aware that, by the end of the late Medieval period (if not earlier), the practice of penance had acquired a chiefly negative and penal focus—penance was the penalty one paid for post-baptismal sin—as distinct from (what I shall later argue as being) an earlier more positive, purgative, and restorative understanding of the sacrament. Most pertinently I am aware (as has already been noted) of the implicit issue between Hugh St. Victor and Peter Lombard of whether penance can properly be reckoned as a sacrament of the Church since penance lacks

---

[39]   For a related discussion of the nature of Church discipline by John Calvin, including the notion of penalty, see *Institutes* IV xii 1-13.

[40]   'Sacramental penance is only external and presupposes inward penance without which it has no value. But inward penance can exist without the sacramental.' Martin Luther, *Explanations of the Ninety-Five Theses* or *Explanations of the Disputation concerning the value of Indulgencies*, in *LW* vol. 31, pp. 83-252 (p. 85); cf. Luther's *Ninety-Five Theses* or *Disputation on the power and efficacy of indulgencies*, in *LW* vol. 31, pp. 25-33, Theses 1-4, and *The Sacrament of Penance* (1519), in *LW* vol. 35, pp. 3-22.

any 'physical or material element set before the external senses'.[41] But the practice of penance, nonetheless, bears witness to the continuing dynamic of disciplined discipleship, to the actuality of post-baptismal sin, to the continuing consequences of human weakness, to the promise and possibility of cleansing and restoration, and to the mediated nature of that restoration through the Church's ministry and through the exercises of prayer and of the spiritual disciplines. All forgiveness, cleansing, and restoration is a consequence of Christ's person, his sacrificial death, his resurrection, his eternal intercession. That we participate in the forgiveness, cleansing, and restoration that are in Christ in this continuing manner is mediated to us by the Spirit. But the Spirit, here as elsewhere, mediates to us that continuing participation in Christ through perceivable means, through verbally expressed confession, through verbally expressed forgiveness and restoration, through penitential prayer that is a participation in the eternal pleading of the Son before the Father.

I am not, at this stage, offering an unqualified argument in favour of a sacrament of penance. I am certainly not (for obvious reasons) arguing that the sacrament of penance is a necessary and defining sacrament of the Church. But I think I am arguing that without some sacramental dynamic of continuing forgiveness and restoration the Church lacks visible sacramental discipline and that a Church lacking discipline is a Church lacking credibility. And since, in this post-Christendom context, the Church seems to have something of a credibility crisis, I shall be arguing in chapter 8 of this book that this sacramental representation of church discipline at very least merits reconsideration amongst Protestant churches.

But, for this author at least, there need be no such hesitation or qualification with respect to the sacrament which is ordained ministry. As will be argued in chapter 10 of this book, ordained ministers—by which I mean those whose ministries are mediated by the Spirit through the ordering of the Church—are gifts of the ascended Christ to his Church precisely as means of the Church's maturity and unity (Ephesians 4.7-13).[42] It is also, then, through such ordained ministers that the Church is gathered, shaped, and commissioned. By the work of the Spirit mediated through such ministers the Church is gathered to Christ before the Father as the Word and the Sacraments are ministered to the Church. And through this mediated ministry of Word and Sacrament the Church is shaped by the Spirit in conformity to the fullness of Christ. And through this mediated ministry of Word and Sacrament the Church is

---

[41]   Hugh of St. Victor, *de sacramentis* IX, 2.

[42]   The significance of this disputed passage will be discussed in ch. 10 of this book.

commissioned by the Spirit to participate in the Son's mission to the world as the one sent by the Father.

And here, as previously, we are not encountering a merely human dynamic: as the Church has concluded since Augustine, the sacramental validity of Christian ministry is not dependent on the purity or merely human skill of those who minister.[43] The sacramental validity of Christian ministry, just as with the sacramental validity of baptism or the Lord's Supper, is an outcome of God's promise to mediate grace to us by his Spirit through such means. The expectation of the reality of such grace here then, as everywhere else, depends entirely on the reality of God's gratuitous promise. Christian ministry is constituted by the promise of God and nothing else, the promise that such men and women will be the means through which the ascended Christ himself ministers to his Church through the Spirit. Perhaps it is this sacramental dynamic that underlies the significance of the enigmatic text with which this chapter began: the ministering of the mystery of the gospel to the nations is itself a participation in the priestly ministry and suffering of Christ; Paul's suffering for the Church is a sign and mediation of Christ's suffering for the Church—not an addition or repetition, but a representation and participation, a sacramental sign, a sacramental mediation.

And also, as previously, Christian ministry is eschatologically orientated. Those who minister are given by Christ so that 'we all reach unity in the faith...and become mature'.[44] And such unity and maturity manifestly are not yet fulfilled; they represent an anticipated future rather than an already perfected present. But here again, as with Holy Communion, we are confronted with the scandal of the Church's present disunity and division—here also in its sharpest form since, while the Lord's Supper is given to the Church (in part) to express its unity, Christian ministry is given to the Church explicitly as the means through which that unity should be established and maintained. Too often those through whom the unity of the Church is to be established have been responsible for its loss. The seriousness of schism, as Thomas Aquinas testifies, cannot be overstated:

---

[43]   '[T]he Lord Christ is the cleanser and the justifier of men that believe in Him that justifieth the ungodly, that their faith may be counted unto righteousness, whether the man who administers the baptism be righteous, or such an impious and deceitful man as the Holy Spirit flees.' Augustine, *In answer to the letters of Petilian, the Donatist*, III 43, in *NPNF* 1, vol. 4, pp. 519-628; cf. Thomas: '...since the minister works instrumentally in the sacraments, he acts not on his own but by Christ's power... Wherefore...even sinners can confer sacraments...'. *ST* III 64 9; cf. Calvin, *Institutes* IV xv 16.

[44]   Ephesians 4.13.

...the sin of schism is, properly speaking, a special sin, for the reason that the schismatic intends to sever himself from that unity which is the effect of charity: because charity unites not only one person to another with the bond of spiritual love, but also the whole Church in unity of spirit.[45]

Interestingly, Thomas continues to define the Church's unity both in terms of the 'mutual connection or communion of the members' and also in terms of the Church's submission (*subordinatio*) to the one head (Christ) of whom the Sovereign Pontiff is viceregent. Baptists generally make much of defining the Church according to the gathering together of two or three in Jesus' name (Matthew 18.20) but tend to pay scant attention to Jesus giving authority to Peter—the one other occasion in the Gospels where the word ἐκκλησία (church) is used (Matthew 16.17ff.). A detailed discussion of this passage, and of its possible implications for a papacy, must also be postponed until chapter 10 of this book, but at very least the passage should focus our attention on the cruciality of Christian ministers for the unity, and therefore for the catholicity, of the Church.

Christian ministry is given as a means and expression of the Church's unity, connectedness, and catholicity. As such, therefore, Christian ministry also is sacramentally defining of the Church; just as the Church is defined through baptism and Holy Communion, so also the Church, in its catholicity and connectedness, is defined through Christian ministry. Irenaeus expresses the matter succinctly:

'For in the Church,' it is said, 'God hath set apostles, prophets, teachers,' and all the other means through which the Spirit works; of which all those are not partakers who do not join themselves to the Church, but defraud themselves of life through their perverse opinions and infamous behaviour. For where the Church is, there is the Spirit of God; and where the Spirit of God is, there is the Church, and every kind of grace... Those, therefore, who do not partake of Him are neither nourished into life from the mother's breasts, nor do they enjoy that most limpid fountain which issues from the body of Christ; but they dig for themselves broken cisterns out of earthly trenches, and drink putrid water out of the mire, fleeing from the faith of the Church lest they be convicted; and rejecting the Spirit, that they may not be instructed.[46]

The Church, therefore, is sacramentally defined: its being gathered, being shaped, and being commissioned, occurs through the sacramental mediation of baptism, Eucharist, ministry, and the continuing spiritual disciplines of discipleship (penance perhaps). Through such sacramental means the Church indwells the gospel story which is the creative word of its existence. Through such sacramental means the Church is made visible within the world.

---

[45]   *ST II-II* 39 1.
[46]   Irenaeus, *Against Heresies*, III xxiv 1.

And as made visible within the world sacramentally, the Church is itself a sacramental means of grace within the world. Probably the most significant and innovative contribution of *Lumen Gentium* (the statement on the constitution of the Church that issued from Vatican II)[47] was its eschatological orientation, its definition of the Church as a 'pilgrim people'.[48] But of at least complementary significance was its explicit definition of the Church as 'in the nature of a sacrament':

> Since the Church, in Christ, is in the nature of sacrament—a sign and instrument, that is, of communion with God and of unity among all men—she here purposes, for the benefit of the faithful and of the whole world, to set forth, as clearly as possible, and in the tradition laid down by earlier Councils, her own nature and universal mission. The condition of the modern world lends greater urgency to this duty of the Church; for, while men of the present day are drawn ever more closely together by social, technical and cultural bonds, it still remains for them to achieve full unity in Christ.[49]

It would seem straightforward to see this recognition of the Church as itself a sacrament as a development of the older Catholic and Lutheran tendency to speak of the Church as Christ's body in the sense of its being a continuation of his incarnation (in fact, I suspect that this is not the case and will argue so later). This would seem to be the assumption of the following quotation from Henri de Lubac:

---

[47]   *Lumen Gentium* or *The Dogmatic Constitution of the Church* (Vatican II, 21 November 1964), in *Vatican Council II: The Conciliar and Post Conciliar Documents*, ed. Austin Flannery (Dublin: Dominican Publications, 1975), pp. 350-426: hereafter referred to as *LG*.

[48]   'Already the final age of the world is with us (cf. 1 Cor. 10:11) and the renewal of the world is irrevocably under way; it is even now anticipated in a certain real way, for the Church on earth is endowed already with a sanctity that is real though imperfect. However, until there be realized new heavens and a new earth in which justice dwells (cf. 2 Pet. 3:13) the pilgrim Church, in its sacraments and institutions, which belong to this present age, carries the mark of this world which will pass, and she herself takes her place among the creatures which groan and travail yet and await the revelation of the sons of God (cf. Rom. 8: 19-22).' *LG* VII 48.

[49]   *LG* I 1; cf. '...God has gathered together and established as the Church, that it may be for each and everyone the visible sacrament of this saving unity.' *LG* II 9. Basil Butler, Abbot of Downside, in his preface to a commentary on the text of *LG* recognises these two emphases as at least qualifying the continuing focus on the Church's institutional hierarchy: the statement 'sees the Church, in her earthly pilgrimage, first and foremost as the spiritual fellowship of her baptized members, and only secondarily, and as it were consequentially, as a hierarchized communion.' In Gregory Baum, *De Ecclesia: The Constitution on the Church of Vatican Council II with commentary* (London: Darton, Longman & Todd, 1965), p. 9. So also Karl Rahner: '...the Church is the primal and fundamental sacrament.' Karl Rahner, *The Church and the Sacraments* (Tunbridge Wells: Burns & Oates, 1963), p. 19.

If Christ is the sacrament of God, the Church is for us the sacrament of Christ; she represents him, in the full and ancient meaning of the term, she really makes him present. She not only carries on his work, but she is his very continuation, in a sense far more real than that in which it can be said than an human institution is its founder's continuation.[50]

Predictably Robert Jenson, as a Lutheran theologian, similarly seizes upon this interpretation:

The teaching of Vatican II, that the church is *'uti sacramentum'*, was intended as an ecumenical contribution. It was intended to take Paul's teaching that the church is the body of Christ with ontological seriousness while avoiding the kind of identification of Christ and church that underlies ecclesial triumphalism.[51]

But what is the warrant for taking as ontological that which within the New Testament appears to be simply metaphorical? The imagery of the Church as Christ's body is unpacked by Paul in 1 Corinthians 12 with respect to the body's various parts: are these various parts of the body also to be taken 'with ontological seriousness'? Are teachers to be ontologically identified as 'mouths'? Is a Christian congregation entirely constituted of 'ears'? And what 'ontologically' are we to make of 'feet' or 'noses', or (more interestingly), of 'our unpresentable parts'?[52] Surely an ontological interpretation of the imagery of the Church as Christ's body is unsustainable if the ridiculous is to be avoided. Elsewhere Jenson presses this notion of the Church as the continuing presence of Christ to the point of speaking of Christ as rising again into the Church.[53] Such language, surely, not only confuses Christ and the Church, it also implicitly identifies the risen one as other than the ascended one—unless, of course, that triumphalism is implicitly admitted that Jenson is so rightly concerned to avoid. The Church is not called to 'be' Christ, even in the

---

[50]   Henri de Lubac, *Catholicism, Christ and the Common Destiny of Man* (London: Burns and Oates, 1950), p. 2. Avery Dulles credits de Lubac with the revival of this notion of the Church within Catholic theology: Avery Dulles, *Models of the Church* (Dublin: Gill and Macmillan, 1976).

[51]   Robert W. Jenson, 'The Church and the Sacraments', in *The Cambridge Companion to Christian Doctrine*, ed. Colin E. Gunton (Cambridge: Cambridge University Press, 1997), pp. 207-225 (p. 212). Note that Karl Rahner also speaks of Christ's 'abiding presence' in the Church: Rahner, *The Church and the Sacraments*, pp. 18-19.

[52]   1 Corinthians 12.23: τὰ ἀσχήμονα ἡμῶν.

[53]   'He needs no other body to be a risen man, body and soul. There is and needs to be no other place than the church for him to be embodied, nor in that other place any other entity to be the "real" body of Christ. Heaven is where God takes space in his creation to be present to the whole of it; he does that in the church'. Jenson, *Systematic Theology*, vol. 1, p. 206.

power of the Spirit; the Church rather is called to witness to Christ in the power of the Spirit; to point away from itself to him; to announce that which is future by proclaiming that which is past.

Moreover, whereas the passage in 1 Corinthians 12 explicitly refers to the Spirit's activity within the Church, mediating the life and ministry of Christ within and through the Church and its members, in these accounts of the Church as the continuation of Christ's incarnation, or as the locatedness and identity of his resurrection body, this mediating work of the Spirit is (to say the least) downplayed. Here all the emphasis is upon the immediate, and that in an unmediated sense. The Church simply *is* the continuing presence and action of Christ; the identification is ontological; the Spirit's mediating action is rendered redundant; there is little room for eschatological deferment. And if the Church simply *is* the continuing presence and action of Christ then such presence and action is no longer truly gracious; it is an ontological 'given' rather than a gratuitous 'being given'; it can be presumed upon rather than anticipated in hope and prayer. Here as elsewhere, the ultimate difficulty of such ontological accounts of Christ's unmediated presence and action, accounts that minimise any mediating work of the Spirit, is that grace ceases to be grace.[54]

Some years ago I wrote a paper (that would benefit from revision) arguing that distinct Anabaptist groups were defined by differing eschatologies (and differing hermeneutical strategies).[55] The perfectionist and inherently schismatic ecclesiology expressed at Schleitheim is the outcome of an over-realised eschatology: the visible purity of the local church anticipates directly and unfeignedly the fulfilment of God's reign; the Church is the presence of the coming kingdom rather than the witness to the coming kingdom; the final division of wheat and weeds, good fish and bad fish,[56] is anticipated in the Church's disciplined gathering; or, to put the matter in terms more pertinent for this particular study, the eschatological future is assumed as immediately (and unmediatedly) present in the locally gathered congregation. Schleitheim's typically dualistic division of Church and world, the rigorous enforcement of the 'ban', the rejection of magistracy, 'sword',

---

[54]   'If we assert that the Church is the body of Christ, that Head and members together constitute the *Totus Christus*, yet it must immediately be added that the Church is not thereby deified nor is its relation to deity ever unmediated'. Neville Clark, *An Approach to the Theology of the Aacraments* (London: SCM Press, 1956), p. 79.

[55]   John E. Colwell, 'A Radical Church?' A Reappraisal of Anabaptist Ecclesiology' (Tyndale Historical Theology Lecture, 1986), *Tyndale Bulletin* 38 (1987), pp. 119-141.

[56]   Matthew 13.24ff.

and oath as outside the 'perfection of Christ', all simply are outworkings of this over-realised eschatology.[57]

The ecclesiological characteristics and characteristic difficulties of this over-realised eschatology are highlighted in the following comments by John Webster:

> ... if the church is a participation in the life of the triune divine society, then it is in the work of the church that the work of the triune God finds its realization and, in an important sense, its continuation. In effect, this constitutes an orientation in ecclesiology which makes the work of the church an actualisation of or participation in the divine presence and action, rather than a testimony to that presence and action. And, as a result, the holiness of the church is no longer sheerly alien, no longer the result of the Word's declaration, but in some sense infused into the church by the church's *koinonia* with God, its perichoretic relation to the holy Trinity.[58]

Webster resists this move as a great danger that itself undermines grace, and he proposes the themes of election and confession as alternative ways of viewing the Church's holiness. But is this not to avoid one danger by falling headlong into another? Is the Church's testimony to 'divine presence and action' a merely human endeavour, or is that testimony itself an outcome of a mediated presence and action? Is the Word's declaration within the Church merely declaratory or is it also performative? Is it the case, then, that the holiness of the Church remains simply 'sheerly alien'?[59] Is the Church's communion with the Father in the Son by the Spirit a reality, albeit a mediated rather than an infused reality? Or, to put the matter more positively, might not a sacramental understanding of the Church offer a middle position between the equally unacceptable poles of this supposed 'either... or...'?

And that which makes *Lumen Gentium* most interesting and attractive to this particular reader is the possibility that, through its identification of the Church as itself a sacrament, and through the eschatological orientation of its understanding of the Church as a pilgrim people, it approximates to this middle position. Certainly there remain elements of

---

[57]   In some respects I repeat this warning concerning seeing the Church too simply as an anticipation of the future, particularly in relation to the work of John Howard Yoder and Stanley Hauerwas, in my *Living the Christian Story*, pp. 195ff.

[58]   John Webster, 'God, Holiness and Election: The Holiness of God and the Holiness of the Church' (as yet unpublished paper delivered to the Conference of the Society for the Study of Theology, 2002).

[59]   This phrase, that echoes Luther, may be helpful inasmuch as it identifies the otherness of the Church's holiness, as that which is purely given rather than in any way inherent; but it is unhelpful inasmuch as it implies that the Church's holiness remains purely other, that it is not given effectively, that it is 'unreal'. See Martin Luther, 'Two Kinds of Righteousness', trans. Lowell J. Satre, in *LW* vol. 31, pp. 297-306.

a more realised, essentialist, and institutional understanding—not least in its discussion of the Church's hierarchy—but these elements are enclosed within a discussion of the Church as 'mystery' and the Church as a pilgrim people. Indeed, the 'hierarchic gifts', like the 'charismatic gifts', are gifts of the Spirit (rather than inherent aspects of the Church as an institution);[60] the Church is explicitly defined not so much by the Incarnation as by Pentecost.[61] And, as such, the Church explicitly is eschatologically orientated, the first-fruits of all humanity,[62] a visible sacrament of a future salvation.[63]

It is this eschatological orientation of the Church which, predictably, is the characteristic emphasis of Irenaeus: the Church, in its sacramental life and witness, points to a coming kingdom; it is the foreshadowing of a future reality rather than the shadow (in any Platonic sense) of an eternal reality.[64] The degree to which Augustine, in his *City of God*, views the Church in this latter sense, as the shadow of an eternal reality, is the basis upon which institutional understandings of the Church in the West were constructed.[65] And the degree to which here, as also in his work on the Trinity, the person and work of the Spirit is minimalised, is the basis upon

---

[60]   'Guiding the Church in the way of all truth (cf. Jn. 16:13) and unifying her in communion and in the works of ministry, he bestows upon her varied hierarchic and charismatic gifts, and in this way directs her; and he adorns her with his fruits (cf. Eph. 4:11-12; 1 Cor. 12:4; Gal. 5:22).' *LG* I 4.

[61]   'When the work which the Father gave the Son to do on earth (cf. Jn. 17:4) was accomplished, the Holy Spirit was sent on the day of Pentecost in order that he might continually sanctify the Church, and that, consequently, those who believe might have access through Christ in one Spirit to the Father (cf. Eph. 2:18). He is the Spirit of life, the fountain of water springing up to eternal life (cf. Jn. 4:47; 7:38-39). To men, dead in sin, the Father gives life through him, until the day when, in Christ, he raises to life their mortal bodies (cf. Rom. 8:10-11).' *LG* I 4.

[62]   '[T]hat messianic people, although it does not actually include all men, and at times may appear as a small flock, is, however, a most sure seed of unity, hope and salvation for the whole human race. Established by Christ as a communion of life, love and truth, it is taken up by him also as the instrument for the salvation of all—as the light of the world and the salt of the earth (cf. Mt. 5:13-16) it is sent forth into the whole world.' *LG* II 9.

[63]   'God has gathered together and established as the Church, that it may be for each and everyone the visible sacrament of this saving unity.' *LG* II 9.

[64]   'The church on earth is not related to a heavenly counterpart as image to reality (a construct that would eventually help to create formidable institutional symbols as mediating and perfecting hierarchies). Rather the relation is an eschatological one; the eucharistic outcome is discoverable only in the grace of the parousia and of the resurrection.' Douglas Farrow, *Ascension and Ecclesia: On the Significance of the Doctrine of the Ascension for Ecclesiology and Christian Cosmology* (Edinburgh: T & T Clark, 1999), p. 72

[65]   Augustine, *The City of* God, in *NPNF* 1, vol. 2, pp. 1-511.

which the Church in the West came to be viewed in an unmediated manner, as an ontological immediate. My point is that a sacramental understanding of Church, as a mediated immediate, while preserving the reality of the Church's mediation of the presence and action of God, militates against any ontological or institutional definition of the Church as an unmediated immediate. A sacramental understanding of the Church as eschatologically orientated precisely is not an outcome or a reinforcement of an understanding of the Church as a continuation of Christ's incarnation. In the quotation from Colossians with which this chapter begins, Paul does speak of the Church as Christ's body, he speaks of Christ 'in' the Church, but he identifies this as 'mystery' and he orientates this mysterious presence to the eschatological future: the mystery which is Christ in the Church is the hope of future glory. The presence and action of the risen Christ in and through the Church is not an unmediated ontological or institutional 'given'; it is rather a pneumatological 'being given'; it is a mediated immediacy; it is a promise anticipating a future fulfilment; it is mystery.[66]

To define the Church as itself sacramental is to live with the prayerful expectation that, just as God has promised to mediate his presence and action by the Spirit within the Church through baptism, Eucharist, ministry, so also God has promised to mediate his presence and action by the Spirit through the Church itself, through its sacramental life and worship. Through the instrumental means of the Church the Holy Spirit mediates the presence and action of God in Christ to the world. In distinction, then, to what is implicit in the Schleitheim Confession, the Church is not constituted as over against the world, as the perfected to the corrupt, as light to darkness; the Church rather is constituted as the first-fruits of the world's future, as the harbinger of a cosmic salvation.[67] Through the mediation of the Spirit the Church represents to the world that which the world is called and invited to become through God's grace in Christ. It is in this sense that the whole creation 'waits in eager expectation for the children of God to be revealed' (Romans 8.19).

And it is in this sense that the Church is the living hermeneut of the gospel, not as an outcome of the 'givenness' of its institutional life, but as

---

[66]   '[I]n this present age, the Church still moves towards that which her Lord already possesses. Dying with him and risen with him, she is not yet glorified with him; she awaits the redemption of the body. Incorporated by baptism into the one man, she does not yet possess his fullness and completion; she remains the *mystical* body of the Christ.' Clark, *An Approach to the Theology of the Sacraments*, p. 80.

[67]   'The church is not directly God's agent for the realization of the kingdom, but rather it is God's harbinger of the kingdom by being the fellowship of the faithful in which the reality of the kingdom is manifest.' Stanley Hauerwas, *Vision and Virtue: Essays in Christian Ethical Reflection* (Notre Dame and London: University of Notre Dame Press, 1981), p. 221.

an outcome of the 'being-givenness' of the Spirit's mediation. The Church is not merely commissioned to proclaim the gospel in the power of the Spirit; the Church is also commissioned as itself a proclamation of the gospel in the power of the Spirit. The Church is a rendering of the gospel story, not in any unmediated or 'given' sense, but by the mediation of the Spirit through its sacramental life and worship.

In response to a previous work in which I made much of the Church as a 'rendering of the gospel to the world' one of my friends objected that such a Church seemed (to him) to be an idealistic abstraction.[68] Where in actuality is this Church so indwelt by the Spirit, so indwelling the gospel story, so rendering that story to the world? Who was I kidding? How might this idealised notion of the Church relate to the local church of which I am a member? This is an appropriate and penetrating challenge but I would suggest (I hope, humbly) that it rather misses the point I am trying to make. It is an appropriate challenge to any notion of the Church as the continuation of Christ's incarnation; to any ontological interpretation of the Church's identity as Christ's body; to any ecclesiology rooted in an over-realised eschatology. But I do not recognise it as a decisive objection to the sacramental notion of the Church that I am attempting to expound. The Church is eschatologically orientated; the fulfilment of its identity lies in its future. The Church mediates a presence; it is not itself that presence in any immediate and unmediated sense. And that mediation of presence through the Church is itself mediated by the Spirit; there is no unmediated immediacy; grace is truly grace. The Church is not called to 'be' Christ; it is called to witness to Christ. But the Church witnesses to Christ, not just in its verbal proclamation of the gospel story, but also in the proclamation of that story that is its sacramental indwelling of that story. Through its sacramental life and worship the Church both indwells that story and renders that story to the world. There is no idealistic assumption of present perfection here; there is rather a prayerful expectation of mediation; a prayerful expectation of God's truly gracious presence and action. The perfection of the Church is a gift of the Spirit that can only be anticipated in hope and prayer.

The sacramentality of the Church, therefore, is truly sacramental, truly mysterious. It is not as if the Church were already a perfected community. It is not as if the presence and action of God within the Church could be rationally discerned by some detached observer. It is rather that, through the mystery of the Church's life and worship, the Spirit mediates the mystery of the gospel to the world. It is as the Church indwells the gospel story through its sacramental life and worship, that the Church itself is a sacrament of that gospel story to the world. It is as the

---

[68]   Colwell, *Living the Christian Story*, see especially chs. 7, 8 and 9.

Spirit mediates the gracious presence and action of God to the Church through its sacramental life and worship that the Spirit also mediates that gracious presence and action through the Church to the world. And through this mediation of the Spirit the Church truly participates in the priestly ministry of the ascended Christ. This priestly ministry is his and his alone, but, just as Paul participates in the ministry and suffering of Christ, so also the Church truly participates in that ministry through the mediation of the Spirit in its sacramental life and worship. The Church, then, which is defined and constituted sacramentally, is itself sacramental through that same mediating work of the Spirit by which it is sacramentally defined and constituted. The Church is sacramental since it is defined and constituted sacramentally:

> Sacramental life and the Word are the fruits, the expression, the result of its ecclesial community and at the same time they are its essential constitutive elements. Without the ecclesial prerequisites there are no sacraments, without the life of the sacraments and the prophetic Word there is no Church.[69]

---

[69]   Gennadios Limouris, 'The Physiognomy of BEM after Lima in the Present Ecumenical Situation', in *Orthodox Perspectives on Baptism, Eucharist, and Ministry*, Faith and Order Papers 128, eds. Gennadios Limouris and Nomikos Michael Vaporis (Brookline, MA: Holy Cross Orthodox Press, 1985), pp. 25-45 (p. 37).

CHAPTER 4

The Sacramentality of the Word

For the word of God is living and active. Sharper than any double-edged sword, it penetrates even to dividing soul and spirit, joints and marrow; it judges the thoughts and attitudes of the heart. Nothing in all creation is hidden from God's sight. Everything is uncovered and laid bare before the eyes of him to whom we must give account. (Hebrews 4.12-13)

The common juxtaposition of the terms 'Word' and 'Sacrament' may itself be suggestive of their distinction rather than their relation; suggestive that the sacraments might be entirely other than verbal or proclamatory; suggestive that the Word might be other than inherently sacramental or mediated. And if there is validity in the observation that notions of the Church and notions of the sacraments have been distorted by assumptions of unmediated immediacy, then this is most certainly true of notions of Scripture. Notwithstanding notions of the Church as ontologically Christ's body, and notwithstanding implicitly manipulative notions of the sacraments, it is difficult to evade the sense that, in both Church and sacraments, we are encountered by mystery; by that which is not entirely at our disposal or in our grasp; by that which is truly gracious. Not so with Scripture. Surely there is nothing mysterious here. The Bible is, after all, an object at our disposal, pages of text bound together in leather or cardboard, human language that can be humanly comprehended—or so we too commonly suppose.

This all too common supposition—which should be recognised as chiefly an Enlightenment phenomenon—is manifest at the popular as well as the academic level. Generally, when Christians read Scripture or listen to Scripture being read they do not convey the impression that they are dealing with that which is sacramental. If there is mystery here it is the mystery of incomprehension rather than the mystery of sacramental presence. If any mediation occurs it is assumed to be simply the human mediation of meaning by a preacher or commentator rather than the divine mediation of God's gracious presence and action by the Spirit. Something is expected to be understood, but nothing is expected to 'happen'. There is expectation to be informed, but little expectation to be transformed.

But it is at a more academic level that this assumption of an unmediated immediacy is consciously and reflectively affirmed. The various interpretative strategies collectively known as historical criticism have in common, for all their distinctions, the assumption that meaning is accessible in an entirely unmediated manner. This is not to say that such critical study is assumed to be easy or straightforward—it requires diligent and scholarly effort—but it does not seek, expect, or require divine mediation. The Bible is simply an object of study, an object of unmediated immediate perception, an object that can be comprehended through careful and thorough human effort.

In practice, of course, such interpretative strategies often display rather limited concern for the text itself, for the structure and connectedness of its final form, presuming rather that the meaning of the text will be discovered by investigating that which lies behind and beneath the text, the historical context of the author of the text, the historical context of the original receivers of the text, supposed sources (written or oral) underlying the text. In all this historical criticism reflects the general Enlightenment assumption that meaning lies behind and beneath immediate perception. But more fundamentally, historical criticism shares the general Enlightenment assumption that such meaning is accessible, that meaning can be discovered (or perhaps 'excavated') merely through diligent study; pure objectivity is possible if only the critic can find a truly detached vantage point.

But a truly detached vantage point is a fanciful illusion; pure objectivity is simply unattainable. What is remarkable is that such optimistic interpretative strategies held sway in biblical studies (and in literary studies more generally) for so long. The sheer variety of assured conclusions emanating from such supposed pure objectivity, of itself, should be a sufficient salvo to sink this proud ship.[1]

Neither are more 'conservative' biblical interpretative strategies immune either from these modernistic assumptions or from their flaws. Merely to have greater reverence for the final form of the text, merely to use the tools of historical criticism in order to arrive at more conservative conclusions, merely to commence such study with prayer for the Spirit's aid, is not of itself to abandon the notion of the unmediated nature of reading or hearing. In the main, throughout the twentieth century, evangelical and conservative approaches to biblical studies were

---

[1]   For perceptive general critiques of historical criticism in its various forms, together with critical assessments of more recent hermeneutical strategies, see Anthony C. Thiselton, *New Horizons in Hermeneutics* (London: HarperCollins, 1992); Francis Watson, *Text, Church and World: Biblical Interpretation in Theological Perspective* (Edinburgh: T & T Clark, 1994); Kevin J. Vanhoozer, *Is There a Meaning in This Text? The Bible, The Reader, and the Morality of Literary Knowledge* (Leicester: Apollos, 1998).

characterised by precisely the same modernistic assumptions as their more liberal counterparts: the meaning of Scripture was assumed to be immediately accessible to diligent historical scrutiny; the Spirit's assistance may have been prayerfully sought, but the Spirit's mediation, in practice, was deemed unnecessary. Evangelical piety proved inadequate immunisation from Enlightenment assumption. And at the most extreme conservative edge of the spectrum this effective dispensing with the mediate was (and is) no less the case: as Harriet Harris has argued, Fundamentalism is simply biblical foundationalism.[2] In Scripture, Fundamentalism assumes, we encounter inerrant propositional truths that are rationally accessible. Through the influence of the Princeton Theologians in general,[3] and B. B. Warfield in particular,[4] inspiration came to be conceived as a quality of the text itself rather than the dynamic through which the text was heard, the Spirit's 'illumination' displaced the Spirit's 'inner testimony'; the unmediated immediate displaced the mediated immediate.[5]

Such interpretative strategies, dependent as they are upon underlying modernistic assumptions of pure objectivity, of accessible meaning, of the correspondence between language and reality, have struggled to withstand the successive assaults of structuralism and post-structuralism. If, as Ferdinand de Saussure maintains,[6] the relationship between words and things is arbitrary, then the meaning of words can only be apprehended within the syntax of a text, within its internal connectedness and

---

[2]   Harris, *Fundamentalism and Evangelicals*.

[3]   For this development see George M. Marsden, *Fundamentalism and American Culture: The Shaping of Twentieth-Century Evangelicalism, 1870–1925* (New York and Oxford: Oxford University Press, 1982), or Mark A. Noll, (ed.), *The Princeton Theology, 1812–1921: Scripture, Science, and the Theological Method from Archibald Alexander to Benjamin Breckinridge Warfield* (Grand Rapids, MI: Baker Book House, 1983).

[4]   B. B. Warfield, *The Works of Benjamin B. Warfield*, vol. 1, *Revelation and Inspiration* (Grand Rapids, MI: Baker Book House, 1981). For a more recent defence of this 'rationalistic' approach to Scripture (specifically in criticism of Karl Barth's approach to Scripture) see Gordon H. Clark, *Religion, Reason and Revelation* (Phillipsburg, NJ: Presbyterian and Reformed Publications, 1961).

[5]   '[M]uch of the history of the doctrine of inspiration is in large measure an attempt to equate inspiration and revelation in such a way that the text in some way replaces or renders redundant the mediating work of the Spirit.' Gunton, *A Brief Theology of Revelation*, p. 66.

[6]   Ferdinand de Saussure, *Course in General Linguistics* (New York: McGraw-Hill, 1959). Saussure (1857–1913), was a Swiss linguist, born in Geneva. He worked chiefly in Paris and Geneva, and was responsible for ideas of linguistic structure that proved programmatic for subsequent literary and linguistic studies.

structures.[7] But if, as Jacques Derrida asserts,[8] there is an inevitable gap (difference) between word and concept, then the meaning of words, even within the internal connectedness and structures of a text, is continually postponed (deferred).[9] David Lodge, in a highly amusing novel, expresses the problem with great clarity:

> To understand a message is to decode it. Language is a code. *But every decoding is another encoding.* If you say something to me I check that I have understood your message by saying it back to you in my own words, that is, different words from the ones you used, for if I repeat *your* own words exactly you will doubt whether I have really understood you. But if I use *my* words it follows that I have changed *your* meaning, however slightly; and even if I were, deviantly, to indicate my comprehension by repeating back to you your own unaltered words, that is no guarantee that I have duplicated your meaning in my head, because I bring a different experience of language, literature, and non-verbal reality to those words, therefore they mean something different to me from what they mean to you. And if you think I have not understood the meaning of your message, you do not simply repeat it in the same words, you try to explain it in different words, different from the ones you used originally; but then *it* is no longer the *it* that you started with. Time has moved on since you opened your mouth to speak, the molecules in your body have changed, what you intended to say has been superseded by what you did say, and that has already become part of your personal history, imperfectly remembered. Conversation is like playing tennis with a ball made of Krazy Putty that keeps coming back over the net in a different shape.[10]

If this is the case with personal conversation then the problem is greatly compounded when we come to read that which has been written—and even more deeply compounded when what we are reading is ancient writing, writing in a language other than our own, writing that has undergone translation (or a series of translations), writing that issues from a culture now entirely inaccessible to us other than through the means of such writings. And all this implies that any claim to have discerned objective meaning is a delusion—or worse, a thinly veiled attempt to exert totalitarian control. Such claims to authoritative meaning, therefore, must

---

[7]   For a helpful overview of the rise of structuralism and post-structuralism see David Lodge, *Working with Structuralism: Essays and Reviews on Nineteenth- and Twentieth-Century Literature* (London and New York: Routledge, 2nd edn, 1991).

[8]   Jacques Derrida, *Writing and Difference* (London and Henley: Routledge and Kegan Paul, 1978); *Of Grammatology* (Baltimore and London: Johns Hopkins University Press, 2nd edn, 1997). Derrida was born in 1930 in Algeria, has taught in Paris and in the United States of America, and is generally recognised as the leading proponent of deconstructionalism.

[9]   Derrida famously makes use of the ambiguity of the French word *differance* which can signify both difference and deference.

[10]   David Lodge, *Small World: An Academic Romance* (1984), in *A David Lodge Trilogy* (London: Penguin, 1993), p. 252

now be exposed as oppressive and tyrannical. We have no objective access to meaning. Despite its appearance as print, paper, and binding, a text is not an object accessible to detached scrutiny; a text only truly exists as 'text' (as not merely print, paper, and binding) in the process of reading.[11] And a text is read by a someone—a someone with past experiences, with opinions, with preferences, with assumptions. To such a someone a text certainly may have 'significance', but such a someone has no objective access to 'meaning'—and to mistake significance for meaning is to assert an authoritarian claim.[12] All this is not to deny, of course, that the author of a text intended a meaning; it is rather to recognise that such intended meaning is no longer accessible to us—the author is dead and post-structuralism in essence is the proclamation of the death of the author.

Contrary to common (and frankly facile) caricatures, all this need not (and should not) issue in radical relativism. Individual readers of texts do not exist in a vacuum, they exist with opinions, with preferences, with assumptions—and these opinions, preferences and assumptions have been historically formed within a community (or within communities). Individual readers of texts do not exist in isolation—and, in this sense, there are no 'individual' readers of texts, there are communities of readers, communities of understanding, traditions of signification. A text, therefore, cannot signify just anything; its significance is attested within an interpretative community, within an interpretative tradition.[13] Consequently, this recognition of the nature of texts and of the inaccessibility of meaning issues in a reassertion of the authoritative function of interpretative communities. A Christian reading of the Exodus narrative inevitably will differ from a Jewish reading of the Exodus narrative, which will differ again from an Islamic reading, from a Marxist reading, or from a late Western-European Liberal reading. Indeed, even within the context of the interpretative community which is the Christian Church there are sub-communities: a liberationist reading

---

[11]   For an entertaining and persuasive account of the nature of texts see the essay by Stanley Fish, 'Is there a Text in This Class?', in *Is There a Text in This Class? The Authority of Interpretive Communities* (Cambridge, MA: Harvard University Press, 1980), pp. 303-321.

[12]   '[N]othing is ever comprehended, but rather designated and distorted'. Derrida, *Of Grammatology*, p. xxiii.

[13]   '[I]f, rather than acting on their own, interpreters act as extensions of an institutional community, solipsism and relativism are removed as fears because they are not possible modes of being. That is to say, the condition required for someone to be a solipsist or relativist, the condition of being independent of institutional assumptions and free to originate one's own purposes and goals, could never be realized, and therefore there is no point in trying to guard against it'. Fish, 'Is there a Text in This Class?', p. 321.

will differ (at least in some respects) from some feminist readings, which will differ again from some 'Anabaptist' or pacifist readings. But, notwithstanding these latter distinctions, if the Christian Scriptures are read as the *Christian* Scriptures they are read as the Church's text, they are read within the context and traditions of the interpretative community which is the Church catholic. And within this catholic community the Scriptures cannot signify just anything: there are theological constraints to reading which, if transgressed, identify a reader as no longer effectively participating in this community.[14]

Indeed, here perhaps we have a practicable definition of this elusive term 'catholic': the term catholic is not simply or merely a synonym for the term 'universal' (less still for the term 'ecumenical'), nor is it used denominationally to refer to one part of the Church as distinct from another (this would be anachronistic within the Early Church), it is used rather to refer to that essence of sameness which identifies the Church's connectedness and continuity in every age and in every place. To transgress this continuity, therefore, is to separate oneself from the community that is recognisably the Church.[15]

But here also perhaps we have an effectual and dynamic first step towards at least qualifying the gap of deferment between author and reader identified by post-structuralism. The confession of the Church's catholicity is the confession of the Church's connectedness in every age. The reading community, as part of the Church catholic, is continuous with that community that first received and read this text. The reading community, more pertinently, is continuous with those through whom and by whom this text came to be written. To affirm this catholic continuity is not to reassert a modernistic claim to detached objectivity—the continuity here identified precisely is not detached—it is rather to affirm an expectation for some continuity of significance within that tradition of signification which is the Church catholic.[16]

One helpful (and generally conservative) response to these trends in hermeneutical theory attempts to develop and apply the 'speech-act'

---

[14]   As Robert Jenson points out, this is the essence of Irenaeus' response to gnosticism: R. W. Jenson, 'Hermeneutics and the Life of the Church', in *Reclaiming the Bible for the Church*, ed. Carl E. Braaten and Robert W. Jenson (Edinburgh: T & T Clark, 1995), pp. 89-105.

[15]   The significance of this term 'catholic' and the controversies concerning that which constitutes this 'sameness' will, of course, be a recurring theme of the subsequent discussion of the sacraments of the Church.

[16]   'As Irenaeus said, we need no special exertions to join the community of which Scripture speaks or to profit from its story, because the community in question is the very one that we, as baptized, already belong to'. Jenson, 'Hermeneutics and the life of the Church', p. 104.

theory proposed by J. L. Austin.[17] Words do not merely encode information: they are performative; they 'do' something. When words are spoken, therefore, there is not merely a locutionary act (the mere utterance of the words), there is also an illocutionary act (that which the speaker intends to do through those words). Moreover, as those words are heard there is a perlocutionary act (that which actually occurs through those words). Here then, it is claimed, we may have the possibility of reaffirming the potency of words without resorting again to the ultimately futile quest for 'meaning'. Indeed, a focus particularly on the perlocutionary act enables an attention to significance and, therefore, to the transformative (rather than merely informative) outcomes of speech.[18]

The obvious flaw in this strategy—a flaw which, though obvious, is rarely acknowledged or treated with sufficient seriousness—is that writing is not speech; the speaker is absent; illocutionary intent here is as elusive as intended meaning; the reader of a text has no more assured access to an author's intended outcome than to an author's intended meaning. One might question, of course, whether, even in speech, illocutionary intent is assuredly accessible: I know the effect of your words on me but I have no assured access to the effect you intended when you spoke those words. Even in spoken conversation I can no more access the illocutionary act through the perlocutionary act than I can access the meaning through the significance. But writing is not speech; the speaker—or rather, the author—is absent. Post-structuralism pronounces the 'death' of the author, and merely to refer to the author as a 'speaker' does not constitute a resurrection. Indeed, to refer to an author as a speaker is disingenuous: an author precisely is not a speaker; a text is not speech. Speech-act theory is immensely helpful in its shift of focus from meaning to performance—in this respect the theory has influenced new approaches to homiletics as much as new approaches to hermeneutics[19]—but speech-act theory, of itself, aids us not at all in overcoming the problem of the author's absence.

---

[17]   J. L. Austin, *How to do Things with Words* (Oxford: Oxford University Press, 2nd edn, 1976).

[18]   For examples of this strategy applied to biblical studies see Craig Bartholomew, Colin Greene and Karl Möller (eds.), *After Pentecost: Language and Biblical Interpretation* (Carlisle: Paternoster Press/Grand Rapids, MI: Zondervan, 2001); Richard Briggs, *Words in Action: Speech Act Theory and Biblical Interpretation: Toward a Hermeneutic of Self-involvement* (Edinburgh: T & T Clark, 2001); John R. Searle, *Expression and Meaning: Studies in the Theory of Speech Acts* (Cambridge: Cambridge University Press, 1985); Nicholas Wolterstorff, *Divine Discourse: Philosophical Reflections on the Claim that God Speaks* (Cambridge: Cambridge University Press, 1995).

[19]   See for example, David Buttrick, *Homiletic: Moves and Structures* (London: SCM Press, 1987); Fred B. Craddock, *Preaching* (Nashville, TN: Abingdon Press, 1985);

At this point, however, it should be recognised that, for most Christians throughout the major part of the Church's history, Scripture has been 'heard' rather than 'read'. This was partly an outcome of widespread illiteracy, but, far more fundamentally, it was an outcome of non-availability: people did not own their own Bibles; copies of Scripture were relatively rare and precious; the printing-press had not yet been invented. One might question, perhaps, whether the ready availability of Scripture is entirely beneficial: there is nothing like having the Bible at one's disposal to foster the assumption that the Bible is at one's disposal; to foster the assumption that the Bible is accessible to unmediated scrutiny.[20] The Bible for the most part, then, was heard. It was heard through the human mediation of a preacher or a lector. One might even say that the reading and hearing of Scripture was performative (a speech-act): it was (and remains) a rite of the Church, a crucial element in the Church's liturgy; Timothy is instructed to 'devote' himself 'to the public reading of Scripture, to preaching and to teaching' (1 Timothy 4.13).[21] And, as performative, the reading and hearing of Scripture was anticipated as transformative: Scripture was not read merely to inform but rather to transform; Scripture was read in order that, through it, the Church might be shaped; Scripture was read with the expectation expressed in the passage cited at the beginning of this chapter.

But if the reading and hearing of Scripture was anticipated as transformative this was certainly not through any incipient awareness of speech-act theory; the reading and hearing of Scripture was anticipated as transformative through the expectation of the presence and action of the risen Christ through the Spirit; the reading and hearing of Scripture was (and should be) anticipated as the living and active word of God.[22] This livingness of the reading and hearing of Scripture is expressed by John Calvin in terms of an 'inward testimony of the Spirit', a testimony that is both informative (instructive) and therefore assuring, and also transformative and shaping of Christian life:

Thomas G. Long, *The Witness of Preaching* (Louisville, KY: Westminster John Knox, 1989).

[20]   It could also be noted that the non-availability of Scripture within the Early Church did not prevent the Church's dramatic growth, and that the ready availability of Scripture in present-day Western Europe has not prevented the Church's inexorable decline.

[21]   πρόσεχε τῇ ἀναγνώσει, τῇ παρακλήσει, τῇ διδασκαλίᾳ.

[22]   'Christ is not the content of the proclamation merely as a passive object, as that *about* which the proclamation speaks. That he is risen, and so can himself speak now in the church, is part of what is narrated.' Jenson, *Systematic Theology*, vol. 1, p. 175.

...the testimony of the Spirit is more excellent than all reason. For God alone is a
fit witness of himself in his Word, so also the Word will not find acceptance in
men's hearts before it is sealed by the inward testimony of the Spirit.[23]

Note in particular here how Calvin distinguishes this testimony of the
Spirit from that which otherwise would be accessible to human reason.
For Calvin, Scripture is to be received as God's Word, not because it can
be established as such through any number of reasonable 'proofs', but
because it is heard and received through this living testimony.[24] There is
certainly no sense here of a Bible at our disposal—and it is in this respect
that Calvin's heirs, in a later Enlightenment context, may have so
seriously departed from his insight—it is rather that, through the means
of the Bible, we are at the Spirit's disposal; he speaks, he witnesses, he
confronts, he assures, he transforms.

In the case of the reading and hearing of Scripture, therefore, the
'author' (or the divine speaker, to be more precise) is neither absent nor
'dead'. It is in this respect that Scripture, for the Church, is distinctive. It
is in this respect that the Church reads and hears Scripture in a manner
that is radically other than the manner in which it reads and hears any
other text. And it is therefore in this respect that contemporary notions of
speech-act theory are particularly pertinent and potentially helpful. As I
have previously admitted, I would follow Edwards and Berkeley in
recognising all perception as divinely mediated. In this respect Scripture
is not unique. I am dependent upon the Spirit for my reading or hearing
of any text or speech, as for any perception—albeit that such mediation
generally passes unacknowledged and unrecognised.[25] That which
renders the Church's reading and hearing of Scripture distinctive is that
the Spirit who mediates the reading and hearing of the text is
correspondingly the mediator of the 'speaking' of that text; the mediator
of the perlocutionary act is similarly the mediator of the illocutionary act
and, indeed, the locutionary act. And in this expectation of the Spirit's
active speaking lies the true basis for the Church's anticipation of the
reading and hearing of Scripture as a performative and transformative

---

[23]   *Institutes* I vii 4.

[24]   '[T]hose whom the Holy Spirit has inwardly taught truly rest upon Scripture, and
that Scripture indeed is self-authenticated; hence it is not right to subject it to proof and
reasoning. And the certainty it deserves with us, it attains by the testimony of the Spirit.
For even if it wins reverence for itself by its own majesty, it seriously affects us only
when it is sealed upon our hearts through the Spirit'. *Institutes* I vii 5.

[25]   In this respect I could not disagree more radically when, in response to an earlier
article by Stephen Wright in the same volume, Brian Ingraffia and Todd Pickett assume
that '...non-Christians understand communicative actions all the time, without the aid of
the Holy Spirit?' Brian D. Ingraffia and Todd E. Pickett, 'Reviving the Power of Biblical
Language', in Bartholomew, Greene and Möller (eds.) *After Pentecost*, pp. 241-262 (p.
245).

event: that which is anticipated is the Spirit's speaking and acting; or, as Kevin Vanhoozer puts it, '[t]here is nothing human authors can do to make sure their recipients "get it". God, however, has no such limits…'.[26]

> As the rain and the snow
> come down from heaven,
> and do not return to it
> without watering the earth
> and making it bud and flourish,
> so that it yields seed for the sower
> and bread for the eater,
> so is my word that goes out from my mouth:
> It will not return to me empty,
> but will accomplish what I desire
> and achieve the purpose for which I sent it. (Isaiah 55.10-11)

That which is distinctive about the Church's reading and hearing of Scripture is not just that it is a mediated hearing (a mediated perception) but that this mediated hearing is in correspondence to a mediated speaking: the Word of God is 'living'. And since the Spirit who is the mediator of the speaking of this Word is simultaneously the mediator of the hearing of this Word the Church, with confidence, can expect the reading and hearing of Scripture to be a performative and transformative event, a mediation of the gracious presence and action of God, a sacramental act. Scripture is a human Word, the event of reading and hearing Scripture is a truly human event, but through the means of this truly human event the Spirit mediates to us the gracious presence and action of God. Scripture, in the event of its being read and heard, is a means of grace.

One recent, significant, and substantial discussion of Scripture as a means of grace occurs in William Abraham's *Canon and Criterion in Christian Theology*[27] in which the distinction is made between ecclesial canon (that which is identified as a means of grace within the Church) and epistemic criterion (that which is identified as normative for Christian faith and practice). The argument of the book is long and detailed, but in essence the author suggests an unfortunate (and relatively early) shift from an identification of Scripture as *a* canon of the Church (a means of grace to the Church) to an identification of Scripture as *the* canon of the

---

[26]   Kevin J. Vanhoozer, 'From Speech Acts to Scripture Acts: The Covenant of Discourse and the Discourse of Covenant', in Bartholomew, Greene and Möller (eds.), *After Pentecost*, pp. 1-49 (p. 38).
[27]   William J. Abraham, *Canon and Criterion in Christian Theology: From the Fathers to Feminism* (Oxford: Clarendon Press, 1998).

Church (the epistemic criterion for Christian theology); that is to say, quite early in the Church's history a change occurred in the notion and significance of 'canon' itself.[28] Now it may be that this distinction between canon as means of grace and canon as criterion is not as straightforward as the book sometimes appears to suggest. It may also be that any notion of canon as 'identified' and 'separated' means of grace inevitably and appropriately issues in a recognition of such canon as normative for Christian faith and practice. But Abraham's thesis is instructive, both in its identification of this earlier notion of canon as a means of grace, and in its identification of the processes through which this earlier notion becomes obscured or effectively abandoned. This is, after all, simply another construal of the move from the dynamic to the static, from the being given to the given, from the mediated immediate to the unmediated immediate. To identify Scripture as criterion—as normative for faith and practice—in any unmediated sense would be to imply again that Scripture was simply an object at our disposal, would be to assent to the presupposition of unmediated accessibility, would be to comply with the epistemic foundationalism of the Enlightenment. If Scripture is to be acknowledged as criterion in any valid manner it must be because firstly and definitively it is acknowledged as a means of grace, as a means through which the Spirit mediates the promised speaking and acting of God.

To acknowledge Scripture as sacramental, as a means of grace, is to acknowledge both the mediating agency of the Spirit and the mediating instrumentality of the human text:

> The scriptural texts converge on this divine speaking because they mediate this divine speaking. God speaks in Jesus in and through the texts of Old and New Testaments. These texts do not merely report the divine speaking, they enact it; and that they do so is the distinctive work of the Holy Spirit.[29]

It is not then that in and through the reading and hearing of Scripture the word and act of God is accessible to us in an immediate and unmediated manner, as pure object, as a 'given' inherent in the text of Scripture itself; it is rather that in and through the reading and hearing of Scripture the word and act of God is mediated to us by the Spirit: there is here a mediated immediacy rather than any unmediated immediacy. But neither is this mediation of the word and act of God by the Spirit unmediated,

---

[28]   '[T]he term "canon" ceased to be seen as a list of concrete items, such as a list of books to be read in worship, and came to be seen as a criterion of justification in theology'. Abraham, *Canon and Criterion*, p. 2.

[29]   Francis Watson, '"America's theologian": an appreciation of Robert Jenson's *Systematic Theology*, with some remarks about the bible', *SJT* 55.2 (2002), pp. 201-223 (pp. 217-218).

immediate other than through the mediating instrumentality of this human text or some other mediating instrumentality. For all the undoubted perceptiveness and helpfulness of Karl Barth's discussion of the threefold form of the Word of God[30]—a perceptiveness and helpfulness rooted precisely in its affirmation of the dynamic of God's speaking and its rejection of any purely objective givenness that renders God's Word at our disposal—the mere distinction of a *three*fold form of God's Word,[31] the mere affirmation of revelation 'itself' as a third 'form' taken by God's Word alongside the form this revelation takes through proclamation and through Scripture, would seem to imply the possibility of an unmediated immediate, the possibility of the Spirit's mediation of God's Word other than through the mediating instrumentality of proclamation, of Scripture, of the flesh of Christ, of some embodied material means.[32] As I argue at various points in this book, the tendency towards an affirmation of an unmediated immediate, of an immediate mediation of the Spirit other than through material sacramental means, vitiates the entirety of Barth's *Dogmatics*.

As with any other sacramental means, the text of Scripture is certainly not God's prison. In the first place, as Karl Barth graphically expresses it, though God has promised to speak here he has not prohibited the possibility of speaking elsewhere, through other material means:

---

[30]   *CD* I/1, pp. 88-247.

[31]   'There is no distinction of degree or value between the three forms. For to the extent that proclamation really rests on recollection of the revelation attested in the Bible and is thus obedient repetition of the biblical witness, it is no less the Word of God than the Bible. And to the extent that the Bible really attests revelation it is no less the Word of God than revelation itself. As the Bible and proclamation become God's Word in virtue of the actuality of revelation they are God's Word: the one Word of God within which there can be neither a more nor a less.' *CD* I/1, pp. 120-121.

[32]   It could be argued that Barth moderates this position in IV/3, both by reasserting the singleness of the Word of God through the forms of proclamation and Scripture (i.e., these are not to be seen as two further 'forms' of God's Word), and also by the recognition of other created means which might be pressed into service as the mediations of this single Word (though, as we will note later, Barth had already intimated the latter): '...we should simply maintain that alongside the first and primary Word of God, and in relation to it, there are at least two other true words which are distinct yet inter-related... If the words of Scripture and the Christian community can be called a true word in the strict sense, in neither case can there be any question of completing, rivalling, systematising or transcending the one Word. These words do not stand beside it in their own right. The one Word itself sets them there. Similarly, they are not independent, but their relationship with it is one of service, and it is only as they are spoken in this ministry of service that there can be any question of their validity, dignity or truth.' *CD* IV/3, p. 114; and again: 'In the course of this action of the Word of God the eternal light can shine, the Word of the covenant of grace be spoken and the saving truth of God be uttered in the lights, words and truths of creation.' *CD* IV/3, p. 157.

God may speak to us through Russian Communism, a flute concerto, a blossoming
shrub, or a dead dog. We do well to listen to Him if He really does. But, unless we
regard ourselves as the prophets and founders of a new Church, we cannot say that
we are commissioned to pass on what we have heard as independent proclamation.[33]

That which renders Scripture distinct from other such possible mediations
is simply and solely the promise of God, the witness of Scripture to itself
as witness to God's speaking and acting, the expectation of God's
mediated speaking in the future on the basis of the recollection of his
mediated speaking in the past.[34] But in the second place, Scripture is
certainly not God's prison in any sense of his word and action being at
our disposal here, to be presumed upon here, to be taken for granted
here: God's speaking here is gracious; God's speaking here is mediated
by the Spirit. The Church expects God's mediated presence and action
here, but it does so—as with any other sacramental means—humbly and
prayerfully.

And in this recollection and prayerful expectation of God's mediated
speaking, the Church and the Scriptures are mutually defining. The
Church, which is defined sacramentally through baptism, Communion,
ministry, is correspondingly defined as that community which recollects
and expects this mediated divine speaking. And Scripture, which is
defined sacramentally through the event of this mediated divine speaking,
is correspondingly defined through the Church's recollection and
expectation of that mediated divine speaking through the means of this
text.

I suspect there will be some who read this book (or who make no
progress beyond the contents' page) who would assume that a chapter on
Scripture should precede a chapter on the Church: the Church is shaped
by Scripture rather than Scripture by the Church; the Church does not
decide upon that which is Scripture (or which is not Scripture), the
Church rather recognises and attests this mediated divine speaking.
Scripture, therefore, must be set above the Church rather than the Church
above Scripture.[35]

But while it should indeed be recognised that God's mediated speaking
precedes the Church this is not to say that Scripture precedes the

---

[33]   *CD* I/1, p. 55.

[34]   'Of the book as we have it, we can only say: We recollect that we have heard in
this book the Word of God; we recollect, in and with the Church, that the Word of God has
been heard in all this book and in all parts of it; therefore we expect that we shall hear the
Word of God in this book again, and hear it even in those places where we ourselves have
not heard it before. *CD* I/2, p. 530.

[35]   Thus Calvin, commenting (rightly or wrongly) on Augustine, notes that '...the
holy man's intention was not to make the faith that we hold in the Scriptures depend upon
the assent or judgment of the church'. *Institutes* I vii 3.

Church—the latter claim would simply be historically false. God's mediated speaking to Abram and Moses is constitutive of Israel as the people of God, but the historical phenomenon of Israel as the people of God precedes and predates the Torah, the Prophets, and the Writings. Jesus' calling of the disciples and the coming of the Spirit at Pentecost is constitutive of the Church, but the historical phenomenon of the Church precedes and predates the Gospels and the Epistles. God's mediated speaking through Scripture may be formative (now) of the Church, but God's mediated speaking through the Church, correspondingly but primarily, is formative of Scripture.[36] Without Scripture there may now be no Church, but without the Church (in the old and new covenant sense) there would be no Scripture. The phenomenon of Scripture presupposes the phenomenon of the Church, not just for that recollection and expectation which is its recognition as Scripture, but for that initial writing which is its formation as Scripture. Scripture, therefore, as the instrumental means of God's mediated speaking, is the Church's text, a human text.

To affirm Scripture as Scripture, then, is simply to affirm the expectation of God's mediated speaking through this text—an expectation grounded in the Church's recollection of that mediated speaking; an expectation grounded in the witness of Scripture to itself; an expectation grounded in the promise of God that this mediated speaking which has occurred through this instrumental means will occur again; an expectation grounded in the Church's recognition of Scripture's sacramentality as this instrumental means of God's mediated speaking. To affirm Scripture as Scripture, then, is to affirm that, through the means of this human word, this word that originates within the Church (in the old and new covenant sense), we are encountered by God's mediated speaking; this human word is the instrumental means of the divine word.[37] But Scripture is the instrumental means of this mediated divine word without ceasing to be a truly human word, a word that originates within the Church—though, even in its human origins, a word that is a mediation of God's mediated speaking.

It is both possible and essential to affirm Scripture's origin in this mediated divine speaking—to affirm Scripture as Scripture is both to expect and to recollect God's mediated speaking; here God will speak by

---

[36] 'When we adopt the Canon of the Church we do not say that the Church itself, but that the revelation which underlies and controls the Church, attests these witnesses and not others as the witnesses of revelation and therefore as canonical for the Church.' *CD* I/2, p. 474.

[37] 'As the Word of God in the sign of this prophetic-apostolic word of man Holy Scripture is like the unity of God and man in Jesus Christ. It is neither divine only nor human only. Nor is it a mixture of the two nor a *tertium quid* between them. But in its own way and degree it is very God and very man...'. *CD* I/2, p. 501.

the Spirit since here God has spoken by the Spirit—but this is not to imply that such initial mediated divine speaking corresponded to any conscious initial human hearing. The recognition of Scripture as Scripture is a matter of recollection and expectation rather than any necessary conscious initial awareness. Or, to put the matter more simply, any divine dictation theory of Scripture's inspiration should be resisted both as fanciful and as undermining of the authentic humanity of this text. It may be that the prophets were aware of the Spirit's mediated speaking—though even here one suspects the dynamic of prophecy to be both more complex and more simple; and here again we must be careful to distinguish the prophets' speaking and the subsequent writing of those words. But in the case of the narratives of Scripture, the Psalms, wisdom literature, the Epistles, there is no reason to suppose any initial conscious hearing of God's mediated speaking: that God mediates his speaking here is 'hidden'; it is 'mystery'; it is recognised only through the subsequent mediation of God's speaking through these human words.

And they are truly human words. Notions of Scripture's inerrancy fail to take account of the limitations of language. Language is imperfect. Words simply are inadequate in relation to concepts. We must heed the critique which is post-structuralism concerning the inevitable deferment of meaning. Even if we had absolute assured access to the 'original' text of Scripture, we have no such absolute assured access to the 'original' linguistic community, and we certainly have no such assured access to the intentions of the author—we may affirm the continuity of the believing community; we may affirm the continuity of a tradition of signification; but we can have no assured access to original meaning. But far more seriously, notions of Scripture's inerrancy fail to take account of the character of theology, of the far deeper limitations of any language with respect to God. If human words are inadequate to human concepts then human words are certainly inadequate to God, even when God himself uses those human words in his mediated speaking. It is in this context that John Calvin writes of God 'accommodating' himself to human language,[38] and, though Calvin never explicitly presses this notion with respect to the limitations of the text, he does seem to allow for the possibility of errors within Scripture.[39]

---

[38]   'For who even of slight intelligence does not understand that, as nurses commonly do with infants, God is wont in a measure to "lisp" in speaking to us? Thus such forms of speaking do not so much express clearly what God is like as accommodate the knowledge of him to our slight capacity. To do this he must descend far beneath his loftiness.' *Institutes* I xiii 1.

[39]   'The scholarly literature on Calvin still puzzles over the question how he can nevertheless—as he plainly does—admit that there are errors in the Bible. But more important for my present purpose is the fact that reverence for Scripture did not prevent Calvin from seeking a word *within* the words, nor from identifying *this* word as the actual

The authority of Scripture within the Church, therefore, cannot be reduced in some legalistic manner in terms of supposedly inerrant propositional truths or supposedly absolute rules; the authority of Scripture within the Church consists rather in its recollection of God's mediated speaking through this text and its prayerful expectation of God's future mediated speaking through this text.[40] The text with which this chapter began concludes a passage in the Letter to the Hebrews in which the writer has been reviewing the wilderness wanderings and rebellions of the people of Israel, as recorded in Exodus and Numbers, in the light of Psalm 95, and warning his readers lest they too 'harden' their 'hearts'. In the course of this exposition the writer reflects on the significance of God's sabbath rest (Genesis 2.2-3), the rest in the promised land that Israel received through Joshua's leadership (Joshua 22.4), and the rest implicit in the invitation of the psalmist (Psalm 95.7-8)—which presumably had significance for the psalm's previous readers and hearers as much as for the readers and hearers of this Epistle. The writer then concludes this exposition with the affirmation of the livingness of God's Word with which this chapter began: the 'today' of the psalm is re-presented as the 'today' of the Letter's readers and hearers; through these human words God has mediated his speaking and will mediate his speaking again; his gracious warning and invitation, mediated through the words of the psalmist, are mediated again through the words of the writer; they are mediated by the Spirit who mediated them before; they are mediated as immediate:

> Today, if you hear his voice,
> do not harden your hearts...

This mediated immediacy should be the expectation of the Church whenever Scripture is read, heard, or preached. Within the Church, Scripture is a means of grace; through this human text God promises to mediate his speaking, acting, and presence by the Spirit. Indeed, the Church may also expect Scripture to be a means of grace within the world: wherever and whenever Scripture is read and heard there is the

---

object of faith. For Calvin the Bible was not a mere compendium of supernaturally communicated information; it was the medium of a divine message.' Gerrish, *Grace and Gratitude*, p. 77.

   [40]   'These texts are foundational to the life of the church, not on the legalistic and biblicistic grounds that they possess an inherent, absolute authority to which we are bound to submit, but on the grounds that in them we encounter the particular life upon which the communal life of the church is founded; the life that is the light not only of the church but also of the world. For that reason and in that sense, preaching, worship and sacraments must conform to these texts.' Francis Watson, *Text and Truth: Redefining Biblical Theology* (Edinburgh: T & T Clark, 1997), p. 1.

possibility (because there is the promise) of the Spirit's mediated speaking; Scripture is a 'converting ordinance'. And it is a 'converting' ordinance: as with the other sacraments of the Church, Scripture is a means of grace in order to change us; the intention and effect of Scripture's sacramentality is our sanctification; through the hearing of Scripture we are changed by the Spirit who speaks through Scripture.[41]

But this change is brought about, not merely through our mediated hearing, but through our mediated indwelling. As with the example cited from the Letter to the Hebrews, we are drawn into the narrative of the text, the story becomes our story, and hence we are shaped by the Spirit through that story.[42] And, by such means, the Church itself becomes a part of the story, a fresh telling of the story, a living hermeneut of the gospel: the Church itself is sacramental, a means of grace to the world, inasmuch as the Church itself indwells this story sacramentally.[43]

And herein lies the connectedness of the sacramentality of Scripture and the sacraments of the Church. The Church's indwelling of Scripture is itself sacramental: it is through its sacramental life and worship that the Church is brought to indwell the gospel story that the Spirit narrates through Scripture; it is through its sacramental life and worship that the Church is shaped by the Spirit in coherence with that gospel story. Within the Church, Scripture is not merely read and heard; it is enacted and indwelt. Therefore, just as the sacramentality of the sacraments is constituted through the promise mediated in Scripture (the promise that these rites of the Church will be means through which the Spirit mediates God's presence and action to us),[44] so also the sacramentality of Scripture is constituted through the sacramental life and worship of the Church; it is

---

[41]   'The proclamation of the Word is a sacramental act par excellence because it is a transforming act. It transforms the human words of the Gospel into the Word of God and the manifestation of the Kingdom. And it transforms the man who hears the Word into a receptacle of the Word and a temple of the Spirit...'. Schmemann, *The World as Sacrament*, p. 38.

[42]   'The true end of the covenant of discourse and the discourse of the covenant is indeed a kind of dwelling—or better, a mutual *indwelling*. The Bible simply calls it *communion*: we in Christ; Christ in us.' Kevin J. Vanhoozer, 'From Speech Acts to Scripture Acts: The Covenant of Discourse and the Discourse of Covenant', in Bartholomew, Greene and Möller (eds.) *After Pentecost*, pp. 1-49 (p. 46).

[43]   'Barth, of course, does not deny that the church is constituted by the proclamation of the gospel. What he cannot acknowledge is that the community called the church is constitutive of the gospel proclamation.' Stanley Hauerwas, *With the Grain of the Universe: The Church's Witness and Natural Theology—Gifford Lectures 2001* (London: SCM Press, 2002), p. 145.

[44]   '[W]e must reaffirm the tradition of both Augustine and the Reformers that there is no sacrament without word, without some word of divine promise that the material creation is able to be the vehicle of divine action in and towards the world.' Gunton, *Christ and Creation*, p. 113.

through the Church's sacramental life and worship that the Church is brought by the Spirit to indwell Scripture's story and to be transformed through that indwelling. It may not be quite true to say that, just as there can be no sacramentality of the sacraments without the promise of Scripture, there can be no sacramentality of Scripture without the sacraments: we must believe that the penitent thief was brought to indwell the story of the Crucified and Risen One without baptism—but this was extra-ordinary, an exceptional circumstance. The mediated means of indwelling the story that is mediated through Scripture is the sacramental life and worship of the Church—and to the sacraments that form this sacramental life we now turn.

PART THREE

PART THREE

CHAPTER 5

The Sacrament of Baptism

Peter replied, 'Repent and be baptised, every one of you, in the name of Jesus Christ for the forgiveness of your sins. And you will receive the gift of the Holy Spirit. The promise is for you and your children and for all who are far off—for all whom the Lord our God will call.' (Acts 2.38-39)

Though one would expect to the contrary, many contemporary Baptists are often strangely muted concerning their defining distinctive. In part this quite recent reticence is an outcome of ecumenical sensitivity: a significant proportion of Baptist churches in England (that is, of those that are in membership with the Baptist Union of Great Britain) practise 'open membership', receiving members from other denominations and connections 'on profession of faith' and without insisting on baptism. This is not a misprint: it is not that most Baptist churches reluctantly accept the validity of the infant baptism of prospective members coming from other denominations—most Baptists (I would guess) would not count infant baptism as valid baptism—it is rather that most Baptist churches, not counting infant baptism as valid baptism, do not ultimately insist on baptism at all. It may be possible, therefore, for former members of the Salvation Army, or the Society of Friends, or for others who (for some reason) have never been baptised in any form, to be received into membership within a local Baptist church simply on profession of their faith—and if, of course, infant baptism is perceived as invalid, to receive those who have not received this rite is entirely consistent; in neither case validly would baptism have occurred.[1] The outcome of this ecumenical openness is the anomalous phenomenon of that connection defined by its baptismal distinctiveness being most lax in its baptismal practice and discipline.[2] It was not always the case of course: this rise of 'open

---

[1]   It should be noted, however, that in most cases an 'unbaptised' member of an open-membership Baptist church would be prohibited from holding office (such as that of elder or deacon) within that church, and that the Baptist Union of Great Britain insists upon the baptism (as a believer) of any candidate for its nationally accredited ministry.

[2]   For a discussion of Baptist life and attitudes to baptism see H. Wheeler Robinson, *The Life and Faith of the Baptists* (London: Methuen, 1927), and Stanley K. Fowler, *More Than a Symbol: The British Baptist Recovery of Baptismal Sacramentalism* (Carlisle: Paternoster Press, 2002).

membership' Baptist churches is relatively recent; in the past both General and Particular Baptists tended to practice closed membership (and closed communion) and even though John Bunyan defended the 'open' baptismal policy of the Bedford Meeting against the criticisms of John Kiffin, he surely would have assumed that those benefiting from this open policy would have been 'baptised' as infants.[3]

But this contemporary reticence is more deeply rooted in longstanding theological controversy and confusion. From their beginnings, Baptists (both General and Particular) have never been able to agree concerning the significance of baptism: they have been united in reserving baptism for believers; they have been united (for the most part) in practising baptism by total immersion;[4] but they have been markedly disunited in their understanding of baptism's significance, in their expectation of whether or not something occurs through baptism, in their recognition or non-recognition of baptism's sacramentality. And while it could be argued (and has been argued)[5] that a more sacramentalist view dominated Baptist beginnings (at least in Great Britain), one suspects that, despite the sterling efforts of some, efforts not without fruit amongst those who have troubled to engage with their work,[6] this is no longer the case amongst Baptists in general. Anecdotally at least, most contemporary members of Baptist churches seem to view baptism as an entirely human event, as a

---

[3]   Bunyan, 'Differences in Judgment about Water Baptism', pp. 616-642; cf. his 'A Confession of my faith', in *Works,* vol. II, pp. 593-616, and 'Peacable Principles and True', in *Works,* vol. II, pp. 648-657; cf. Michael A. G. Haykin, *Kiffin, Knollys and Keach: Rediscovering the English Baptist Heritage* (Darlington: Carey, 1996); D. M. Lloyd-Jones, 'John Bunyan: Church Union', in *Light from John Bunyan and other Puritans* (London: Westminster Conference, 1978), pp. 86-102; and B. R. White, *The English Baptists of the Seventeenth Century* (London: Baptist Historical Society, 1983).

[4]   The 'Declaration of Principle' of the Baptist Union of Great Britain defines baptism as 'the immersion in water into the name of the Father, the Son, and the Holy Ghost, of those who have professed repentance towards God and faith in our Lord Jesus Christ...'. Unsurprisingly this defines baptism in relation to repentance and faith, but bizarrely it also defines baptism explicitly according to its mode, and implicitly in relation to the quantity of water available.

[5]   For a full and engaging account of this historical debate see Fowler, *More Than a Symbol*; cf. Anthony R. Cross, 'Dispelling the Myth of English Baptist Sacramentalism' *Baptist Quarterly* 38 (2000), pp. 367-391.

[6]   In this respect contributions of particular note have been brought by Ernest A. Payne, *The Fellowship of Believers: Baptist Thought and Practice Yesterday and Today* (London: Carey Kingsgate Press, 2nd edn, 1952); Clark, *An Approach to the Theology of the Sacraments*; G. R. Beasley-Murray, *Baptism in the New Testament*; P. S. Fiddes (ed.), *Reflections on the Water: Understanding God and the World through the Baptism of Believers* (Oxford: Regent's Park College, 1996); Anthony R. Cross, *Baptism and the Baptists: Theology and Practice in Twentieth-Century Britain* (Carlisle: Paternoster Press, 2000).

testimony to an event of Christian conversion that has already occurred in some unmediated sense.

In contrast to this vacuous but all too common assumption, Luke's account of Peter's appeal on the day of Pentecost is pregnant with expectation: '...you will receive the gift of the Holy Spirit...[t]he promise is for you and your children and for all who are far off'. Baptism is approached with expectation because baptism is constituted by promise.

As has already been noted, the sacraments are *res promissa* (a matter of promise). While the Holy Spirit may mediate God's presence and action through the means of any aspect of the material creation God has not promised to do so. God may speak to Moses through a burning bush but he has not promised that this will be the case; he has not constituted burning bushes as means of grace. That which is truly sacramental is constituted as such through a specific promise of God. God has promised to speak and act through the Church. God has promised to speak and act through the reading and hearing of Scripture. God has promised to speak and act through baptism. And here, at the conclusion of Peter's sermon, the promise is specific: '...you will receive the gift of the Holy Spirit'.

While this account of Peter's Pentecost sermon is appropriately focused on Christ (on his ministry, death, resurrection, and ascension), its starting point, understandably in the circumstances of the narrative, is this giving of the Spirit. The ascending Christ promises his disciples that, just as John baptised with water, they will be baptised with the Holy Spirit (Acts 1.5), and the beginning of Peter's sermon, with its extended quotation from the prophecy of Joel, suggests that the disciples interpreted the events of Pentecost morning as the fulfilment of this promise. This quotation from Joel is significant, not primarily for its ecstatic references,[7] but for its eschatological orientation: this is the fulfilment of God's promise to pour out his Spirit 'in the last days' (Acts 2.17); this is the precursor to 'the coming of the great and glorious day of the Lord' (Acts 2.20). And this promise is 'for you and your children...'; this promise is for all those who respond in repentance and baptism.

This link between water baptism and the eschatological outpouring of the Spirit occurs, at least negatively, in the narrative of John's baptism; it is he who first contrasts a baptism with water for repentance and a baptism of the Holy Spirit effected by the one who comes after him (Matthew 3.11). Notwithstanding this explicit contrast, there has been much debate concerning whether John's baptism might properly be identified as

---

[7]   'Your sons and daughters will prophesy, your young men will see visions, your old men will dream dreams' (Acts 2.17).

Christian baptism.[8] In the first place (and most strikingly) Luke employs precisely the same phraseology to describe John's baptism (Luke 3.3) as he later employs on the lips of Peter (Acts 2.38): both are described as a baptism of repentance for the forgiveness of sins ($\epsilon\dot{\iota}\varsigma$ $\ddot{\alpha}\phi\epsilon\sigma\iota\nu$ [$\tau\tilde{\omega}\nu$] $\dot{\alpha}\mu\alpha\rho\tau\iota\tilde{\omega}\nu$). Secondly there is no record of any of the disciples of Jesus being re-baptised. And thirdly there is the enigmatic reference in John's Gospel to the disciples of Jesus baptising during his earthly ministry,[9] a reference rendered the more extraordinary given the Gospel's unequivocal denial of the Spirit's outpouring prior to Christ's exaltation.[10] But, on the other hand, John the Baptist is unequivocally portrayed in the Gospels as the herald of the Christ; one who prepares the way for the Christ; the last of the 'old' rather than the first of the 'new'.[11] Perhaps John's baptism should be understood as anticipative of Christian baptism inasmuch as, within the context of John's proclamation, it was a baptism into the coming Christ. This may be the reason underlying Paul's 're-baptism' of disciples in Ephesus: on the basis of the surrounding narrative it would appear that they had received John's baptism without hearing John's message (Acts 19.1ff.).

But that which radically distinguishes John's baptism (or any baptism prior to Christ's exaltation) from Christian baptism is this explicit promise of the eschatological outpouring of the Spirit. Those baptised by John (other than Jesus himself) do so simply as a sign of their repentance, with the hope of forgiveness, and in anticipation of the coming Christ who—unlike John—will baptise with the Holy Spirit and with fire. Those baptised on the day of Pentecost do so as a sign of repentance and with the hope of forgiveness but also with the expectation of the imminent fulfilment of this promise of the outpouring of the Spirit. And it is through the means of baptism that this promise is effected. As distinct from John's baptism, the significance of Christian baptism in water is a baptism with and by the Spirit.[12]

Perhaps the strongest (though also perhaps the most contested) New Testament witness to this significance of baptism occurs within the Johannine narrative of Jesus' conversation with Nicodemus:

---

8   See for instance Ulrich Zwingli, *Refutation of the Tricks of the Baptists (In catabaptistarum strophas elenchus*: 1527), in *Selected Works*, pp. 123–258; cf. *Institutes* IV xv 7.

9   John 3.22; cf. 4.1-2.

10      $o\ddot{\upsilon}\pi\omega$ $\gamma\dot{\alpha}\rho$ $\ddot{\eta}\nu$ $\pi\nu\epsilon\tilde{\upsilon}\mu\alpha$, $\ddot{o}\tau\iota$ $'I\eta\sigma o\tilde{\upsilon}\varsigma$ $o\dot{\upsilon}\delta\acute{\epsilon}\pi\omega$ $\dot{\epsilon}\delta o\xi\acute{\alpha}\sigma\theta\eta$ (John 7.39).

11   See especially Matthew 11.11ff.

12   Some years ago I recall Tom Wright commenting that where the New Testament mentions baptism we should assume that it is to baptism that it is referring. On this simple (though strangely contested) basis, then, I assume that when Paul states that '...we were all baptised by one Spirit into one body...' (1 Corinthians 12.13) he is referring to a baptism of the Spirit mediated through a baptism in water.

Jesus declared, 'I tell you the truth, no-one can see the kingdom of God without being born again.'

'How can anyone be born in old age?' Nicodemus asked. 'Surely they cannot enter a second time into their mother's womb to be born!'

Jesus answered, 'I tell you the truth, no-one can enter the kingdom of God without being born of water and the Spirit. Flesh gives birth to flesh, but the Spirit gives birth to spirit.' (John 3.3-6)

The mention within the passage of flesh giving birth to flesh has afforded opportunity for some to conclude that a birth of water here refers simply to physical birth; in other words, Jesus is telling Nicodemus that physical birth (being born of water) is insufficient, he must also be born of the Spirit, born again.[13] In the light of the previous and subsequent references to water baptism within the Gospel, and in the light of the immediately preceding narratives of the wedding at Cana and the cleansing of the Temple with their clear eschatological (and sacramental) significance, but principally in the light of the overwhelming sacramental emphasis of the Gospel (as also the first Epistle of John and the Book of Revelation), I find this reasoning breathtakingly wooden. I can only assume that some of my fellow Protestants are so resistant to anything sacramental that they will resort to any degree of special pleading in order to evade such significance. More commonly a distinction is assumed between being born of water and being born of the Spirit: according to this interpretation the passage is clarifying that water baptism, of itself, is insufficient; a separate and distinct baptism with the Spirit must also occur. Surely a more simple reading of the text is that to be 'born again' (γεννηθῇ ἄνωθων) is to be born of water and the Spirit (γεννηθῇ ἐξ ὕδατος καὶ πνεύματος), that to be born of water and to be born of the Spirit are inextricably linked, that the significance of the former is the reality of the latter.

On the day of Pentecost Peter articulates a promise. He does so on the basis of a previous promise of Jesus. It is a promise to those coming to baptism. It is the promise of the eschatological outpouring of the Spirit. It is the promise of new life. And it is not an empty promise. Those coming to baptism, therefore, may come with the humble yet confident expectation of that promise being fulfilled. Baptism is a means of this

---

[13]   George Beasley-Murray makes reference to such ideas (and dismisses them) in his commentary on the Gospel: George R. Beasley-Murray, *John*, Word Biblical Commentary 36 (Waco, TX: Word Books, 1987), pp. 48-49.

grace: it does not effect this grace; but it is the ordained means through which this grace is effected.[14]

Karl Barth concludes the final *Fragment* of his *Church Dogmatics* with an exposition of 1 Peter 3.21 since (in his view) this text more than any other offers us an explicit definition of baptism and does so by defining baptism as a prayer:[15]

> If this is not a definition of the meaning of baptism, it is a description not unlike a definition; it is the only baptismal verse of this kind in the New Testament.... [I]t justifies us in bringing our whole doctrine of baptism to a climax in what is expressly stated here, namely, that baptism is a prayer to God.[16]

Barth's assumption that the word commonly translated 'pledge' (ἐπερώτημα) should be interpreted rather in terms of 'prayer' (an 'appeal' to God) has not passed unchallenged,[17] but, as I have argued at length elsewhere,[18] when the word in question appears here and nowhere else in the New Testament, linguistic arguments should proceed with great caution. Moreover, while there may be extra-biblical historical reasons for interpreting the word in terms of contractual pledge,[19] there are certainly

---

[14]   'Baptism and new birth are inseparably bound together, for the gift of the Holy Spirit involves a radical change at the centre of man's being. The divine promises attached to the sacraments are not empty promises; what God says, "goes".' Clark, *An Approach to the Theology of the Sacraments*, p. 82.

[15]   '[T]his water symbolises baptism that now saves you also—not the removal of dirt from the body but the pledge of a good conscience towards God. It saves you by the resurrection of Jesus Christ...' (1 Peter 3.21).

[16]   *CD* IV/4, p. 211.

[17]   Bo Reicke, for instance, describes the idea as 'actually quite unthinkable in this connection': Bo Reicke, *The Disobedient Spirits and Christian Baptism: A Study of 1 Pet. III. 19 and its Context* (København: Ejnar Munksgaard, 1946), p. 182; similarly R. E. O. White comments that '[a]ll attempts to make baptism a prayer or appeal, or to regard a good conscience as something that can be had for the asking, fail both on general and on linguistic grounds'. R. E. O. White, *The Biblical Doctrine of Initiation* (London: Hodder & Stoughton, 1960), p. 232.

[18]   John E. Colwell, 'Baptism, Conscience and the Resurrection: A Reappraisal of 1 Peter 3:21', in *Baptism, the New Testament and the Church: Historical and Contemporary Studies in Honour of R. E. O. White*, eds. S. E. Porter and A. R. Cross (Sheffield: Sheffield Academic Press, 1999), pp. 210-227.

[19]   See for instance J. N. D. Kelly, *A Commentary on the Epistles of Peter and of Jude* (London: Adam and Charles Black, 1969), p. 162; J. D. G. Dunn, *Baptism in the Holy Spirit: A Re-examination of the New Testament Teaching on the Gift of the Spirit in Relation to Pentecostalism Today* (London: SCM Press, 1970), p. 217; W. J. Dalton, *Christ's Proclamation to the Spirits: A Study of 1 Peter 3:18–4:6*, Analecta Biblica, 23 (Rome: Editrice Pontificio Istituto Biblico, 2nd edn, 1989), pp. 206ff.; Peter H. Davids, *The First Epistle of Peter* (Grand Rapids, MI: Eerdmans, 1990), p. 145; Norbert Brox, *Der*

theological reasons for resisting such an interpretation.[20] In the light of the gospel, the prospect of a 'good conscience towards God' (συνειδήσεως ἀγαθῆς...εἰς θεόν) could never be a merely human possibility; that it is a possibility—as the text itself indicates—is an outcome of Christ's resurrection. If baptism, then, is in any sense a 'pledge' of a 'good conscience' it is so because God has first promised such to us in the resurrection of Christ: baptism can only be a human 'pledge' of a 'good conscience' if it is firstly understood as an 'appeal' or prayer in the light of this divine promise:

> They can only await it as God's free gift. Hence they can only pray for it. The divine work of their justification and sanctification, the divine work of the presence and action of the Holy Spirit can alone create and give them the good conscience which they need. The human work of baptism is the request for this, the petition that God will create and give it to those who ask and pray for it.[21]

On this basis it may be possible to interpret each of the sacraments of the Church (with the possible exception of marriage) as enacted prayer. The resurrection of Jesus Christ is God's promise of a new (sanctified) humanity, a promise made present to us by the Spirit through the sacraments. God has promised to effect this promise by his Spirit through these ordained means. We therefore come to the sacraments in the prayerful expectation of the fulfilment of this promise. This is not at all to reduce the sacraments to merely human events of prayer: such genuinely human events are only meaningful as human events of prayer

---

erste Petrusbrief: Evangelisch-Katholischer Kommentar zum Neuen Tetament (Zürich: Benziger Verlag/Neukirchen-Vluyn: Neukirchener Verlag, 1979), p. 178.

[20]   See for instance Wayne A. Grudem, The First Epistle of Peter (Leicester: IVP, 1988), p. 164; cf. Paul J. Achtemeier, A Commentary on First Peter (Minneapolis, MN: Fortress Press, 1996), p. 272. Note that G. R. Beasley-Murray, in his Baptism Today and Tomorrow, pp. 31-32 and 96, and I. Howard Marshall, in 1 Peter (Leicester: IVP, 1991), p. 131, admit the possibility of interpreting the word as 'pledge' or as 'appeal' while, like Barth, Pheme Perkins, in Interpretation: A Bible Commentary for Teaching and Preaching: First and Second Peter, James, and Jude (Louisville, KY: John Knox Press, 1995), p. 66, simply assumes the word refers to an 'appeal'.

[21]   CD IV/4, p. 212; cf. 'Die Taufe hat ihre rettende Kraft. Doch ist sie—gemäß 1 Petr—nur Bitte um Gottes Wirken. Ihre Kraft hat sie nur aus dem Heilswerk Christi. Gott und sein Christus geben ihr je ihre Wirklichkeit und Wirksamkeit'. Karl Hermann Schelkle, Herders Theologischer Kommentar zum Neuen Testament XIII, 2, Die Petrusbriefe der Judasbrief (Freiburg, Basel und Wien: Herder, 1980), p. 109; cf. 'Die durch die Taufe geschehende Rettung ist Gottes Gabe auf des Menschen Bitte. Diese rettende Wirkung der Taufe aber hängt an der Auferstehung Jesu Christi, wie die Wiederholung der Verbindung von Taufe und Auferstehung zeigt'. Horst Balz U. Wolfgang Schrage, Das Neue Testament Deutsch 10, Die "Katholischen" Briefe (Göttingen: Vandenhoeck & Ruprecht, 1980), p. 108.

in the expectation of a genuinely divine event mediated by the Spirit. But it is to affirm the sacraments in general as genuinely human events albeit in response to the promise that such will also be genuinely divine events. Within the sacraments, as in Christ himself, the human and the divine occur together albeit that the divine, here as elsewhere, has priority.

Sadly, by the time he writes this final *Fragment* of the *Church Dogmatics*, it is the expectation of a genuinely divine event mediated through a genuinely human event that Barth is committed to deny.[22] Barth himself attributes this final rejection of a Reformed (and catholic) understanding of sacramentality in part to exegetical discussions with his son Markus,[23] but, as John Webster observes, this rejection is more radically grounded in a general and programmatic rejection of any form of creaturely mediation.[24] Barth eventually arrives at the notion that Jesus Christ himself is the only true sacrament and that, as such, he stands in no need of creaturely mediation;[25] the pure objectivity of his work includes its own subjective efficacy within it;[26] he alone communicates his

---

[22]   'What takes place in baptism is neither the work of salvation nor the revelation of salvation. There could be no clearer rejection of every sacramental understanding of baptism than that given here. As the building of the ark saved the eight souls, baptism saves them as their own human act, namely, the act of their faith and obedience'. *CD* IV/4, p. 212.

[23]   *CD* IV/4, p. x.

[24]   'Barth became convinced over the course of the 1950s that liberal Protestant theology, represented by Bultmann and having its roots in Schleiermacher and in the younger Luther, and also classical Roman Catholic and even Reformed sacramental theology, had seriously mishandled the question of how the objectivity of Jesus Christ and his salvation becomes subjectively real to the Christian believer. These schools of thought and practice, Barth came to believe, envisaged the transition from the *extra nos* to the *in nobis* to be accomplished by the mediation of creaturely agencies...'. John Webster, *Barth's Ethics of Reconciliation* (Cambridge: Cambridge University Press, 1995), p. 126.

[25]   'The confession of Christians, their suffering, their repentance, their prayer, their humility, their works, baptism, too, and the Lord's Supper can and should attest this event but only attest it. The event itself, the event of the death of man, is that of the death of Jesus Christ on Golgotha: no other event, no earlier and no later, no event which simply prepares the way for it, no event which has to give it the character of an actual event. This is the one *mysterium*, the one sacrament, and the one existential fact before and beside and after which there is no room for any other of the same rank.' *CD* IV/1, p. 296. Hence John Webster comments that '[a]s Barth pursued this train of thought, he began to leave behind some of his own earlier affiliation with Reformed sacramental doctrine. Where he had at one time spoken of a continuity between Jesus Christ as the "first sacrament" and creaturely signs...Barth now moves to a significantly different affirmation: Jesus Christ is not the first but the only sacrament...'. Webster, *Barth's Ethics of Reconciliation*, p. 127.

[26]   '[T]his means that the perfection of Jesus Christ's work is such that it stands in need of no human or created mediation. Christ's work is characterised by what might be

perfected work by the Spirit to the human subject—and that in an immediate and unmediated manner:[27]

> Barth did not believe that Christian theology requires a supplementary theory of how the objective is mediated to the human historical existence—whether the theory be an anthropology, a phenomenology of sacramental signs, or a philosophical hermeneutics. He denies the necessity of such strategies, on the grounds that Jesus Christ himself, the living Word of God, is immediately present and active in his Holy Spirit. Language about the Spirit constitutes for Barth not only a necessary, but also a sufficient, explanation of how it is that the Christian life comes to be.[28]

Barth's concern, then, is both to affirm the divine action as truly divine by preserving it from any creaturely mediation of that divine action, and similarly to affirm the human action as truly human (and therefore as truly ethical) by preserving it from any overarching divine action.[29] But in the first place (and again as I have argued at some length elsewhere), in the light of Barth's own theological effort it is difficult to see how any human action can be *authentically* human without, at the same time, being authentically divine—the denial of such constitutes a denial of Barth's own more formative Christological insights since it is precisely as the one who is truly divine that Jesus Christ is truly human.[30] But in the

---

called "inclusive perfection": its completeness is not only its "being finished", but its effective power in renewing human life by bringing about human response to itself. Consequently, the relation of "objective" and "subjective" shifts. The objective is not a complete realm, separate from the subjective and, therefore, standing in need of "translation" into the subjective. Rather, the objective includes the subjective within itself, and is efficacious without reliance on a quasi-independent realm of mediating created agencies.' Webster, *Barth's Ethics of Reconciliation*, pp. 127-128.

[27]   'Barth seeks to secure a theology of Christian existence and ecclesial action against forgetfulness of the primacy of divine agency. His appeal to language about the Holy Spirit is in effect a denial of the communicability of the perfect work of Jesus Christ by agents other than Jesus himself...'. Webster, *Barth's Ethics of Reconciliation*, p. 129.

[28]   Webster, *Barth's Ethics of Reconciliation*, p. 146. Note in contrast that William Stacy Johnson attributes this rejection of the sacramental to an underlying rejection of 'foundationalism' in Barth: William Stacy Johnson, *The Mystery of God: Karl Barth and the Postmodern Foundations of Theology* (Louisville, KY: Westminster John Knox Press, 1997), p. 170.

[29]   'To fail to grasp the character of baptism with water as a human work is to confuse divine and human action by envisaging the real meaning of water-baptism as some "immanent divine work". And to do this is either to swallow up "that which men will and do" in a divine work, or to make water-baptism itself into the accomplishment of the divine work in a way which in effect renders the latter superfluous.' Webster, *Barth's Ethics of Reconciliation*, p. 156.

[30]   Colwell, *Living the Christian Story*, pp. 149ff.

second place (and with more immediate pertinence for this study),
Barth's assumption of an unmediated immediate, that the presence and
action of the Spirit is effected without creaturely mediation, similarly
offends the Christology that lies at the centre of his theological effort.
While Barth might be correct in recognising the limited and non-technical
use of the word μυστήριον within the New Testament,[31] and while he
might also be correct in the suspicion that 'pagan' notions were
subsequently imported to the term,[32] the mediate (rather than
unmediated) manner of divine presence and action is ubiquitous in the
narrative of Scripture. The ultimate mediation of the divine through the
human which is the Incarnation of the eternal Son is certainly unique, but
it is so in a definitive and determinative manner: God's presence and
action is mediated by the Spirit through creaturely means; there is little
Scriptural record of any unmediated immediacy.

By effectively detaching a baptism with the Spirit from a baptism with
water, Barth has placed an unmediated immediacy at the centre of his
understanding of Christian existence (and, by implication, of
ecclesiology) and has finally reduced water baptism as merely a witness to
this unmediated immediacy rather than as the mediating means of this
immediacy.[33] Barth continues to perceive baptism with water in terms of
prayer, but now not as a prayer for the effecting of a divine promise but
rather for the continuation of an effecting of a divine promise that
primarily has been effected elsewhere and in some unmediated manner.
All this represents not merely a rejection of sacramentality but, more
fundamentally, a return to that dualism which Barth previously was so
strenuous in denying.[34]

---

[31]   Barth notes that it is never used in relation to 'Christian obedience, nor love,
nor hope, nor the existence and function of the ἐκκλησία, nor its proclamation of the
Gospel, nor its tradition as such, nor baptism, nor the Lord's Supper.' *CD* IV/4, p. 109.

[32]   *CD* IV/4, p. 109.

[33]   T. F. Torrance criticises this as a return to a sacramental dualism, and, though
John Webster offers his own criticisms of Torrance's proffered alternative, this counter-
criticism (even if valid) rather evades the charge of dualism which surely is difficult to
gainsay. T. F. Torrance, 'The one baptism common to Christ and his church', in
Theology in Reconciliation (London: Geoffrey Chapman, 1975), pp. 82-105 (p. 99); cf.
Webster, *Barth's Ethics of Reconciliation*, p. 171.

[34]   Webster tries to defend Barth from the charge of dualism but concedes that
Barth's rejection of the sacraments is 'unnecessary': '[i]t would not be impossible to
construct an account of Spirit-baptism and water-baptism as a differentiated unity without
threatening either the uniqueness and incommunicability of the work of Jesus Christ or
the full reality of the human response. A carefully phrased notion of sacramental
mediation could allay Barth's fears about overinflation of ecclesial activity and, at the
same time, avoid the overschematic separation of divine and human work which afflicts
his exegesis. Indeed, Barth's pre-war writings on sacraments elaborate just such a notion
of mediation, insisting, with the classical Reformed tradition, upon the rooting of any

But, as has already been admitted, by belittling baptism with water merely as a witness to a previous and unmediated 'conversion' event, Barth is simply endorsing a notion of baptism apparently espoused by a significant proportion of contemporary Baptists. Indeed, Pilgram Marpeck,[35] one of the most perceptive of the early Anabaptist thinkers, offers this ordering as a key reason for rejecting the validity of paedo-baptism: whereas circumcision was given to Abraham as a symbol (*Zeichen*) of that covenant hope which was not yet fulfilled, water baptism is given as an external witness (*Zeugnis*) of that which already has been fulfilled, a witness 'to the inner conviction that one's sins are forgiven'.[36] For water baptism to precede a baptism with the Spirit, then, is (according to Marpeck) to reduce the Spirit to a secondary witness:[37]

> If one is previously baptized by Christ, by the kindled fire of the Holy Spirit in fire and spirit, then one may also make a testimony concerning the forgiveness of sins by the sprinkling of the baptismal water, which follows the belief in the outward preached Word.[38]

It would seem (to this writer at least) quite impossible to reconcile this view of baptism—as a testimony to a previous and unmediated baptism of the Spirit—with the recorded words of Peter on the day of Pentecost. Certainly those who had heard his testimony to Christ were 'cut to the heart' (Acts 2.37); certainly the invitation to water baptism was juxtaposed with an invitation to 'repent' (Acts 2.38); certainly I would want to attribute conviction and repentance to the mediating work of the Spirit (here mediated through Peter's preaching); but the promised 'gift of the Holy Spirit', the promise prophesied by Joel and fulfilled in an apparent 'violent wind' and seeming 'tongues of fire', is here

---

consideration of sacrament in Christology and pneumatology.' Webster, *Barth's Ethics of Reconciliation*, p. 172.

[35]   Pilgram Marpeck (c.1495–1556) was born in Rattenberg and served as Mayor and then as 'mining magistrate' until his support for Anabaptists led him to resign his post and leave the city for Strasbourg. Following debates with Bucer and Capito he was banished from Strasbourg and gained employment as an engineer in Augsburg where later his death is recorded. Although (unlike many early Anabaptist leaders) he appears to have had no formal theological education his writings are marked by an extraordinary clarity and perception—and also unlike many early Anabaptist leaders he appears to have died of 'natural causes'. For a comparison of Marpeck and Barth see John Colwell, 'Alternative Approaches to Believer's Baptism (from the Anabaptists to Barth)', *The Scottish Bulletin of Evangelical Theology*, 7 (1989), pp. 3-20.

[36]   Pilgram Marpeck, 'Confession of 1532', in *The Writings of Pilgram Marpeck*, trans. and ed. William Klassen and Walter Klaassen (Scottdale, PA: Herald Press, 1978), pp. 107-157 (p. 153).

[37]   Marpeck, 'Confession of 1532', p. 138.

[38]   Marpeck, 'A Clear and Useful Instruction', in *Writings*, pp. 69-106 (p. 88).

proclaimed to Peter's hearers as a consequence of baptism rather than as its precursor. Now a sacrament is not God's prison, he can give his Spirit in other ways and through other means (and a brief discussion of the Cornelius narrative will follow later in this chapter), but a sacrament is the instrumental means of God's promise and it is in this manner that Peter here seems to speak of water baptism (he certainly doesn't counsel the crowd to wait until they have received this gift before they are baptised). This notion of water baptism, then, as a witness or testimony to a preceding (and unmediated) baptism of the Spirit would seem to lack credible or sustainable Scriptural testimony.

And it is inherently dangerous. It is elusive, beguiling, and confusing. The unmediated, by definition, is indefinable, inaccessible, non-assessable. To sever this promised gift of the Spirit from water baptism is to restrict its perceptibility to the vagaries of felt religious experience. To sever this promised gift of the Spirit from water baptism is implicitly to gainsay the mediate manner of God's relatedness to creation. In context this focus may be understandable (albeit superficial and inexcusable): the focus of the narrative, after all, is on the phenomenal, the apparent 'violent wind' and seeming 'tongues of fire', the speaking 'in other tongues' and apparent drunkenness, the being convicted and 'cut to the heart'. Such phenomena are not to be dismissed or belittled, but to retain a focus on such phenomena is to ignore virtually every other New Testament reference both to the Spirit and to baptism; to retain a focus on such phenomena is to be preoccupied with the charismatic and the ecstatic rather than with the Christological and the ecclesiological. If here baptism with water is identified as a mediation of the promised gift of the Spirit, then everywhere else both baptism with water and this promised gift of the Spirit are identified as a mediation of our inclusion in Christ and in his Church. The charismatic and the ecstatic are 'accidental'; the essence of baptism and the gift of the Spirit is Christological and ecclesiological.

> ...don't you know that all of us who were baptised into Christ Jesus were baptised into his death? We were therefore buried with him through baptism into death in order that, just as Christ was raised from the dead through the glory of the Father, we too may live a new life. (Romans 6.3-4)

Overwhelmingly Paul's preferred manner of referring to Christians is as those who are 'in Christ': such references are ubiquitous in the Pauline corpus and therefore are far too many to enumerate. For Paul, to be a Christian is to be identified with Christ, or rather, to be incorporated in his identity—not in the sense that our distinct identity is lost but rather in the sense that Christ's identity is now defining of our identity; our distinct identity is only authentically apprehended in his identity. It is not that we become him (notwithstanding the metaphorical references to the Church as Christ's body, Paul is never guilty of obscuring the distinction between the ascended Christ and his Church), it is rather that we have been included in him, included in his unique sonship before the Father, included in his death, included in his resurrection. Here again a distinction of identity can be maintained simply because the intimate union effected is a mediated union, a mediated intimacy: our identity 'in Christ' is mediated by the Spirit. And, for Paul, baptism is the means through which the Spirit mediates this inclusion in Christ. Here again, the sacramental realism of biblical language can only be avoided through extreme special pleading: in this text from his letter to the Romans (as similarly in a parallel text in the letter to the Colossians[39]) Paul is arguing from this realistic understanding of baptism rather than towards it; he is arguing on the assumption that his readers will already acknowledge this realistic and narratival significance of baptism.

Elsewhere I have argued that the sacraments of the Church are promised means through which we are brought by the Spirit to indwell the gospel story.[40] Such a conclusion is supported by the realistic language of these Pauline passages: through baptism it is not that we are brought to indwell Christ in some abstracted sense; we are rather brought to indwell the story of Christ's passion; we are buried with him and raised with him; we become part of his story; his story becomes our story. In response to the question posed by the song, *Were you there when they crucified my Lord*, the answer is 'Yes: (for me) on 2 December 1962 when I was baptised into his death and, subsequently, whenever I share in the bread and wine of Communion'. As I claimed in the previous chapter: the narrative of Scripture is not merely read and heard, it is indwelt, and it is indwelt sacramentally. Through the sacrament of baptism, then, the Spirit brings us to indwell the Christ narrated in the gospel story; to indwell his life, death and resurrection; to indwell his eternal relatedness to the Father.

And in this sense, therefore, the narrative of Jesus' baptism is the narrative of our baptism: just as he comes to baptism (as he also comes to the Cross[41]) identifying with repentant sinners, so we come to his Cross through baptism, identifying ourselves as those with whom he identifies and for whom he dies; just as the Father speaks at his baptism, identifying him as the beloved Son, so the Father mediates his speaking at our

---

[39]   'In him you were also circumcised, in the putting off of the sinful nature, not with a circumcision done by human hands but with the circumcision done by Christ, having been buried with him in baptism and raised with him through your faith in the power of God, who raised him from the dead.' (Colossians 2.11-12).

[40]   Colwell, *Living the Christian Story*, chs 7–9 (especially chapter 8).

[41]   Note that more than once within the Gospels Jesus speaks of his suffering and death in terms of a 'baptism' (Mark 10.38ff.; Luke 12.49-50).

baptism, identifying us as those included in his sonship;[42] just as the Spirit descends on him at his baptism, separating and empowering him to fulfil his mission, so also the Spirit comes to indwell us, separating and empowering us as those now included in his life and witnessing to his mission. Or, as Paul puts it:

> God made him who had no sin to be sin for us, so that in him we might become the righteousness of God…. (2 Corinthians 5.21)

> For you know the grace of our Lord Jesus Christ, that though he was rich, yet for your sakes he became poor, so that you through his poverty might become rich. (2 Corinthians 8.9)[43]

That which we are made by our inclusion in Christ through baptism is 'the righteousness of God'. The promised power of the Spirit is primarily and essentially the power by which to live and only secondarily and 'accidentally' the power by which to exercise charismatic gifts. In each of his letters, the focus of Paul's discussion in relation to baptism is ethical rather than ecstatic. That which the Spirit mediates through baptism is not primarily a feeling of 'in-Christness', but rather a new orientation of life issuing in trust and obedience.[44] The significant phenomenal outcome of the gift of the Spirit through baptism, then, is a life being shaped in faithfulness, hopefulness, and lovingness—felt experience or ecstatic phenomena, though not to be belittled, are never more than 'accidental'.[45]

---

[42]   'For you did not receive a spirit that makes you a slave again to fear, but you received the Spirit of adoption. And by him we cry "*Abba*, Father." The Spirit himself testifies with our spirit that we are God's children.' (Romans 8.15-16).

[43]   'Athanasius's aphorism, "He became man in order that we might become God," while indeed true just as it stands, can be misleading out of its context. Irenaeus can supply the needed precision: the God who becomes what we are is the God-man; what he becomes is what we actually are, "fallen and passible man, condemned to death"; and we become what he is, humans so united with God as to "receive and bear God."' Jenson, *Systematic Theology*, vol. 2, p. 341.

[44]   Or, in more catholic terms, a sacramental character is imparted through baptism: *ST* III 63; cf. III 69.

[45]   The work of Jonathan Edwards is often misappropriated in these respects. Throughout the progression of his writings on 'revival' Edwards is concerned to affirm the appropriateness of religious phenomena—to be encountered by God through the Spirit is to be 'affected' by that encounter—but, as he makes plain in his *Treatise concerning the Religious Affections*, such phenomena are never decisive, primary, or essential; the definitive outcome of such an encounter is rather a life re-orientated in love for God. Jonathan Edwards, *Religious Affections*, in *YE* vol. 2. A more sustained discussion of Edwards' contribution in this respect occurs within the next chapter of this book.

But if the essential outcome of our inclusion in Christ through baptism is ethical, then its ultimate fulfilment (or perfection) lies in the future: the orientation of baptism is eschatological. We have been baptised into Christ's death and resurrection, we have already 'crossed over from death to life' (John 5.24), but our ultimate resurrection has not yet occurred. We have been baptised into Christ's filial relatedness to the Father, but the entire creation awaits the final revelation of the children of God (Romans 8.19). We have been baptised into that perfected humanity which is already Christ's ascended humanity, but the ultimate perfecting of Christ's humanity in us is yet to come:

> Dear friends, now we are children of God, and what we will be has not yet been made known. But we know that when he appears, we shall be like him, for we shall see him as he is. All who have this hope in them purify themselves, just as he is pure. (1 John 3.2-3)

At various points throughout the Pauline corpus we encounter the notion of the ascended humanity of Christ as inaugurating a new humanity: he is the 'last Adam' whose 'heavenly' likeness we shall bear (1 Corinthians 15.47ff.); those joined to him are a 'new creation' (2 Corinthians 5.17); in him a single 'new humanity' has been created (Ephesians 2.15). For Paul, as indeed for the entire New Testament, the most radical and unthinkable outworking of this single new humanity is the uniting of Jew and Gentile in Christ: that God should graft the Gentiles into the 'olive tree' that is Israel is entirely 'contrary to nature' (παρὰ φύσιν).[46] In comparison with this most radical outcome of a covenantal redefining of humanity in Christ all other such redefinings—of slave and free, of male and female—are relatively trivial. In Christ all such distinctions of gender, race, age, class, or status, are transformed and transcended; his ascended humanity, which is now definitive of our humanity, is inclusive of, but greater than, all such distinctions.[47]

Which, of course, brings us back to Peter's sermon on the day of Pentecost and to his explanation of this promised gift of the Spirit with reference to Joel's prophecy. As Jürgen Moltmann has indicated,[48] this

---

[46] For a provocative discussion of the implications of this reference to that which is contrary to nature, particularly with reference to questions of human sexuality, see Eugene F. Rogers, Jr., *Sexuality and the Christian Body* (Oxford: Blackwell, 1999).

[47] Galatians 3.28; cf. Colossians 3.11.

[48] 'The eschatological hope for experience of the Spirit is shared by women and men equally. Men and women "will prophesy" and proclaim the gospel. According to the prophecy in Joel 2, through the shared experience of the Spirit the privileges of men compared with women, of the old compared with the young, and of masters compared with "men-servants and maidservants" will be abolished.' Moltmann, *The Spirit of Life*, p. 239.

promised outpouring of the Spirit, anticipating the 'coming of the great and glorious day of the Lord',[49] is without prejudice to race, sex, age, or class. The Church, those united with Christ by the Spirit through baptism, can only anticipate the fulfilment of this eschatological humanity of the ascended Christ—but anticipate it they can and must. The Church is not called to be Christ, but the Church is called to witness to Christ and therefore to witness to this new and transformed humanity defined in him. The Church has not yet arrived at its eschatological goal but it is called to witness to this eschatological goal in its committed discipleship, in its ethical identity, and in its inclusivity—and it is called to do so in the power of the Spirit promised through baptism.

To summarise then, baptism is the means through which we are promised this gift of the Spirit, and the promised gift of the Spirit is the means through which we become united with Christ and defined by his ascended humanity, albeit eschatologically. Moreover, to be incorporated in Christ through baptism is to be incorporated in his Church—or rather, to be incorporated in Christ's Church through baptism is the means through which we are incorporated in Christ by the Spirit.[50] One cannot, therefore, be incorporated in Christ without being incorporated in his Church and one cannot be incorporated in the Church without being incorporated in Christ—these two ways of identifying the Christian are in reality but one and, just as the Spirit is the agent by whom this single identity is effected, baptism is the instrument through which it is effected.

Or, at least, this is generally the case. As has already been stated, the sacraments are not God's prison. He has promised to act by his Spirit through these ordained means but he is not entrapped by such means, he remains free to act elsewhere and through other means (though he has not promised to do so). Just as there may have been extraordinary reasons for Peter and John needing to travel to Samaria in order for the believers there to receive the Spirit (an enigma to which we shall return in the next chapter), so there may also have been extraordinary reasons for the Spirit coming upon Cornelius and those gathered with him prior to baptism. As was noted earlier, the inclusion of Gentiles into Christ and his Church was an astounding and disquieting occurrence the shock of which we cannot now begin to comprehend. Only the assurance that 'the Holy Spirit came on them as he had come on us at the beginning' (Acts 11.15) seems to have been sufficient to silence Peter's detractors and to vindicate, not just his baptising of these Gentiles, but his entering their house in the first place. But Cornelius and those with him were

---

[49]   Acts 2.20.

[50]   'Being in Christ, being in the Church, being in the Spirit—these are but different ways of asserting the same one great reality. For the Spirit is the Spirit of Christ, and the Church is the body of Christ.' Clark, *An Approach to the Theology of the Sacraments*, p. 25.

nonetheless baptised—not now perhaps as a means of baptism with the Spirit, but certainly as a sign of such and of their inclusion in Christ and his Church. There is no New Testament record of anyone being included in the Church (and hence being identified as included in Christ) other than through baptism—Luke's story of the penitent thief (Luke 23.39ff.) occurs before the resurrection, before the ascension, before Pentecost, and therefore, though there can be no question of this man's ultimate salvation, he must at least be considered anomalous in relation to the New Testament Church.

But such anomalies now abound. If the Church is defined sacramentally, in what meaningful sense might the Salvation Army or the Society of Friends be deemed valid expressions of the Church? This is not to doubt the ultimate salvation of those included in these 'connections' (any more than it is to doubt the ultimate salvation of the penitent thief): ultimately we are saved by the mercy of God *and nothing else*; the sacraments are not God's prison. Nor is it to doubt the inclusion of such in Christ by the Spirit (any more than it is to doubt the reality of the Spirit's work in Cornelius and those with him): the Spirit is free to mediate our inclusion in Christ with or without baptism; once again the sacraments are not God's prison. But it is to doubt whether, without sacramental ordering, such connections can properly be deemed 'Church'. The Church is made visible through the sacraments and without the sacraments it is not visible as 'the Church'. Precisely because the Church on earth is called to be 'visible' it was appropriate for Cornelius and those with him to be baptised as the sign of that which, for them, had already occurred—and only so were they included in the visible Church.

Moreover, we are physical beings inhabiting a physical world. God has chosen to mediate his presence and action through physical means and we seem congenitally disposed to such physical mediation. It would appear to be extraordinarily difficult to maintain for long any unmediated expectation of God's presence and action. Abandon baptism and the Lord's Supper as means of grace and their place is quickly usurped by notions of simplicity, by the layout of chairs, by tables, by flowers, or by a 'mercy seat', by a banner, by 'articles of war', by uniforms, or (more commonly) by appeals to 'come to the front', by the signing of decision cards, or by the investing of ecstatic phenomena with definitive significance. Is there not something strangely perverse in such departures? When God has ordained means of grace, what disingenuity beguiles us to abandon them and to invent our own (as if such were possible)? In no sense would one want to detract from the extraordinary and self-sacrificial witness and work of the Salvation Army and the Society of Friends (or necessarily from other unbaptised groups of believers). Indeed, one might even be sympathetic to the rejection of hierarchical clericalism and vacuous ritualism that prompted this abandonment of sacramental worship and identity. But, nonetheless, such abandonment remains unnecessary, inappropriate, and confusing. Such connections cannot be deemed 'Church' without fundamentally redefining the term both biblically and theologically.

The preceding discussion, of course, implies a rather different assumption than the traditional conclusion espoused by the Church catholic that there can be no salvation outside of the Church (*extra ecclesiam nulla salus*). This exclusive conclusion was classically expressed by Cyprian,[51] was dogmatically formulated at the Fourth Lateran Council,[52] and was repeated at the Council of Florence (1438–45): '...no-one outside the Church catholic...can be a partaker of eternal life; but will be in the everlasting fire prepared for the devil and his angels'.[53] Though this assumption was reaffirmed at the second Vatican Council, explicitly identifying the Church with the Roman Catholic communion,[54] it was significantly moderated, both by the recognition of other sacramental ecclesial communities,[55] and by the

---

[51] Cyprian, *Epistle to Jubaianus*, in *The Epistles of St. Cyprian: Library of the Fathers of the Holy Catholic Church* (Oxford: John Henry Parker, 1844), Epistle LXXIII 18; cf. 'He can no longer have God for his Father, who has not the Church for his mother.' *Treatise On the Unity of the Church*, in *ANF*, vol. 5, pp. 421-429, Treatise 1.6.

[52] '*Una vero est fidelium universalis Ecclesia, extra quam nullus omnino salvatur*' cited in *ES*, Num. 430 (p. 200).

[53] '...*nullos intra catholicam Ecclesiam non existentes, non solum paganos, sed nec Iudaeos aut heaereticos atque schismaticos, aeternae vitae fieri posse participes; sed in ignem aeternum ituros, qui paratus est diabolo et angelis eius...*', cited in *ES*, Num. 714 (p. 295). Note a remarkably similar (though more positive) passage in Calvin: '...let us learn even from the simple title "mother" how useful, indeed how necessary, it is that we should know her. For there is no other way to enter into life unless this mother conceive us in her womb, give us birth, nourish us at her breast, and lastly, unless she keep us under her care and guidance until, putting off mortal flesh, we become like the angels. Our weakness does not allow us to be dismissed from her school until we have been pupils all our lives.' *Institutes*, IV 1 4.

[54] 'This Church, constituted and organized as a society in the present world, subsists in the Catholic Church, which is governed by the successor of Peter and by the bishops in communion with him.' *LG* I 8; cf. 'Basing itself on scripture and tradition, it teaches that the Church, a pilgrim now on earth, is necessary for salvation: the one Christ is mediator and the way of salvation; he is present to us in his body which is the Church. He himself explicitly asserted the necessity of faith and baptism (cf. Mk. 16:16; Jn. 3:5), and thereby affirmed at the same time the necessity of the Church which men enter through baptism as through a door. Hence they could not be saved who, knowing that the Catholic Church was founded as necessary by God through Christ, would refuse either to enter it, or to remain in it.' *LG* II 14.

[55] 'The Church knows that she is joined in many ways to the baptized who are honored by the name of Christian, but who do not however profess the Catholic faith in its entirety or have not preserved unity or communion under the successor of Peter. For

affirmation of the possibility of ultimate salvation for those who 'through no fault of their own, do not know the Gospel of Christ or his Church, but who nevertheless seek God with a sincere heart, and, moved by grace, try in their actions to do his will as they know it through the dictates of their conscience'.[56]

There are two key issues raised by the traditional exclusion, both relate to its assumed correlation between the visible Church and ultimate salvation, and both are implicitly qualified by the statements issuing from this second Vatican Council. In the first place (and an issue to which we shall return in chapter 8 of this book), the Church has never taught that participation in the Church and its sacramental life precludes the possibility of future judgement;[57] the negative conclusion of the *extra ecclesiam nulla salus* was never intended as implying a corresponding positive presumption; judgement begins 'with the family of God' (1 Peter 4.17).[58] But secondly, and more pertinently at this point of the discussion, surely we ought to understand the Church as established by the Spirit through the sacraments, not over against the world, but rather on behalf of the world, as the first-fruits of the world. The Church is established as a means of grace for the world, as a means through which the world is brought towards the goal of cosmic redemption in Christ.[59] Consequently, it may be appropriate to note the ambiguity of the term 'without' (*extra*) in this catholic assertion (as least when lifted from its context),[60] an ambiguity that could be resolved in this more inclusive

---

there are many who hold sacred scripture in honor as a rule of faith and of life, who have a sincere religious zeal, who lovingly believe in God the Father Almighty and in Christ, the Son of God and the Savior, who are sealed by baptism which unites them to Christ, and who indeed recognize and receive other sacraments in their own Churches or ecclesiastical communities.' *LG* II 15; cf. 'Nevertheless, many elements of sanctification and of truth are found outside its visible confines. Since these are gifts belonging to the Church of Christ, they are forces impelling towards Catholic unity.' *LG* I 8.

[56]   *LG* II 16.

[57]   Whatever may have been intended by the belief that baptism bestows an 'indelible character' (*character indelebilis*) it was certainly without prejudice to the possibility of ultimate apostasy; cf. Berkouwer, *The Sacraments*, p. 144; 'Baptism involves both gift and response. It is not just a "ticket" to automatic salvation; a response is also involved to what has been received in Baptism.' Paul Haffner, *The Sacramental Mystery*, p. 49.

[58]   'Even though incorporated into the Church, one who does not however persevere in charity is not saved. He remains indeed in the bosom of the Church, but "in body" not "in heart".' *LG* II 14.

[59]   Surely this is at least a possible interpretation of Ephesians 1.9-10 and Colossians 1.18ff.?

[60]   Cyprian's context is unambiguous: '...if not even the Baptism of a public Confession and of blood can profit a heretic to salvation, because salvation is not without the Church, how much rather will it avail him nothing, that, in a lurking place

direction by substituting the word '*sine*' for the word '*extra*': there is no salvation other than through the Church (*sine ecclesiam nulla salus*)?

This latter issue has some pertinence, of course, to arguments for or against paedo-baptism. If we maintain a traditional understanding of the *extra ecclesiam nulla salus*, that those outside the Church cannot be saved—and if we continue to define the Church sacramentally, understanding baptism as the means through which the Spirit incorporates us into the Church and into Christ—then must we not conclude that unbaptised infants (like unbaptised members of the Salvation Army and unbaptised Quakers) cannot be saved?[61]

Strangely, B. A. Gerrish, in his otherwise quite excellent account of Calvin's understanding of the sacraments, attributes this fear concerning the fate of unbaptised infants to Calvin.[62] Conversely, the text of the *Institutes* suggests that Calvin (mistakenly at least in some cases) attributed such a view to his Anabaptist opponents.[63] Calvin's concern rather is that the Anabaptists, by withholding baptism from children, were

---

and den of robbers, bedewed with a defiling and adulterous water, he has not only not laid aside his old sins, but even gathered upon him new and greater!' Cyprian, *Epistle* LXXIII 18.

[61]   The notion of Limbo as the destiny of unbaptised infants is discussed in the 'Supplement' to the *Summa Theologica*, probably compiled by Rainaldo da Piperno on the basis of Thomas' commentary on the *Sentences* of Peter Lombard: 'The limbo of the Fathers and the limbo of children, without any doubt, differ as to the quality of punishment or reward. For children have no hope of the blessed life, as the Fathers in limbo had, in whom, moreover, shone forth the light of faith and grace.' *ST* Suppl. 69 6; cf. 'Unbaptized children are not detained in limbo save because they lack the state of grace. Hence, since the state of the dead cannot be changed by the works of the living, especially as regards the merit of the essential reward or punishment, the suffrages of the living cannot profit the children in limbo.' *ST* Suppl. 71 7. The seventh session of the Council of Trent includes the following anathema against any who deny the necessity of baptism for salvation: '*Si quis dixerit, baptismum liberum esse, hoc est non necessarium ad salutem: anathema sit.*' Canon 5 *de sacramento baptismi* (3 March 1547), cited in *ES*, Num. 861 (p. 302).

[62]   '...Calvin was convinced that the logical consequence of believer baptism was the abandonment of infants wholesale to damnation.' Gerrish, *Grace and Gratitude*, p. 120.

[63]   '[W]e must utterly reject the fiction of those who consign all the unbaptized to eternal death.' *Institutes*, IV xvi 26. Note that, earlier in the *Summa Theologica*, Thomas distinguishes between those unbaptised in reality and those unbaptised in desire. Here he follows Augustine in maintaining that it may be possible for someone (in the former rather than the latter case) to obtain salvation without baptism. *ST* III 68 2; cf. 'The Church's teaching on the necessity of Baptism for salvation is completed by a consideration of how, in certain circumstances, this necessity can be supplied also by baptism of desire or baptism of blood. While God has bound salvation to the sacrament of Baptism, "He Himself is not bound by His sacraments.' Haffner, *The Sacramental Mystery*, p. 51; cf. *CCC*, 1257 and 1260.

depriving both children and their parents of assurance, of the sign of God's promise, of a means of grace.[64] Calvin defends the practice of paedo-baptism, not on the basis of a too-simple equation between sacramental participation in the Church and participation in eternal salvation, but rather because the practice of reserving baptism for 'believers' would issue in the exclusion of infants from the Church and its sacramental life, from the very means through which God's grace is mediated to us.

Which, of course, is not a conclusion you would expect a Baptist writer to affirm—but it is a conclusion which this (admittedly idiosyncratic) Baptist writer finds increasingly difficult entirely to refute. Some years ago I took part in a debate on baptism held at Tyndale House.[65] In the course of the concluding plenary session one of my paedo-baptist friends issued the public challenge that, in reality, I practised 'adult baptism' rather than 'believer's baptism'. Most Baptists are accustomed to this common misrepresentation and I confidently refuted it. But my confidence was ill-founded, my friend knew me rather too well: 'At what age then, John, should you have been baptised? When did you first believe?' He knew, you see, that I was brought up in a devout home and that I have no recollection of ever having not believed the gospel. When then, if I am really committed to the practice of believer's baptism, ought I to have been baptised?

Faith is perhaps the hardest of the three theological virtues to define. While surely it must include some measure of understanding (trust in God implies some minimal knowledge of the one to be trusted) it would be as perilous to belittle the unformed (and uninformed) faith of an infant as to belittle the unformed (and uninformed) faith of the penitent thief.[66] Faith, like hope and love, is relational; it is formed within connectedness. If 'faith comes from hearing' (Romans 10.17) it comes correspondingly (as was argued in the last chapter) through indwelling, and baptism is the ordained means through which the Spirit brings us to indwell Christ by indwelling Christ's Church. I am grateful to Anthony R. Cross for painstakingly demonstrating that nothing is affirmed within the New Testament of baptism that is not also affirmed of faith and that nothing is

---

[64]   '[O]nce this testimony of God's grace is taken away from us, the promise which, through it, is put before our eyes may eventually vanish little by little. From this would grow up not only an impious ungratefulness toward God's mercy but a certain negligence about instructing our children in piety. For when we consider that immediately from birth God takes and acknowledges them as his children, we feel a strong stimulus to instruct them in an earnest fear of God and observance of the law.' *Institutes* IV xvi 32.

[65]   Tyndale House, Cambridge, is a library and study centre for Evangelicals.

[66]   'Let the children come to me, and do not hinder them, for the kingdom of God belongs to such as these. I tell you the truth, anyone who will not receive the kingdom of God like a little child will never enter it.' Mark 10.14-15.

affirmed within the New Testament of faith which is not also affirmed of baptism.[67] But surely this begs the question rather than resolves it: it might represent grounds for reserving baptism for believers; contrarily, it might represent grounds for recognising baptism as a means through which faith is formed.[68]

To contest a notion of the efficacy of the sacraments *ex opere operato* by a notion of the efficacy of the sacraments *ex opere operantis* (an efficacy dependent upon those receiving the sacraments) is no advance; it is simply another way of denying the graciousness of grace:[69] if the *ex opere operato* notion of sacramental efficacy denies grace by qualifying the freedom of God's presence and action within the sacraments, the *ex opere operantis* notion of sacramental efficacy denies grace by implying sacramental efficacy to be dependent upon us.[70] We are not saved *by* faith anymore than we are saved *by* the sacraments;[71] we are saved *by* God *through* faith and *through* the sacraments—and these instrumental means of salvation ought not be opposed as rivals or alternatives (as will be

---

[67]   '[I]t is undoubtedly true that in the New Testament it is everywhere assumed that faith proceeds to baptism and that baptism is for faith...for *in the New Testament precisely the same gifts of grace are associated with faith as with baptism*.' G. R. Beasley-Murray, *Baptism in the New Testament*, p. 272; cf. Anthony R. Cross' summary of Beasley-Murray's various expositions of this in 'Faith-Baptism: The Key to an Evangelical Baptismal Sacramentalism', *Journal of European Baptist Studies* 4.3 (2004), pp. 5-21 (pp. 12-18), and *Baptism and the Baptists*, pp. 30ff.

[68]   Calvin speaks of baptism as given 'for the arousing, nourishing, and confirming of our faith'. *Institutes* IV xv 14.

[69]   'The intent of the formula *ex opere operato* is sometimes explained by contrasting it with *ex opere operantis*, which means an efficacy that comes from the belief of the recipient. The sacraments do not work in that way. They are effective by virtue of the work wrought, objectively.' Berkouwer, *The Sacraments*, p. 63.

[70]   '[T]he subject's preparation for the sacraments is not the effective cause of the grace of the sacraments, it only removes obstacles to their reception. Opening a window allows fresh air to enter a room, but does not produce the freshness; it is the breath of air which causes that. An obstacle on the part of the subject can invalidate the sacrament, such as the case in which a person is baptized or ordained against their will. For the validity of a sacrament, the intention to receive it is the basic condition in the adult subject.' Haffner, *The Sacramental Mystery*, p. 18.

[71]   'It is often said by Protestants, in opposition to the *ex opere operato* doctrine, that the efficacy of the sacraments depends on the faith of the recipient. But is that quite a safe way of putting it? Does not that suggest that the human part comes first, is prevenient? Would that not be to forget that 'all is of God', that even the faith by which we accept God's grace is itself a gift of God, that it is wrought in us by His grace, and partly *by means of* the sacraments?' Donald M. Baillie, *The Theology of the Sacraments* (London: Faber and Faber, 1957), p. 53.

discussed in the next chapter, these two 'instrumental' means function in quite different ways).[72]

Calvin was fully aware of this complex relationship between faith and baptism.[73] His unease with the *ex opere operato* notion of the sacraments (at least as he perceived it in contemporary practice and assumption) focused on the tendency to treat God as an automaton and thereby to render grace graceless.[74] A sacrament is given as a sign of God's grace, a seal of God's promise. The validity of the sacrament as such a sign is not annulled by lack of faith. Though such promise only comes to benefit us through faith, that faith itself is God's gift and it is aroused and awakened through the sacrament. The precise manner, then, in which Calvin relates faith and baptism, as encouraging rather than precluding the practice of paedo-baptism, is entirely coherent—baptism, as a sign of God's promise, is a means to faith since it is a means of grace, a means of that gracious promise being heard and received:

> ...it is not my intention to weaken the force of baptism by not joining reality and truth to the sign, in so far as God works through outward means. But from this sacrament, as from all others, we obtain only as much as we receive in faith. If we lack faith, this will be evidence of our ungratefulness, which renders us chargeable before God, because we have not believed the promise given there.[75]

Baptism, therefore, is not so much a first step on the pathway of discipleship and obedience as it is the means through which we are set on that pathway of discipleship and obedience in the first place. Through baptism we are included in Christ by being included in his Church, we are placed in the context through which discipleship can happen, a context through which the theological virtues of faith, hope, and love can be nurtured and can grow. Jesus commands his apostles to make disciples by baptising and teaching (Matthew 28.19-20) and, though Alan Kreider

---

[72]   'Sometimes the question is asked (by people who are more 'evangelical' than 'sacramentalist'): Are we saved by faith or by sacraments? Surely that is a false antithesis and alternative. The truth is that we are saved by neither, but by God. But He saves us through faith, and therefore partly through sacraments, which He uses to awaken and to strengthen our faith.' Baillie, *The Theology of the Sacraments*, p. 101.

[73]   'We therefore confess that for that time baptism benefitted us not at all, inasmuch as the promise offered us in it—without which baptism is nothing—lay neglected. Now when, by God's grace, we begin to repent, we accuse our blindness and hardness of heart—we who were for so long ungrateful toward his great goodness. But we believe that the promise itself did not vanish.' *Institutes* IV xv 17; cf. IV xiv 16: '...the sacraments have effectiveness among us in proportion as we are helped by their ministry sometimes to foster, confirm, and increase the true knowledge of Christ in ourselves... But that happens when we receive in true faith what is offered there'.

[74]   *Institutes* IV xiv 14.

[75]   *Institutes* IV xv 17.

and others rue the loss of the lengthy catechumenate that came to characterise the Early Church,[76] it might be more coherent with the biblical narrative and with a sacramental theology of baptism to rue its inception.

We do not become disciples by being taught without being baptised anymore than we become disciples by being baptised without being taught. We do not become disciples in detachment from the Church and the means of grace that constitute its sacramental life; rather we are shaped in the habits and virtues of discipleship precisely through our participation in the Church and its sacramental life. Baptism therefore, properly conceived, should mark the beginning of a life-long 'catechumenate' rather than the conclusion of a preliminary and 'qualifying' catechumenate. Indeed, the very notion of a 'qualifying' catechumenate offends a doctrine of grace. Though a genuinely human act, baptism is never a meritorious act, it is not an award for achievement. It is in opposition to such tendencies that Colin Gunton questions the notion of baptism as an 'ethical' act:

> Here the efforts of the self-consciously Anabaptist end of the Free Church spectrum, encouraged as its representatives are by Barth's theology of baptism, can militate against an ethic of grace. Joining, or being joined to, the Church is not an ethical act but one whose stress is on that which is received: the turning round of the old Adam symbolised by the water which drowns. The strengths of the traditions of infant baptism are that they stress that the path of virtue is one on which we have been set, by others, as they place us in a community oriented to the death of Christ, a death which was, though finally chosen after much struggle, imposed upon him by his Father.[77]

Unusually perhaps for a Baptist writer I gladly affirm the 'strengths of the traditions of infant baptism' alluded to here by Gunton and outlined in these preceding paragraphs—but with two hesitations.

In the first place, any affirmation of paedo-baptism according to the preceding argument assumes that the child is baptised and nurtured fully within the context of the Church and its sacramental life. Whether this is ever the case in Anglican and Catholic contexts, anymore than in Baptist contexts, will be discussed in the next chapter in relation to the practice of confirmation. But this assumption of meaningful ecclesial context certainly precludes indiscriminate paedo-baptism, the practice of baptising infants without prejudice to the future participation of the child

---

[76]   Alan Kreider, *The Change of Conversion and the Origin of Christendom* (Harrisburg, PA: Trinity Press International, 1999).

[77]   Colin Gunton, 'The Church as a School of Virtue? Human Formation in Trinitarian Framework', in *Faithfulness and Fortitude: In Conversation with the Theological Ethics of Stanley Hauerwas*, ed. Mark Thiessen Nation and Samuel Wells (Edinburgh: T & T Clark, 2000), pp. 211-231 (p. 224).

and the child's family in the life and worship of the Church. And in the present post-Christian context of the Church in Britain (if for no other reason) there is surely justification for acknowledging 'adult' baptism as the more normal form of the rite.[78]

But secondly and more fundamentally, Gunton, in the above quotation, seems to be in danger of lapsing into the very same dualism of which Barth becomes guilty (albeit at its other polar extreme): to deny that baptism is at all an ethical act is effectively to deny that baptism is at all a human act, albeit a human act of prayer—once again here the divine and the human are in jeopardy of being sundered in a manner that is dissonant with the heart of the gospel. Baptism is a sacrament; it is a means of grace; it is a human event through which a divine event is promised to occur. Baptism, therefore, is genuinely a human act; it is a human act of prayer in the context of a specific divine promise. As a human act of prayer it is genuinely a human ethical act—indeed, as Barth rightly affirms, as a human act of prayer it is *the* genuinely human ethical act. And as a human act of prayer it surely cannot be exclusive of the praying of the person baptised.

At this point, of course, the paedo-baptist will usually accuse the credo-baptist of rampant individualism: the event of infant baptism occurs (or, at least, properly occurs) in the context of the prayers of the Church and the faith of the Church; it is a corporate event of incorporation. All of which is entirely valid—but can this truly corporate event be exclusive of the praying of the one being baptised? We are not brought to baptism, we come to baptism; we come to baptism empty-handed; our coming to baptism is not itself a meritorious act; but we do come to baptism; we are not brought.

Which brings us back again to the narrative of Acts 2: through Peter's preaching the Spirit evokes conviction within many of his hearers; on asking what they then should do, they are called to repent and to be baptised for the forgiveness of their sins, and they are assured that they too will receive the Spirit; through baptism they are added to the Church and thereby incorporated in Christ. No-one here is brought to baptism; they come to baptism. They do not baptise themselves but neither are

---

[78] Without prejudice to this present context, the Liturgical Commission of the Church of England has acknowledged 'Adult' baptism as the 'norm': '[i]n the New Testament Adult Baptism is the norm, and it is only in the light of this fact that the doctrine and practice of Baptism can be understood. The Commission has therefore rearranged the present services of Baptism and Confirmation so as to set forth their theological meaning as well as to make them more flexible in the present pastoral situation. The Baptism and Confirmation of Adults is treated as the archetypal service, and is printed first.' *Baptism and Confirmation: A Report submitted by the Church of England Liturgical Commission to the Archbishops of Canterbury and York in November 1958* (London: SPCK, 1959), p. x.

they baptised unconsciously, as if in their sleep (as Barth put it).[79] All that
has been said in this chapter concerning the significance of baptism as the
means through which we are included by the Spirit in Christ and his
Church, together with all that has been more briefly said here of the
nature of faith and the nature of indwelling, renders it impossible for this
Baptist writer to dismiss infant baptism as entirely invalid. But all that has
been said in this chapter concerning baptism as a human act of prayer
and, as such, as a means of this grace, renders it impossible for this Baptist
writer not to continue to discourage the practice of infant baptism as
'irregular'.[80]

Other than in these closing paragraphs my concern within this chapter
has been hardly at all with the debate concerning the appropriateness of
credo-baptism or paedo-baptism. My concern rather has been to discuss
the significance of baptism as a basis from which these distinct baptismal
disciplines can be considered. And since, at least in some respects, the
practice of confirmation (together with its implications) impinges upon
these distinct baptismal disciplines, it is under this heading that these
discussions will now continue.

---

[79]   'It is the perverted ecclesiastical practice of administering a baptism in which
the baptised supposedly becomes a Christian unwittingly and unwillingly that has
obscured the consciousness of the once-for-allness of this beginning, replacing it by the
comfortable notion that there is not needed any such beginning of Christian existence,
but rather that we can become and be Christians in our sleep, as though we had no longer
to awaken out of sleep.' *CD* IV/3, pp. 517-518.

[80]   Barth concludes his discussion of baptism in the *Fragment* of IV/4 with an
appeal to abandon the practice of infant baptism as 'profoundly irregular'. *CD* IV/4, p.
194.

CHAPTER 6

The Sacrament of Confirmation

When the apostles in Jerusalem heard that Samaria had accepted the word of God, they sent Peter and John to them. When they arrived, they prayed for them that they might receive the Holy Spirit, because the Holy Spirit had not yet come upon any of them; they had simply been baptised into the name of the Lord Jesus. Then Peter and John placed their hands on them, and they received the Holy Spirit. (Acts 8.14-17)

Scripture can be infuriatingly silent at points where we might long for further elucidation—though such silences may alert us to the possibility that what we consider significant was not considered significant by the authors of these narratives (and that maybe our attention and interests are mis-focused). In this passage, for instance, we might covet more information concerning this apparent absence of the Spirit. Was this lack of the Spirit's outpouring until a subsequent laying-on of hands by the apostles entirely normal? Was there something defective in Philip's message or ministry? Was there something irregular in the baptism these Samaritan believers received? The passage, after all, draws attention to the fact that they 'had simply been baptised into the name of the Lord Jesus': was such a non-trinitarian baptism deficient? Certainly the Church would come to view as invalid any baptism other than in the name of the Trinity,[1] but, though Luke here draws attention to this form of baptism, he doesn't suggest it was unusual or invalid (the Samaritans were not re-baptised), and he repeats the formula elsewhere, with respect to the baptism of Cornelius (Acts 10.48), and (most surprisingly) with respect to the 're-baptism' of disciples at Ephesus (Acts 19.5).[2] So, if there was nothing flawed in Philip's ministry or in the baptism these Samaritans received, ought we to conclude that this two-stage process—a baptism with water and a subsequent laying-on of hands—was normal? Notwithstanding the impression gained from the narrative that there is

---

[1]   So, for instance, '...Christ commanded the sacrament of baptism to be given with the invocation of the Trinity. And consequently whatever is lacking to the full invocation of the Trinity, destroys the integrity of Baptism.' *ST* III 66 6.

[2]   In this latter case the narrative surely does imply that there was something defective about the rite of baptism, a defect evidenced initially by their non-reception of the Spirit. Yet Paul is still recorded as baptising them 'into the name of the Lord Jesus'.

something other than the ordinary here, the normality (and therefore normative force) of this passage came to be assumed in the Western catholic tradition and (as will be discussed later in this chapter) by Pentecostalism.

The origins of a distinct and separate rite of confirmation are cloudy and uncertain. There is clear (though far from unanimous) evidence in the Early Church of baptism being accompanied by an anointing with oil and a laying-on of hands in prayer (and preceded by a formal exorcism).[3] There is no evidence for such accompaniments to baptism in any of the Pauline catholic epistles; the references to a laying-on of hands in the pastoral epistles may or may not refer to an adjunct to baptism; and there may (or more probably may not) be allusions to an anointing with oil in 1 John and Revelation. As in this narrative of the Samaritan conversion, there are explicit references in the Acts of the Apostles to both an accompanying and a subsequent laying-on of hands, though this is not always the case: it is absent from the narrative of Acts 2, and even F. H. Chase admits (despite seeming to find allusions to confirmation throughout Scripture, and despite viewing the Acts 2 narrative as 'wholly abnormal') that 'we have no right to assume that to have happened which is not recorded'.[4] Nonetheless, Chase assumes that '...Confirmation scenes in the Acts are chosen, we cannot doubt, from many similar scenes'.[5] Frankly, I find no difficulty in doubting this whatsoever: the New Testament is not a blue-print for ecclesial practice; the diversity evidenced by Luke in the narratives of Acts is indicative of yet developing and non-formalised processes; and to read a formal and normative significance into this narrative of the Samaritan conversion is therefore inappropriate.

According to Donald Baillie (following Gregory Dix), the first reference to the term 'Confirmation' occurs in the fifth century, and Baillie ponders whether this development marked 'a change of emphasis

---

[3] So for instance, 'And afterward, when he has come up [out of the water], he is anointed by the presbyter with the oil of thanksgiving...'. Hippolytus, *The Apostolic Tradition*, trans. Burton Scott Easton (Cambridge: Cambridge University Press, 1934), 21 19; cf. 'The flesh, indeed, is washed, in order that the soul may be cleansed; the flesh is anointed, that the soul may be consecrated; the flesh is signed (with the cross), that the soul may be fortified; the flesh is shadowed with the imposition of hands, that the soul also may be illuminated by the Spirit...'. Tertullian, *On the Resurrection of the Flesh*, in *ANF*, vol. 3, pp. 545-594, viii; cf. 'After this, when we have issued from the font, we are thoroughly anointed with a blessed unction'. Tertullian, *On Baptism*, vii, in *ANF*, vol. 3, p. 672; cf. viii, p. 672.

[4] Frederic Henry Chase, *Confirmation in the Apostolic Age* (London: Macmillan, 1909), p. 24.

[5] Chase, *Confirmation in the Apostolic Age*, p. 23.

in the rite of initiation'.[6] John Macquarrie similarly acknowledges that '...Christian initiation...was originally a single sacrament, and continues to be ministered as such in the Eastern church'.[7] It is impossible to conceive of how an originally single rite could be divided without some 'change of emphasis' at the very least. For Thomas Aquinas, while baptism remains the sacrament of regeneration through which we receive the life of the Spirit, confirmation is the sacrament of maturity, of the 'fulness of grace', marking the 'perfect age' of the spiritual life.[8] L. S. Thornton similarly identifies confirmation as the 'completion' of baptism.[9] However, Paul Haffner represents the Catholic assumption that confirmation 'confers grace beyond that already received in Baptism and also imparts a new sacramental character'.[10] Similarly, P. T. Forsyth appears to distinguish between a promise of the Spirit in baptism and a subsequent appropriation of the Spirit,[11] while Gregory Dix seems to reduce baptism to a mere 'preliminary rite'.[12] And yet more radically,

---

[6]   'The word seems to occur first in the fifth century—in 441, and again in a letter of Pope Leo I in 458.' Baillie, *The Theology of the Sacraments*, p. 90 n. 1; cf. Gregory Dix, *The Theology of Confirmation* (London: Dacre Press, 1946), p. 21.

[7]   Macquarrie, apparently in some tension with Baillie and Dix, continues that '...[i]n the West, the chrismation after the washing eventually became the sacrament of confirmation. The process had begun early in the third century and was established by the end of the fourth.' Macquarrie, *A Guide to the Sacraments*, p. 80.

[8]   *ST* III 72 1.

[9]   L. S. Thornton, *Confirmation: Its Place in the Baptismal Mystery* (London: Dacre Press, 1954), p. 171. Chase similarly identifies confirmation as the 'complement of Baptism, conveying to those who have been engrafted into Christ a full participation in the divine fellowship of the regenerate life.' Chase, *Confirmation in the Apostolic Age*, p. 107.

[10]   Haffner, *The Sacramental Mystery*, p. 71.

[11]   'Spiritual blessings come to belong to us in two stages: first, as they are made possible to us by God's grace, as they surround us, and they are sealed to us; second, as they are actual, as we appropriate them, as we are sealed to them. The baptized child represents the first stage, the confirmed youth the second.' Forsyth, *The Church and the Sacraments*, p. 218.

[12]   Gregory Dix, *The Theology of Confirmation in Relation to Baptism* (London: Dacre, 1946); cf. his *Confirmation or the Laying On of Hands*, Occasional Paper (London: SPCK, 1936). For an assessment of the contribution of Gregory Dix, together with the dispute with G. W. H. Lampe, see Kenneth W. Stevenson, *Gregory Dix 25 Years On*, Grove Liturgical Study 10 (Bramcote: Grove Books, 1977), and John Macquarrie, 'Baptism, Confirmation, Eucharist', in *Signs of Faith, Hope and Love: The Christian Sacraments Today*, eds. John Greenhalgh and Elizabeth Russell (London: St Mary's Bourne Street, 1987), pp. 57-70 (pp. 65ff.).

while joining together the rites of baptism and chrismation, Orthodoxy views the former as 'paschal' and the latter as 'pentecostal'.[13]

All of which only serves to confirm Calvin's conclusion that the supposed sacrament of confirmation, 'cutting off from baptism the promises proper to baptism, conveys and transfers them elsewhere'.[14] This, of course, is not at all to deny that, throughout Scripture, the laying-on of hands or an anointing with oil are commonly identified as signs of a giving of the Spirit and, consequently, that such can be generally characterised as sacramental.[15] But it is to repudiate this diminishing of the significance of baptism; it is to question (as Thomas Aquinas seems to acknowledge[16]) any explicit dominical ordaining of confirmation as a sacrament (as distinct from the general sacramentality of anointing and the laying on of hands); and it is to reaffirm baptism as unequivocally the sacrament of the giving of the Spirit and, thereby, the sacrament of our inclusion in Christ and his Church.

As elsewhere in his discussion of the 'five other ceremonies, falsely termed sacraments', Calvin affirms an appropriateness—albeit here a non-sacramental appropriateness—for an act of confirmation in which 'children or those near adolescence would give an account of their faith before the church'.[17] This notion of confirmation as a human confirming (as distinct from a divine confirming) crept into common consciousness, as F. H. Chase notes, through (to him) an unfortunate wording of the 1662 *Prayer Book* in which the words 'ratify and confess' were replaced by the words 'ratify and confirm', thereby giving some cause for misunderstanding concerning whether the act of 'confirming' was divine or human.[18] But in either case—whether a rite of confirmation is

---

[13]   Schmemann, *The World as Sacrament*, p. 92; cf. Thomas Hopko, 'Tasks Facing the Orthodox in the "Reception" Process of BEM', in Limouris and Vaporis (eds.), *Orthodox Perspectives on Baptism, Eucharist, and Ministry*, pp. 135-147 (p. 87).

[14]   *Institutes* IV xix 8.

[15]   L. S. Thornton makes much of this as a general sign of the Spirit. Thornton, *Confirmation*, pp. 76ff. For a series of discussions of the uses of oil in Christian traditions see Martin Dudley and Geoffrey Rowell (eds.), *The Oil of Gladness: Anointing in the Christian Tradition* (London: SPCK, 1993).

[16]   *ST* III 72 1.

[17]   *Institutes* IV xix 13. Calvin continues: 'A child of ten would present himself to the church to declare his confession of faith, would be examined in each article, and answer to each; if he were ignorant of anything or insufficiently understood it, he would be taught. Thus, while the church looks on as a witness, he would profess the one true and sincere faith, in which the believing folk with one mind worship the one God.'

[18]   Chase, of course, repudiates this mistaken change of emphasis: 'The essence of the rite lies in the prayer for the gift of the Spirit and in the laying on of hands... The renewal of the Baptismal vows on the other hand is an accident of the rite, appropriate only in the case of those whose Confirmation is separated from their Baptism by an interval of time.' Chase, *Confirmation in the Apostolic Age*, p. 13.

understood sacramentally as a means of the giving of the Spirit, or whether the rite is understood simply as a human confirmation of baptismal vows—something surely is implied as 'lacking' in the rite of baptism. And in either case a separate and distinct rite of confirmation would seem (to this author at least) to be an inevitable outcome of the practice of paedo-baptism.

Perhaps I should clarify that the question here is not that of the appropriateness or otherwise of accompanying baptism with the laying-on of hands or with an anointing with oil—though biblically and theologically unnecessary (given the biblical and theological significance of baptism itself) neither accompaniment need be deemed inappropriate or unhelpful. The problem is rather this dividing of a single rite of Christian initiation by the introduction of a second rite that can only issue in some form of diminishing of baptism's significance.[19]

As has already been acknowledged, many Baptist churches divide this single rite of Christian initiation, not by the introduction of a supplementary sacramental rite signifying the giving of the Spirit, but by a distinct rite of reception into the membership of the local church. For Baptists, of course, such distinction implies no sacramental restriction: as has also been acknowledged previously, 'open' membership Baptist churches practice 'open' communion, even the lack of any form of baptism, not to mention the lack of formal church membership, is perceived as no bar to communion in such contexts. However, though those baptised but not yet received into formal church membership may freely participate in the Eucharist, and in this respect this distinction represents no sacramental restriction, since full membership of the local church is itself a means of grace perhaps the distinction does represent some sacramental restriction after all? If this strange distinction can be defended (and I realise that such a distinction is incomprehensible to most other denominations) this may be attempted on two grounds. In the first place, and most obviously, the distinction implies some distinction

---

[19]   Even when anointing follows baptism immediately there remains the danger that this anointing, rather than the baptism itself, is the real means of the Spirit's bestowal. This is illustrated by the following account, by Kallistos Ware, of the Orthodox practice: 'The newly-baptized, whether infant or adult, is marked by the priest on the forehead, eyes, nostrils, mouth, ears, breast, hands and feet, with the words, "The seal of the gift of the Holy Spirit". This is for each one a personal Pentecost: the Spirit, who descended visibly upon the Apostles in tongues of fire, descends upon every one of us invisibly, yet with no less reality and power. Each becomes an "anointed one", a "Christ" after the likeness of Jesus the Messiah. Each is sealed with the *charismata* of the Comforter. From the moment of our Baptism and Chrismation the Holy Spirit, together with Christ, comes to dwell in the innermost shrine of our heart. Although we say to the Spirit "Come", he is already within us.' Kallistos Ware, *The Orthodox Way* (New York: St. Vladimir's Seminary Press, 1979), p. 100.

between the Church and the church, between full participation in the universal and catholic and full participation in the local and particular. But while I preserve some distinction between the catholic and the particular and acknowledge this by referring to the Church and the churches (albeit struggling to maintain this consistently), this distinction (if it validly can be made at all) is surely invalid at this point: to participate in Christ and his Church must surely imply full participation in any local church, just as full participation in any local church should imply full participation in Christ and his Church. Any distinction between the Church and the church is deeply unhelpful here. But in the second place (and perhaps more helpfully), in the context of congregational church government, the distinction between baptism and full membership of the local church represents the recognition of a limitation of responsibility and, thereby could be construed as one aspect of the recognition of a 'journey' of faith, a recognition that could have the outcome of admitting to baptism those who might not yet be ready to bear the full responsibilities of local church membership.[20] My response to this distinction between baptism and local church membership, as implied previously, is that it jeopardises far more than it is likely to maintain; that it would be better to permit younger people to participate in church meetings than to convey the impression that they were less than fully members of Christ and his Church. Indeed, this common practice may simply reinforce the impression amongst other Christians that Baptists exclude children from the Church.

And this is a common accusation levelled against Baptists by paedo-baptists, that the former implicitly (and explicitly) exclude children from the Church by their baptismal practice. Certainly it would not be difficult to cite instances where this has been the case—British Baptists, in the main, have not been prominent in developing theologies of children and childhood.[21] But, having pleaded guilty to the charge (at least in a general and corporate sense), I want to suggest (as irenically as possible) that paedo-baptists (at least those inhabiting a Western catholic tradition) are similarly guilty and therefore have little room to make the charge. As a Baptist, and affirming entirely the biblical and theological conclusions of

---

[20]   This notion of a 'journey' of faith has been developed by Paul Fiddes in various contexts and occurs in his book, *Tracks and Traces: Baptist Identity in Church and Theology* (Carlisle: Paternoster Press, 2003).

[21]   Though see, for instance, G. R. Beasley-Murray, 'The Church and the Child', *The Fraternal* 50 (1943) 9-13; W. M. S. West, 'The Child and the Church: A Baptist Perspective', in W. H. Brackney, P. S. Fiddes and J. H. Y. Briggs (eds.), *Pilgrim Pathways: Essays in Honour of B. R. White* (Macon, GA: Mercer University Press, 1999), pp. 88-92; Anne Dunkley, *Seen and Heard: Reflections on Children and Baptist Tradition* (Oxford: Whitley Publications, 1999); or (more broadly) Keith J. White, *A Place for Us* (London: Mill Grove, 1981).

the previous chapter, I acknowledge baptism as the instrumental means through which we receive the Spirit and are thereby incorporated into Christ and his Church. I therefore cannot conceive of how anyone who has been baptised can appropriately be excluded from the sacramental life of the Church. Yet, by excluding children from full participation in the Lord's Supper until they have been confirmed, this is precisely the common Western catholic paedo-baptist practice.[22] The life of the Church *is* its sacramental life and, therefore, to exclude a child from the Lord's Supper *is* effectively to exclude that child from the life of the Church. I am aware, of course, of the manner in which this bizarre practice is justified: that to receive the Lord's Supper is a matter of great seriousness and that Paul has grave things to say concerning those who eat and drink 'in an unworthy manner' or who receive the bread without 'recognising the body of the Lord' (1 Corinthians 11.27ff.). But is baptism not also a matter of great seriousness? Is not the invitation to baptism similarly accompanied by a call to repentance? Or, conversely, if we affirm the priority of God's promise and of God's grace in the sacrament of baptism on what basis do we implicitly deny that priority at the Lord's Supper; do we suddenly become semi-Pelagians at communion having so resisted any trace of Pelagianism at the font?[23] As a Baptist, as a 'sacramentalist', and as (I hope) a catholic Christian, I want to affirm the priority of God's promise and of God's grace both in baptism and in the Lord's Supper. As a Baptist (and I hope still as a 'sacramentalist' and a catholic Christian) I also want to recognise an element of human prayer and promise in baptism, in the Lord's Supper, and indeed in every sacramental rite. Wherever else, as a Baptist, I might be deficient, this understanding of baptism and the Lord's Supper appears (admittedly to me) to have the merit of consistency. Which is more than I can recognise in common Western catholic paedo-baptist practice.

There are, of course, those within the Western catholic tradition who resist this withholding of Communion from baptised children, there are those (like Calvin) within the Western catholic tradition who dispute a separate rite of confirmation and reject this implicit belittling of baptism and its significance. This (apparently minority) position is at least consistent—though, as stated above, I would hold an element of prayer and human promise to be inherent in the sacraments and would therefore consider such consistent practice to be irregular albeit valid. But the

---

[22]   This is in contrast to the Eastern practice that considers the child, once baptised and chrismated, a full communicant member of the Church.

[23]   Pelagianism, named after Pelagius, though probably owing more to the thought of Caelestius and Rufinus, was a movement promoting asceticism in the fifth century, refuted by Augustine for teaching that men and women remain unaffected by Adam's fall, are capable (of themselves) of responding to grace, and are capable of living virtuous lives.

separation of confirmation as a distinct sacramental rite, together with the withholding of the Lord's Supper from baptised infants, is not only irregular (biblically and theologically), it also implicitly invalidates baptism by detracting from its significance. Indeed, what significance remains for baptism if it no longer signifies our reception of the Spirit and our incorporation into Christ through our incorporation into his Church and into its sacramental life? Or what in actuality is the status of a baptised child in relation to the Church if baptism is no longer deemed to signify the actuality of that child's reception of the Spirit and if that child is excluded from full participation in the Church by being excluded from full participation in the Lord's Supper?

Nor is it entirely fair to accuse all Baptists of lacking a theology of childhood. Though this feature of their teaching remains virtually unknown to the majority of British Baptists, several amongst the Anabaptists of the sixteenth century developed a coherent and consistent theology of childhood and of the place of the child within the Church. In the first place this was achieved either by a severe qualification of the Augustinian doctrine of original sin, or, more commonly, by the belief that original sin (our universal sharing in Adam's sin and guilt) was remitted solely and completely through the merits of Christ and his suffering without baptism. In the second place, while none denied an enduring bias to sin in infants, children were considered to be 'innocent' until such a time that they themselves, like Adam, sinned consciously and wilfully, fully knowing that such an action offended God and God's law. Thus, in a letter to Thomas Müntzer, Conrad Grebel[24] affirms that children are saved simply through the suffering of Christ, without either faith or baptism, and also develops this notion of a child's innocence before that child reaches an 'age of discernment', a personal knowledge of good and evil.[25] Both these ideas are further developed by Pilgram Marpeck who similarly argues that children are accepted and included simply on the basis of Christ's promise:

> Christ has accepted the children without sacrifice, without circumcision, without faith, without knowledge, without baptism; He has accepted them solely by virtue of the word: 'To such belongs the kingdom of heaven.'[26]

The notion of a child's innocency is also developed by Marpeck who argues that, since Adam's sin consists in a knowledge of good and evil, a

---

[24]   Conrad Grebel (1498–1526) was among the first Anabaptist leaders in Zürich and was the first to be 're-baptised'.

[25]   Conrad Grebel and Friends, 'Letters to Thomas Müntzer', in *Spiritual and Anabaptist Writers*, ed. George Huntston Williams and Angel M. Mergal (Philadelphia, PA: Westminster Press, 1957), pp. 73-85 (p. 81).

[26]   Marpeck, 'Confession of 1532', p. 130.

child lacking such knowledge must be deemed innocent; only when a child attains personal knowledge of good and evil do 'sin, death, and damnation begin' and does repentance and baptism become meaningful:

> All true simplicity of infants is bought with the blood of Christ, but without any law, external teaching, faith, baptism, Lord's Supper, and all other Christian ceremonies, for theirs is the kingdom of heaven without admonition to change. But to those who claim to know good and evil...the Lord says: 'You must become as children.' He is condemned who is not born again through faith and baptism for the forgiveness of sins, and who is not born again into the obedience of faith, the simplicity and innocence of the child.[27]

Similarly Dietrich Philips[28] relates the 'age of discretion' to the ability to 'distinguish good from evil' and speaks of the death of Christ as being a sufficient payment for original sin: though children have a 'tendency' towards evil this 'does not damn them', by the 'grace of God' it is 'not accounted as sin to them'.[29] I suspect that, for most contemporary Baptists, the phrase 'age of discretion' is taken to refer simply to an age of understanding—baptism should be postponed until the one coming to baptism understands the significance of what is happening—though, on this basis, I suspect that few Baptists ought ever to have been baptised. It should be emphasised, therefore, that Philips and other early Anabaptists are using the phrase in a wholly different manner: the age of discretion is the age of wilfulness; the age at which a child becomes personally aware of good and evil, right and wrong; the age at which a child becomes aware that to act in such a way is to act rebelliously against God (rather than merely rebelliously against parents). Until such an awareness is attained, these Anabaptists argue, though a child may certainly display a bias to sin, sin as a wilful act (sin, that is, in the likeness of Adam's sin) is incoherent. And if the notion of wilful sin in the child is incoherent then so is the notion of repentance, and so also is the rite of baptism.

While I find this latter line of argument coherent and attractive I remain unpersuaded. Perhaps my experience as a parent leads me to suspect that the possibility of wilful sin, like the possibility of genuine

---

[27]   Pilgram Marpeck, 'Judgment and Decision', in *Writings*, pp. 309-361 (p. 337); cf. '...they have not yet been perverted by their own fleshly mind and thus, do not know the difference between good and evil... [O]riginal sin is inherited only when there is a knowledge of good and evil'. Pilgram Marpeck, 'Admonition of 1542', in *Writings*, pp. 159-302 (pp. 204-205).

[28]   Dietrich (Dirk) Philips (1504–68) was an associate of Menno Simons with whom he came to disagree concerning the strictness of the ban. He was one of the leaders of the Anabaptist movement in the Netherlands and in the northern parts of Germany.

[29]   Dietrich Philips, 'Christian Baptism' (1564), quoted in Klaassen (ed.), *Anabaptism in Outline*, p. 187; cf. Dietrich Philips, 'Regeneration and the New Creature', (1556), quoted in Klaassen (ed.), *Anabaptism in Outline*, pp. 63ff.

faith, can pertain at a very young age. I am, however, considerably more impressed and persuaded by the first line of argument, that the merits of Christ and of his suffering are entirely and solely sufficient for the salvation of the child—and, indeed, for the salvation of the world.

Contrary (I suspect) to the assumptions of many Baptists, and perhaps of many paedo-baptists, and certainly contrary to the assumptions underlying Catholic notions of Limbo, we are saved neither by baptism nor by faith; we are saved solely and sufficiently by the mercy of God in Christ. Both baptism and faith are instrumental means through which we are brought to participate in this salvation; but neither faith nor baptism effect that salvation; salvation is effected by God alone; he alone is the efficient cause of grace through the sacraments—or, indeed, without them. Baptism, as an instrumental means of grace, is not God's prison; he is not confined there; he cannot be manipulated there; his mercy and grace are broader and wider than our most extravagant imaginings. The promise of the kingdom of God to children, the receiving of children by Jesus, and the command that we should receive children, all are integral to the gospel story. By being brought to the Church, the communion of Christ's disciples, children are brought to Jesus. Moreover, in being brought to Jesus by being brought to his Church, by being raised and nurtured in awareness of God's grace, or merely by virtue of being born to Christian parents, children are declared 'holy' (1 Corinthians 7.14). Like Marpeck,[30] most Baptists encourage a rite of infant presentation in which thanksgiving is offered for this new life, in which promises are made by parents and by the gathered church, in which prayers are said for parents and child, and in which the Aaronic blessing is pronounced (Numbers 6.24ff.). Such a rite should be recognised as truly sacramental (though perhaps not as a dominically ordained sacrament), as prayer and promise in the light of God's promise, as a means of his grace. But such a rite is not baptism, nor is it a substitute for baptism. No-one in Scripture is brought to baptism. Those coming to baptism do so repentantly, prayerfully, and expectantly. They come expecting this rite to be the means through which they receive the Spirit and through which they are incorporated into Christ through being incorporated fully into his Church and its sacramental life. The mere existence of a rite of confirmation testifies to a deficient incorporation in Christ through baptism through a deferment of full participation in the Church's sacramental life; it testifies to a deferment of an expectation of the Spirit; it testifies therefore to a belittling of baptism.

---

[30]   'We admonish the parents to cleanse their conscience, as much as lies in them, with respect to the child, to do whatever is needed to raise the child up to the praise and glory of God, and to commit the child to God until it is clearly seen that God is working in him for faith or unfaith. Any other way is to be like thieves and murderers and to be ahead of Christ.' Marpeck, 'Confession of 1532', p. 147.

But if an expectation for the receiving of the Spirit is muted through the practice of paedo-baptism, it is muted just as effectively through the non-sacramental (or even 'anti-sacramental') notion of baptism that seems to hold sway amongst many contemporary Baptists. When baptism is reduced to a merely human and ethical event, to a public testimony to an inward conviction, to a human prayer and promise devoid of any notion of participating in a divine promise, then expectation for anything at all is minimalised or entirely negated. And if a demeaning of the significance of baptism by paedo-baptists is evidenced formally by the rite of confirmation, this demeaning (by both paedo-baptists and credo-baptists) is evidenced informally and more radically by the rise of Pentecostalism. Pentecostalism, like the rite of confirmation, is testimony to a lack, a perceived deficiency.

Clearly there are several differing strands and streams of Pente-costalism: there are Pentecostal denominations; and there are charismatic streams within older, non-Pentecostal denominations. But whether a baptism with the Spirit is perceived as a receiving of charismatic power, as an experiential seal of assurance, or as an impartation of holiness, Pentecostalism generally attests a second and subsequent experience of the Spirit and, thereby, implicitly diminishes the significance of baptism.

Though his work remains largely unknown and rarely acknowledged (even by Pentecostalists), the writings of Edward Irving, the nineteenth-century Scottish Presbyterian,[31] offer perhaps the most coherent justification for a 'second blessing' theology. Irving roots his interpretation Christologically by drawing attention to Christ's birth by the Spirit (by virtue of which he was preserved holy) and Christ's baptism by the Spirit (by virtue of which he was anointed with power for public ministry). Tracing a similar distinction between the first disciples' belief in Jesus (by virtue of which he pronounced them 'clean') and their subsequent receiving of the Spirit on the day of Pentecost (by virtue of which they were empowered as his witnesses), Irving concludes that the Christian's experience of the Spirit ought properly to be determined by that of Christ.[32] One suspects, nonetheless, that the driving force for the

---

[31] Edward Irving (1792–1834), perhaps best remembered for teaching that the flesh assumed by Christ was the fallen flesh of Adam (a view for which, on 30 November 1830, the London Presbytery of the Scottish Presbyterian Church found him guilty of heresy), became intrigued by manifestations of 'spiritual gifts'. On being deposed from the ministry of the Caledonian Chapel in Regent's Square, London, for permitting unordained men and women to 'lead' worship, Irving joined with others in founding the 'Catholic Apostolic Church'.

[32] Edward Irving, *The Day of Pentecost or The Baptism with the Holy Ghost* (Edinburgh: John Lindsay, 1831). For an engaging and full summary of Irving's contribution see Gordon Strachan, *The Pentecostal Theology of Edward Irving* (London: Darton, Longman & Todd, 1973).

distinction between these two works of the Spirit was experiential: Irving became increasingly impressed by what he interpreted as a restoring to the Church of the spiritual gifts listed in 1 Corinthians 12; but he observed such signs as a separate and subsequent receiving of the Spirit. And, like Irving (though not consciously dependent upon him), Pentecostalism is empirically driven: second blessing theologies derive from second blessing experiences; the phenomena of charismatic gifts draw attention to their previous absence. Irving, however, was a sufficiently perceptive thinker (and sufficiently committed to a sacramentalist theology) to identify both works of the Spirit within the significance of Christian baptism.[33] Unlike Irving, Pentecostalism generally lacks a sacramentalist theology and, consequently, this phenomenon of charismatic experience is usually affirmed without specific relation to water baptism (within Pentecostal denominations, water baptism and Spirit baptism are usually radically distinguished).

This response to charismatic phenomena—or rather, this response to a perceived lack of charismatic phenomena—is all very understandable. In the narrative of the Samaritan conversion, and in the verses immediately following the passage cited at the beginning of this chapter, we encounter the story of a man called Simon who offered Peter and John money in exchange for the 'ability' to confer this gift of the Spirit. We tend to focus on the outcome of this story for Simon (from whom derives the canonical crime of simony). We notice that he had previously 'practised sorcery' and that he probably mistook a sacramental laying-on of hands for magical power. However, the implication of this story surely is that something observable occurred when Peter and John laid their hands on these Samaritan believers—indeed, something so extraordinary and impressive that Simon was prepared to part with money to gain this 'ability'. Now would you give money for what you observed happening at the average confirmation—or at the average baptism, for that matter?

Perceivable phenomena are prominent throughout the narrative of the Acts of the Apostles: it was in response to perceivable phenomena on the day of Pentecost that a crowd gathered in amazement; it was in response to perceivable phenomena that Peter urged the baptism of Cornelius and of those with him; and the perceivable phenomena following Paul's baptism of the Ephesian disciples serves to emphasise the lack of such

---

[33]   'For baptism, Christ's ordinance, containeth two things, the working away of our sin, and the baptism with the Holy Ghost; the former holding of redemption and satisfaction, the latter holding of the new acquisition which our nature made on the morning of Christ's baptism.' Edward Irving, *Christ's Holiness in Flesh, The Form, Fountain Head, and Assurance to us of Holiness in Flesh* (Edinburgh: John Lindsay, 1831), pp. 109-110; quoted in Gordon Strachen, *The Pentecostal Theology of Edward Irving*, p. 97.

phenomena previously.[34] Such phenomena, therefore, ought not to be lightly dismissed or repudiated; rather the absence of such phenomena—given the prominence of such phenomena in these narratives—ought to give cause for concern. But to accord such phenomena determinative and definitive theological or personal significance is nevertheless a harmful delusion. And it is in this respect that the work of Jonathan Edwards is again often misunderstood or misappropriated.

Edwards' series of reflections on the phenomena accompanying the 'revival' in New England were prompted at least partly by the need to respond to those, like Charles Chauncy of Boston, who were entirely dismissive of such phenomena. Chauncy, together with other critics of the 'revival', maintaining that true religion was entirely a matter of reason and sound judgement, refuted the 'carnal enthusiasm' excited by promoters of the 'revival' such as James Davenport. While Edwards was similarly critical of Davenport and of any artificial exciting of emotionalism, his unified account of knowledge—that we are affected by that which we know—provided a philosophical and theological basis for accepting, and indeed for expecting, phenomenal signs of affectedness. Edwards had previously outlined this theological basis for explicitly religious 'affections' in a sermon on divine revelation,[35] and his first explicit response to the 'revival' was a simple description of the manner in which this awakening affected two members of his Northampton congregation: Abigail Hutchinson, an adult who had died by the time Edwards wrote his account; and Phebe Bartlet, a five-year old child.[36] Edwards' subsequent reflections, however, represent ever more cautious and circumspect attempts to assess the significance of such 'affections':[37] while not finally dismissive of 'inconclusive signs', Edwards is here concerned to identify those affections which might be recognised as sure

---

[34]   For a discussion (and possible interpretation) of these narratives see Dunn, *Baptism in the Holy Spirit*, pp. 38-102.

[35]   Jonathan Edwards, 'A Divine and Supernatural Light' (1733), in *Sermons and Discourses 1730–1733*, in *YE* vol. 17, pp. 408-426.

[36]   Jonathan Edwards, *A Faithful Narrative of the Surprizing Work of God in the Conversion of Many Hundred Souls in Northampton, and the Neighbouring Towns* (1737), in *The Great Awakening*, in *YE* vol. 4, pp. 144-211.

[37]   Jonathan Edwards, *The Distinguishing Marks of a Work of the Spirit of God. Applied to that uncommon Operation that has lately appeared on the Minds of many of the People of this Land* (1741), in *The Great Awakening*, pp. 226-288; *Some Thoughts concerning the present Revival of Religion in New-England, and the Way in which it ought to be acknowledged and promoted* (1742), in *The Great Awakening*, pp. 291-530; *A Treatise concerning the Religious Affections* (1746), in *YE* vol. 2, pp. 91-461.

signs of grace.[38] And here Edwards accords with Thomas Aquinas and all true catholic theology: true Christian conversion consists in 'a sanctification of the will',[39] in virtues of humility and holiness, in unfeigned love for God and for all that he loves—but such signs are both more profound and more elusive than the more immediate 'affections' accompanying 'revival'. While Edwards remains convinced that 'holy affections' are a necessary part of true religion, he appears to have increasing difficulty in identifying such in a manner that renders them assessable.

If we accept Edwards' unified theory of knowing—that there is no knowledge without affection—then surely we should expect phenomenal outcomes in any genuine mediation of grace. Indeed, the absence of such, though not decisive, should be deemed both surprising and concerning. But if we accept Edwards' pneumatological epistemology in its entirety—that all knowledge is a gift mediated by the Spirit, and that to know is to participate by the Spirit in the divine knowing and loving—then the definitive phenomenal outcomes in any genuine mediation of grace will be reflections of the divine character and the divine loving. This is not to be dismissive of more immediate phenomena—of swooning, of shaking, of weeping, of laughing, or even of glossolalia—but though such may be expected they are merely secondary; they are never decisive; they may be delusory. Nor, though such are to be expected, is their absence decisive: we respond in different ways to the mediation of God's grace, and some responses—indeed, the truly significant responses—are not immediately perceivable.[40]

But though the absence of such immediately perceivable phenomena is indecisive, it is often problematic, and Pentecostalism remains an inevitable (though inappropriate) response to this problem of apparent lack. It is an inappropriate response, not merely because it tends to focus on the wrong phenomena (on the secondary phenomena of immediate physical and emotional response), but primarily because it focuses on perceivable phenomena at all rather than on the mediated promise of God. I trust readers will forgive a very personal digression.

---

[38]   Note that, in *Distinguishing Marks*, Edwards repeats the common assumption that the gifts of the Spirit listed in 1 Corinthians 12 had ceased. This was initially Irving's assumption almost a century later until he became convinced to the contrary. Nonetheless, glossolalia, which became so significant for Irving and for later Pentecostalism, was discounted by Edwards.

[39]   Jenson, *America's Theologian*, p. 73.

[40]   For more recent discussion of such phenomena see David Middlemiss, *Interpreting Charismatic Experience* (London: SCM Press, 1996); see also Douglas McBain, *Discerning the Spirits: Checking for Truth in Signs and Wonders* (Basingstoke: Marshall Pickering, 1992).

I write not just as a Baptist but also as one who does not lack experience of charismatic phenomena. Yet I write also as one who has wrestled with a form of chronic depression throughout adult life—as one who remains bemused that he should ever have served as pastor of a charismatic Baptist church when extended periods of personal discipleship have lacked any form of 'felt' experience. And without prejudice to the preciousness of charismatic phenomena, by far my most profound recollection of mediated grace is entirely devoid of any such phenomena or of any form of 'felt' experience. During one sustained bout of acute depression two very dear friends invited me and my wife to stay with them until I could cope again with everyday life (without their generosity I would probably have needed to spend time in hospital). Returning from an evening service of communion, these friends, together with my wife, determined that I too should share in communion. They produced bread and (very excellent) wine, and we celebrated while squatting around their coffee table. Any who have any experience of serious depressive illness will understand that, at the time, I was entirely without any form of religious feeling—indeed, it was a struggle to believe at all. Yet as we sat around that table I realised, perhaps truly for the first time, that the bread and wine, and the body and blood of Christ that the elements re-presented, were there on the table for me whether I 'felt' anything—or even 'believed' anything—or not. In the absence of any perceivable phenomena, in the absence of any 'feeling' of faith, I recognised the significance of grace that evening more deeply and truly than ever before.

As has already been admitted, faith is perhaps the most difficult of the theological virtues to define: but faith is not a feeling; faith is more properly an attitude of trust in relation to the promises of God. Christian assurance, therefore, is grounded in the veracity of those promises rather than in our ability to believe them in any 'felt' sense. If faith is rightly defined as an instrumental cause of salvation it is so in a quite different manner to the sacraments. As means through which the promises of God are made present to us by the Spirit, the sacraments are instrumental causes of grace in a quite primary sense. Faith, though a gift of God, a fruit of the Spirit, is not at all an instrumental cause of grace; faith is responsive; it is an instrumental means through which, by the Spirit's mediation, grace is recognised and enjoyed. Through faith grace becomes effective in a human life, but faith is not in any sense a cause of that grace. And if this is the case with faith (properly defined), it is certainly the case with any form of religious feeling, affection, or phenomenon.

When responding to the issue of assurance, notwithstanding his emphasis on justification by faith alone, Martin Luther's response was sacramental: I am baptised (*baptismus sum*).[41] And in this respect the entire effort of Jonathan Edwards to ponder the religious affections could be considered mistaken, or at least insufficient. Unlike the later reflections of Edward Irving, there is in Edwards' work very little focus on the sacraments and on the promises of God effected through them.[42] While (agreeing with Edwards) religious affections are not to be despised or dismissed but are rather to be expected, they are neither decisive nor definitive and, therefore, it is inappropriate and misleading to focus attention here and to this degree. If today I believe myself to be filled with the Spirit and incorporated in Christ, that belief is not grounded in any felt experience or charismatic phenomena (precious though such may be) but is grounded rather in the promises of God imparted through baptism and reaffirmed through the Lord's Supper. This is not to dispute anything Edwards says concerning the religious affections, neither is it to belittle the preciousness and appropriateness of charismatic phenomena, but it is to set such in proper context. The promises of God are rendered to us sacramentally and confidence in God—the passive trust that, for Luther, is the essence of faith—rests on those promises *and on nothing else.*

The point at issue here is central to the argument of (and the motivation for) this entire study. Writing towards the beginnings of the Enlightenment, and responding to its philosophical assumptions so effectively in other respects, Jonathan Edwards nonetheless appears here merely to echo an Enlightenment preoccupation with assessable (and verifiable) empirical phenomena. Affirmation of such phenomena, of course, predates Edwards: it is ubiquitous in the writings of the Puritans; it is certainly acknowledged in Thomas Aquinas, Augustine, the Cappadocians, Athanasius, Irenaeus; it is prominent—as we have seen—in the Acts of the Apostles. But, at least when Acts is read in the context of the Epistles, it is never the primary focus for attention, nor is it the primary focus for an understanding of Christian identity. Paul does not remind the Christians at Rome that they once spoke in tongues (if indeed they did); he reminds them rather that they were once baptised into Christ Jesus—this, and this alone, is deemed decisive for their identity.[43] Yet a preoccupation with empirical phenomena, with 'felt' experience, with unmediated immediacy, vitiates Evangelicalism in general and the Charismatic movement in particular: it characterises the teaching of George Whitefield; it characterises the teaching of John Wesley; it is

---

[41]   'I have been baptized and I have the Word, and so I have no doubt about my salvation as long as I continue to cling to the Word'. *LW* vol. 54, *Table Talk*, No. 365 (1532), pp. 55-58 (p. 57).

[42]   For some intimation of this criticism see Jenson, *America's Theologian*, pp. 175-176.

[43]   Romans 6.3-4.

central to the teaching of John Wimber. Whatever theological language may be used to define such experience, the 'felt' experience of conversion or of receiving the Spirit is accorded priority over the promises of God mediated sacramentally.

And all this is both erroneous and dangerous. It is erroneous because it ultimately grounds faith and assurance in self rather than in God, in felt experience rather than in promise. It is dangerous because felt experience can be delusory and its absence, though surprising, can never be definitive. One encounters far too many delightful disciples who are disturbed because their spiritual experience doesn't conform to the perceived 'norm' (ironically, Edwards himself was aware that his own experience did not 'fit').[44] And the very notion of a perceived 'norm' is presumptuous: the Spirit blows wherever he wills; those born of the Spirit defy categorisation;[45] to presume any felt experience as normative engenders pomposity, exclusivity, and division.

But if this preoccupation with felt experience is an Evangelical echo of the Enlightenment, it is also, I would argue, an outcome of impoverished sacramental practice.[46] As long as baptism continues to be administered, by paedo-baptists or by credo-baptists, devoid of explicit expectation for the fulfilment of divine promise, an assurance of that fulfilment will be sought elsewhere and through other means. As long as some Baptists continue to belittle baptism as merely an act of obedience, as an external witness to a previous (and unmediated) inner reality, that previous unmediated felt experience will remain the focus for faith and assurance. And if that previous unmediated felt experience is deemed inadequate, the remedy will be sought, not sacramentally, but through further unmediated felt experiences. And as long as paedo-baptists continue to undermine the significance of baptism through a subsequent sacrament of confirmation, and as long as both rites are administered in a formalised manner that militates against any phenomena of religious affection, the remedy will be sought, either again through some unmediated felt experience that becomes the actual focus for faith and assurance, or through 're-baptism'.

There can, of course, be no such rite as 're-baptism'. There is but one baptism and baptism, validly, can occur but once.[47] To 're-baptise', therefore, is explicitly to deny the validity of any previous 'baptism'. And it is hardly surprising, where baptism is understood simply as an act

---

[44]   Jonathan Edwards, 'Diary', in *YE* vol. 16, *Letters and Personal Writings*, pp. 759-789.

[45]   John 3.8.

[46]   For an excellent discussion of the properly sacramental mediation of faith and assurance, particularly within a Baptist context, see Stephen R. Holmes *Tradition and Renewal in Baptist Life* (Oxford: Whitley Publications, 2003).

[47]   Ephesians 4.4ff.

of obedience, as an external witness to a previous (and unmediated) inner reality, that infant baptism is dismissed as entirely invalid. If, however, baptism is recognised, not just or even primarily as a human act of prayer and promise, but primarily as a mediation of divine promise, then infant baptism, for all its deficiency and irregularity (as undermining those properly human elements of prayer and promise) cannot be dismissed as entirely invalid. Therefore, if the significance and validity of baptism as a mediation of divine promise is not to be undermined (by re-baptism), but if the deficiency and irregularity of infant baptism (through its undermining of the human elements of prayer and promise) is to be admitted, then the continuance and appropriateness (albeit a consequential appropriateness) of a sacramental rite of confirmation is inevitable. But let that sacramental rite of confirmation, as in the narrative of the Samaritan conversion, be truly sacramental, be pregnant with expectancy. And let that sacramental rite of confirmation, as in the narrative of the Samaritan conversion, be acknowledged as an admission of a lack—a lack which may yet occur (as in the narrative of the Samaritan conversion), but which should not be actively courted through the continuance of the practice of infant baptism.

The folly of attempting a mediating position, of course, is that one loses friends on both sides of the debate: I do not expect my begrudging acceptance of infant baptism as 'valid but irregular',[48] together with my begrudging advocacy of a sacramental rite of confirmation as a means of accommodating this irregularity, to impress either my paedo-baptist or credo-baptist associates. As long as the practice of infant baptism continues there will be those who count it as invalid and either seek or administer 're-baptism' as a consequence. As long as the practice of 're-baptism' continues there will be those who repudiate it as offensive and as inherently 'Pelagian'. In response to this impasse my (modest?) proposal is firstly that any baptism, understood primarily as a mediation of the promise of God, should be acknowledged as valid, no matter how 'irregular',[49] and secondly that, in response to this narrative of the Samaritan conversion, a sacramental rite of confirmation should be acknowledged as an appropriate means of dealing with this 'irregularity'. An alternative mediating possibility would be the proposal of a rite for

---

[48]   As was acknowledged in the previous chapter, this understanding of infant baptism as valid but irregular remained Barth's position throughout his writing on the theme, both before and after his rejection of baptism's sacramentality: 'Baptism without the willingness and readiness of the baptized is true, effectual and effective baptism, but it is not correct; it is not done in obedience, it is not administered according to proper order, and therefore it is necessarily clouded baptism.' Karl Barth, *The Teaching of the Church Regarding Baptism*, trans. Ernest A. Payne (London: SCM Press, 1948), p. 40.

[49]   This begrudging acceptance is by no means original. See for instance, G. R. Beasley-Murray, *Baptism Today and Tomorrow*, pp. 145ff. see especially pp. 166-169.

renewing baptismal vows through total immersion:[50] but I cannot see how such could occur without an implicit undermining of baptism (at least in the mind of the candidate), and the focus for this proposal seems to be a human confirming rather than the sacramental mediation of a divine confirming. However, to fail to acknowledge this 'irregularity', and to fail to address this 'irregularity' sacramentally—whether through confirmation or through 're-baptism'—would be to reinforce the Evangelical habit of locating an assurance of Christian identity in unmediated 'felt' experience.

I am grateful (once again) to my friend and colleague, Steve Holmes, for drawing attention to the fact that controversies concerning baptismal discipline are far from novel.[51] Within the Early Church—and within any single local church—there were conflicting views of infant baptism, of baptism *in extremis*, and (for them most problematically and divisively) of the validity or otherwise of 'heretical' baptism. The Early Church suffered schisms concerning the validity of 'heretical' baptism but it does appear that some, while expressing differing convictions on the matter, managed to remain together, united in the one catholic Church (and even within a single local church). My reasons for remaining a Baptist have far more to do with an understanding of the nature of the Church's apostolicity and of its relationship to the State than with an understanding of baptism. I simply cannot accept that differing views of baptism are sufficient grounds for continued denominational separation (I struggle with the notion that there could ever be *sufficient* grounds for separation). And, at risk of offending my paedo-baptist friends still further, perhaps we should remember that 're-baptism' is not the unforgivable sin: the grace of God is not ultimately hampered by our sacramental indiscipline.

There may be, however, quite different significance to draw from this narrative of the Samaritan conversion as recorded in Acts. Clearly the author of this narrative is not offering us a comprehensive account of the first thirty years of the Church's history (as if such were either possible or desirable). Rather events are recorded (as in any 'history') because they are indicative of particular significance to the author or (in the author's opinion) to the author's intended readers. Now it may be that Luke intends to draw attention to the sheer variety of spiritual phenomena accompanying Christian initiation and, thereby, to the freedom of the Spirit and the non-manipulable nature of grace. He therefore narrates the events of the day of Pentecost, the Samaritan conversion, the conversion of the Ethiopian eunuch, the conversion of Paul, the conversion of Cornelius, the 'instruction' of Apollos, the 're-baptism' of Ephesian

---

[50]　Colin Buchanan, *Adult Baptisms*, Grove Worship Series 91 (Bramcote: Grove Books, 1985), pp. 23-24.

[51]　Holmes, 'Baptism: Patristic Resources for Ecumenical Dialogue', in *Listening to the Past*, pp. 108-121.

disciples, simply to convey this variety. Alternatively, Luke may record
some of these events in this manner because, for him, they mark key
stages in the narrative; stages emphasised by the journey of Peter and
John to Samaria, by the conversion of Paul, by the sending of Barnabas to
Antioch, by the council of Jerusalem, by the accelerating spread of the
gospel amongst the Gentiles. In other words, Luke is drawing attention to
the controversies accompanying Gentile conversion and his concern (like
the probable underlying concern in so many of the Pauline Epistles) is
for the unity of the Church. Who knows (and are the alternatives, or any
number of other possible interpretations, mutually exclusive)? Whatever
Luke's intention it is not inappropriate for us to recognise the
significance of the second, as well as the first, possibility. It may be
appropriate, therefore, to read the narrative of the Samaritan conversion,
not primarily as drawing attention to a 'lack' in the Samaritans' initial
experience, but rather (and primarily) as drawing attention to the unity of
these Samaritan Christians (as later of Gentile Christians) within the one
Church; this 'confirmation' through Peter and John is not merely a
response to a perceived lack but is also a mark of unity.

And if there is validity in such a reading of the narrative, then there
may also be validity in recognising this rite of confirmation (perhaps the
most 'questionable' of the seven Catholic sacraments) as an expression of
unity rather than of division. And if, within baptistic churches, a
sacramental rite of confirmation could be acknowledged as an
appropriate response to any 'irregularity' of infant baptism, then a
significant step towards unity would have been taken.[52]

---

[52] I have not, at all, discussed the appropriate ministers of this rite and, in some
respects, this issue will be revisited in chapter 10 of this book. One could simply say (for
the present) that bishops are the appropriate ministers of this rite within churches that
recognise this order of ministry. It should be noted, as Paul Haffner acknowledges, that
the Catholic church acknowledges priests as 'extraordinary' ministers of this rite: '[i]n
the West however, Confirmation could also be imparted by priests under special
circumstances, so that they were regarded as extraordinary ministers of this sacrament.
Papal authority extended the necessary permission. From the time of St. Gregory the
Great onwards, many Popes gave the faculty of administering Confirmation to priests of
the Latin rite, including missionaries, abbots and cardinals. When the Councils of
Florence and Trent spoke of the bishop as the ordinary minister of the sacrament, this
implied that there could be an extraordinary minister, namely the priest.' Haffner, *The
Sacramental Mystery*, pp. 69-70.

CHAPTER 7

The Sacrament of the Lord's Supper

Therefore, my dear friends, flee from idolatry. I speak to sensible people; judge for yourselves what I say. Is not the cup of thanksgiving for which we give thanks a participation in the blood of Christ? And is not the bread that we break a participation in the body of Christ? Because there is one loaf, we, who are many, are one body, for we all partake of the one loaf.

Consider the people of Israel: Do not those who eat the sacrifices participate in the altar? (1 Corinthians 10.14-18)

It is the assumption of this passage, rather than its underlying argument, that is so startling. Without apology, explanation, or equivocation, Paul here compares the Corinthians' participation in the Lord's Supper to their (previous and apparently continuing) participation in pagan sacrifices. Nor is the argument for the sacrificial nature of the Lord's Supper based on an understanding of the sacrificial nature of pagan rites—the argument, in fact, is entirely the other way round. Earlier in this letter, perhaps reflecting the argument of the 'libertines' at Corinth, Paul has conceded that 'an idol is nothing at all in the world' and that 'there is no God but one' (1 Corinthians 8.4). He warns, however, that not everyone has this understanding (γνῶσις) and that 'knowledge' is secondary to love (ἀγάπη): perhaps those who do have this 'knowledge' should waive their 'rights' (ἐξουσία) for the sake of others. Paul then seems to interject an extended excursus (if it is, indeed, an excursus) on his waiving of rights (ἐξουσία) as an apostle, including the 'right to food and drink' (ἐξουσίαν φαγεῖν καὶ πεῖν). He returns, in chapter 10, to the question of eating meat that has been offered to idols by first reminding his readers that those who ate and drank spiritual food and drink through Moses later fell under judgement through eating and drinking in the context of 'pagan revelry' (1 Corinthians 10.7). And then, beginning with the passage cited at the commencement of this chapter, he reminds the Corinthians that, just as to participate in the bread and wine of the Lord's Supper is to participate in the body and blood of Christ, so also to participate in meat that has been offered to idols is to participate in pagan altars, and is possibly to participate in 'demons' (v. 20). That is to say, Paul seeks to establish the possible significance of participating in pagan sacrifices on the basis of the actual (and apparently accepted) significance of participating in the bread and wine of the Lord's Supper; the effectiveness of the Supper as a participation in Christ's sacrifice is used to establish the effectiveness of eating meat offered to idols as a participation in pagan sacrifices.

All attempts to interpret Eucharistic language symbolically flounder on this text. A symbol, by definition, is symbolic of something and here that 'something' is identified as a participation in Christ's body and blood. Moreover, the reality of that participation in Christ's body and blood is the basis on which Paul's entire argument concerning participation in pagan altars rests. What is spoken of here is not a symbolic participation in Christ but a real participation in Christ. Therefore, even if the bread and wine of the Lord's Supper are designated as 'symbolic', we are yet left with the need to account for how our participation in Christ's body and blood, through the means of these 'symbols', is 'real'.

One major obstacle for our contemporary understanding of this passage is our almost total unfamiliarity with the language and dynamic of sacrifice—an unfamiliarity compounded by notions of penalty and propitiation that came to dominate atonement theologies during the late Medieval period and thereafter. When we think of a sacrifice we tend to think of a victim, slain on an altar, and wholly consumed by fire, as a propitiatory offering to a 'deity'. We tend not to think of a votive offering or of a sacrifice in the form of a participatory meal such as probably underlies the 'pagan' context addressed here by Paul. Which, of course, raises the question of the manner or type of sacrifice that Paul assumes here as an appropriate defining of the Lord's Supper—and which, in turn, raises the question of the relationship between the Lord's Supper and the Passover meal.

It is not ultimately possible, nor is it necessary or even desirable, to determine the precise historical relationship between the Passover and Christ's instituting of the Supper—whether he reinterpreted elements of the Passover meal in terms of his own body and blood, or whether he accorded this significance to elements that were not themselves elements of the Passover ritual. Nor is it even necessary to establish, despite the rather different chronology of John's Gospel, that the 'Last Supper' was itself a Passover meal—the issues have been definitively and exhaustively (though not, perhaps, entirely persuasively) discussed by Joachim Jeremias.[1] All that is required is to establish that the Passover, as a sacrificial meal, formed the context in which the New Testament (and thereby the earliest Church) came to understand the Lord's Supper. And this, surely, is indisputable. In the first place, and without prejudice to the

---

[1]   Joachim Jeremias, *The Eucharistic Words of Jesus*, trans. Norman Perrin (London: SCM Press, 1966). Note that Gregory Dix had previously followed the Johanine chronology in his understanding of the Eucharist: Gregory Dix, *The Shape of the Liturgy* (London: Dacre, 1945).

exact point in the celebrations at which Jesus gave significance (or new significance) to the bread and the wine, the testimony of the Synoptic Gospels is clear that this occurred in the context of Passover celebration. Similarly the Pauline epistles seem to assume a 'paschal' context of understanding (or, at least, never relate anything that explicitly undermines it).[2] Moreover, though John's Gospel suggests a rather different chronology according to which the crucifixion of Jesus coincides with the slaughter of the Passover lambs, this only serves to make the identical point in a rather different manner: Christ's death on the Cross is to be interpreted in the light of the Passover sacrifice; he is 'the Lamb of God' the one who truly 'takes away the sin of the world' (John 1.29).[3] And, if Christ dies as the eschatological Passover lamb, we would expect—if the imagery is to be maintained and meaningful—that Christ's death would issue in a participatory sacrificial meal (since this was the nature of the Passover). Though John's Gospel contains no explicit account of the institution of the Lord's Supper, the narrative of Jesus' sermon at Capernaum, following the feeding of the 5,000, is astonishing in its paschal imagery and—at least in the thinking of some commentators—fulfils the same function:[4] the evangelist clarifies that 'the Jewish Passover Feast was near' (John 6.4), and Jesus here uses the Eucharistic language of eating his flesh and drinking his blood.

The Jewish Passover Feast was and is a participatory sacrificial meal (which, interestingly, required and requires no 'priest'), and, as such, the Jewish Passover Feast was and is no mere memorial: it was and is not merely a means of remembering the once-for-all events of the Exodus; it was and is more profoundly a means of participating in those events. To share in the Jewish Passover Feast is to be identified with the people of Israel who were brought up out of Egypt: it is to participate in the bitterness of their sufferings; it is to participate in the joy of their deliverance. Through means of the Passover ritual the past is made

---

[2]   Most clearly, perhaps, earlier in this Epistle: '...Christ, our Passover lamb, has been sacrificed. Therefore let us keep the Festival, not with the old yeast, the yeast of malice and wickedness, but with bread without yeast, the bread of sincerity and truth.' (1 Corinthians 5.7-8).

[3]   I am aware of George Beasley-Murray's suggestion (following J. C. O'Neill) that this reference, together with the reference to the 'slain' lamb of Revelation 5, should be understood primarily in terms of the conquering ram alluded to in the *Testament of Joseph* (19.8-9). I found the suggestion surprising when I first heard it and it only seems more bizarre on reflection, not least when the imagery of the Paschal Lamb seems to dominate the Johannine corpus. George R. Beasley-Murray, *John*, pp. 24-25; cf. J. C. O'Neill, 'The Lamb of God in the *Testaments of the Twelve Patriarchs*', *Journal for the Study of the New Testament* 2 (1979), pp. 2-30.

[4]   For example see Edwyn Clement Hoskyns, *The Fourth Gospel*, ed. Francis Noel Davey (London: Faber and Faber, 2nd edn, 1947), pp. 304ff.

present; the present becomes a participation in the past. Moreover, inasmuch as the Passover Feast is celebrated with the expectation of the fulfilment of God's kingdom and the gathering of the Jewish people, the Passover Feast is also a prayerful anticipation of the future: 'next time in Jerusalem'.

Now it would be remarkable, given the overwhelming paschal imagery and allusions of the New Testament, if this background notion of a participatory sacrificial meal as a means of sharing in a past event did not, at least to some degree, inform an understanding of the Lord's Supper. But even if the influence of this paschal background were to be considered indecisive, the combined significance of the language of John 6, the language of the narratives of 'institution' in the Synoptic Gospels and 1 Corinthians 11, and the language of the passage cited at the beginning of this chapter, is overwhelming: the elements of bread and wine are given by Christ to his Church as means of participating in him and in his sacrificial death. Through participating in the bread and wine of communion we are brought to participate in the sacrifice of Calvary, the past becomes present, we in the present participate in the past. Or, to put the matter in terms I have employed previously, by means of this sacrament we are brought to indwell the gospel story: the story becomes present to us; it is not merely heard, it is indwelt. A sacrament is a means of grace, a means through which the Holy Spirit indwells our lives in order to renew us and transform us. And the Spirit's indwelling of our lives occurs through our indwelling of the gospel story. As we indwell the story so we are indwelt through the story and so we are changed; this story becomes our story, the defining truth of our lives.

And consequently, if the Lord's Supper is to be understood as a participatory sacrificial meal, it is highly unlikely that the term ἀνάμνησις should be interpreted merely in terms of a remembrance. Even if we were to discount the possible use of the term within the Septuagint in sacrificial context,[5] the context of its use within the words of institution, in relation to the declarations that 'this is my body' and 'this cup is the new covenant in my blood', is more suggestive of an interpretation in terms of a 're-presenting' of Christ's once-for-all sacrifice than a mere remembering of Christ's once-for-all sacrifice; what occurs is a genuine participation rather than just a recollection. There is no question here, of course, of a 'repeating', less still of a 'rivalling'—the sacrifice at Calvary is unrepeatable and utterly unique—and it should be noted that the Council of Trent uses the term

---

[5]   See especially Leviticus 24.7: 'Καὶ ἐπιθήσετε ἐπὶ τὸ θέμα λίβανον καθαρὸν καὶ ἅλα, καὶ ἔσονται εἰς ἄρτους εἰς ἀνάμνησιν προκείμενα τῷ Κυρίῳ'; cf. Numbers 10.10. D. M. Baillie may be rather too quick in dismissing the possibility of some sacrificial import for the words 'do' and 'remember' within the Septuagint. Baillie, *The Theology of the Sacraments*, pp. 116ff.

representatio and avoids the term *repetitio*.[6] But an unrepeatable and unique event (or, to be more precise, this unrepeatable and unique event) can nonetheless be re-presented; it is a once-for-all historical event but it is not thereby entrapped in its historical pastness; through the mediation of the Spirit it can be made present to us again and again; we can indwell this story.

Moreover, just as the Passover Feast includes a prayerful anticipation of a future fulfilment, so also the Lord's Supper, as a means of participating in a past event, is given as a means of prayerfully anticipating the future. In identifying bread and wine as means of participating in his sacrifice, Jesus promises not to drink wine again until he drinks it, with his disciples, in his Father's kingdom (Matthew 26.29);[7] John's account of the Capernaum sermon has Jesus promising to raise up on the last day those who eat his flesh and drink his blood (John 6.54); and Paul's account of the instituting of the Lord's Supper identifies it as a proclaiming of 'the Lord's death until he comes' (1 Corinthians 11.26). To participate in the bread and wine of the Lord's Supper, then, is not just to participate in the once-for-all sacrifice of Calvary, it is also to anticipate the future fulfilment of that sacrifice in the eschatological kingdom of God. As with every sacramental rite, the Lord's Supper is both genuinely (and primarily) a divine act and also genuinely (though secondarily) a human act: it is a divine act of promise and fulfilment through the means of a human act of promise and prayer. And here, as with baptism, the prayer is both for a present and immediate fulfilment of promise, a real participation in Christ, and also for a future and eschatological fulfilment of promise, a participation in the coming kingdom.[8]

The Letter to the Hebrews is unequivocal in its affirmation that, unlike the Aaronic priesthood, Christ's sacrifice was once-for-all ($\H{\alpha}\pi\alpha\xi$): 'Christ did not enter a sanctuary made with human hands...[n]or did he enter heaven to offer himself again and again...' (Hebrews 9.24-25). But the Epistle is similarly unequivocal in its affirmation of Christ's eternal high priestly office, his unceasing intercession, his continual mediation. Indeed, according to the argument of this letter, it is precisely because Christ's sacrifice was once-for-all, precisely because he is now risen and seated at the Father's right hand, that his sacrifice is eternally sufficient

---

6   *Doctrina de sanctissimo Missae sacrificio*, Council of Trent, session 22/1 (1562), cited in *ES*, Num. 938 (p. 330); cf. Macquarrie, *A Guide to the Sacraments*, pp. 139-40.

7   λέγω δὲ ὑμῖν, οὐ μὴ πίω ἀπ' ἄρτι ἐκ τούτου τοῦ γενήματος τῆς ἀμπέλου ἕως τῆς ἡμέρας ἐκείνης ὅταν αὐτὸ πίνω μεθ' ὑμῶν καινὸν ἐν τῇ βασιλείᾳ τοῦ πατρός μου; cf. Mark 14.25; Luke 22.18.

8   Note Jeremias' intriguing proposal that the Eucharist is a memorial before God of the sacrifice of the Son, an enacted prayer for the coming of the kingdom. Jeremias, *The Eucharistic Words of Jesus*, pp. 237ff.

and effective; he 'has a permanent priesthood'; he 'is able to save completely those who come to God through him' (Hebrews 7.24-25). It is, of course, by no means certain that the terminology of 'approach', recurring throughout this letter, is Eucharistic—but neither can such a possibility be excluded, indeed, there is much incidental material here to render such a context and interpretation likely. In the Lord's Supper we approach God through the mediation of this eternal high priest, humbly confident of receiving mercy and finding grace (Hebrews 4.16). In the Lord's Supper we approach one who, through his once-for-all sacrifice, can 'cleanse our consciences from acts that lead to death' (Hebrews 9.14; cf. 10.22). In the Lord's Supper we approach one who 'has made perfect for ever those who are being made holy' (Hebrews 10.14). And in the Lord's Supper we approach, not a tangible mountain and burning fire, but the 'heavenly Jerusalem'; 'thousands upon thousands of angels in joyful assembly'; the 'church of the firstborn'; and God himself, the 'judge of all people' (Hebrews 12.18ff.). By sharing in the Lord's Supper we participate through the Spirit in the once-for-all sacrifice of Christ and in the grace and mercy that are its outcome. By sharing in the Lord's Supper we participate through the Spirit in the eternal communion of the Father and the Son. By sharing in the Lord's Supper we participate in the communion of the saints, the one, holy, catholic, and apostolic Church; we share communion with 'the spirits of the righteous made perfect' (Hebrews 12.23). The once-for-all nature of Christ's sacrifice is not the denial but rather the affirmation and possibility of present participation and future fulfilment.

It should be no surprise, therefore, that this Letter to the Hebrews concludes by speaking of an 'altar' ($\theta\nu\sigma\iota\alpha\sigma\tau\eta\rho\iota\sigma\nu$) which we now have (Hebrews 13.10), of a 'sacrifice of praise' ($\theta\nu\sigma\iota\alpha$ $\alpha\iota\nu\epsilon\sigma\epsilon\omega\varsigma$) which we now may offer continually (Hebrews 13.15), and of good acts ($\epsilon\nu\pi\sigma\iota\iota\alpha\iota$) and of communion ($\kappa\sigma\iota\nu\omega\nu\iota\alpha$) which are 'sacrifices' ($\theta\nu\sigma\iota\alpha\iota$) with which God is pleased (Hebrews 13.16). As has already been admitted, there can be no certainty that such language constitutes a deliberate allusion to the Lord's Supper—indeed, given the absence of any explicit reference to the Supper within the letter it could be argued that such language is a deliberate evasion of reference to the Supper—but it is difficult (if not perverse) for us to evade such significance, just as probably it would have been difficult for the first readers of this Letter.

And in the light of the language with which the Letter to the Hebrews closes it is, at very least, appropriate to identify the Lord's Supper as a 'sacrifice of praise': it is a 'Eucharist', an expression of thanksgiving offered to God.[9] But it is surely also appropriate, not just in the light of such language, but also in the light of the participatory language that

---

[9]   Cf. Baillie, *The Theology of the Sacraments*, pp. 114ff.

recurs throughout the New Testament, to identify the Lord's Supper as a 'communion', as a sharing in Christ's once-for-all sacrifice, as a sharing in the altar that is his Cross.[10] And it is therefore appropriate, albeit in a specifically defined sense, to identify the Lord's Supper as a 'sacrifice'.

However, to identify the Lord's Supper as a sacrifice is not quite to identify it as an offering of Christ again, albeit 'bloodlessly', by priest or by Church.[11] Certainly we bring the bread and the wine and, in the act of communion, we offer ourselves afresh to God as 'living sacrifices' (Romans 12.1). But that Christ is truly offered again here (or better, that Christ's offering is re-presented here) is no mere human act: it is a divine act mediated through a human act by the Spirit; if it is a divine act in response to human prayer it is more fundamentally a human prayer in response to a divine promise. If, by our prayers, we move the Father, by the Spirit, to re-present the offering of the Son, it is most basically because we gather and pray in the light of the preceding promise that Christ's sacrifice will be re-presented here for us.[12] This question of that which we do within the Lord's Supper—whether we merely 'give thanks' or whether we 'consecrate'—will be re-engaged later in this chapter, of greater pertinence for this present discussion is the recognition that to identify the Lord's Supper as a sacrifice is not in any sense to detract from the once-for-all nature of Christ's Cross (indeed, I remain unaware of any key Catholic text that does so detract);[13] it is rather to identify the Lord's Supper as a sacrificial meal, as a genuine participation in that once-for-all sacrifice.[14]

And it is a genuine participation: to share in the bread and wine of the Lord's Supper is truly and really to share in the body and blood of Christ—his flesh is 'real food' and his blood is 'real drink'[15]—or, to express the matter in more traditional terms, the sacramental sign really

---

[10] Cf. Baillie, *The Theology of the Sacraments*, pp. 116ff.

[11] *'Et quoniam in divino hoc sacrificio, quod in Missa peragitur, idem ille Christus continetur et incruente immolatur, qui in ara crucis* semel se ipsum *cruente* obtulit...'. Council of Trent, session 22/2 (1562), cited in *ES*, Num. 940 (p. 332).

[12] '...Luther's thoughts carry him a step further (he is thinking out loud, as we say): he finally ventures to assert that, if we move Christ by our prayers to offer himself for us, then we do, in a way, offer Christ to God... In his commentary on a passage in the Book of Numbers (Num. 19:1-10), Calvin too speaks of "offering Christ," and he means by the expression much the same as Luther.' Gerrish, *Grace and Gratitude*, p. 153; cf. Martin Luther, *A Treatise on the New Testament, that is, the Holy Mass*, in *LW* vol. 35, 75-111, pp. 99ff.

[13] 'Rome wants to accept the mass-offering without devaluating the "once only" of Hebrews.' Berkouwer, *The Sacraments*, p. 260.

[14] For further discussion of the nature of the Eucharist as truly a sacrifice see Jenson, *Systematic Theology*, vol. 2, pp. 217-18.

[15] ʻἡ γὰρ σάρξ μου ἀληθής ἐστιν βρῶσις, καὶ τὸ αἷμά μου ἀληθής ἐστιν πόσιςʼ.

and actually contains and communicates that which it signifies; the participation in the body and blood of Christ attested by Paul in 1 Corinthians 10 and by Christ himself in the Synoptic Gospels and in John 6 is actual and real, it is no empty sign and no ineffective sign; we are truly changed here because we truly participate in Christ here.

There has been, of course, a forceful tendency amongst some Protestant commentators to deny any Eucharistic significance to the Capernaum sermon recorded in John 6: Jesus' language of eating and drinking are metaphors for coming to him and believing in him (v. 35); flesh (and blood?) 'count for nothing'; it is the Spirit who 'gives life' (v. 63).[16] Such evasions are extraordinary. Even if we read the narrative as an unembellished relating of an historical event, and even if we acknowledge (as the narrative leads us to acknowledge) that Jesus' first 'hearers' would have perceived no Eucharistic significance but would rather have found these words strange and confusing, it is surely unlikely that Jesus would have used such language without conscious reference to his coming sacrificial death and to the celebration he would institute as a means of participating in that sacrifice. But even if such 'original intention' cannot be established, surely it is entirely unthinkable that the first hearers of this Gospel would have missed such significance given both the blatancy of the language and the prominence of the Lord's Supper from the very earliest days of the Church. And for us now to deny such significance is simply disingenuous.

The language of this passage is wholly uncompromising (which, one suspects, is the underlying reason for its evasion now as much as for its recorded offensiveness then). For Jesus to speak of himself as the 'bread of life' caused his hearers to grumble (vv. 35-42). For Jesus to speak of eating this bread, which is his flesh, as a means to life caused his hearers to 'argue sharply' (vv. 48-52). For Jesus to speak (most starkly of all) of the necessity of chewing ($\tau\rho\omega\gamma\omega\nu$) his flesh and drinking ($\pi\iota\nu\omega\nu$) his blood caused 'many of his disciples' to turn back and to follow him no longer (vv. 53-66). Maybe one cannot entirely dismiss the possibility that this is just extraordinary metaphorical language for coming and believing (any more than, in these post-modern days, one can entirely dismiss the possibility that the narrative is an encrypted time-table for Judean camel trains), but a more straight-forward reading of the narrative identifies eating Christ's flesh and drinking Christ's blood as means of participating in eternal life (v. 54), as means of mutual indwelling (v. 56).

It is the reality of the Lord's Supper as a participation in Christ's body and blood, in his once-for-all sacrifice, that the overwhelming majority of the Church, for the overwhelming majority of its history, and from its

---

[16]   See for instance William Hendriksen, *The Gospel of John* (Edinburgh: Banner of Truth Trust, 1954), pp. 240ff.

earliest extant confessions, has unequivocally affirmed: the risen Christ is made present here in a unique manner and to a unique degree.[17] At risk of gross oversimplification, difficulties and controversies have tended to occur when the Church has sought to define this 'mystery' more closely. In the West, the doctrine of transubstantiation was dogmatically affirmed at the Fourth Lateran Council in 1215.[18] As Edward Schillebeeckx helpfully indicates, this interpretation of the mystery of the Lord's Supper by means of distinctions between Aristotelian notions of 'substance' and 'accidents' was both novel and a reaction to more popular 'sensualistic' understandings of the mystery.[19] By means of this distinction between 'substance' and 'accidents' Thomas Aquinas and others were clarifying that, while the 'substance'—the true identity of the bread and wine—was transformed into the body and blood of Christ, the 'accidents' of bread and wine—the outward appearance, texture, taste, smell, of the bread and wine (perhaps we now could say their empirical qualities, or even their 'physicality')—remained unchanged.[20] This interpretation was novel, as Schillebeeckx clarifies, not just in its rejection of any popular view of a 'sensual' change in the elements, but more radically in its use (or misuse) of these Aristotelian categories: Wycliffe (following Berengar)[21] disputes this doctrine of transubstantiation precisely because, in its separating of 'substance' from 'accidents', it

---

[17]   For confirmation of the antiquity of this understanding see Edward B. Pusey, *The Doctrine of the Real Presence, as Contained in the Fathers from the Death of St. John the Evangelist to the Fourth General Council* (Oxford and London: J. H. Parker, 1855); also J. Betz, *Die Eucharistie in der Zeit der Griechischen Väter* (Freiburg: Herder, 1955); both cited by Edward Schillebeeckx, *The Eucharist* (London: Sheed & Ward, 1968), pp. 66-67.

[18]   '[C]uius corpus et sanguis in sacramento altaris sub speciebus panis et vini veraciter continentur, transsubstantiatis pane in corpus, et vino in sanguinem potestate divina'. Fourth Lateran Council (1215), chapter 2, cited in *ES*, Num. 430 (p. 200).

[19]   'A completely new theological interpretation of the eucharistic presence arose in the thirteenth century in reaction to the "sensualistic" interpretation of the quite unique presence of Christ in the Eucharist ("in communion I really bite the true body of Christ") which had been generally prevalent although not accepted entirely without criticism, in the Middle Ages.' Schillebeeckx, *The Eucharist*, p. 11. This interpretation of Thomas Aquinas is similarly acknowledged by Rowan Williams in his essay on 'The Nature of a Sacrament', in John Greenhalgh and Elizabeth Russell (eds), *Signs of Faith, Hope and Love: The Christian Sacraments Today* (London: St Mary's Bourne Street, 1987), pp. 32-44 (p. 43).

[20]   *ST* III 75-77.

[21]   Berengar of Tours (c.999–1088) responded to Lanfranc of Bec (c.1005–89) with respect to the previous Eucharistic debate between Radbertus (786–c.860) and Ratramnus (d. c.868), disputing the doctrine of transubstantiation. John Wycliffe (c. 1329–84) anticipated several Reformation themes along with a restatement of Berengar's arguments.

offends Aristotelian assumptions.[22] But, as Wycliffe and later Zwingli were to demonstrate, once such a distinction and separation had been introduced its denial effectively evacuated the Supper of Christ's real presence.[23]

It would be all too easy, at this point, to lose one's way in a labyrinth of Aristotelian arguments, and to lose sight of the foundational confession that Thomas and others were trying to preserve—that Christ is truly present here and that we truly partake of his body and blood by means of this bread and wine, even though the physicality of the bread and the physicality of the wine appear to remain unchanged.[24] The more helpful question, surely, is whether, within a society where Aristotelian distinctions are less familiar, we can identify alternative means of expressing this same truth. And the urgency for such alternative expressions is reinforced by the suspicion that, at a popular level, this doctrine of transubstantiation is misappropriated (both by its proponents and more especially by its critics) as affirming precisely that all too 'physical' and 'sensual' change that it was formulated to deny.

In his very helpful book on this theme, Edward Schillebeeckx briefly discusses the proposal of F. J. Leenhardt that the reality of any entity is determined, not empirically, but by God's intention for that entity, an intention that can only be grasped by faith—or, in other words, something is whatever God says it is despite its appearance.[25] Though Schillebeeckx is uneasy concerning its apparent 'extrinsicism',[26] there is surely something both simple and attractive about this suggestion. If, following George Berkeley and Jonathan Edwards, we affirm an absolute

---

[22]   Schillebeeckx, *The Eucharist*, pp. 58ff.

[23]   Gerrish draws attention to Zwingli's reluctance to refer to any form of instrumentality: 'Zwingli was reluctant to acknowledge any other causality than that of God, the first cause. Hence the very notion of *sacramental* causality was offensive to him. It seems to detract from the immediacy of the divine activity if one assigns even an instrumental function to the creaturely elements of water, bread, and wine. Signs, for Zwingli, are not instrumental, but indicative or declarative. They have a twofold use: they signal the fact that something has already been accomplished by the activity of God, and they declare the commitment of the redeemed to live in faithfulness to the God who has redeemed them.' Gerrish, *Grace and Gratitude*, p. 164.

[24]   '[I]t seems very important to realize that the doctrine of transubstantiation itself was an attempt, however unsuccessful and unsound, to avoid crude and materialistic conceptions of what happens in the sacrament, and even to save the idea of the Real Presence from a crudely spatial interpretation.' Baillie, *The Theology of the Sacraments*, p. 100.

[25]   '[T]he substance of a reality is in the divine intention which is realised in it'. F. J. Leenhardt, *Ceci est mon corps* (Neuchâtel: Delachaux & Niestle, 1955), p. 31; quoted in Schillebeeckx, *The Eucharist*, p. 77.

[26]   '[T]he Catholic view of reality cannot admit the "extrinsicism" of the creative word of God'. Schillebeeckx, *The Eucharist*, p. 78.

and continuing dependence of all reality on God and on his creative word, then we must conclude that reality can only be that which God declares it to be. Nor is this (for Berkeley and Edwards, if not for Leenhardt) mere 'extrinsicism' or 'idealism' — divine perception is the sole ground, rather than the denial, of created reality. That God declares that this bread and wine, despite its continuing appearance as bread and wine, is truly and really the body and blood of Christ, a means of sharing in his once-for-all sacrifice, should foreclose all discussion (whether this accords with or offends Aristotelian categories is, frankly, irrelevant).

Schillebeeckx grants rather more space to a consideration of the notion of 'transsignification' as a contemporary means of accessing that which is being confessed through the doctrine of transubstantiation:[27] though the physical appearance of bread and wine remain unchanged, their true significance is no longer as bread and wine but as the body and blood of Christ. But here, surely (and as Schillebeeckx finally acknowledges), there is even greater danger of 'extrinsicism'.[28] In a context increasingly dominated by post-structuralism, 'significance' has come to displace 'meaning' (the latter being deemed inaccessible) and is seen as indicative of the 'response' of a reader, hearer (or partaker?). The reality of Christ's presence within the Lord's Supper, as with the reality of Christ's resurrection, simply is not dependent upon the Church's response of faith. The statement 'this is my body', like the statement 'Christ is risen', may call for faith, may be accessed and appropriated by faith, may be perceptible to faith and imperceptible without faith, but it is not dependent upon faith for its reality and truth. Christ's presence at the Lord's Supper, like Christ's resurrection, may be dependent upon divine perception but it is certainly not dependent upon our perception. The reality of Christ's presence at the Supper through the means of bread and wine may be received and appropriated by faith, but this reality cannot ultimately be dependent upon faith; it is ultimately dependent upon the determination and promise of God.[29]

---

[27]   Schillebeeckx cites Piet Schoonenberg and L. Smits as proponents of 'transsignification' or 'transfinalisation': Schillebeeckx, *The Eucharist*, pp. 117-18; cf. Joseph Powers, *Eucharistic Theology* (London: Burns and Oates, 1968), and Macquarrie, *A Guide to the Sacraments*, p. 133.

[28]   'The event in which Christ, really present in the Eucharist, appears, or rather, offers *himself* as food and in which the believer receives him as food therefore also includes a projective act of faith. This act does not bring about the real presence, but presupposes it as a metaphysical priority.' Schillebeeckx, *The Eucharist*, p. 150.

[29]   Hence Schillebeeckx concludes, '...I cannot personally be satisfied with a *purely* phenomenological interpretation without metaphysical density. Reality is not man's handiwork — in this sense, realism is essential to the Christian faith.' Schillebeeckx, *The Eucharist*, pp. 150-51.

For Martin Luther, famously, the words of Christ—'this is my body'—are non-negotiable.[30] Accordingly, for Luther, the 'Mass'—as a real partaking in Christ's body and blood—is constituted by God's promise.[31] Yet Luther's proposal—that Christ's body and blood are 'consubstantial' with the bread and wine of the Supper—tends to confuse rather than to clarify. Luther's alternative formula was motivated partly (one suspects) simply by the quest for an acceptable compromise, but more seriously by the desire to avoid Aristotelian categories in favour of a 'theological' category employed in the Nicene Creed, and subsequently crucial within the Chalcedonian definition—that Christ is 'consubstantial' with the Father according to his deity and 'consubstantial' with us according to his humanity.[32] But herein lies the first source of confusion: are we really to affirm that Christ, who is consubstantial with the Father and consubstantial with us, now also and similarly becomes consubstantial with bread and wine? Can we really affirm the mystery of the Eucharist in precisely the same terms as the mystery of the Incarnation?[33] Moreover, this maintaining of the terminology of 'substance', while rigorously avoiding the Aristotelian distinction between 'substance' and 'accidents', only serves to confuse that which the doctrine of transubstantiation was seeking to clarify. Luther's formula not only affirms that both Christ's body and the bread are substantially present at the Supper, it also inadvertently admits the possibility that Christ's body, like the bread, is 'accidentally' present—in other words, it reintroduces the possibility of an all too 'sensualistic' and 'physical' presence of Christ along with the 'physical' presence of the bread and wine.

But it is Luther's notion of the ascended Christ's ubiquity that (from the perspective of a Reformed tradition, at least) issues in most confusion (and adds weight to the suspicion of an all too 'physical' presence of Christ within the elements). One outcome within the Western Church of

---

[30]   The Marburg colloquy (1529) involved Luther, Melanchthon, Zwingli and Oecolampadius (among others) in disputation concerning the Eucharist. Luther refused to consider the bodily presence of Christ at the Eucharist as non-essential. 'The Marburg Colloquy and The Marburg Articles' (1529), in *LW* vol. 38, pp. 3-89.

[31]   Cf. Luther's description of the Mass in terms of 'promise' in Martin Luther, *The Babylonian Captivity of the Church* (1520), in *LW* vol. 36, pp. 3-126, esp. pp. 38ff.

[32]   The Council of Constantinople (381) affirms the Son as 'consubstantial' with the Father (*Et in unum Dominum Iesum Christum...consubstantialem Patri*), cited in *ES*, Num. 86 (p. 41). Subsequently, the Council of Chalcedon extended the definition to affirm Christ's true humanity (*consubstantialem Patri secundum deitatem, consubstantialem nobis eundem secundum humanitatem*), cited in *ES*, Num. 148 (p. 70).

[33]   Here, of course, we find another instance of the tendency in Lutheranism (and Catholicism) that was noted earlier in discussion of the Church, the tendency to qualify the uniqueness of Christ and Christ's incarnation by the manner of affirming Christ's presence in the Church and at the Supper.

the decisions of the Council of Chalcedon was an increasing focus of the doctrine of the *communicatio idiomatum*—generally this formula was interpreted in terms of the full participation of the single person of Christ in the distinctive characteristics of both his divine nature and his human nature; but occasionally the doctrine seems to have been expressed more radically (and problematically) in terms of the participation of Christ's assumed human nature in all of the distinctive characteristics of his divine nature and, correspondingly, the participation of Christ's divine nature in all of the distinctive characteristics of his human nature. In its more general expression this was little more than a dogmatic development and formulation of an idea that occurs generally amongst the Early Church Fathers, that the incarnate Christ was able to work miracles simply because he was the incarnate Christ.[34] The appropriateness and helpfulness of even this understanding of a *communicatio idiomatum*, both as a means of comprehending Christ's miracles and as a means of comprehending the reality of his humanity, was to be questioned generally within the Reformed tradition,[35] but this questioning seems to have been initiated by Calvin's unease with the use made of the doctrine by Luther with reference to Christ's Eucharistic presence. In several places Luther argues that, since the human nature assumed by Christ was made capable of the distinctive properties of the divine nature, and since, therefore, Christ's resurrection body participates in the ubiquity that is characteristic of his deity, the ascended Christ can be bodily present along with the bread and wine.[36] But if Christ's presence at the Eucharist is simply an instance of a general ubiquity there is nothing distinctive, less still unique, about his presence at the Eucharist.[37]

By way of contrast, Thomas Aquinas had spent much space discussing whether Christ's body is present in the sacrament 'as in a place' and concluded that this cannot be so:

> Christ's body is not in this sacrament in the same way as a body is in a place, which by its dimensions is commensurate with the place; but in a special manner which is proper to this sacrament. Hence we say that Christ's body is upon many altars, not as in different places, but *sacramentally:* and thereby we do not understand that

---

[34] See for instance Athanasius, *On the Incarnation*, trans. A Religious (London: Mowbray, 1953), III 18; cf. Augustine, *On the Holy Trinity*, I xii 23-24.

[35] See for instance *Institutes*, II xiii 4; John Owen, *A Discourse concerning the Holy Spirit*, pp. 159ff.

[36] See for instance Martin Luther, *Against the Heavenly Prophets in the Matter of Images and Sacraments* (1525), in *LW* vol. 40, pp. 73-223.

[37] As Douglas Farrow notes, '[w]hat is sacrificed for the sake of this *Christus praesens*, as Calvin noticed long ago, is his specificity as a particular man. Christ everywhere really means Jesus of Nazareth nowhere. In the ascension he becomes ἀ τόπος in the most literal sense: he is unnatural, absurd, for he has no place of his own.' Farrow, *Ascension and Ecclesia*, pp. 12-13.

Christ is there only as in a sign, although a sacrament is a kind of sign; but that
Christ's body is here after a fashion proper to this sacrament...'[38]

That which is clear here, as elsewhere in Thomas' discussion, is that to
speak of this sacramental presence is to say something entirely distinctive,
something entirely other than any general spatial presence: Christ's
presence here is unique; he is present here in a manner in which he is
present nowhere else; he is present here 'sacramentally'. For Thomas, as
for the tradition he represents, Christ is spatially (or locally) present in
heaven, at the right hand of the Father; he is present at the Eucharist,
therefore, in an entirely different manner; he is present at the Eucharist
'sacramentally' rather than spatially.[39] And it is this unique
distinctiveness of Christ's presence at the Eucharist that is obscured, if not
forfeited, by Luther's appeal to a general ubiquity (whether such
ubiquity, as an outcome of the *communicatio idomatum*, is an appropriate
assumption or not). Ironically, when Calvin (following Zwingli) refutes
this appeal to Christ's ubiquity, reaffirming that Christ is spatially (or
locally) present in heaven, he appears to be unaware that he is reiterating
one aspect of Thomas' previous argument.[40]

Unlike Zwingli (and contrary to the manner in which he has sometimes
been caricatured),[41] Calvin is certainly not content to reduce the Supper to
a mere memorial but attests a 'true and substantial partaking of the body
and blood of the Lord'.[42] Ultimately, Calvin is willing to leave the reality
of this partaking unexplained, simply believing that which here has been
promised:

---

[38]   *ST* III 75 1; cf. 76 3-6.

[39]   '[I]n no way is Christ's body locally in this sacrament' *ST* III 76 5; '...Christ's
body is at rest in heaven. Therefore it is not moveably in this sacrament.' *ST* III 76 6.

[40]   '[W]e do not doubt that Christ's body is limited by the general characteristics
common to all human bodies, and is contained in heaven...so we deem it utterly unlawful
to draw it back under these corruptible elements or to imagine it to be present
everywhere.' *Institutes* IV xvii 12; and again: '...Christ's body was circumscribed by the
measure of a human body...by his ascension into heaven he made it plain that it is not in
all places, but when it passes into one, it leaves the previous one.' *Institutes* IV xvii 30.

[41]   Berkouwer defends Calvin against Catholic and Lutheran doubts that he truly
held Christ to be 'really' present at the Eucharist. Berkouwer, *The Sacraments*, pp. 219ff.
Similarly Gerrish comments that 'Calvin was at no time a pure Zwinglian. From the very
first, he was convinced that Zwingli was wrong about the principle agent in both baptism
and the Lord's Supper. A sacrament is first and foremost an act of God or Christ rather
than of the candidate, the communicant, or the church.' Gerrish, *Grace and Gratitude*, p. 8.

[42]   '...I freely accept whatever can be made to express the true and substantial
partaking of the body and blood of the Lord, which is shown to believers under the sacred
symbols of the Supper—and so to express it that they may be understood not to receive it
solely by imagination or understanding of mind, but to enjoy the thing itself as
nourishment of eternal life'. *Institutes* IV xvii 19.

Now, if anyone should ask me how this takes place, I shall not be ashamed to confess, that it is a secret too lofty for either my mind to comprehend or my words to declare. And, to speak more plainly, I rather experience than understand it. Therefore, I here embrace without controversy the truth of God in which I may safely rest. He declares his flesh the food of my soul, his blood its drink... I offer my soul to him to be fed with such food. In his Sacred Supper he bids me take, eat, and drink his body and blood under the symbols of bread and wine. I do not doubt that he himself truly presents them, and that I receive them.[43]

Nevertheless, though this simple confidence in the promise that Christ's body and blood are truly here and truly partaken here should suffice, Calvin has previously indicated his distinctive understanding of the 'means' by which this real presence occurs, an understanding referring more overtly to the Spirit's mediating action than is common within the Western tradition:[44]

But if we are lifted up to heaven with our eyes and minds, to seek Christ there in the glory of his Kingdom, as the symbols invite us to him in his wholeness, so under the symbol of bread we shall be fed by his body, under the symbol of wine we shall separately drink his blood, to enjoy him at last in his wholeness. For though he has taken his flesh away from us, and in the body has ascended into heaven, yet he sits at the right hand of the Father—that is, he reigns in the Father's power and majesty and glory. This Kingdom is neither bounded by location in space nor circumscribed by any limits. Thus Christ is not prevented from exerting his power wherever he pleases, in heaven and on earth. He shows his presence in power and strength, is always among his own people, and breathes his life upon them, and lives in them, sustaining them, strengthening, quickening, keeping them unharmed, as if he were present in the body. In short, he feeds his people with his own body, the communion of which he bestows upon them by the power of his Spirit. In this manner, the body and blood of Christ are shown to us in the Sacrament.[45]

For Calvin, therefore, it is not that the ascended Christ is ubiquitous but rather that, though Christ is spatially located at the right hand of the Father, he can nonetheless mediate his presence to his people by his Spirit and, supremely and uniquely, he can mediate the reality of his body and blood by the Spirit through the bread and wine of the Supper. Moreover, while Calvin (like Thomas) denies that the substance of the bread and the

---

[43]   *Institutes* IV xvii 32.

[44]   Calvin's emphasis upon the mediation of the Spirit as the means through which the body and blood of Christ are made present to us, together with his overall understanding of the Supper as the means through which, by the Spirit, we are caught up into Christ's ascended life, is all remarkably reminiscent of a typically Eastern understanding of the Eucharist.

[45]   *Institutes* IV xvii 18.

wine is annihilated through its consecration,[46] he does not deny that through consecration 'a secret conversion takes place, so that there is now something other than bread and wine'.[47] Indeed, as B. A. Gerrish continually opines,[48] one can but wonder whether Thomas ought to be included amongst the 'older writers' whose interpretations Calvin admits.[49] And accordingly, notwithstanding Calvin's rantings against a doctrine of transubstantiation, one must ask whether his affirmation that the Supper 'consists of two parts, the earthly and the heavenly',[50] radically differs in significance from Thomas' affirmation of the 'substance' of Christ's body and blood and the 'accidents' of bread and wine.[51] Calvin's discussion is continually undermined, as Gerrish acknowledges, by an inconsistent use of the term 'substance' and by inadequate recognition of the distinctions between the various views he refutes.[52] Nevertheless, notwithstanding these limitations, it should be clear that this is no mere memorialism: while Calvin (like Zwingli) affirms the Supper as the means through which we are caught up into the ascended life of Christ, the means through which we commune with the Father, in the Son, and by the Spirit, he also affirms (unlike Zwingli) a real presence of Christ and a real partaking of Christ inasmuch as he affirms a real

---

[46]   *ST* III 73 3: '...in this sacrament the substance of the bread or wine is not annihilated'. The editor of this edition of the *Institutes* notes that it was William of Ockham who introduced the notion of the annihilation of the substance of the elements: '...*substantia panis non remanet post consecrationem*'. *Institutes* IV xvii 14, fn. 42 referring to William of Ockham, *The De sacramento altaris of William of Ockham*, ed. and trans. T. B. Birch (Burlington, Iowa: Lutheran Literary Board, 1930), pp. 182-83. Interestingly, the canon of Trent dealing with the doctrine of transubstantiation reaffirms the language of 'conversion': '*per consecrationem panis et vini conversionem fieri totius substantiae panis in substantiam corporis Christi Domini nostri, et totius substantiae vini in substantiam sanguinis eius*'. Council of Trent, session 13/4 (1551), cited in *ES*, Num. 877 (p. 306).

[47]   *Institutes* IV xvii 14.

[48]   Gerrish, *Grace and Gratitude*, p. 168; cf. p. 97.

[49]   'Indeed, I admit that some of the old writers used the term "conversion" sometimes, not because they intended to wipe out the substance in the outward sign, but to teach that the bread dedicated to this mystery is far different from common bread, and is now something else.' *Institutes* IV xvii 14.

[50]   *Institutes* IV xvii 14.

[51]   I gladly acknowledge my indebtedness to Varujan Smallwood, one of my students, for a quite excellent dissertation in which he explores in detail the similarities between Thomas and Calvin with respect to the Eucharist. Varujan Richard Smallwood, 'A comparison of Thomas Aquinas' and John Calvin's understanding of the Eucharist' (Spurgeon's College, the University of Wales: Unpublished BD dissertation, 2003).

[52]   Gerrish notes that the manner in which Calvin 'used the term "substance" and its cognates was, to say the least, confusing'. Gerrish, *Grace and Gratitude*, p. 178.

presence and action of the Spirit, mediating the body and blood of Christ to us under the signs of bread and wine.[53]

However, even if it is conceded that Calvin's distinction between the heavenly and the earthly, as a means of distinguishing between inner identity and outward form, may lack the precision of Thomas' distinction between 'substance' and 'accidents', it ought correspondingly to be conceded that Thomas' account lacks the explicit affirmation of the Spirit's mediating rôle that is predominant for Calvin:

> ...a serious wrong is done to the Holy Spirit, unless we believe that it is through his incomprehensible power that we come to partake of Christ's flesh and blood.[54]

Such reference to the Spirit is not entirely lacking in Thomas, it is at least implicit throughout his discussion and, insightfully, Thomas explicitly attributes the preservation of the 'accidents' of the bread and wine, as much as the conversion of 'substance' to Christ's body and blood, to the 'unlimited power' of God.[55] Nonetheless (and as has been noted previously) the tendency of Thomas (and of the tradition he represents) to speak of 'grace' where Calvin tends to speak of the mediating presence and action of the Spirit can only issue in an obscuring of the personal and 'free' character of God's presence and action within the sacrament. Too quickly we think of 'grace' as a 'something', and hence a 'something' at our disposal. The Holy Spirit is a 'someone' rather than a 'something'; the Holy Spirit is never at our disposal. Ironically, the tendency to objectify 'grace' itself undermines the gratuitousness of the Spirit's presence and action within the sacrament; it undermines the genuine graciousness of grace. And this tendency to objectify 'grace' inevitably issues in a corresponding tendency to focus upon our 'action' within the Supper, our 'disposing' of this 'grace', at the expense of the Spirit's free and gratuitous action.

All of which serves to draw attention to the other key issue raised by the passage cited at the beginning of this chapter since, alongside its starkly 'realist' language of our participation in Christ's body and blood under the signs of bread and wine, it identifies our 'action' within the Supper in terms of 'blessing' and 'breaking'. Indeed, the editors of the *NIV* have drawn attention to the controversy surrounding this second issue by their translation of the words εὐλογίας and εὐλογοῦμεν in terms

---

[53]   For an excellent discussion of the problems of Calvin's position (and an eschatalogical means of resolving them) see Douglas Farrow, 'Between the Rock and a Hard Place: In Support of (something like) a Reformed View of the Eucharist', *IJST* 3 (2001), pp. 167-86.

[54]   *Institutes* IV xvii 33.

[55]   'God...the first cause both of substance and accident, can by His unlimited power preserve an accident in existence when the substance is withdrawn...'. *ST* III 77 1.

of 'thanksgiving' and the giving of 'thanks' (rather than the more traditional translation in terms of 'blessing'). Do we simply give thanks for bread and wine and for that which they signify, or do we 'bless' bread and wine in a manner through which they become means of participating in that which they signify? And, if the latter, who are the 'we' who have the authority to bless the bread and the wine in this way?

P. T. Forsyth holds Cyprian responsible for the first explicit move towards sacerdotalism (an emphasis on priestly authority and action in the sacraments),[56] yet the tenor of Thomas' discussion, for all its affirmation of priestly authority, represents a significant qualification of that authority. Notwithstanding his tendency, following Augustine, to speak of grace rather than explicitly of the presence and action of the Spirit, Thomas consistently affirms God and God alone as the first or efficient cause of grace within the sacraments; God mediates this power through the priest, but the power remains God's own.[57] Moreover, even when Thomas affirms the priest's 'power' to consecrate the sacrament, he identifies this explicitly again as an instrumental power[58]—indeed, the instrumental (rather than agential) nature of priestly authority remains the basis on which Thomas can continue to affirm the validity of the sacrament even when celebrated by a 'wicked' priest.[59] John Macquarrie, therefore, is more probably correct in identifying the Council of Constance (1414–18) as representing the significant move towards a focus on the power of the priest by its unqualified reference to the priest as the one who consecrates (rather than the one through whom this consecration occurs).[60]

---

[56]   'When Cyprian described the priest as "imitating Christ's sacrifice, and offering a true and full sacrifice to God the Father," he was the chief culprit in effecting the change from a *sacrificium laudis* by the Church to a *sacrificium propitiatorium* by the priest.' Forsyth, *The Church and the Sacraments*, p. 272.

[57]   'There are two ways of producing an effect; first, as a principal agent; secondly, as an instrument. In the former way the interior sacramental effect is the work of God alone... In the second way, however, the interior sacramental effect can be the work of man, in so far as he works as a minister. For a minister is of the nature of an instrument...'. *ST* III 64 1; cf. III 62 1.

[58]   'The sacramental power is in several things, and not merely in one... Accordingly the consecrating power is not merely in the words, but likewise in the power delivered to the priest in his consecration and ordination... *For instrumental power lies in several instruments through which the chief agent acts*' (my emphasis). *ST* III 82 1.

[59]   '[T]he priest consecrates this sacrament not by his own power, but as the minister of Christ, in Whose person he consecrates this sacrament.' *ST* III 82 5.

[60]   '*Item, utrum credat, quod post consecrationem sacerdotis in sacramento altaris sub velamento panis et vini non sit panis materialis et vinum materiale, sed idem per omnia Christus, qui fuit in cruce passus et sedet ad dexteram Patris*'. Council of Constance, session 15 (1415), cited in *ES*, Num. 666 (p. 249); cf. Macquarrie, *A Guide to the Sacraments*, p. 129.

This move may appear subtle but it constitutes a move from instrumentality to agency, and a move from instrumentality to agency implicitly denies the unique agency of the Spirit. Both an agential and an instrumental understanding of priesthood imply a derived authority, both identify the priest as standing in the stead of Christ within the Supper; but whereas an agent acts independently on behalf of another, an instrument acts in an explicitly dependent manner, as the means through which another acts. A priest acting as an agent acts on behalf of Christ immediately; a priest acting as an instrument is one through whom Christ himself acts mediately. Or to put the matter more simply: does the priest at the Supper consecrate bread and wine on behalf of Christ, or does Christ at the Supper, through the Spirit, consecrate the bread and wine through the priest; does the priest, through ordination, receive a delegated authority to act in Christ's name, or does the priest, through ordination, receive a promise that Christ will act, by the Spirit, through the priest; does the priest possess a delegated authority to act, or does the priest pray, in the light of a sacramental promise given at ordination, for Christ to act through the Spirit? This quite fundamental question concerning the nature of Christian ministry (here termed 'priesthood' simply for the sake of the present discussion) will be discussed more fully in chapter 10 of this book—yet a response to this question must be anticipated here for the sake of this current question: is the genuine communion that occurs within the Supper an outcome of a delegated authority to consecrate through the uttering of words of institution, or an outcome of prayer in the light of a promise; is consecration a matter of incantation, or is consecration a matter of prayer; are we dealing here with 'magic', or with 'mystery'?

This distinction between consecration and prayer represents not so much the distinction between Catholic and Reformed understandings of the Supper as the distinction between Western and Eastern understandings of the Supper. Without prejudice to Calvin's definition of a sacrament in terms of promise and prayer, and without prejudice to Calvin's emphasis on the Spirit's mediation within the Supper, Reformed Eucharistic practice—as an outcome of its proper insistence upon the juxtaposition of Word and Sacrament—tends to focus on the significance (if not the efficacy) of the words of institution to no less a degree than does Catholic Eucharistic practice.[61] It is within the liturgy of Eastern Orthodoxy that

---

[61]   Hence Berkouwer comments that '[w]hen the Second Helvetic Confession speaks of the relation between Word and sacrament, it emphasizes strongly what the elements *become* through the Word. That "becoming" is the key to the specific relation between Word and sacrament. Evidently the Word and the sacraments may not be placed side by side, for the signs become sacraments only by virtue of the Word of God. The Reformed confessions also say that the elements are "consecrated" by the Word. That does not mean that the elements are changed or transubstantiated, but rather, this term

dependence upon the Spirit's mediation is made explicit through the 'epiklesis', the calling-upon the Spirit at the climax of the Eucharistic prayer.[62] Here there would seem to be an explicit celebration of an immediacy mediated by the Spirit through the priest. Indeed, through its tendency to focus upon the entire Eucharistic event, rather than on the detailed elements of that event, an Eastern liturgy would seem to draw attention away from anything we do here (or anything a priest does here) in a sustained celebration of the ascended Christ.[63]

It must be admitted that, apart from one possible interpretation of the act of 'blessing' (εὐλογέων) mentioned in 1 Corinthians 10.16, there is little within the New Testament to encourage the recitation of the words of institution specifically as an act of consecration (it should also be noted that the Passover ritual outlined in Exodus 12 and Deuteronomy 16 includes no specific act of consecration). Moreover, if the 'blessing' mentioned here reflects the 'blessing' spoken by Christ as he broke the bread at the 'Last Supper', we should also note that this 'blessing' of the bread is paralleled by a 'giving thanks' (εὐχαριστέων) for the wine in Matthew and Mark, and that Luke and Paul seem to substitute the latter term for the former in relation to the bread (all of which would seem to support the *NIV* translation of 1 Corinthians 10.16).[64] Rather than as an act of consecration, the recitation of the words of institution ought perhaps to be seen simply as a recounting of the story and, implicitly, as an invitation to indwell the story through coming and believing, and through eating and drinking with thanksgiving. Communion, therefore, occurs throughout the entire Eucharistic context and liturgy rather than solely at its conclusion; the reality of our participation in Christ occurs as an outcome of the entire Eucharistic process rather than through any

---

(which Rome also employs for the "consecration") is used to indicate the very important fact that the elements become seals by virtue of divine grace, and thus receive their functions in the acts of God.' Berkouwer, *The Sacraments*, pp. 46-47.

[62]   'It should speak explicitly about the action of the Holy Spirit and state clearly that *anamnesis is essentially inseparable from epiklesis*. The Holy Spirit in the eucharist actualizes that which Christ has performed once and forever.' Archbishop Kirill, 'The Significance and Status of BEM in the Ecumenical Movement', in Limouris and Vaporis (eds), *Orthodox Perspectives on Baptism, Eucharist, and Ministry*, pp. 79-95 (p. 85).

[63]   '[T]he whole liturgy is *sacramental*, that is, one transforming act and one ascending movement. And the very goal of this movement of ascension is to take us out of "this world" and to make us partakers of the *world to come*.' Schmemann, *The World as Sacrament*, p. 50.

[64]   In Matthew 26.26-27 Jesus takes the bread and blesses it (λαβὼν ὁ Ἰησοῦς ἄρτον καὶ εὐλογήσας), then takes the cup and gives thanks (λαβὼν ποτήριον καὶ εὐχαριστήσας). Similar wording is found in Mark 14.22-23. Both Luke 22.14ff. and 1 Corinthians 11 23ff. record Jesus 'giving thanks' (εὐχαριστήσας) for the bread and record no parallel thanksgiving for the wine.

single formulaic pronouncement.[65] The ultimate goal of the Supper, after all, is not the transformation of the elements but rather the transformation of the participants through their partaking of those transformed elements.[66] The ultimate goal of the Supper is our participation in Christ and our transformation through that participation—and that participation and transformation occurs through the entirety of our sacramental indwelling of Christ, through our indwelling of the gospel story, and through the mediating presence and action of the Spirit.

And if this is the case, if the reality of our participation in Christ's body and blood is an outcome of the Spirit's mediation in response to the entire Eucharist act as an act of prayer (without in any sense denying a proper priestly prerogative within that act of prayer), rather than an outcome of an incanted act of consecration, then the practice of venerating the reserved sacrament must be severely questioned. The problem here is not with the reservation of the sacrament as such—as John Macquarrie indicates, the practice of 'reserving' the sacrament, in order that those unable to attend the full Eucharistic celebration might nonetheless participate, is well-attested within the documents of the Early Church.[67] The problem here is rather with the supposition that Christ's body and blood are really present other than in the sacramental context of the Eucharistic celebration. Edward Schillebeeckx notes that '...Luther

---

[65] The point is made similarly by David McCarthy Matzko: 'In the Mass...if Christ is not present, then the eucharistic meal is unintelligible. Christ's presence and ritual performance sustain the intelligibility even of theories, like transubstantiation or trans-signification, which intend to explain what is going on. The theories are inadequate as explanations of the transformation of bread and wine into the body and blood of Christ insofar as they divide appearance from reality. The philosophical accounts are strained and offer little help in articulating the means by which Christ is present rather than hidden behind the attributes of bread. They show how bread is Christ despite its qualities of bread, rather than how the attributes of bread offer and can be seen as the presence of Christ in the concrete. In short, the theories are mere words, while Christ is present in the Eucharist, appearing through the words and actions *of celebrant and congregation*. The grammar and language of bodily movements and verbal expressions acknowledge a social and linguistic space where this particular bread and wine are Christ. Through action we are *oriented* to God's grace. The presence of Christ is *seen* in bread when a set of practices occasions possibilities for *seeing* by conforming the human agents to the events of God. Christ's presence is an event which transpires in space and time, through the worshipping community and by means of ritual action which establishes a world of social, linguistic, and metaphysical possibilities. In the doing of the "Do this in remembrance of me," Christ *is* our bread. Christ is present, and our ritual performance establishes the linguistic and material possibilities for bread and wine to be *recognized* as the body and blood of Christ.' David McCarthy Matzko, 'The Performance of the Good: Ritual Action and the Moral Life', *Pro Ecclesia* 7 (1998) pp. 199-215 (pp. 208-209).

[66] *ST* III 79; cf. *Institutes* IV xvii 2-3.

[67] Macquarrie, *A Guide to the Sacraments*, pp. 146ff.

accepted this unique presence only during the liturgy and therefore at communion (only *in usu*) and was sharply opposed to the Roman practice of "reserving" the sacrament'.[68] It would seem possible, however, to affirm a reservation of the sacrament as a means of including within the Church's celebration those who might otherwise be excluded without offending this '*in usu*' principle: such reservation is merely an extension of the act of communion. But the practice of venerating the reserved sacrament (which Macquarrie also robustly defends)[69] cannot be so readily accepted: this would be to affirm the unique sacramental presence of Christ other than *in usu*; other than within the sacramental context; other than within the context of participation and prayer; other than through the immediate mediating work of the Spirit. Thomas Aquinas argues persuasively that the body and blood of Christ are substantively present within the sacrament without dimensive extension in space.[70] Following Einstein (not to mention Augustine) it would seem entirely reasonable to expand the argument with respect to dimensive extension in time. Christ is present within the Supper sacramentally and substantively rather than 'physically' or empirically. His presence is mediated by the Spirit in the context of Eucharistic prayer and participation. The genuine conversion that takes place here occurs within this sacramental context and not beyond it. I do not doubt the devotional utility of this practice of venerating the reserved sacrament—but I do doubt its wisdom and appropriateness. Here, surely, there is the greatest danger of mistaking a sacramental presence for a physical presence; of mistaking a mediated presence for an unmediated presence; of mistaking a Eucharistic prayer for a magical incantation.

The greatest irony, the greatest tragedy, and perhaps the greatest apostasy of the Church is that the Lord's Supper, the central celebration of the Church's life and essence, given as a sign and focus of its unity, has become the principal sign and expression of its division. Both the immediate and the broader context of the passage cited at the beginning of this chapter constitute a sustained appeal for the Church's unity: '...we, who are many, are one body, for we all partake of the one loaf'. It should be noted that our unity with one another is an outcome of communion: it is not that we share communion as an expression of our unity (a unity defined and discovered in some other place or manner); it

---

68   Schillebeeckx, *The Eucharist*, p. 52.

69   Macquarrie, *A Guide to the Sacraments*, pp. 146ff.

70   '[B]ecause the substance of Christ's body is in this sacrament by the power of the sacrament, while dimensive quantity is there by reason of real concomitance, consequently Christ's body is in this sacrament substantively, that is, in the way in which substance is under dimensions, but not after the manner of dimensions, which means, not in the way in which the dimensive quantity of a body is under the dimensive quantity of place'. *ST* III 76.3 cf. 75 1.

is rather that we are united by virtue of sharing communion. Our participation in Christ is both the possibility and the manner of our participation in one another. For this reason those who, like Zwingli, undermine the reality of our participation in Christ at the Supper, inadvertently also undermine the reality of our unity with one another. It may be historically true that groups that have most stressed the Supper as a celebration of our unity with one another have tended to be groups that have qualified the unique reality of Christ's presence here—but in so doing they have redefined the nature of the Church's unity.[71]

This issue of the Church's unity, which is necessarily an issue of the Church's sacramental unity, will be revisited at the conclusion of this book. But for the present it must be conceded that, until, without hesitation, we can share communion together, every ecumenical pretension remains no more than pretension (for a denial of our sharing in communion can be no less than a denial of the validity of our common identity as the Church): we do not share communion as an expression of our unity; we share communion as the means of our unity; to seek unity through agreeing forms of words is to seek an inadequate form of unity and to seek it by inadequate means.

And differences of understanding, even 'confessional' differences (such, at least, that do not offend the catholic creeds of the Church) are a wholly inadequate basis for continuing such disunity: I have tried to demonstrate within this chapter that it is the reality of our participation in Christ, rather than the manner in which that participation is expressed or analysed, that is crucial. Indeed, since we are dealing here with the central sacramental mystery we must concede that this ultimately will defy all analysis; our forms of words will never be adequate. It is remarkable that, beyond the simple reference 'for us and for our salvation', the major confessions of the Church catholic make no attempt to define a doctrine of the atonement. In part, of course, this is simply because they would not have recognised the wholly regrettable disjunction between the person of Christ and the work of Christ that has increasingly come to characterise Western accounts of the atonement. But might it not also be because they recognised it as being beyond definition, because at the heart of the liturgy of the Early Church the atonement was celebrated as 'mystery'? Participation in this mystery is the means to confessional unity rather than

---

[71]   I am not thinking just of Zwingli and of some of the early Anabaptists: I am thinking more immediately of an attitude to the Supper that seems to dominate contemporary Free Church life. For a thoughtful account of the Supper as a celebration of ecclesial unity see Balthasar Hubmaier, 'A Form of the Supper of Christ' (1527), in *Balthasar Hubmaier: Theologian of Anabaptism*, trans. and ed. H. W. Pipkin and J. H. Yoder (Scottdale, PA: Herald Press, 1989), pp. 393-408; cf. J. D. Rempel, *The Lord's Supper in Anabaptism: A Study in the Christology of Balthasar Hubmaier, Pilgram Marpeck and Dirk Philips* (Waterloo, ON: Herald Press, 1993).

its outcome. To fail to receive one another as we have been received by Christ is itself apostasy.[72]

Nor, given that Judas was present in the Upper Room—and given that Jesus 'knew' Judas—can I conceive of any basis sufficient to exclude any baptised person or persons from participating here and from the grace that is offered here. But this latter point introduces the next theme for discussion.

---

[72]   'Accept one another, then, just as Christ accepted you, in order to bring praise to God.' Romans 15.7.

CHAPTER 8

The Sacrament of Cleansing

[Jesus] came to Simon Peter, who said to him, 'Lord, are you going to wash my feet?'

Jesus replied, 'You do not realise now what I am doing, but later you will understand.'

'No,' said Peter, 'you shall never wash my feet.'

Jesus answered, 'unless I wash you, you have no part with me.'

'Then, Lord,' Simon Peter replied, 'not just my feet but my hands and my head as well!'

Jesus answered, 'Those who have had a bath need only to wash their feet; their whole body is clean. And you are clean, though not every one of you.'

For he knew who was going to betray him, and that was why he said not every one was clean. (John 13.6-11)

The first difficulty encountered in any discussion of a sacrament of cleansing (or, more commonly, of penance) is a matter of identification and definition. Thomas Aquinas identifies three distinct 'parts' to the sacrament—contrition, confession, and satisfaction[1]—though when he defends the rite as truly a sacrament he does so not only by noting that, as with all sacraments, here we have an outward rite that is indicative of an inner reality, but also by affirming the sacramental dynamic of priestly absolution.[2] But how does this absolution relate to penance itself, as contrition, confession, and satisfaction, and are we, in fact, identifying two sacraments here rather than one?[3] As with the notion of the Mass as a sacrifice, it is the notion of penance as providing 'satisfaction' for sin that is generally resisted amongst Protestants as undermining the once-for-all

---

[1]   *ST* III 90 2.

[2]   *ST* III 84 1.

[3]   'Now it is evident that in Penance something is done so that something holy is signified both on the part of the penitent sinner, and on the part of the priest absolving...'. *ST* III 84 1. While John Calvin is entirely dismissive of penance as a sacrament he appears more tolerant of the sacramental nature of absolution: '...if any sacrament is to be sought here, can it not be far more plausibly boasted that the priest's absolution is more of a sacrament than penance, either inward or outward? For it could readily be said that it is a ceremony to confirm our faith in forgiveness of sins, and has the promise of the keys...'. *Institutes* IV xix 16.

nature of Christ's sacrifice at Calvary. And here too, as with discussions of the Lord's Supper, the matter is compounded by penal notions of sacrifice and retributory notions of justice.[4] More recently, as both John Macquarrie and Paul Haffner indicate, the sacrament has tended increasingly to be referred to as the sacrament of 'restoration' and Haffner notes that, historically, a 'medicinal' understanding of the sacrament has been stressed in the Eastern Church as distinct from the predominantly juridical emphasis of the West.[5] But if the 'medicinal' is stressed it becomes difficult ultimately to distinguish this sacrament of penance or cleansing from the sacrament of anointing or healing to be considered in the next chapter.

The narrative of Jesus washing his disciples' feet is cited at the beginning of this chapter, not merely by virtue of its undoubted poignancy, nor as possible justification for a sacrament of penance—penance, as such, is absent from the narrative (or at least explicitly absent) and though the rite of foot-washing has continued within the Church it has not ever (as far as I am aware) been granted sacramental status or been specifically linked to the sacrament of penance. It is cited rather, and simply, for its witness to the need for those already 'clean', who 'have had a bath', to have their feet washed. The imagery is graphic and transparent: it simply was not possible to walk the dusty roads of Judea without getting dirty feet—and dirty feet need washing, indeed, unless our dirty feet are washed by Christ we can have no continuing part in Christ. Our identity as already 'clean' does not negate the need to have our feet washed, it rather identifies that need: if we were wholly unclean our dirty feet would be a matter of consistency rather than of inconsistency; it is our essential and underlying identity as 'clean' that itself identifies the need and necessity of having our feet washed by Christ. And only by Christ: he calls us to wash one another's feet but unless he himself, as our Lord and Teacher, washes our feet, we have no part with him.

This tension between being 'clean' and 'having dirty feet', however, stands in contrast to the probable origins of a sacrament of penance (or, more properly in the historical context of its origins, a rite of reconciliation) which appears to have been more focused on the problem of apostasy, the possibility of losing one's salvation, than on the problem of dealing with that which was inconsistent with one's salvation. The *Shepherd of Hermas* allows for the restoration of the penitent after a single instance of post-baptismal sin—and, remarkably, it appears that

---

[4]   As, for instance, appears to be assumed in the Supplement to the Summa: *ST* Suppl. 12 2.

[5]   'The juridical tendency has been more evident in the West and the medicinal approach has been more stressed in the East.' Haffner, *The Sacramental Mystery*, p. 129; cf. Macquarrie, *A Guide to the Sacraments*, p. 89.

others adopted a less lenient stance.[6] And while a debate over whether, after baptism, one could sin *at all* without losing one's salvation might appear strange to us, it remains an entirely understandable response to the seriousness with which the New Testament treats both baptism and sin. The Letter to the Hebrews comprises a sustained appeal not to apostatise, but it appears to assume apostasy to be both possible and irrevocable:

> If we deliberately keep on sinning after we have received the knowledge of the truth, no sacrifice for sins is left, but only a fearful expectation of judgment and of raging fire that will consume the enemies of God. Anyone who rejected the law of Moses died without mercy on the testimony of two or three witnesses. How much more severely do you think those deserve to be punished who have trampled the Son of God under foot, who have treated as an unholy thing the blood of the covenant that sanctified them, and who have insulted the Spirit of grace? (Hebrews 10 26-29)

Nor should we too quickly sanitise the passage by emphasising a possible significance of the present continuous participle ἁμαρτανόντων (rendered in the *NIV* translation as 'keep on sinning'), or by drawing attention to the ultimate character of the sin envisaged, or by reinterpreting the passage through a focus on the implications of its probable context.[7] This Letter is not alone in the New Testament in treating with the greatest seriousness both the gravity of sin and the possibilities and responsibilities consequent upon baptism as truly a new birth. In the First Letter of John similarly we find the tension between the incongruity of sin in one baptised,[8] and the incongruity of the claim to be without sin.[9] But here too, and as a basis both for confession and absolution, we find an unqualified assurance of forgiveness and cleansing:

> If we confess our sins, he is faithful and just and will forgive us our sins and purify us from all unrighteousness...

---

[6] *The Pastor of Hermas*, in *ANF*, vol. 2, pp. 9-55; cited in Macquarrie, *A Guide to the Sacraments*, p. 92.

[7] If a possible context of the Epistle is an appeal to Jewish converts, fearful of the consequences of post-baptismal sin, not to resort to a continuation of the Jewish sacrificial system—since this would constitute a rejection of the once-for-all sacrifice of Christ—then the statement that there remains 'no sacrifice for sins' could be simply a reference to the sufficiency and ultimacy of Christ's sacrifice. Cf. Barnabas Lindars, *The Theology of the Letter to the Hebrews* (Cambridge: Cambridge University Press, 1991).

[8] 'Those who are born of God will not continue to sin, because God's seed remains in them; they cannot go on sinning, because they have been born of God.' 1 John 3.9. Note how the editors of the *NIV* again have made much of the present continuous tense of the verbs.

[9] 'If we claim to be without sin, we deceive ourselves and the truth is not in us...we make him out to be a liar and his word has no place in our lives.' 1 John 1.8ff.

My dear children, I write this to you so that you will not sin. But if anybody does sin, we have one who speaks to the Father in our defence—Jesus Christ, the Righteous One. He is the atoning sacrifice for our sins, and not only for ours but also for the sins of the whole world. (1 John 1.9 and 2.1-2)

As I have intimated previously, I would argue for a strongly sacramentalist reading of both these letters, for an implicit Eucharistic context underlying much of the argument of Hebrews, and for the explicit baptismal and eucharistic allusion of 1 John 5.6ff. as identifying the assumptions of the entire Letter. The problem of post-baptismal sin is inherently sacramental and it is therefore appropriate for the Church to identify a sacramental resolution. The problem of post-baptismal sin is inherently sacramental since through baptism we are included in Christ, we receive a new nature, we receive a 'sacramental character' which is indelible. Post-baptismal sin therefore, as is evident in both of these Epistles, is deeply incongruous with this sacramentally mediated character; it is a denial of sacramental identity. But it does not constitute a loss of sacramental identity—sacramental identity is indelible—the indelibility of sacramental identity is precisely that which constitutes the seriousness of post-baptismal sin: judgement begins 'with the family of God' (1 Peter 4.17). Herein lies the basis for the deadly warnings concerning the consequences of participating in the Lord's Supper 'in an unworthy manner' (1 Corinthians 11.27ff.); herein lies the horror of Judas (presumably) accepting the bread and wine at the Last Supper whilst betrayal was already festering in his heart. We fall under judgement precisely because of who we are; because sin—any sin, mortal or venial—conflicts with our sacramentally mediated identity in Christ.

To some degree the developing distinction between mortal sin and venial sin—or at least the manner in which mortal sin came to be designated—could be interpreted (or misinterpreted) as militating against the indelibility of sacramental character. Thomas Aquinas distinguishes mortal sin from venial sin both in respect of its nature and its effect: mortal sin militates against love,[10] and mortal sin separates us from God's grace. This language of 'separation', however, is problematic: we may be 'God-forsaking', we may radically turn away from his grace and act in a manner that repudiates his love and does violence to our neighbour, but are we ever 'God-forsaken'? We may be 'faithless', but he 'will remain faithful'; he cannot 'disown' himself even when we disown him and, in that act, are disowned by him (2 Timothy 2.12-13). Even in Israel's utter unfaithfulness to God, and even in the exile and in his disowning of them in their unfaithfulness, he remains their God and they remain his people;

---

[10]   '[E]very mortal sin is contrary to charity'. *ST* I-II 71 4; cf. I-II 88; and II-II 184 2.

they are not ultimately rejected;[11] there is no 'certificate of divorce'.[12] God's judgement here (if not everywhere) is purgative rather than 'repudiative'. In a sacrament of restoration it is not God who needs to be reconciled with us but we with him. God is not fickle or double-minded; his attributes or 'perfections' are not in tension; he is 'simple'; his wrath is not the opposite of his grace but rather the form that his grace takes when it is opposed.[13] The essence and gravity of judgement, then, is an outcome of the presence and persistence of God in his utter faithfulness, it is not an outcome or manifestation of his absence. Like Job, we may even long for God to 'look away' from us—but he never will,[14] and that is what renders his judgement so grave.

This is not to deny the helpfulness and appropriateness of the distinction between mortal sin and venial sin; between that which militates against love and that which, though offensive and objectionable, does not of itself militate against love; between that which is entirely incompatible with our identity in Christ and that which, though a fault or failing, is not itself a repudiation of that identity. But it is to resist the language of separation. And it is to re-affirm (with Thomas Aquinas) that sacramental character is indelible,[15] that not even mortal sin can nullify that which has been mediated by the Spirit through baptism, and that this indelible identity itself marks the gravity of the mortal sin which denies it:

> It is impossible for those who have once been enlightened, who have tasted the heavenly gift, who have shared in the Holy Spirit, who have tasted the goodness of the word of God and the powers of the coming age, if they fall away, to be brought back to repentance, because to their loss they are crucifying the Son of God all over again and subjecting him to public disgrace. (Hebrews 6.4-6)

That which is declared impossible in this deeply disturbing passage is not the prospect of forgiveness but the prospect of being brought back to repentance (πάλιν ἀνακαινίζειν εἰς μετάνοιαν). The finality of the language in this passage, together with the discouragement from praying for those who sin in a manner 'that leads to death' (1 John 5 16-17), may lead us to conclude that the sin here envisaged is more radical and extreme than that subsequently identified as 'mortal sin' within the Christian tradition: here is an act so decisive as to place one beyond the possibility of repentance; here therefore is an apostasy that refuses reconciliation and resists grace even into eternity. But the problem

---

11   E.g., Isaiah 41.8-9 and elsewhere throughout Isaiah.

12   Isaiah 50.1; cf. Hosea 2.

13   'The love of God burns where they are, but as the fire of His wrath which consumes and destroys them'. *CD* IV/1, pp. 220f.

14   Job 7.19ff.

15   *ST* III 63 5.

explicitly identified here is not the reconciliation of God to the apostate but rather the reconciliation of the apostate to God—to those who confess their sin there is unequivocal assurance of forgiveness. But the first part of penance, of restoration, is contrition: the penitent need not be disturbed by such passages, but not so the impenitent.[16] There is here no basis for a cheapening of grace: sin must be confessed; we cannot come to God other than in repentance; other than as those identified with Christ's Cross as the means to his resurrection and ascension.[17]

Ironically it was the common charge of the Reformers that the penitential system itself, together with the sale of indulgences, had issued actually in a cheapening of grace; that which had been intended to enable contrition had come to militate against it.[18] Indeed, whenever grace is misconstrued as a 'something' at our disposal, and whenever the Christian minister (or priest) is perceived as an agent administering that 'something' rather than as an instrument through whom the Spirit mediates true grace, genuine contrition is bypassed and the Holy Spirit is reduced to an automaton. All too easily an appropriate notion of *ex opere operato*, as a reference to the objective 'being-givenness' of grace through the sacrament, is misappropriated as a reference to the objective 'givenness' of grace within the sacrament; the mediated is reduced to the unmediated; the objective is reduced to the manipulable; the external displaces the internal.[19]

But the late Medieval period had no monopoly on such potential cheapening and, with doubled irony, one charge of the Council of Trent

---

[16]   'It is...erroneous to say that any sin cannot be pardoned through true Penance. First, because this is contrary to Divine mercy... Secondly, because this would be derogatory to the power of Christ's Passion, through which Penance produces its effect, as do the other sacraments... Therefore we must say simply that, in this life, every sin can be blotted out by true Penance.' *ST* III 86 1.

[17]   'The worthiness demanded by the Lord's Supper consists, then, in acknowledging one's unworthiness and in knowing that the Supper has been instituted for the "unworthy" who proclaim in the Lord's Supper the death of Christ, not their righteousness. The "unworthiness" can keep us from the Lord's table only if it reveals itself in a disregard of guilt and forgiveness.' Berkouwer, *The Sacraments*, p. 258.

[18]   It ought to be noted that John Calvin begins his brief discussion of penance by ruing the deterioration from the extreme seriousness with which the rite of reconciliation was practised in earlier times. *Institutes* IV xix 14. Cf. Martin Luther, *Ninety-Five Theses or Disputation on the power and efficacy of indulgencies*, in *LW* vol. 31, pp. 25-33, Theses 1-4; cf. Martin Luther, *Explanations of the Ninety-Five Theses or Explanations of the Disputation concerning the value of Indulgencies*, in *LW* vol. 31, pp. 83-252; cf. Luther's *The Sacrament of Penance* (1519), in *LW* vol. 35, pp. 3-22.

[19]   'The design of the penitential system, no doubt, was to encourage moral seriousness both before and after the reception of grace. But it failed, in the eyes of the reformers, to display either the severity of God's judgment on sin or the wholly unconditioned character of God's grace.' Gerrish, *Grace and Gratitude*, p. 90.

against the Reformers (whether justly or unjustly made) was that the Reformation doctrine of justification by faith alone itself cheapened grace.[20] And it would be difficult to conceive of anything more liable to cheapen grace than the all too common contemporary notion that one becomes a Christian by signing a 'decision card', and that once such a 'confession' has been made one is eternally secure.[21] Both the seriousness of sin and the graciousness of grace are belittled here. It is the argument of this book that any notion of unmediated immediacy, whether through a focus on individual 'felt experience' or through an objectifying of grace, not only issues in an obscuring of the Spirit's mediation of God's grace but also misrepresents the grace which is God's eternal nature and the mediated form of God's relatedness to the world. And in this present discussion it must also be concluded that both presumptions—the presumption of unmediated 'felt experience' as much as the presumption of a grace at our disposal—militate against true contrition and thereby militate against true renewal and the possibility of spiritual growth. Indeed, any form of presumption, by definition, militates against progress: the prerequisite for genuine progress is an honest recognition of where we are. Whatever objections may justly be levelled against the legalism and unkindness of the implementation of the 'ban' amongst some early Anabaptists (and, in context, it should be remembered—as was noted earlier—that the 'ban' was significantly less unkind than the burning of an offender at the stake), at least it was indicative of a disciplined seriousness, of a refusal to treat incoherence lightly, of a recognition that to be a Christian was to follow Jesus. Perhaps the test of the authenticity of any spirituality is the seriousness with which it treats the incoherence that is sin.

And such seriousness begins with confession:

> If we confess our sins, he is faithful and just and will forgive us our sins and purify us from all unrighteousness…. (1 John 1.9)

To affirm the necessity of confession, of repentance, is not quite the same thing as affirming the necessity of the rite of penance.[22] Valid confession can be made, and has been made within the Church catholic, through other forms than the private and oral confession of the late Medieval rite of penance. As has already been noted, John Calvin expresses regret at the demise of the practice of public confession that characterised the Church's earlier discipline, together with the reservation of a rite of

---

[20]   Council of Trent, session 6 (1547), cited in *ES*, Num. 792-843 (pp. 284ff.).

[21]   See for instance R. T. Kendall, *Once Saved, Always Saved: Biblical Assurance for Every True Believer* (London: Hodder and Stoughton, 1983).

[22]   Such equivalence is a poorly grounded assumption made by Thomas Aquinas: *ST* III 84 5.

restoration to a bishop (rather than a priest)—here issues of sin and restoration were treated with the greatest seriousness.[23] But here also there may be some disingenuity since, as Calvin would have been aware, there is little evidence of this older rite of open confession and public restoration being implemented in cases of venial sin, or indeed in many cases that would later be categorised as mortal sin. There certainly is an appropriateness for the public restoration of one who has previously and publicly turned entirely away from Christ—and, within churches that recognise episcopacy, it is appropriate that a bishop should officiate at such rites of public restoration. Similarly it may be appropriate for any 'open' sin to be openly confessed and for a public declaration of absolution and restoration to be made. But there is no merit in the public confession of the 'private' sins, frailties, and temptations with which we all struggle—indeed, there may be great harm in such potential self-indulgence. And here, to one for whom (as a Baptist) the Catholic rite of private penance is entirely foreign, the rite of private penance seems both appropriate and helpful.

Of course I am not denying that through Christ, and through Christ alone, we have access 'into this grace in which we now stand' (Romans 5.2); that there is but one mediator between God and us (1 Timothy 2.5); and that we can approach this sympathetic high priest and receive his mercy and grace (Hebrews 4.14ff.). But I am also aware that the central thesis of this book is that God mediates this mercy and grace, by his Spirit, through human and created instrumentality; that we are encouraged to confess our sins to one another and to pray for one another (James 5.16); and that we are human persons with an inherent desire for a human listener and for a spoken word of assurance, albeit as mediating a divine listener and a divine word of assurance. Moreover, though I write as a Baptist for whom the Catholic rite of private penance is entirely foreign, I would have been a very great fool had I not, over the years, sought out a series of 'soul-friends' in whom I confidently could confide, receiving the discipline of counsel and of rebuke, and receiving the grace of assurance. And though I write as a Baptist there have been many occasions when, whether I have thought of myself as a 'priest' or not, I have acted as a priest, hearing on behalf of Christ and speaking on behalf of Christ in the confidence of pastoral ministry. And though I am, of course, aware that even within the context of a formal practice of penance, spiritual (and highly public) disasters can occur and have occurred, I cannot help but wonder how many spiritual disasters (some of them highly public) may have been averted had some formal discipline of spiritual direction and confession been in place. A discussion of the nature of Christian ministry will follow in chapter 10 of this book—but it

---

[23]   *Institutes* IV xix 14.

is high time some Evangelical ministers abandoned delusory notions of themselves as senior managers or spiritual entrepreneurs and rediscovered the responsibilities of pastoral care, of the 'cure of souls'.

And without inappropriately anticipating the discussion reserved for chapter 10, Jesus commits to his disciples, and not just to Peter, the responsibility and the authority of binding and loosing (Matthew 18.18ff.), the responsibility and the authority of forgiving sins (John 20.21ff.). It can be argued that this responsibility and authority is inherently 'apostolic'. It can be argued that this responsibility and authority is therefore 'appropriate' to those called and separated for Christian ministry. But without prejudice to this later argument, this is a mediated responsibility and authority, mediated by the Spirit, mediated through the Church, mediated through the ministers given to the Church by the ascended Christ. Only Christ has the authority to forgive sin, only Christ has the authority to wash our dirty feet and to pronounce us clean—but Christ mediates this authority, by his Spirit, through those he has so called. In Christ's name and in the power of the Spirit the Christian minister has the authority (and the responsibility) to say 'I absolve you' (*ego te absolvo*), to pronounce forgiveness, to enact restoration. Here surely without doubt (and as Calvin seems to concede) there is a truly sacramental act, an act explicitly ordained by Christ, an act that is a mediation of grace, an act through which that which is signified is effected.

But confession and absolution appropriately occur corporately and publicly just as they appropriately occur individually, whether privately or publicly. And, in particular, confession and absolution appropriately occur corporately within the context of the liturgy of the Lord's Supper. The Anglican liturgy of the Supper begins with the prayerful recognition that our lives are open to God and that we come to him in need of the cleansing that is mediated by his Spirit. It continues with a general confession and a general absolution. And without gainsaying all that has been said previously concerning the helpfulness and appropriateness of private confession, this general confession and absolution should be accepted as valid and sufficient. Indeed, in some respects it is more sufficient simply by virtue of being 'general'. An insistence upon a detailed and comprehensive private confession inevitably issues in legalism, selectivity and artificiality: inevitably we focus on specific 'commands' that have been broken; inevitably we omit to itemise the dispositions and the struggles that are continuous and, often, apparently trivial. But more pertinently, we tend to focus on that which ought not to have been done rather than on that which ought to have been done—and it is the latter that lies at the foundation of the former:

> Jesus replied: '"Love the Lord your God with all your heart and with all your soul and with all your mind." This is the first and greatest commandment. And the second is like it: "Love your neighbour as yourself." All the Law and the Prophets hang on these two commandments.' (Matthew 22.37-40)

A general confession is comprehensive by its very nature but it need not thereby be insincere or cursory. Rather, by identifying the essence of sin—that we have not done that which we ought to have done—a general confession identifies that which can too easily be overlooked within private confession and yet which lies at the root of all that there is confessed.

As was noted previously, John's Gospel includes no account of the institution of the Lord's Supper other than the allusion to the Supper in Jesus' sermon at Capernaum. Rather, in the place where we would expect an account of the Supper, we find this narrative of Jesus washing his disciples' feet. And maybe (and no more than maybe), by including this narrative at this point, the evangelist is drawing attention to a further aspect of the significance of the Supper. Here, where Christ offers himself to us again through the agency of the Spirit and the physicality of bread and wine, he repeatedly stoops to cleanse us, and thereby to assure us afresh that we are his, participating in him, loved by him. If the Supper is a participation in his Cross, then this narrative is an anticipation of his Cross and a storied exposition of its significance. Pointedly, the evangelist introduces the story with a series of participles identifying the context in which Jesus did what he did: he did what he did knowing that his time had come; he did what he did loving his own; he did what he did during the Supper; he did what he did the devil having already prompted Judas to betray him; he did what he did knowing that the Father had given him everything, that he had come from God and was going to God.[24] Jesus' washing of his disciples' feet was a deliberate act in the context of this consciousness. And perhaps most astonishingly it was a deliberate act in the full knowledge of Judas' imminent betrayal. Judas was still present. Jesus stooped before Judas and washed his feet—and Judas made no protest. Jesus (presumably) offered bread and wine to Judas and he accepted them. And Jesus knew. When Thomas Aquinas ponders whether a priest should withhold the bread and wine from sinners he concludes that, though the priest should withhold bread and wine from 'notorious' sinners, the priest ought not to deny bread and wine to those who 'ask for it' and who are not 'open sinners'.[25] Of course there is a pastoral responsibility to discourage hypocrisy and to guard the sacrament from

---

24   John 13.1ff.

25   'A distinction must be made among sinners: some are secret; others are notorious, either from evidence of the fact, as public usurers, or public robbers, or from being denounced as evil men by some ecclesiastical or civil tribunal.' *ST* III 80 6.

mockery—but Jesus knew the betrayal in the heart of Judas and Jesus yet gave him bread and wine and stooped to wash his feet. To eat the bread or to drink the wine 'in an unworthy manner' is to 'be guilty of sinning against the body and blood of the Lord' (1 Corinthians 11.27),[26] but the responsibility for such sin, and the responsibility for self-examination, is placed explicitly upon the participant rather than upon the officiating minister. The guilt belongs to Judas in receiving bread and wine, not to Jesus in offering bread and wine, even though he knew what he knew.

To withhold bread and wine from anyone is the gravest imaginable censure and should only occur, as Thomas indicates, in response to the most notorious lack of repentance. It is the gravest censure because it is a withholding of the means of grace, the means of cleansing, the means of restoration. We are not restored through some other means or in some other place in order that we might participate in the sacraments; we are restored through our participation in the sacraments; we are restored sacramentally. And therefore it is not merely appropriate, it is imperative that the liturgy of the Lord's Supper includes a pause for prayerful self-examination, includes a general confession, includes a general absolution. Such constitute sufficient penitence, but such are imperative and irreducible. No one offering such penitence and receiving such absolution need be excluded from communion, but each must have opportunity to exclude themselves, and anyone participating without sincere penitence only compounds their estrangement from the grace of God. We either judge ourselves here or we render ourselves liable to devastating judgement.

And we do judge ourselves here: just as in baptism and in the Lord's Supper we participate in Christ's resurrection and ascension by participating in his death, so also in contrition and confession we identify ourselves again with the one who knew no sin and yet was made sin for us (2 Corinthians 5.21). Christ comes to stand in the place of judgement, the place that is rightfully ours, as both judge and judged.[27] And through the sacraments of baptism and the Lord's Supper, as also through true penitence, we identify with him and participate in his bearing of that judgement in our place. John McLeod Campbell writes of Christ offering a 'vicarious repentance' on our behalf and, whether or not we might consider this to be a sufficient account of atonement theology (or even an explicitly biblical notion), Christ's baptism, in anticipation of his Cross, is

---

[26]   '[I]t is manifest that whoever receives this sacrament while in mortal sin, is guilty of lying to this sacrament, and consequently of sacrilege, because he profanes the sacrament: and therefore he sins mortally.' *ST* III 80 4.

[27]   For an expounding of such language see Barth's discussion of the 'Judge Judged in Our Place', *CD* IV/1, pp. 211ff.

an identification with repentant sinners.[28] Therefore, when we come again in confession as repentant sinners, just as we came previously in baptism, we identify again with him and enter again into the sacrifice he offers and the judgement he bears. And here perhaps we may have grounds for speaking of the 'satisfaction' which Thomas Aquinas identifies as the third part of penance and, consequently, grounds for speaking of the sacramentality of penance alongside the undoubted sacramentality of absolution.

As was mentioned earlier, an understanding of penance, and in particular an understanding of 'satisfaction' as the third part of penance, was rendered more problematic by the gradual confusion of the notion of satisfaction and the notion of penalty. In his book *Christus Victor*, Gustav Aulén argued that a 'classical' account of the atonement that characterised the early years of the Church and that focused on the victory of Christ over sin, death, and the devil, came to be replaced during the Medieval period, and particularly following the work of Anselm of Aosta,[29] by a penal theory, a notion of Christ bearing the penalty incurred by human sin.[30] Aulén is making a crucial point but one suspects the matter to be somewhat more complex and the book is flawed in at least two major respects: firstly it overstates the consensus within the Early Church concerning the work of Christ; secondly it assumes too great a correlation between Anselm's 'satisfaction' theory and the 'penal' theories that were to emerge around the time of the Reformation.[31] Anselm's theory, simply put, is that through our sin we have dishonoured God, rendering ourselves subject to punishment, and that Christ, through his perfect obedience even to death, has offered to God the honour we failed to offer and greater honour besides, thereby satisfying God's honour and averting the punishment to which otherwise we would be liable. For Anselm, therefore, satisfaction is the alternative to punishment rather than a synonym for punishment.[32] By the time of the Reformation,

---

[28]   John McLeod Campbell, *The Nature of the Atonement and its Relation to Remission of Sins and Eternal Life* (London: James Clarke, 1959).

[29]   Anselm (1033–1109) was born at Aosta, Savoy, and, following service first as Prior and then as Abbot at Bec, in Normandy, was consecrated Archbishop of Canterbury in 1093.

[30]   Gustav Aulén, *Christus Victor: An Historical Study of the Three Main Types of the Idea of the Atonement*, trans. A. G. Herbert (London: SPCK, 1931).

[31]   For a rather different account of these developments see T. J. Gorringe, *God's Just Vengeance: Crime, Violence and the Rhetoric of Salvation* (Cambridge: Cambridge University Press, 1996).

[32]   Anselm, *Why God became Man*, trans. E. R. Fairweather, in *A Scholastic Miscellany: Anselm to Ockham. Library of Christian Classics X* (London: SCM Press, 1956). For excellent analyses of Anselm's argument see chapter 4 of Colin E. Gunton's *The Actuality of Atonement: A Study of Metaphor, Rationality and the Christian*

and especially in the work of John Calvin, the notions of punishment and of satisfaction had become confused and Christ's death was perceived as his bearing our punishment in our place.[33] But there is considerable difference between Christ doing on our behalf that which we have failed to do and Christ bearing on our behalf the punishment consequent upon that which we have done.[34]

At the root of this confusion there would seem to be a confusion between two distinct understandings of law and of justice, a confusion between *Torah* and *Lex*, a confusion between law as a means of maintaining a covenant relationship and law as a means of retributive justice. And, of course, any confusion concerning the nature of the satisfaction offered by Christ on our behalf is inevitably reflected in a confusion concerning the nature of the satisfaction offered in penance (though it is probably impossible now to determine which development came first or whether the confusion was simultaneous).[35] Indeed the confusion here is at least partly semantic: the English word 'penance' is related both to the English word 'penitence' and the English word 'penalty'—but penalty does not necessarily imply penitence and penitence does not necessarily imply penalty.[36]

This tension (if not confusion) is amply illustrated within the *Summa Theologica* of Thomas Aquinas—or rather within an apparent distinction between the text of the *Summa* itself and the text of the Supplement to the *Summa* compiled on the basis of Thomas' earlier commentary on Peter Lombard's fourth book of *Sentences*—a commentary completed by Thomas before he was thirty years of age. In the first place, within the *Summa* itself, Thomas expounds the passion of Christ in terms of the deliverance and redemption effected through that passion, in terms of sacrifice, and in terms of satisfaction (in language reminiscent of that of

---

Tradition (Edinburgh: T & T Clark, 1988), or Stephen Holmes' essay 'The Upholding of Beauty: A Reading of Anselm's *Cur Deus Homo*', in his *Listening to the Past*, pp. 37-49.

[33]   '[U]nless Christ had made satisfaction for our sins, it would not have been said that he appeased God by taking upon himself the penalty to which we were subject.' *Institutes* II xvii 4; cf. II xvi 5.

[34]   It is certainly possible to read several New Testament texts in the light of a notion of penal substitution—but it is not necessary to read them in this way. Indeed, even the text of Isaiah 53.5—'...the punishment that brought us peace was upon him...'—could be read more appropriately as reference to a purifying chastening than a retributive penalty. For a discussion of this see John Goldingay, 'Old Testament Sacrifice and the Death of Christ', in John Goldingay (ed.), *Atonement Today: A Symposium at St John's College, Nottingham* (London: SPCK, 1995), pp. 3-20.

[35]   It is at least possible that a penal notion of penance was bequeathed to Catholicism by Celtic Christianity.

[36]   Note the similar relation between the Latin words *poena* and *paenitentia* (*poenitentia*).

Anselm).[37] And when Thomas comes to speak of the penalty and punishment due to God on account of our sin he speaks of Christ, not bearing this punishment, but rather paying the debt and fulfilling the obligation that releases us from this punishment.[38] But more pertinently, Thomas defines penance, not as a 'penalty', but as a 'virtue', that is to say, as a habit or disposition.[39] And similarly, when earlier he speaks of the necessity of penance, he refers both to the power of Christ's Passion operating through the priest's absolution and the co-operation of the penitent in the destruction of sin (rather than a sharing of the penitent in the punishment for sin)—and here Thomas compares penance with medicine.[40] However, within the Supplement to the *Summa*, satisfaction, as the third part of penance, is identified both as a virtue and as an act of justice—and justice is defined in explicitly Aristotelian terms as the restoring of an 'equality of proportion'.[41] Moreover satisfaction, while

---

[37]   '[B]y suffering out of love and obedience, Christ gave more to God than was required to compensate for the offense of the whole human race. First of all, because of the exceeding charity from which he suffered; secondly on account of the dignity of His life which He laid down in atonement, for it was the life of the One who was God and man; thirdly, on account of the extent of the Passion, and the greatness of the grief endured...therefore Christ's Passion was not only a sufficient but a superabundant atonement for the sins of the human race...'. *ST* III 48 2.

[38]   'Since, then, Christ's Passion was a sufficient and a superabundant atonement for the sin and the debt of the human race, it was as a price at the cost of which we were freed from both obligations. For the atonement by which one satisfies for self or another is called the price, by which he ransoms himself or someone else from sin and its penalty... Now Christ made satisfaction, not by giving money or anything of the sort, but by bestowing what was of greatest price—Himself—for us. And therefore Christ's Passion is called our redemption.' *ST* III 48 4.

[39]   'Now the offense of mortal sin is due to man's will being turned away from God, through being turned to some mutable good. Consequently, for the pardon of this offense against God, it is necessary for man's will to be so changed as to turn to God and to renounce having turned to something else in the aforesaid manner, together with a purpose of amendment; all of which belongs to the nature of penance as a virtue.' *ST* III 86 2; cf. III 85.

[40]   *ST* III 84 5.

[41]   *ST* Suppl. 12 2; cf. '...there is due satisfaction when the punishment balances the fault...', *ST* Suppl. 13 1; or again, '...in order that compensation be made, something by way of satisfaction that may conduce to the glory of God must be taken away from the sinner. Now a good work, as such, does not deprive the agent of anything, but perfects him: so that the deprivation cannot be effected by a good work unless it be penal. Therefore, in order that a work be satisfactory it needs to be good, that it may conduce to God's honor, and it must be penal, so that something may be taken away from the sinner thereby', *ST* Suppl. 15 1.

still defined as 'a medicine healing past sins and preserving from future sins', is explicitly defined as (or confused with) punishment.[42]

Now if the satisfaction which is penance is understood as a bearing of punishment, on the part of the penitent, for post-baptismal sin, though such bearing of punishment might be regarded as a participation in Christ's bearing of punishment, it is difficult to perceive how this would not issue in synergy, in some addition to the atoning work of Christ (itself understood as a vicarious bearing of punishment) which thereby implies some lack in the sufficiency of that atoning work of Christ. But if the satisfaction which is penance is understood as a virtue, as a change of disposition, as an offering to God that love, honour, and worship that was God's due in the first place, then such satisfaction can be perceived not only as a participation in the sacrificial obedience of Christ but also as an outcome of that sacrificial obedience. Here, then, is a means of participating in Christ's sacrifice without implicitly detracting from that sacrifice. There is chastening here but not retribution. There is purging here but not deprivation. There is satisfaction here but not penalty. There is justice here, not in the sense of the restoring of equilibrium, but in the more biblical sense of an establishing of righteousness. But given this historical confusion between satisfaction and penalty—and given the difficulty of unravelling that which has been confused for so long—there may be much merit in preferring to speak of a sacrament of cleansing, restoration, or reconciliation rather than a sacrament of penance.

As with baptism and the Lord's Supper, a sacrament of cleansing or penance is a means of participating in Christ: a means of participating in his once-for-all atoning work; a means of participating by the Spirit in his relatedness to the Father. Indeed, no act of prayer, of worship, or of service is ever offered independently of him: all our praying is a participation by the Spirit in his praying; all our worship is a participation by the Spirit in his adoration of the Father; all our service is a participation by the Spirit in his apostolic mission. Consequently acts of penance (or better, penitence) need imply no more a detraction from the sufficiency of Christ's sorrow, passion, and priestly intercession, than our praying, our worship, or our acts of service. The apostle Paul, in a passage notoriously troublesome to most Protestants, speaks of filling up in his flesh 'what is still lacking in regard to Christ's afflictions, for the sake of his body, which is the church' (Colossians 1.24). This need not be interpreted as signifying any 'lack of sufficiency' in the afflictions of Christ—Paul is rather recognising his suffering, not as independent of Christ, but as a participation in Christ's suffering; a means through which, by the Spirit, Christ's suffering is re-presented within the Church and the

---

[42]   'Wherefore satisfaction which is the act of justice inflicting punishment, is a medicine healing past sins and preserving from future sins...'. *ST* Suppl. 12 3.

world. Similarly, when James and John request (or their mother requests on their behalf)[43] to sit either side of Christ in his kingdom, Jesus responds by asking whether they can drink of his cup and be baptised with his baptism; and when they say that they can, he affirms that they will indeed share his cup and his baptism (Mark 10.35ff.). The suffering that James and John were to endure would not in any sense detract from the suffering endured by Christ—it was rather a participation in his suffering, in his cup, in his baptism; and, as such, it was a re-presenting of his suffering, his cup, his baptism. Indeed, perhaps we should infer from these words that all suffering for Christ's sake is a participation in his suffering and, consequently, that all suffering for Christ's sake is sacramental, a means of his grace to us inasmuch as it is a means of participating in him.[44]

And if the latter is the case, then the sorrow I feel for my sin, the human restitution I seek to make to any I may have wronged, and the prayer and spiritual discipline I offer as a means of Christ's cleansing being effected in me, are all means of participating in the once-for-all suffering of Christ; they are means of participating in his praying, they are means of participating in his act of judgement that cleanses and restores. And all are, thereby, sacramental, they are means of grace inasmuch as they are means of participation. But perhaps, strictly speaking, they are not to be identified as a sacrament. If a distinction is to be maintained between that which is a sacrament and that which is sacramental, particularly with respect to the explicit ordaining of a rite by Christ, then, while there is little difficulty in affirming absolution as a sacrament, there is greater difficulty in affirming satisfaction, as the third part of penance, as a sacrament: it is sacramental; it is a participation in the gospel story; it is a means through which the Spirit imparts God's grace to us; but it might not be a sacrament in this strict sense of the definition. And, consequently, the argument is reinforced for referring to this rite as the sacrament of cleansing, restoration, or reconciliation rather than the sacrament of penance.

But all this implies, of course, an understanding of penance, as also an understanding of the atonement, in terms of a satisfaction rather than a penalty, in terms of a purging rather than a punishment, in terms of a restoring of a covenant rather than a bearing of retribution. Overwhelmingly in Scripture, words translated as judgement signify a crisis through which that which is wrong is set right again, words translated as punishment signify a chastening that restores, the metaphor

---

[43]   Cf. Matthew 20.20ff.

[44]   Once again I am grateful to one of my students, James Webb, for a dissertation that reinforces this conclusion. James Webb, 'What are the consequences of a sacramental understanding of suffering?' (Spurgeon's College, the University of Wales: Unpublished MTh dissertation, 2003).

of fire signifies a purging and a cleansing—the words of Jesus imply that the fire that consumed Sodom was not God's final word (Matthew 11.24). Indeed, how could it be God's final word? God is 'simple'. He is not divided. His wrath is not in tension with his covenantal love but is rather an expressing of that covenantal love in the context of our sin and of our rejection of that love:[45]

> If the fire of His wrath scorches us, it is because it is the fire of His wrathful love and not His wrathful hate.[46]

This is certainly not to ignore the finality of judgement implicit in the words of Jesus (Mark 9.48; Matthew 25.46) and echoed in passages of the Book of Revelation (Revelation 14.10-11; 20.15); but it is to posit the question of whether the significance of judgement and of fire should be understood differently here; and it is, consequently, to admit the possibility that the fires of final judgement also imply a (final) purging possibility. The twentieth chapter of the Book of Revelation is followed by the twenty-first and the twenty-second which speak of the nations walking in the light of the new Jerusalem (Revelation 21.24ff.) and of the leaves of the tree of life as a means of healing for the nations (Revelation 22.2). More significantly (and less figuratively), the witness of Scripture as a whole is to the ultimate triumph of God's kingdom, the vindication of his faithfulness, the ultimate restoring of all things to him in Christ. If here and now through true penitence, as through baptism and the Lord's Supper, we participate in Christ's suffering and dying, in a judgement that is a cleansing and a restoring, then perhaps (just perhaps) we do so in anticipation of an ultimate judgement, entered through physical death, that is similarly (though ultimately) a cleansing and a restoring.[47] I am merely suggesting (and certainly not concluding) a thoroughly Scriptural (rather than sentimental) basis for a universalistic hope:

For God has bound everyone over to disobedience so that he may have mercy on them all.

> Oh, the depth of the riches of the wisdom and knowledge of God!
> How unsearchable his judgments,

---

[45] For a more sustained discussion of the relationship between divine judgement and divine mercy, particularly in relation to the theology of Jonathan Edwards, see my Drew Lecture, published as 'The Glory of God's Justice and the Glory of God's Grace: Contemporary reflections on the doctrine of Hell in the Teaching of Jonathan Edwards', in John E. Colwell (ed.), *Called to One Hope: Perspectives on Life to Come* (Carlisle: Paternoster Press, 2000), pp. 113-29.

[46] *CD* III/2, p. 609.

[47] For a highly imaginative but winsome expression of this interpretation of heaven, hell, and purgatory, see C. S. Lewis, *The Great Divorce* (London: G. Bles, 1952).

and his paths beyond tracing out!
'Who has known the mind of the Lord?
Or who has been his counsellor?'
'Who has ever given to God,
that God should repay the gift?'
For from him and through him and to him are all things.
To him be the glory for ever!
Amen. (Romans 11.33-36)

CHAPTER 9

The Sacrament of Healing

Is any one of you in trouble? You should pray. Is anyone happy? Sing songs of praise. Is any one of you sick? Call the elders of the church to pray over you and anoint you with oil in the name of the Lord. And the prayer offered in faith will make you well; the Lord will raise you up. If you have sinned, you will be forgiven. Therefore confess your sins to each other and pray for each other so that you may be healed. The prayer of a righteous person is powerful and effective. (James 5.13-16)

The explicit conjunction of sin and sickness within this passage is doubly problematic: it is problematic in its implications with respect to sin and it is problematic in its implications with respect to sickness. But not withstanding any degree of contemporary embarrassment or unease with this conjunction, it is precisely the associatedness of sickness and sin that identifies the issue of healing as sacramental.

In some respects, of course, an identification of sin as sickness resonates with a culture of modernity. Not that modernity is at all comfortable with the language of sin—sin, after all, is a theological concept and is entirely meaningless other than within the context of an articulation of our relatedness to God—but modernity, nonetheless, constructs notions of wrong-doing, of misdemeanour, of fault, of failing; and modernity is predisposed to explain such wrongs pathologically in terms of sickness, dysfunction, or disorder. If all were healthy, wealthy, and wise, then society would function altruistically; if all were well-nourished, well-adjusted, and well-educated, then all would be well-intentioned—or so runs the modernistic myth, failing (apparently) to notice that, within the last hundred years, remarkably healthy and wealthy societies have perpetrated great wrong and, though highly and widely educated, have signally lacked wisdom (at least as it is defined biblically). We are urged to be not just 'tough on crime', but also 'tough on the causes of crime' as if crime could be explicated in terms of societal causality. Such simplistic political clichés, needless to say, are deeply offensive to those who, lacking health or wealth, nonetheless disavow criminality—but behind such crass slogans lies the foundational modernistic assumption that all can be explained and that, implicitly, all (or almost all) can be excused, and all (or almost all) can be redeemed (albeit without reference to a redeemer). One must admit the 'almost all' since, notwithstanding its pervasive foundationalist disposition, society stubbornly persists in demonising its Hitlers, its Saddam Husseins, its Charles Mansons, its Myra Hindleys—yet even here not without liberal protest: perhaps even Hitler was a victim of circumstance.

What is remarkable in such a context is that anyone ever is convicted of crime. Commenting on Jonathan Edwards' treatment of sin and sinfulness in his treatise on the *Freedom of the Will*, Robert Jenson surmises that Edwards foresaw (and repudiated) an age in which a criminal act in itself would constitute excuse for such criminal act: how could anyone act criminally unless they themselves were criminally deprived or disordered?[1] If I am violent, greedy, selfish, cruel, it is because I was inappropriately disciplined as a child (or not disciplined as a child), it is because I was deprived (or over-indulged), it is because I was discriminated against (or over-privileged).

As with most deceptive distortions, this pathological account of human misdemeanour is beguiling inasmuch as it is partially accurate: we are social creatures and we are affected by our environment, our background, our genetic inheritance. Consequently, a moralistic reaction to this pathological account of human wrong-doing, rooted in the complementary modernistic assumptions of indeterminate freedom and radical individualism, is at least as fallacious as the error it seeks to repudiate. Indeterminate individualistic freedom is every bit as much a modernistic myth as the explanatory causality it seeks to refute. Our identity as human persons is rendered in the narrative of our lives: a narrative rooted in our communal relationships and familial connectedness; a narrative which, by identifying the connectedness of our lives, identifies our choices as truly our own—as I have argued elsewhere (following the argument of Jonathan Edwards and others), the notion of indeterminate freedom is simply incoherent; only as a choice can be comprehended within the narratival sequence of my life can that choice be identified as authentically *my* choice.[2] This pathological account of human wrong-doing is fallacious, therefore, not because it (properly) takes account of human connectedness, but because it assumes such connectedness to be exonerating and, more basically, because its fails (inevitably) to identify the more profound sickness at the heart of the human condition. Or, to put the matter more straightforwardly, the diagnosis is wrong because (as Stanley Hauerwas opines) it is implicitly atheistic.[3]

---

[1]   Jenson, *America's Theologian*, p. 164.

[2]   See for instance, Colwell, *Living the Christian Story*, pp. 175ff.

[3]   'Before exploring how sickness manifests our sin I need to make clear why for most people the language of being sick seems more intelligible than the language of being a sinner. I think the answer is simple—we are atheists. Even if we say we believe in

Following Augustine, and with remarkably few exceptions, the Christian tradition witnesses that we sin because we are sinners rather than that we are sinners because we sin; that our sin is an outworking of a deeply rooted disorientation of our nature; that, to use the terminology adopted by Stanley Hauerwas, we are 'sinsick'.[4] The form this recognition takes in Augustine's thought, most notably in his *Anti-Pelagian Writings*, has justly been criticised: that I share in Adam's sin and guilt is not an outcome of genetic descent, nor is the distortion of my nature an outcome of concupiscence within the act of procreation; it is rather (and far more simply) that Adam's sin, in its form and consequence, is defining of the disorientation of my life and of the life of every human person. Perhaps the more basic flaw in Augustine's analysis is the non-Christological form of his notion of original righteousness: the underlying instinct here is perceptive and crucial—sin is a distortion, a disorientation of human nature, it is secondary rather than primary, penultimate rather than ultimate—but the narrative in which authentic original righteousness is defined is not that of a pre-fallen Adam in Eden but rather that of the resurrection and ascension of Christ. In this respect Irenaeus offers an older and more Christologically focused account of human identity and destiny: it is not that Christ assumes the humanity previously defined in Adam, but rather that Adam is formed in the humanity that Christ would assume.[5] When, in Romans 5.12ff., Paul speaks of sin and death entering the world through one man, his focus is ultimately and definitively on Christ as the one through whom the many are made righteous, and only penultimately and derivatively on the one through whom the many were made sinners (Romans 5.19); Adam's humanity was a 'type' of Christ's humanity, and not the other way around;[6] in Christ's resurrection and ascension our original destiny and identity is defined; in Christ's Cross the distortion of that original destiny and identity is exposed in all its unspeakable horror:

God, most of our lives are constituted by practices that assume that God does not exist'. Stanley Hauerwas, 'Sinsick', in *A Better Hope: Resources for a Church Confronting Capitalism, Democracy, and Postmodernity* (Grand Rapids, MI: Brazos Press, 2000), pp. 189-199 (p. 190).

[4]   Stanley Hauerwas derives the term from the revivalist hymn 'There is a balm in Gilead', but it occurs also in the hymn 'Christ for the world! we sing' (Samuel Wolcott, 1813–86): here the 'sin-sick and sorrow-worn' are listed as those who are to be brought to Christ. Hauerwas, 'Sinsick', p. 192.

[5]   '[I]t was said that man was created after the image of God, but it was not [actually] shown; for the Word was as yet invisible, after whose image man was created.' Irenaeus, *Against Heresies* V xvi 2.

[6]   Hence Rom. 5 14: ὅς ἐστιν τύπος τοῦ μέλλοντος. The *NIV* translation of τύπος as 'pattern' here seems especially lame.

In that He takes our place it is decided what our place is.[7]

We were not created to sin. The humanity assumed by Christ, as definitive of humanity, reveals sin to be 'unnatural' to human nature. That which is 'natural' to human nature, as defined in Christ's human nature, is a mediated participation in divine nature (2 Peter 1.4); a mediated communion with the Father, in the Son, through the Spirit. Sin (for Christ as for us) was a possibility but was not an inevitability. As Douglas Farrow comments, it is the non-inevitability of sin that renders it so devastating,[8] having been created for glory we have, 'in Adam', turned away; we have turned back to corruption. And this corruption of human nature, this disruption of our relatedness to God and, consequently, to one another, is all pervasive: it is not that we all are as corrupted as we could be (this would be to misunderstand a doctrine of total depravity); it is rather that there is no aspect of human nature, no aspect of our societal relationships, no aspect of our life within creation, that is not in some way affected by this fundamental distortion.[9] Human sin is not merely nor foundationally a matter of that which we have done and ought not to have done, it is rather a matter of that which we have not done and ought to have done inasmuch as this lack, this refusal to glorify God and render thanks to him (Romans 1.21), this refusal to love God with all our heart, soul, and strength (Deuteronomy 6.5), has issued in a radical and total distortion of human nature. Our being in sin, therefore, is a matter of fundamental disorientation, of fatal sickness, of spiritual death (Ephesians 2.1ff.).

And since this is the reality of the human condition, all modernistic attempts to account for human fault and failure, precisely because they are implicitly atheistic, cannot but fall short of persuasiveness and coherence: even when a malaise is acknowledged its nature and depth are

---

[7]   *CD* IV/1, p. 240.

[8]   '...Irenaeus does indeed confess...the imperfection of creation, an imperfection that makes the fall possible, not inevitable. The "imperfection" is this: The love for God which is the life of man cannot emerge *ex nihilo* in full bloom; it requires to grow with experience. But that in turn is what makes the fall, however unsurprising, such a devastating affair. In the fall man is "turned backwards." He does not grow up in the love of God as he is intended to. The course of his time, his so-called progress, is set in the wrong direction.' Douglas Farrow, 'St. Irenaeus of Lyons: The Church and the World', *Pro Ecclesia*, 4/3 (1995), pp. 333-55 (p. 348).

[9]   Much is commonly made of a perceived distinction between the manner in which Thomas Aquinas, Martin Luther, and John Calvin represent this human distortion. However, while Martin Luther proffers a most radical account of human corruption, it is plainly incorrect to suggest that Thomas holds human reason to be unaffected by the Fall. Martin Luther, *The Bondage of the Will*, in *LW* vol. 33, pp. 15-295; cf. *ST* I-II 85 and I-II 109.

misconstrued and understated.[10] And since this is the reality of the human condition a proper account of the Christian doctrine of salvation will focus not just on forgiveness, nor just on a merely forensic account of justification, but on the healing, renewal, and re-creation of human nature in Christ through the agency of the Spirit. Sin, whether venial or mortal, distorts and contaminates: it contaminates the whole creation; it contaminates human society; it contaminates the life of one not yet joined to Christ by the Spirit; it contaminates the one in Christ—the one who is clean but who nonetheless has dirty feet. And consequently, when one joined to Christ by the Spirit through baptism sins and seeks restoration in true penitence, the need is not merely for forgiveness and absolution but also for cleansing and healing. And for this reason, not just this sacrament of anointing, but similarly the sacraments of baptism, Eucharist, and penance, are sacraments of healing. To confess and to be forgiven, accordingly, is inclusive of being healed.

But if the association of sin with sickness is contentious, the association of sickness with sin is more so. This is the more dominant point of the essay by Stanley Hauerwas who opines that '...the assumption that we are made sick by sin is theologically right no matter how much it may offend our sensibilities'.[11] And 'offend our sensibilities' it most certainly does: for the cultures of modernity, sickness may be a 'cause' of 'sin', but 'sin' is most certainly not a 'cause' of sickness; sickness and death are pointless, meaningless interruptions of human freedom to be overcome through scientific endeavour. Consequently, Hauerwas gives significant space to the discussion of the matter by Thomas Aquinas and to the latter's assertion that, while in one sense sickness and death are 'unnatural' to human beings—we 'were not created to die'—in another sense 'corruptibility is a necessary consequence' of the physical actualities of our existence and of the 'loss of the Divine favor preserving man from death'.[12] For Thomas then, in contrast to popular contemporary assumptions, sickness and death are not 'pointless' but are rather 'an indication of the distorting effect sin has in our lives': we are made sick by sin; we are 'sinsick'.[13] This is not in any sense to suggest

---

[10]   Hence, in a highly persuasive example of genuinely 'applied' theology, Alistair McFadyen expounds an Augustinian doctrine of original sin, in comparison with secular pathologies, as a more persuasive and coherent account of the human condition: '[t]he meaninglessness of the language of sin in our secular culture issues a challenge to Christian faith and theology: to show that reference to God holds explanatory and descriptive power; that it invokes and enables a more truthful relation to reality in both theory and practice.' Alistair McFadyen, *Bound to Sin: Abuse, Holocaust and the Christian Doctrine of Sin* (Cambridge: Cambridge University Press, 2000), p. 10.

[11]   Hauerwas, 'Sinsick', p. 192.

[12]   Hauerwas, 'Sinsick', pp. 193ff.; referring to *ST* I-II 8 1 and II-II 164 1.

[13]   Hauerwas, 'Sinsick', p. 195.

some comprehensive theodicy—as Colin Gunton would often comment, evil and suffering are surds, to seek to explain them is foolish and blasphemous—it is more minimally to acknowledge their connectedness as indicative of the disorientation of creation and of our lives within it, a connectedness demonstrated in the ultimate overcoming of both sin and death in the resurrection of Jesus Christ.

> Surely he took up our infirmities and carried our sorrows,
> yet we considered him stricken by God, smitten by him, and afflicted.
> But he was pierced for our transgressions, he was crushed for our iniquities;
> the punishment that brought us peace was upon him,
> and by his wounds we are healed. (Isaiah 53.4-5; cf. Matthew 8.17).

This connectedness of sickness and sin, of course, is similarly (though rather differently) contentious within the narratives of Scripture. On the one hand psalms of lament confess sickness and descent into death in juxtaposition with sin as that which disrupts relatedness to God; Jesus, before healing a paralysed man, tells him that his sins are forgiven (Matthew 9.1ff.); and, having healed a man at the pool of Bethesda, Jesus warns him to stop sinning lest something worse happens to him (John 5.14). Conversely, whatever else may be the significance of the book of Job, it represents a sustained rebuttal of any simplistic theodicy and of any necessary association of personal guilt (as distinct to a context of universal sinfulness) and personal suffering. And perhaps most significantly, when confronted by a man blind from birth, and by his disciples' insistent question of whether this blindness was an outcome of the man's sin or the sin of his parents, Jesus dismisses both possibilities, attesting rather that 'this happened so that the work of God might be displayed in his life' (John 9.3). Reflections upon the significance of this story give shape to the closing section of Stanley Hauerwas' essay, itself responding to the compelling discussion of the narrative by James Alison.[14] It is difficult to resist Alison's response to the passage as a narrative of exclusion: one formerly excluded through his blindness (and presumed sinfulness) is subsequently, though healed and 'seeing', excluded through prejudice; and so we are left with the question of who is truly 'blind'—the man born blind or those who exclude him; the narrative which begins with the question of the association of the man's guilt (or his parents' guilt) and the man's blindness, concludes with the question of the association of the guilt of those who exclude him and their 'blindness'.

---

[14]   Hauerwas, 'Sinsick', pp. 196ff.; cf. James Alison, *The Joy of Being Wrong: Original Sin through Easter Eyes* (New York: Crossroad, 1998), pp. 120ff.; cf. James Alison, *Faith Beyond Resentment: Fragments Catholic and Gay* (London: Darton, Longman and Todd, 2001), pp. 3ff.

As with other 'miracle' narratives within John's Gospel, the evangelist's telling of this story is eschatologically orientated: miracles here are not simply works of power (δύναμεις) but signs (σημεῖα) of Jesus' identity and mission. Jesus heals the man born blind as the one who is the 'light of the world'; the one who delivers those who follow him from darkness; the one who is himself the light of life to all who accept him (John 8.12). Those who are truly blind, therefore, are those who reject this light which is Jesus himself, those who love darkness rather than light (John 3.19), those who claim already to be free (John 8.33), those who claim already to see (John 9.40). Thus understood, this narrative, by its juxtaposition of physical blindness and spiritual blindness, far from undermining the associatedness of sickness and sin, actually reinforces it, albeit in an eschatological rather than a particularised sense. Here as in the other Gospels, sickness, like sin, is confronted by Jesus in anger and compassion. Here as in the other Gospels, sickness, like sin, is that which Jesus comes to defeat and to destroy. Here as in the other Gospels, sickness, like sin, is a symptom of the human condition that Jesus comes to heal and to restore. It is not that this man's blindness was an outcome of his sin (or the sin of his parents); it is rather that this man's blindness, like all sickness, is symptomatic of this fundamental distortion of the human condition that is sin. We are not merely sick, we are 'sinsick', and consequently only in Christ can genuine healing and restoration be found.

And as in the other Gospels, healing is miraculous, it is extra-ordinary. There were other blind beggars pleading for sustenance in the streets of Jerusalem and Jericho. There were other sick men and women dreaming of a miracle at the pool of Bethesda. The miracles of Jesus narrated here are remarkably selective. They are extra-ordinary. This extra-ordinariness of healing, though implicit in the Synoptics, is made explicit by the eschatological orientation of the healing narratives within the Fourth Gospel. The healing miracles of Jesus are interpreted here as 'signs', not as ends in themselves, acts of compassion and power, but as events pregnant with eschatological significance, pointing away from themselves to the glory of Christ and the ultimate deliverance to be found in him. Only with and in the resurrection of Jesus comes ultimate deliverance; any instance of cleansing and healing now is penultimate, an anticipation of that ultimate cleansing and healing that are an outcome of his glory. That which is revealed as ultimately normal for the human condition in the narratives of the gospel story is cleansing, healing, and resurrection. That which is 'normal' for the human condition in its fallenness is sin, sickness, and death.

Nowhere is this eschatological 'not yet' more clearly expressed than in the narrative of the raising of Lazarus. Contrary to countless pietistic sermons on the relative priorities of Mary and Martha (Luke 10.38ff.),

Mary here greets Jesus with a reproachful (?) 'Lord, if you had been here, my brother would not have died' (John 11.32). It is Martha who earlier, and following a similar reproach, adds the trustful anticipation '[b]ut I know that even now God will give you whatever you ask' (vv. 21-22). When Jesus responds to Martha that her brother 'will rise again', Martha recites the eschatological hope, 'I know he will rise again in the resurrection at the last day' (v. 24). Moreover, when Jesus replies that he *is* the resurrection and the life (vv. 25-26) Martha answers with a confession similar to that which, in the Synoptic Gospels, is found on the lips of Peter: 'Yes, Lord,...I believe that you are the Christ, the Son of God, who was to come into the world' (v. 27). Within this interchange, even without the actual raising of Lazarus, the evangelist has established the point: Jesus himself is the eschatological hope; he is the resurrection; he is the life. The subsequent raising of Lazarus is illustrative of this—the raising of Lazarus is a 'sign' of Jesus' claimed identity as the resurrection and the life—but the raising of Lazarus is neither the fulfilment of this hope nor the issue of the narrative. To state the obvious, Lazarus would die again; he was 'raised' rather than 'resurrected'; the fulfilment of Jesus' words occurs in chapter 20 of this Gospel with the resurrection (rather than mere raising) of Jesus himself. The miracle of the raising of Lazarus, for all its extra-ordinariness, was penultimate rather than ultimate, a sign of an eschatological fulfilment rather than the fulfilment itself.

And what is true of the raising of Lazarus is similarly true of all Jesus' healing miracles. We can only assume that, though Jesus raised Jairus' daughter and the widow of Nain's son, they both subsequently died. And for all we know, blind Bartimaeus may subsequently have lost his sight and the man whose sins Jesus forgave may subsequently have lost the use of his limbs—what is certain is that they all subsequently died. The healing miracles of Jesus are penultimate rather than ultimate, extra-ordinary rather than ordinary: they confront the normality of our fallenness with that ultimate normality which is not yet, but not in such a manner as to establish that ultimate normality here and now. The resurrection and ascension of Jesus, as the revelation of true humanity, demonstrates sin, sickness, and death as abnormal, as inauthentic. But short of the eschatological fulfilment of that resurrection and ascension, sin, sickness, and death remain as symptomatic both of human and of cosmic fallenness.

Strangely, and perhaps contradictorily, modernity struggles to accept the present normality of sickness and death. We speak of less developed nations suffering a high mortality rate—as if the mortality rate were not universally one hundred percent. We speak of a 'right' to life as if such a right were within our power to deliver. Less ultimately, we speak of 'rights' to health, wealth, and the pursuit of happiness, as if it were the responsibility of society, or more particularly the nation state, to ensure the fulfilment of such aspirations. And we enshrine these delusory expectations in citizens' charters that reinforce the notion that health, wealth, happiness, and life itself are 'rights' to be demanded. In many respects such expectations are an outcome of the amazing advances in medical science that have gathered pace since the beginnings of the twentieth century. The highly advanced technology that characterises the contemporary medical profession (notably usually now termed a 'profession' rather than a 'vocation') soars as monumental testimony to the presumed triumph of modernistic optimism. And when death does finally occur—too often perceived as a failure of the medical services for which someone must be blamed—we deal with it as expeditiously as possible, in a fifteen minute slot, within the squeaky-clean efficiency of a crematorium, thus avoiding the pathos of a graveside in the drizzle and a slowly decaying cadaver.

All this, of course, is relatively recent. In the early years of ordained ministry I had a friend who had already retired from general practice. He once told me, perhaps with some exaggeration, that when he began his medical career (in the 1920s) there were really but two things he could prescribe and neither of them achieved very much. Even allowing for hyperbole, it is difficult for us now to imagine a world—such as his—without antibiotics. My maternal grandmother was one of seventeen children, only nine of whom survived to adult life. Neo-Gothic graveyards remain as increasingly neglected monuments of an age less successful in denying mortality.

How quickly we take for granted that which a hundred years ago would have been unimaginable. Stanley Hauerwas, in an excellent and perceptive series of articles, identifies this shift of perceived responsibility from care to cure.[15] A hundred years ago there was but limited prospect of cure and a sober acknowledgement of that limitation; the vocation of those in medical care was precisely to care since the prospect of cure was remote; a doctor was judged on the basis of 'bedside manner'. The possibility of cure—especially when the inevitable provisionality of that cure is disregarded—issues in a change of priority and expectation: a change from the commitment to care to the challenge to cure; a change from caring vocation to skilled profession. The two identities, that of caring vocation and curing profession, need not be held in tension, they could easily coinhere—but it is instructive to note where priority is given, and it is difficult not to conclude, in contemporary Britain at least, that an increase in the possibility of cure has been paralleled by a decrease in the quality of care.

---

[15] Stanley Hauerwas, *Suffering Presence: Theological Reflections on Medicine, the Mentally Handicapped, and the Church* (Edinburgh: T & T Clark, Edinburgh: 1988).

The eloquent exception to this trend, of course, is the hospice movement: a context in which the ultimate impossibility of medical cure is acknowledged; a context in which, correspondingly, medical skill and resources are devoted rather to palliative care. And perhaps it is no coincidence that, to a significant degree, the impetus for the hospice movement was religious, was a faithful acknowledgement of the naturalness of death within this penultimate context as that to be faced hopefully rather than optimistically (though vainly) deferred.[16] For more fundamentally, a contemporary expectation for health, wealth, happiness, and life itself, as of right, is an outcome of the refusal to recognise that we are 'sinsick', a refusal to recognise that the 'cure of souls' is more basic than the cure of bodies, a refusal to face death with hope rather than with vacuous optimism, a refusal to recognise, therefore, the sacramental context of authentic healing.

Ironically (though hardly surprisingly) this modernistic demand for health, wealth, and happiness, is mirrored within the Church in a manner that parodies the hope of the gospel. Perhaps it is also no coincidence that the rise of Pentecostalism, and the subsequent rise of the Charismatic Movement within existing denominations, occurs simultaneously with the advances in medical science already noted and a consequent secular expectation for imminent cure. And again, as with all beguiling errors, this distortion gains its impetus from a valid insight, that we are made sick by sin and that, therefore, sickness as much as sin is at issue in any theology of the atonement. The Church throughout its history, as attested not least by the sacrament that is the theme of this chapter, has affirmed that God continues to heal miraculously—but the Church has consistently viewed such miraculous healing as extra-ordinary and, consequently, the Church has consistently perceived its primary pastoral task as a 'cure of souls', as a preparing of men and women for death in the light of Christ's resurrection and ascension. The novelty represented by the more extreme strands of Pentecostalism and the Charismatic Movement is that of perceiving the Church's primary pastoral task as a 'cure of bodies' as much as a 'cure of souls', of perceiving sickness and death as defeat or failure, of perceiving miraculous healing as the ordinary rather than the extra-ordinary, as a 'right' to be claimed rather than a mediated anticipation of the ultimate to be sought humbly and prayerfully.[17]

---

[16]   I am reminded again of Stanley Hauerwas' definition of optimism as 'hope without truth': 'Optimism—hope without truth—is not sufficient for dealing with the pretentious powers that determine a person's existence in the world.' Stanley Hauerwas, *Christian Existence Today: Essays on Church, World, and Living in Between* (Durham, NC: Labyrinth, 1988), p. 211.

[17]   For helpful discussions of appropriate forms of healing ministry within the Church see Church of England, General Synod, *A Time to Heal: A Report for the House of*

While it is difficult to evade the possibility that culturally this phenomenon is a mere mirroring of the optimism of secular modernism, theologically it is indicative again of an over-realised eschatology and of an insufficient delineation between Christ and his Church. The Church exists between the ascension of Christ and the final coming of Christ, in an 'even now' which is nonetheless still a 'not yet', and within this time between the times sin, sickness, and death remain the normal conditions of human life in its fallenness; perfected holiness, miraculous healing, and the raising of the dead remain extra-ordinary. And when such extra-ordinary events occur, as in the ministry of Jesus himself, they do so penultimately rather than ultimately: no saint yet attains the perfection of glory;[18] Lazarus was yet to die again. Such extra-ordinary events therefore, though genuinely mediations of God's compassion and power, are never ends in themselves but, as John's Gospel attests, they are 'signs' of that which is truly ultimate.

Moreover, as signs of the ultimate such extra-ordinary events are more proper to the ministry of Jesus—as himself the presence of the ultimate—than to the ministry of the Church. Even for Jesus such extra-ordinary events are mediated acts of the Spirit—he drives out demons 'by the Spirit of God' (Matthew 12.28)—but, though mediated acts of the Spirit, they are nonetheless indicative of Jesus' identity as also of the ultimate future anticipated in him. However, when such extra-ordinary events occur in the life of the Church they do so, not primarily as indicative of the Church's identity as Christ's body, but as indicative of the authority of the risen and ascended one in distinction from that 'body'. When Peter and John speak healing to a lame man they emphasise that his healing was not an outcome of their own 'power or godliness' but an outcome of trust in the ascended authority of Jesus. Here again the Church is not called to be Christ but is called rather to witness to Christ.

And here again it is the mediated and gracious (or gratuitous) nature of such extra-ordinary events that is obscured and finally forfeited by the delusion that health (not to mention wealth and happiness) can be claimed as of right. Such presumption reduces the Holy Spirit to the status of an automaton, an impersonal force subject to the bidding of the agential (rather than instrumental) authority of the 'healer' or the measure of faith of the one who is sick. And in the context of such presumption, the absence of immediate healing can only be perceived as failure: failure on the part of God; failure on the part of the 'healer'; or

---

Bishops on the Healing Ministry (London: Church House Publications, 2000), and Ernest Lucas (ed.), *Christian Healing: What can we Believe?* (London: Lynx, 1997).

   [18]   Thomas Aquinas is careful to distinguish between a perfecting of love attainable in this life and that perfecting of love characteristic of glory since 'the conditions of the present life do not allow of a man always tending actually to God'. *ST* II-II 184 2.

(and is more often implicitly the case) failure on the part of the one seeking healing—the pastoral tragedies consequent on this presumption are legion. To identify healing as sacramental is to acknowledge the human instrumentality—rather than human agency—implicit in the process. To identify healing as sacramental is to acknowledge the mediate—rather than unmediated—dynamic of the process. To identify healing as sacramental is to acknowledge the gratuitous—rather than constrained—nature of the process. To identify healing as sacramental is to acknowledge the process as a matter of prayer rather than as a matter of claimed right.

The discussion of this chapter has continued to this point with little explicit mention of the sacrament which is its claimed focus—a postponement necessitated by a societal context that assumes sickness and death to be other than religious phenomena. It is hardly necessary to yield space to protracted discussions of the theological nature of our incorporation in Christ, our participation in his sacrifice, our cleansing from sin—indisputably these are religious themes. But in a societal context where sickness and death are persistently and increasingly considered as merely secular concerns it is both necessary and appropriate to affirm their theological significance and rootedness—an apologetic that would have been unnecessary in previous generations. Sickness and death are symptomatic of the disorientation consequent on human sinfulness: we are 'sinsick' and therefore every instance of healing is theologically significant, is a mediation of grace, is extra-ordinary.

> Praise the LORD, O my soul;
> all my inmost being, praise his holy name.
> Praise the LORD, O my soul;
> and forget not all his benefits—
> who forgives all your sins
> and heals all your diseases,
> who redeems your life from the pit
> and crowns you with love and compassion,
> who satisfies your desires with good things
> so that your youth is renewed like the eagle's. (Psalm 103.1-5)

One of the several unhelpful and fallacious consequences of the common Reformed distinction between special grace and common grace—a fallacious assumption even more pronounced in the common Catholic distinction between grace and nature—is a blurring of the mediate and gratuitous nature of *all* healing. Here the psalmist confesses the God of Israel as the source, not just of forgiveness, but of healing, of every means of sustenance, and of life itself. Whether I am healed through prayer, or whether I am healed through medical intervention, I am healed by God—my healing, therefore, is both mediate and gratuitous. The mediate and gratuitous dynamic of such healing may not be acknowledged, of course, by those through whom it is mediated—to such the process may appear 'natural' and 'ordinary'—but health, healing, and life itself are simply not at human disposal: Jesus Christ alone is the resurrection and the life. In such a secular and reductionist context, therefore, the Church is called especially to witness to the mediate and gratuitous nature of healing—and to do so sacramentally. A sacrament of healing or anointing ought not to be perceived as an alternative to appropriate medical processes but rather as defining and identifying a context of trustfulness and hopefulness (not to mention faithfulness) in which such processes appropriately occur.[19] To receive the sacrament of healing or anointing, then, is to face sickness and death in the light of the mediated gospel promise of healing and resurrection; it is to confess that sickness and death are theological issues, consequences of our 'sinsickness'; it is humbly to acknowledge that both penultimate and ultimate health and life are divine gifts rather than human rights.[20]

And as an act of prayer, the sacrament of healing or anointing, like every sacrament, is eschatologically orientated: that which is mediated here is not principally a promise of penultimate healing but of ultimate resurrection. The ambiguity of this sacrament—as an anointing for healing that gradually transmogrifies as an anointing for death[21]—has proved a focus for consternation if not derision in some Pentecostalist circles, but the identical ambiguity occurs in the passage that defines the sacrament:

> ...the prayer offered in faith will make you well; the Lord will raise you up. If you have sinned, you will be forgiven. (James 5.15)

The word here translated 'will make you well' ($\sigma\acute{\omega}\sigma\varepsilon\iota$) is notoriously broad in its reference, signifying both penultimate and ultimate deliverance; and the word here translated 'will raise...up' ($\dot{\varepsilon}\gamma\varepsilon\rho\varepsilon\hat{\iota}$) again

---

[19]   Martin Israel, at the beginning of his study of healing as sacrament, makes the point that the human person is an integrated whole. This, of course, is the case but it is rather a different point to that being asserted here. Martin Israel, *Healing as Sacrament: The Sanctification of the World* (London: Darton, Longman and Todd, 1984).

[20]   An account of the beginnings of a sacrament of healing occurs on pp. 30ff. of the Church of England report, *A Time to Heal*. Nonetheless, this helpful report is remarkable for how little it discusses the sacramental nature of healing.

[21]   Paul Haffner includes a useful discussion concerning the development of a sacrament of anointing, its distinction from penance, its identity as a sacrament (as distinct from a sacramental) and its gradual association with an anointing for death (especially during the Carolingian era). Haffner, *The Sacramental Mystery*, pp. 145ff.

could refer to a penultimate raising or an ultimate resurrection. To administer this sacrament, therefore, is not to be the agent of immediate healing—though penultimate healing may occur—it is rather to be the instrument through which the assurance of ultimate healing, cleansing, forgiveness, and resurrection are mediated. This, after all, is the authentic Christian hope, not necessarily for an immediate deliverance, but for an ultimate deliverance: 'to depart and be with Christ...is better by far' (Philippians 1.23).[22] That an anointing for healing should have transmogrified into an anointing for death is, of course, to be regretted. But that death should ever now be perceived as defeat is to be regretted far more, indeed, to imply such is to apostatise. Here and now there can only be penultimate deliverance—ultimate deliverance is yet to come; ultimate deliverance awaits a general and universal resurrection. Any penultimate deliverance, then, and any sacrament of anointing that may be the means of that penultimate deliverance, points away from itself to this ultimate deliverance. And it is with reference to this ultimate deliverance that an anointing for healing should always be administered. Death, in the light of the resurrection of Christ, can never signify defeat. Real and deep grief at parting is now encompassed by resurrection hope. This, after all, is the essence of the pastoral task, to be a means through which the entirety of life, sickness, and death can be brought into the compass of Christ's death and resurrection.

---

[22]   Note how Athanasius cites the manner in which Christians face death as testimony to the truth of Christ's resurrection. Athanasius, *On the Incarnation*, V 27.

CHAPTER 10

The Sacrament of Christian Ministry

...to each one of us grace has been given as Christ apportioned it. This is why
it says:
'When he ascended on high,
he led captives in his train
and gave gifts to people.'
(What does 'he ascended' mean except that he also descended to the lower,
earthly regions? He who descended is the very one who ascended higher than all
the heavens, in order to fill the whole universe.) It was he who gave some to
be apostles, some to be prophets, some to be evangelists, and some to be
pastors and teachers, to prepare God's people for works of service, so that the
body of Christ may be built up until we all reach unity in the faith and in the
knowledge of the Son of God and become mature, attaining to the whole
measure of the fulness of Christ. (Ephesians 4.7-13)

To speak of Christ's ascension is to speak not just of his authority and
glory, but to speak also of his priestly office and ministry; he now lives
eternally not just to reign but also to intercede (Hebrews 7.25); he is not
only our resurrected and ascended king, he is also our priest and our
prophet.[1] Indeed, the danger of speaking, with the tradition, of this
threefold office of Christ is precisely the danger of implying a division
and distinction within that which is itself single and united: it is not that
Christ reigns, and also intercedes, and also mediates that word to us which
is his person; his priestly intercession is the form of his reign, his kingly
servanthood is the manner of his intercession, and as this priestly king
and kingly priest he is himself the single and eternal word of God to us.
Christ is not divided; every legitimate expectation within ancient Israel,
and every anticipatory office, comes to fruition and fulfilment within his
true humanity. In response to every authentically prophetic and
covenantal word, and in contradistinction to every false prophecy and
inauthentic word, Jesus Christ is the word of God made flesh; he is the
truth and, as such, he is the way and the life (John 14.6). In relation to
every legitimate covenantal king within Israel and Judah, and in

---

[1]   '...Christ, as being the Head of all, has the perfection of all graces. Wherefore,
as to others, one is a lawgiver, another is a priest, another is a king; but all these concur
in Christ, as the fount of all grace'. *ST* III 22 1; cf. *Institutes* II xv 1.

contradistinction to every human form of government and pretentious claim to authority, Jesus Christ is Lord and King; he is the true Lord who is the true servant (John 13.13-14); to him every knee will bow in heaven, on earth, and under the earth, and every tongue will confess his lordship (Philippians 2.10). And in fulfilment of Israel's priesthood, and in refutation of every deceptive and delusory claim to mediatorial office, Jesus Christ is the one true high priest who meets our need (Hebrews 7.26); he is the one effective mediator between us and God (1 Timothy 2.5).

This final affirmation, of course, prompted the understandable protest of the Reformation against any agential notion of ecclesial priesthood that implicitly rivals or qualifies the unique and sufficient priesthood of Christ. Through him, and through him alone, we 'have gained access...into this grace in which we now stand' (Romans 5.2). No one, therefore, may claim to supplement or complement his mediating work without undermining and implicitly denying its uniqueness and sufficiency. Rightly or wrongly the Reformers perceived the clericalism of the late Medieval Church as implying an agential and supplementary mediation and, in parody of the apostasy of the mob before Pilate, protested that we have no priest but Jesus.

But to deny any supplementary or complementary notion of priesthood is not necessarily to deny a participatory or representational notion of priesthood, to deny an agential mediation is not necessarily to deny an instrumental mediation. Notwithstanding their resounding and unanimous protest, the Magisterial Reformers, together with several of their more radical critics,[2] retained a high view of ministerial office within the Church, not as a supplement or complement to Christ's unique priesthood, but as a participation in that unique priesthood, as a mediation by the Spirit of Christ's unique mediation. It is precisely as the sole mediator between God and humankind that the ascended Christ gives apostles, prophets, evangelists, pastors and teachers to his Church, not as rivals to his unique apostolic office, but as means through which that

---

[2]   So for instance, the fifth article of the Schleitheim Confession (a confession made by Swiss and South German Anabaptists in 1527) states that '[w]e have been united as follows concerning shepherds in the church of God. The shepherd in the church shall be a person according to the rule of Paul, fully and completely, who has a good report of those who are outside the faith. The office of such a person shall be to read and exhort and teach, warn, admonish, or ban in the congregation, and properly to preside among the sisters and brothers in prayer, and in the breaking of bread, and in all things to take care of the body of Christ, that it may be built up and developed, so that the name of God might be praised and honored through us, and the mouth of the mocker be stopped.' Quoted from 'Brotherly Union of a Number of Children of God Concerning Seven Articles', in *The Legacy of Michael Sattler*, trans. and ed. John H. Yoder (Scottdale, PA: Herald Press, 1973), pp. 34-43.

unique apostolic office is mediated; as he is sent by the Father into the world so he sends his apostles into the world (John 20.21); and those so sent are given as mediations of the kingly, priestly, and prophetic office of the ascended Christ.

This is not, of course, to deny the kingly, priestly, and prophetic identity of the Church in its entirety and wholeness. Like Israel, the Church is constituted a 'royal priesthood' (1 Peter 2.9);[3] the Church itself, like Israel, is sacramental, a mediation of God's gracious presence and action within the world; just as Israel as a whole anticipates the kingly, priestly, and prophetic ministry of Christ, so now the Church as a whole participates in that kingly, priestly, and prophetic ministry. As with every other instance of a sacramental dynamic (and as argued in chapter 3 of this book), this participation by the Church in the ministry of Christ, together with the Church's consequent mediation of that ministry of Christ, is a matter of promise and of grace. The Church is not the agent of this mediation but rather the instrument through which this mediation is effected through the agency of the Spirit. This sacramental mediation, then, which is the Church's true calling and essence, remains always a matter of prayer in response to divine promise. The risen Christ has promised to be present, to speak, and to act, through the mediating agency of the Spirit and through the mediating instrumentality of the Church. The Church, therefore, worships, prays, and witnesses in confident expectation of the fulfilment of this promise. The Church's mediation of the ministry of the risen Christ is sacramental; it is μυστήριον; it cannot be presumed upon; it cannot be demonstrated to empirical observation; it can only be hoped for in prayer and obedience.

And, as members of the Church, as those included in Christ through baptism, all Christians participate in this corporate mediation of Christ's presence and action, all Christians worship, pray, and witness in the context of this sacramental promise. But once again I am grateful to my friend and colleague, Steve Holmes, for drawing attention to the subtle shift within Baptist churches (if not more widely) from speaking of the 'priesthood of all believers' to speaking of 'every member ministry':[4] a shift from 'all' in this participatory sense to 'every' (or 'each') in an individualistic sense. As I have argued elsewhere, in speaking of the priesthood of all believers it was Luther's intention to affirm every aspect of life as vocational, as a means of service, as a means of participating in

---

[3]   '...Ὑμεῖς δὲ γένος ἐκλεκτόν, Βασίλειον ἱεράτευμα, ἔθνος ἅγιον, λαὸς εἰς περιποίησιν'; cf. Exodus 19.5f. and Deuteronomy 7.6.

[4]   Stephen R. Holmes, 'Towards a Baptist Theology of Ordained Ministry', in Anthony R. Cross and Philip E. Thompson (eds), *Baptist Sacramentalism* (Carlisle: Paternoster Press, 2003), pp. 247-262 (p. 254).

the single priestly ministry of Christ.[5] This phrase, then, is entirely misappropriated when it is cited as justification for any individualistic notion of ministry, for any notion of 'my' ministry as if such were my possession and prerogative, as if such were distinct from or independent of the single corporate ministry of the Church and the undivided though mediated ministry of the ascended Christ. And a notion of the priesthood of all believers similarly is entirely misappropriated when it is cited as implicit denial of any separated or distinct ministry within the Church—nothing could be further from Luther's discernible intention or actual practice.

Jesus calls all to follow him and to love him, but he does not call all to feed his sheep (John 21.15ff.). Jesus called many disciples but few apostles (Mark 3.13ff.). The ascended Christ gives some—but not all—as apostles, prophets, evangelists, and pastors and teachers (Ephesians 4.11). There has been not a little discussion, both in the past and the present, concerning whether this last reference should be understood as historically descriptive or as continuously descriptive; whether, that is to say, apostles and prophets were given to the Church by Christ at the beginning of the Church's history or whether these terms remain appropriate designations of the Church's continuing ministry. More recently there has been some (less interesting and significant) discussion concerning whether 'pastors and teachers' constitute a single office and ministry or two distinct offices and ministries.[6] However a third apparent ambiguity of the text—whether such are given to the Church for a single or a multiple goal—tends to be overlooked: are apostles, prophets, evangelists, and pastors and teachers given for ($\pi\rho\dot{o}s$) the preparation of God's people, for ($\varepsilon\dot{i}s$) the work of ministry, and for ($\varepsilon\dot{i}s$) the building up of the body of Christ (i.e., a threefold goal); are they given for the preparation of God's people for the work of ministry and the building up of the body of Christ (i.e., a single goal fulfilled through the ministry of the Church as a whole); or are they given (as, for instance, the *NIV* concludes) for the preparation of God's people for the work of ministry, and for the building up of the body of Christ (i.e., a dual goal, the first being fulfilled through the ministry of the Church as a whole)?[7] In other

---

5   John E. Colwell, 'The Sacramental Nature of Ordination: An Attempt to Re-engage a Catholic Understanding and Practice', in Cross and Thompson (eds), *Baptist Sacramentalism*, pp. 228-246 (pp. 242-43).

6   The question turns of the use of the conjunction καὶ here as distinct from the simple δὲ that is used previously: καὶ αὐτὸς ἔδωκεν τοὺς μὲν ἀποστόλους, τοὺς δὲ προφήτας, τοὺς δὲ εὐαγγελιστάς, τοὺς δὲ ποιμένας καὶ διδασκάλους.

7   καὶ αὐτὸς ἔδωκεν τοὺς μὲν ἀποστόλους, τοὺς δὲ προφήτας, τοὺς δὲ εὐαγγελιστάς, τοὺς δὲ ποιμένας καὶ διδασκάλους, πρὸς τὸν καταρτισμὸν τῶν ἁγίων εἰς ἔργον διακονίας, εἰς οἰκοδομὴν τοῦ σώματος τοῦ Χριστοῦ, μέχρι καταντήσωμεν οἱ πάντες εἰς τὴν ἑνότητα τῆς πίστεως καὶ τῆς ἐπιγνώσεως τοῦ

words, are the prepositions πρὸς and εἰς to be interpreted here as of synonymous significance and weight (the first option); are they to be interpreted here as of distinct significance and weight (the second option); or is the preposition εἰς to be interpreted with rather different significance in each of its occurrences (the third option)? Or, to put the matter more simply still, is the work of ministry (according to this passage) the prerogative of apostles, prophets, evangelists, and pastors and teachers; or is the work of ministry the prerogative of the whole Church? The matter, of course, cannot be decisively resolved (though, to this author at least, the first possibility seems the more likely)—but what is interesting is that, in a context where the ministry of the whole Church is increasingly stressed, the matter receives relatively little discussion, the third possibility generally being assumed.[8]

The ministry of the whole Church—its participation in Christ's ministry and its mediation of that ministry—is, of course, clearly affirmed elsewhere in the New Testament. The mere possibility, however, that ministry within this passage is attested as the prerogative of those distinctly given by the ascended Christ to the Church ought further to militate against any affirmation of the Church's ministry as a means of belittling or even negating this separated and distinct ministry. That Israel as a nation was called and constituted a 'kingdom of priests' did not exclude the calling and constituting of a separated Aaronic priesthood within Israel and for Israel.[9] That the Church as a chosen people and a holy nation similarly is called and constituted a 'royal priesthood' should not be misappropriated as excluding or belittling the calling and constituting of a separated ministry within the Church and for the Church. It has been the argument of this book that a contemporary belittling (or repudiating) of the sacraments is, at least in part, an outcome of a modernistic preoccupation with an expectation for the unmediated immediate. One suspects, therefore, that John Webster is accurate in his conclusion that modernity's 'assertions of the primacy of private (or perhaps congregational) judgement', together with its assumption of 'the fundamental reality of unmediated encounter with God in Christian experience' issues similarly in a relegating of orders of ministry.[10] The calling and separation of the apostles by Jesus (Mark 3.13ff.), the specific

---

υἱοῦ τοῦ θεοῦ, εἰς ἄνδρα τέλειον, εἰς μέτρον ἡλικίας τοῦ πληρώματος τοῦ Χριστοῦ....

[8]   For a full discussion of this see Ernest Best, *A Critical and Exegetical Commentary on Ephesians*, The International Critical Commentary (Edinburgh: T & T Clark, 1998), pp. 388ff.; cf. Andrew T. Lincoln, *Ephesians*, Word Biblical Commentary 42 (Dallas, TX: Word Books, 1990), pp. 248ff.

[9]   Exodus 19.6.

[10]   John Webster, 'The Self-Organizing Power of the Gospel of Christ: Episcopacy and Community Formation', *IJST* 3 (2001), pp. 69-82 (p. 70).

commission given to Peter (Luke 22.31-32; John 21.15ff.), Paul's parting speech to the Ephesian elders (Acts 20.17ff.), the instructions given to Timothy and to Titus, together with this attestation of apostles, prophets, evangelists, and pastors and teachers as the gift of the ascended Christ, all imply a separated ministry given to the Church (and to the world) as a means through which the Church becomes that to which it has been called and for which it has been constituted.

In a most engaging and perceptive sermon preached in Spurgeon's College Chapel, my friend and colleague Susan Stevenson suggested the rôle of the midwife as a metaphor for Christian ministry.[11] This seems (to me) to be a most helpful analogy, accentuating at least one implication of a properly sacramental understanding of Christian ministry. A Christian minister, like a midwife, possesses no power or possibility for the creation and birth of a new life; a Christian minister, like a midwife, can only be a means through which the birth of that new life, through all the inevitable messiness and pain of the process, is assisted. The analogy effectively draws attention to the instrumental and mediatorial nature of Christian ministry but, like all analogies, it ultimately fails: the competency of a midwife to assist in the birth of a new life is an acquired skill; the competency of a Christian minister cannot be acquired, it is a gift of God, an outcome of divine calling, an outcome of divine promise.

There may be many ways in which a Christian minister is competent—a competent leader, a competent speaker, a competent liturgist, a competent theologian, a competent biblical scholar, a competent counsellor, a competent arranger of chairs, a competent sweeper of floors, a competent strategic thinker, a competent designer of church programmes—but with respect to the promise which is the essence of Christian ministry no-one is competent. The Christian minister may be competent in all of the senses already listed and more besides, but such competencies are no more than means through which God may choose to be present and to act through the Spirit—and no such competency, nor the sum of such competencies, qualifies or constitutes a man or a woman as a Christian minister. No man or woman is competent to bring the Church to maturity in Christ. Competence as a minister of the gospel, competence as one through whom the Spirit gives life, comes from God (2 Corinthians 3.4ff.). The distinctive competency of a Christian minister—a competency that cannot be acquired, a competency that is divinely promised and divinely given—is the competency to be an instrumental means through which the Spirit gives new life to men and women, the competency to be an instrumental means through which the Church is brought to maturity in Christ. It is the graciously given

---

[11]   Sermon preached at Spurgeon's College, 2 December 2003, by Rev. Susan A. Stevenson, Minister of West Norwood Baptist Church (1990–).

competency to be a living mediation of the presence and action of the Spirit. It is the graciously given competency to be a priest.

It may be thought unusual (if not incoherent) for a Baptist to affirm the priestly nature of Christian ministry—as has already been noted, one of the clarion calls of the Protestant Reformation was the confession of Jesus Christ as our sole and sufficient mediator and priest. But whatever term be used (and in this positive sense 'presbyter is but priest writ large'[12]) Protestantism properly has always understood Christian ministry in priestly terms, as a mediation of the priestly ministry of Christ, as a means of grace through Word and Sacrament. The Protestant minister represents God to the people in Word and Sacrament, and similarly represents the people to God in prayer and Sacrament—though never in such a manner that displaces or qualifies the unique and sufficient priesthood of Christ. It is the duty of Protestant ministers to pray for the people, to speak the word of God to the people, to administer the sacraments to the people, and themselves to be means of God's grace to the people—all of which implies a priestly function. This priestly character of Protestant ministry (and surely also of Catholic ministry) is never intended as a denial of the immediate access of every man or woman to the Father, in the Son, and by the Spirit—it is rather a mediation (an instrumental rather than agential mediation) of that immediate access; it militates not against immediacy but against unmediated immediacy (though without ultimately denying the possibility of an unmediated immediacy). I might hear God's word directly but generally I hear God's word mediated through the human words of Scripture or the human words of a preacher or pastor. I might have an unmediated sense of God's presence and grace but generally such presence and grace are mediated sacramentally. I might have an immediate sense of assurance and forgiveness but generally such assurance and absolution are mediated through the words of a human minister.

It is necessary to emphasise that which has been *properly* understood concerning Protestant ministry since, within the contemporary Church, this Protestant understanding of a ministry of Word and Sacrament appears to be under some degree of threat. The 'anyone can' culture arising generally from modernity and post-modernity, compounded by the Charismatic Movement's emphasis on the ministry of the whole body of Christ and its individual members, has issued in an ecclesial context where it has become common for the non-ordained—not to mention the non-trained and non-licensed—to preach and, at least in a Free Church

---

[12]   'New *Presbyter* is but old *Priest* writ large'. John Milton, 'On the New Forcers of Conscience under the Long Parliament' (1646), in *Milton: Poetical Works*, ed. Douglas Bush (Oxford: Oxford University Press, 1966), pp. 175-76.

context, to preside at the Eucharist. And within a context where a ministry of Word and Sacrament is no longer recognised as appropriately reserved to those separated within the Church to this ministry it is hardly surprising that such separated ministry becomes undervalued and both its focus and essence become confused. It might seem one of the great mysteries of the twentieth-century Church that a Charismatic Movement with such emphasis on the gifts of the Spirit as described in 1 Corinthians 12—a passage affirming the variety of gifts within the Church and the appropriateness of particular gifts to particular members of the body—should serve to reinforce this 'anyone can' culture: surely such an emphasis should have served to reinforce the appropriateness of a separated ministry and the appropriateness of certain gifts to those so separated? But the greater focus of the Charismatic Movement, as a phenomenon of modernity and post-modernity, was (and is) upon the unmediated immediate, upon the immediacy of charismatic experience and charismatic giftedness, itself unmediated by the structures and orders of the Church in its continuity and connectedness. Herein is located the source of a charismatic belittling of ordained ministry and of ordination—notwithstanding the apostle's appeal for appropriate order, an underlying expectation for the unmediated prevails in contemporary charismatic readings of the passage.

Ironically, many of the 'new churches' that were born out of the Charismatic Movement have developed strong leadership structures, in many respects more overtly clericalist than the clericalism they previously repudiated. But this is no priestly ministry, the emphasis here is but rarely on a ministry of Word and Sacrament, the emphasis rather is upon leadership, governance, authority—and all this more often than not in a strongly hierarchical sense. Neither is this notion of ministry as leadership confined to 'new churches' of charismatic disposition: notions of the Christian minister as primarily a leader or a counsellor are the inevitable outcome of a democratising of the ministry of Word and Sacrament,[13] and such 'democratising' is rampant beyond the confines of these 'new churches'; throughout Protestant churches (at least) there seems to be an increasing emphasis on management and leadership skills and upon counselling skills as the focus of a separated ministry.[14]

---

[13]   Thus Paul Beasley-Murray contends that '[l]eadership is the distinguishing mark of the ordained' and specifically maintains that ordination is *not* to a ministry of Word and Sacrament. P. Beasley-Murray, 'The Ministry of All and the Leadership of Some: A Baptist Perspective', in P. Beasley-Murray (ed.), *Anyone for Ordination?* (Tunbridge Wells: Marc, 1993), pp. 157-174 (pp. 161 and 167-68).

[14]   So John Macquarrie notes that '[t]oday we still have bishops who might laugh at the idea of a prince bishop, but who act like managing directors, the modern equivalent of older power figures.' Macquarrie, *A Guide to the Sacraments*, p. 196.

But leadership skills and counselling skills are acquirable competencies. I can be trained as a leader and I can be trained as a counsellor—just as I can be trained as a speaker, as a liturgist, as a biblical scholar. All such competencies may serve as means of God's grace—but they are not inherently and necessarily such. All such competencies may be appropriate to a Christian minister—but they are not the essence of a separated and ordained ministry. The essence of a separated and ordained ministry is a ministry of Word and Sacrament and such is not an acquirable competency; such is inherently and necessarily a gift of God's grace.[15] I may (or may not) be an accomplished and compelling speaker, but only the Holy Spirit can cause a sermon to be a means of transforming grace. I may (or may not) be able to celebrate Holy Communion beautifully and reverently, but only the Holy Spirit can cause the celebration to be the means of the presence of the ascended Christ. The essence of Christian ministry, thus defined, simply cannot be acquired—it is a matter of calling and of promise.

And, as a matter of calling and promise, it is a matter of being rather than merely a matter of doing; it is ontological and not merely functional; a Christian minister is one who has been separated to be something rather than merely one who has been separated to do something. In this sense a focus on a ministry of Word and Sacrament, just as much as a focus on a ministry of leadership or counselling, might be misleading. The apostle Paul, writing to the church at Corinth at least partly in defence of his apostleship, speaks of himself and of those with him in ministry as being 'the aroma of Christ among those who are being saved and those who are perishing' (2 Corinthians 2.15). It is for this ministry of 'being' (rather than merely doing) that Paul considers himself unequal. It is for this ministry of 'being', the ministry of a new covenant of the Spirit, that Paul and those with him have been made competent by God (2 Corinthians 3.6). To affirm a sacramental understanding of ministry is not just to affirm that one has been separated to perform a series of kerygmatic, liturgical, and sacramental functions—it is rather that one has been separated to be oneself a living sacrament, a living instrumental means of God's grace, a priest.

During the month preceding my ordination, and as a concluding aspect of my training, I attended a 'clinical' course designed to introduce

---

[15]   'The minister is much more than a leading brother as the Church itself is more than a fraternity. He is neither the mouthpiece of the Church, nor its chairman, nor its secretary. He is not the servant, not the employee, of the Church. He is an apostle to it, the mouthpiece of Christ's gospel to it, the servant of the Word and not of the Church; he serves the Church only for that sake. The ministry is a prophetic and sacramental office; it is not a secretarial, it is not merely presidential. It is sacramental and not merely functional. It is the outward and visible agent of the inward gospel Grace.' Forsyth, *The Church and the Sacraments*, pp. 132-33.

ordinands to the work of hospital chaplaincy. The course was ecumenical and, since all the participants were preparing for imminent ordination, it afforded opportunity for some lively (and heated) conversations concerning the nature of the ministry for which we were preparing. During one such conversation a delightful Anglo-Catholic brother very graciously conceded that he could accept the validity of my ordination as a Baptist minister in precisely the terms that I myself understood it, as a separation to perform certain functions within a particular denomination, as a separation to preach and to celebrate the Lord's Supper (the latter in a merely memorialist sense). The problem with this attempt at ecumenical compromise was that even then I did not subscribe to a merely memorialist understanding of the Eucharist and that I can no longer subscribe to a merely functional understanding of Christian ministry. In fact now my understanding of ordination would be almost exactly that of my then conversation partner. To be ordained implies a change of being and not merely a change of function. Those ordained are not just separated to perform certain sacramental functions, they are separated themselves to be sacramental mediations of God's presence and action.

As with a sacramental understanding of marriage, a sacramental understanding of Christian ministry implies both a sacramental understanding of a continuing reality and a sacramental understanding of the means through which that reality is established: a sacramental understanding of marriage implies both a sacramental understanding of the marriage relationship and a sacramental understanding of the rite of marriage through which that relationship was established; a sacramental understanding of Christian ministry implies both a sacramental understanding of the minister—of one in holy orders—and a sacramental understanding of the rite of ordination through which that minister is established as such. Christian ministry is a matter of gracious calling and promise—but how do such occur?

Early in his Letter to the Galatians we find one of several accounts of Paul's calling as an apostle, and one can hardly fail to notice the tension within the account—a tension between Paul's confidence in the immediacy of his own calling on the one hand, and, on the other hand, his concern to receive the affirmation and commendation of James, Peter, and John, of those who were apostles before him; a tension between an unmediated revelation and a mediated recognition (Galatians 1.13–2.10). And if a mediated recognition was important to Paul, lest he be found to be running in vain (Galatians 2.2), such must be foundational for all since Paul—for how many of us can truly lay claim to an unmediated encounter with the risen Christ? A sense of personal vocation is as crucial now as it was for Paul—it is such that is tested by the Church during a process of preparation and attested by the Church within a rite of ordination—but, unlike Paul, few today see a light or hear a voice: the potential for delusion is considerable. And if the potential for delusion is considerable so, consequently, is the potential for self-doubt and uncertainty. Again I acknowledge that I write as one beset with recurring depression: though I recall with gratitude a clear sense of personal vocation, I have good reason to doubt my felt experiences. If today I have confidence in a calling to Christian ministry it is not simply based on a felt experience (a felt experience I have often doubted) — it is based rather on the affirmation of that calling by the local church of which I was a member; on the testing of that calling by the Ministerial Recognition Committee of the (then) Kent and Sussex Baptist Association, by the Council of Spurgeon's College, and by the entire process of ministerial training and preparation; and, ultimately, on the definitive uttering of that calling at my ordination. Here again a contemporary predisposition to the unmediated immediate must be resisted and rejected. That which God does here he does both graciously and mediately, in a manner that cannot be manipulated, but also in a manner that does not bypass the physical instrumental means he has established; that is to say, in a manner that does not bypass his Church in its continuity and connectedness. A calling to Christian ministry — together with the promise of mediated grace consequent upon that calling — though initially and necessarily personal and direct, is ultimately and definitively mediated through the Church.

Ordination, therefore, is a mediation of calling and promise, it is a mediation of God's grace, it is sacramental, it is a sacrament. Indeed, as a dominical ordinance, ordination surely should be acknowledged as a sacrament without equivocation.[16] Jesus specifically calls and separates the first apostles (Mark 3.13ff.), he promises that whatever they bind on earth will have been bound in heaven (Matthew 18.18),[17] he breathes on them and promises them the Spirit, affirming that whomever's sins they forgive are truly forgiven (John 20.21ff.). It is this calling and promise of Jesus that is mediated by the Spirit through the Church in the act of ordination — it may be responsive to and affirming of a previous sense of personal vocation, but it is within this act that this calling is decisively and effectively uttered. In the act of ordination a man or woman is separated as a minister of Word and Sacrament. In the act of ordination a man or

---

[16]   Note that John Calvin, though dismissive of a sacrament of holy orders as he perceived it within the Roman Catholic Church, clearly affirms the laying on of hands in ordination as 'a sacrament in true and lawful ordinations' (*Institutes* IV xix 31). Earlier Calvin had written of ordination as being 'no empty sign if it is restored to its own true origin' (*Institutes* IV iii 16). For a more sustained discussion of Calvin's consistency in this see Colwell, 'The Sacramental Nature of Ordination', pp. 236-37.

[17]   As the marginal note for the *NIV* acknowledges, the participles here are in the perfect tense: ὅσα ἐὰν δήσητε ἐπὶ τῆς γῆς ἔσται δεδεμένα ἐν οὐρανῷ, καὶ ὅσα ἐὰν λύσητε ἐπὶ τῆς γῆς ἔσται λελυμένα ἐν οὐρανῷ. Cf. Matthew 16.19.

woman is separated as themselves a living sacrament, an instrumental means of the gracious presence and action of the Holy Spirit.

The act of ordination, therefore, implies and effects not merely the possibility of a new function but the actuality of a new being. As with baptism, in the act of ordination a sacramental character is bestowed. Indeed, it is within the course of a work on Christian baptism that Gregory of Nyssa draws a parallel between the consecration of the bread in the Eucharist and the consecration of a priest—in both acts a sacramental change occurs.[18] And, as with the bread and wine of the Eucharist, it is a *sacramental* change that occurs—there is no analogy for this change; it is unique; it is a gracious work of the Spirit that cannot be presumed upon or manipulated; it is not a 'magical' change. The act of ordination occurs as an attestation by the Church that the ordinand truly has been called by God to this ministry. The act of ordination occurs in response to the promise that what is done in the name of Christ upon earth will have been done by God. The act of ordination occurs as an act of prayer in response to that promise. It is an act of humble confidence rather than presumption or manipulation. It is an act of trust that the Holy Spirit will effect that which here is sought in prayer and declared in the name of Christ. It is a receiving of the ordinand as a gift of the ascended Christ to his Church.

And as with marriage (as will be argued in the next chapter of this book), just as also with baptism, this act of ordination is indelible. That which God promises to do here by his Spirit cannot be undone. There is no sacrament of 'un-ordination' any more than there is a sacrament of divorce or a sacrament by which baptism can be set aside. An ordained minister may sully that ordination, may be unfaithful to that ordination, may betray that ordination, may disown that ordination, may deny that ordination—but that ordination cannot be undone; an ordained minister cannot be un-ordained. Certainly it may prove necessary and appropriate to bar an ordained minister from active ministry, to remove a name from a list of accredited ministers, to impose a public censure; but if and when such an offender is restored to active ministry there is never a rite of 're-ordination'.[19] The Church is the means rather than the source of the calling to Christian ministry—it cannot, therefore, abnegate that calling; there may be a suspension of function but there cannot be a rescinding of calling and identity.[20]

---

[18]   Gregory of Nyssa, *On the Baptism of Christ*, in *NPNF* 2, vol. 5, pp. 518-24.

[19]   Yet again I am grateful to Steve Holmes for drawing attention to the implication of this lack of a rite of re-ordination: Holmes, 'Towards a Baptist Theology of Ordained Ministry', p. 258.

[20]   In this respect, despite significant agreement, I find myself in disagreement with my friend Paul Fiddes (arguably the most able contemporary Baptist theologian). I suspect this disagreement concerning the indelibility of ordination rests upon a more

Moreover, if Christian ministry is a way of being rather than merely a way of doing, then this, as John Macquarrie notes, carries implications for the manner in which ordinands should be prepared and for the manner in which those engaged in Christian ministry should be supported:

> If we see the development of a certain character as the important *res* of ordination, then we shall see also that talk of 'training' the clergy is unfortunate, and quite inadequate. We train people (and even some animals) to perform certain actions. Talk of 'training' clergy reinforces the merely functional view. If beyond the functions there is a priestly character and a priestly heart, formation as well as training is needed.[21]

Without in any way belittling the appropriateness of theological and biblical studies, of a familiarity with the history of the Church, of the development of pastoral and leadership skills and of liturgical competence (I presently teach doctrine and ethics in a Baptist seminary, after all), the focus and priority for ministerial preparation surely should be an encouragement of spiritual disciplines and the formation of habits of character that enable an authentic and sustainable spirituality. And without in any way belittling the appropriateness of continual professional development (which rightly those engaged in ministry are now encouraged to pursue), if Christian ministry is primarily a matter of character, then character is developed through spiritual discipline, through mentoring, through spiritual direction. We must recognise the danger, both before and after ordination, of focusing on skills and understanding that can be acquired rather than upon a spirituality that develops through processes of formation. In this respect perhaps the traditional language of 'holy orders' should be encouraged: John Wesley expected certain disciplines of character and spirituality amongst his band of preachers just as Dominic and Francis respectively expected such from their orders of friars.[22] One of the principal besetting weaknesses of a Free Church ecclesiology is a lack of any clear and formal structure of ministerial accountability (though for such to exist formally does not necessarily imply that it functions effectively).

Christian ministry is a matter of character because Christian ministry is priestly, a participation in the priestly ministry of the ascended Christ and a mediation of that priestly ministry within the Church *and within the*

---

foundational difference concerning the essence of Christian ministry: by defining ministry in terms of ἐπισκοπή Fiddes is continuing to work primarily with a functional rather than ontological designation. Paul S. Fiddes, *Tracks and Traces: Baptist Identity in Church and Theology* (Carlisle: Paternoster Press, 2003), p. 101

[21] Macquarrie, *A Guide to the Sacraments*, pp. 185-86.

[22] See A. B. Lawson, *John Wesley and The Christian Ministry: The Sources and Development of His Opinions and Practice* (London: SPCK, 1963).

world. Christian ministry is priestly because it is apostolic and it is apostolic because it is priestly. Those called and separated as Christian ministers are not just the gifts of the ascended Christ to his Church, they are also sent by the ascended Christ into the world. I was taught and now teach in a college founded by one who modelled the ministry of the pastor and the evangelist.[23] Just as it is unhelpful (and illegitimate) to divide the single office and ministry of the ascended Christ, so surely it is unhelpful (if not illegitimate) too rigidly to distinguish various forms of Christian ministry. There may be pastors and there may be evangelists but, just as I find it impossible to conceive of an effective evangelist without pastoral skills, I find it impossible to conceive of a pastor without an evangelistic calling and responsibility. The danger of colleges establishing distinct courses for pastors and for evangelists is that of conveying the impression that one might be called to be the one without in any respect being called to be the other. The same danger occurs more widely in the now common distinction between ministry and mission—there simply is no mission that is not a mediation of the priestly ministry of Christ, just as there is no ministry that is not an outcome of being sent into the world as he himself was sent into the world.

And just as a priestly understanding of Christian ministry ought not in any way to detract from the uniqueness of Christ as our sole and sufficient priest so also an understanding of the apostolicity of Christian ministry ought not in any way to detract from the uniqueness of Christ's apostleship as the one sent by the Father into the world. Christian ministry is no more a simple continuation of the sending of the Son by the Father than the Church is a simple continuation of the Son's Incarnation. But just as the Church existing within the world witnesses to the incarnation of the Son and is enabled to mediate his risen presence by the Spirit, so also Christian ministry is itself an echo of the sending of the Son and, by the power of the Spirit, is a mediation of his mission and ministry. But neither (perhaps more controversially) is Christian ministry as truly apostolic a simple continuation of the apostolic ministry of the first apostles.[24] The first apostles, as witnesses of the resurrection, stand in a unique relationship to Christ as those entrusted with the gospel: we live, speak, and act in continuity with their unique testimony rather than in simple continuation of their unique office. The Church and its ministry are truly apostolic, not in repetition or prolongation of this unique apostolate, but in faithfulness to this unique apostolate. The Church is not at liberty to

---

[23]   C. H. Spurgeon, *Lectures to My Students* (London: Marshall, Morgan & Scott, 1954), pp. 22ff.

[24]   'The ministry is, therefore, not the canonical prolongation of the Apostolate any more than the Church is the prolongation of the Incarnation.' Forsyth, *The Church and the Sacraments*, pp. 138-39. Earlier (p. 138) Forsyth speaks of the minister as the 'surrogate of the Apostles rather than their successor'.

distort this unique witness or to compromise the gospel. Our responsibility, more simply, is to continue 'to contend for the faith that was once for all entrusted to the saints' (Jude 3).[25]

Within this responsibility for faithful resonance with the first apostles lies the principle source of Catholic unease with the ordination of women. Christ himself was male and Christ only appointed male apostles, consequently those who represent Christ in ministry and who stand in continuity with those first apostles must similarly be male: according to the late Pope John Paul II, '...the Church has no authority whatever to confer priestly ordination on women...'.[26] Such arguments appear (to this author) to be astoundingly disingenuous. In the first place, remarkably little is made within the Gospels of the maleness of Jesus; apart from the reference to his circumcision on the eighth day (Luke 2.21) the stress of the Gospel accounts is upon his humanity rather than his maleness. But more fundamentally the maleness of Jesus has little theological significance: the particularities of the Incarnation, including Christ's maleness, are crucial aspects of his historical locatedness, it could indeed be argued that such particularities were appropriate to his historical locatedness, but they do not constitute the central significance of the Son's incarnation. The second person of the Trinity assumes this particular humanity in order to define and to redeem all humanity: '...that which He has not assumed He has not healed; but that which is united to His Godhead is also saved...'.[27] Since Christ, then, represents a woman in his incarnation, in his death, in his resurrection, and in his ascension, it is difficult to understand why a woman cannot represent Christ in Word and Sacrament. And in the second place, while it is true that Christ, in his historical locatedness, chose only male apostles, it is also true that he chose only Jewish apostles—but I know of no-one who argues that only Jewish males should be ordained as Christian ministers. And this point is far from trivial. When today we read in Galatians 3.28 that, in Christ, there 'is neither Jew nor Greek, slave nor free, male nor female', we often fail to acknowledge that it was the first of these distinctions that was Paul's focus and that was the source of such contention within these first churches. The distinction between Jew and Gentile, in Paul's context, was of far greater significance than any

---

[25]   Note again the significance of the 'once for all' ($\H{\alpha}\pi\alpha\xi$) of this passage.

[26]   Pope John Paul II, *Ordinatio sacerdotalis* (Apostolic Letter) 4, cited in Haffner, *The Sacramental Mystery*, p. 174. Haffner continues on p. 188 to list six reasons militating against women's ordination: (1) that this has been the constant practice of the Church; (2) that Jesus only chose male apostles; (3) that the apostles didn't appoint female apostles; (4) that this precedent is normative; (5) that the priest must bear a 'natural resemblance' to Christ; (6) that this is not an issue of human rights.

[27]   Gregory Nazianzus, *Epistle to Cledonius the Priest Against Apollinarus*, in *NPNF* 2, vol. 7, pp. 439-443 (p. 440).

distinction between slave and free or between male and female. Too easily
we overlook the starkness of Paul's rhetoric in Romans: for God to graft
the Gentiles onto the olive tree that is Israel is simply contrary to nature
(παρὰ φύσιν), as 'contrary to nature' as the 'shameful lusts' cited
previously by Paul as manifestations of God's 'giving up' of men and
women to the outcomes of sin.[28] Besides which, in John's Gospel, a
Samaritan woman is the first evangelist; Martha confesses Jesus to be the
Christ, the Son of God; and Mary Magdalene, as the first witness of the
resurrection, is sent by Jesus to announce his resurrection to his
'brothers'—remembering that the apostles are never listed in John's
Gospel one cannot entirely dismiss the possibility that the Gospel was
written in this manner to draw attention to the inclusivity of Jesus. It is
more common for Protestant arguments against the ordination of women
to focus upon apparently prohibitive biblical texts (typically 1
Corinthians 14.34-35 and 1 Timothy 2.11ff.), but such strategies rest
upon the hermeneutical assumption that Scripture's authority for the
Church is prescriptive and proscriptive rather than descriptive—that the
Bible is primarily a book of rules rather than primarily a book of
stories—and consequently take inadequate account of the cultural and
textual locatedness of these apparent prohibitions. Whether or not women
were included in the Church's separated ministry within some of the
earliest churches (as some would argue[29]), the majority of the Church for
the majority of its history has not ordained women. Therefore the
remaining difficulty in the Church now deciding to ordain women is that
of how the Church in its present visible disunity can validly and
definitively decide upon anything at all. The genius of the papacy is
precisely that it affords the Roman Catholic Church the means to reach
such a definitive decision—which renders incomprehensible the papal
statement on this issue cited previously.

The remaining issues deriving from the necessary continuity of
Christian ministry with the first apostles concern the appropriate
expression of that continuity both within the act of ordination and with
respect to distinct orders of ministry: by whom are we appropriately
ordained and to what are we appropriately ordained?

The second question is the far easier to resolve. My early years as a
Christian were marked by the unquestioned assumption that Scripture's

---

[28]   Compare Romans 1.26-27 and Romans 11.17ff. I am grateful to Eugene Rogers
for drawing attention to this rhetoric that, on reflection, seems crucial to Paul's argument
in Romans. God, who gives us up (παρέδωκεν) in wrath to the outcomes of sin (Romans
1.24, 26 and 28), gives up (παρέδωκεν) his Son for us all (Romans 8.32); when we act
contrary to nature (παρὰ φύσιν) God responds by acting contrary to nature (παρὰ φύσιν).
cf. Eugene F. Rogers Jr., *Sexuality and the Christian Body* (Oxford: Blackwell, 1999).

[29]   Elisabeth Schüssler Fiorenza, *In Memory of Her: A Feminist Theological
Reconstruction of Christian Origins* (New York: Crossroad, 1984).

authority was that of a book of rules and that, therefore, the Bible offered a sufficient and comprehensive blueprint for the Church and its ministry. Reading Eduard Schweizer's *Church Order in the New Testament* was just one part, albeit a significant part, in the undermining of this naïve and distorting assumption.[30] The Bible is not a Hayne's Manual (car enthusiasts will understand the allusion) and comparison with any work intended as a blueprint will quickly clarify that this simply is not the genre of Scripture. The Bible, as overwhelmingly a narratival account of God's interaction with his people, is authoritative more in the manner of a case book than a rule book (the 'rules' which unquestionably occur generally relate to a specific context). The Bible, therefore, though sufficient in its witness to the gospel and to God as revealed in the gospel, makes no claim to comprehensiveness: it makes no claim to tell us all there is to know. And consequently, as Schweizer ably demonstrates, it simply is not possible to trace a single and consistent 'order' of ministry (of bishops, elders, and deacons—or of any other order for that matter) within the New Testament. It may be possible to trace a development from an informal recognition of ministry to a more formal recognition of ministry,[31] but it is neither possible nor valid to read a developed ordering of ministry back into the New Testament. The appropriate question, then, is not whether a pattern and ordering of ministry conforms to a supposed New Testament blueprint, but rather whether a contemporary pattern and ordering of ministry is a consistent and appropriate response to the New Testament witness.[32]

In the absence of any clear and consistent biblical delineation of orders of ministry perhaps the first inference to be drawn (as has been assumed throughout this chapter) is that Christian ministry, as a mediation of the ministry of Christ, is singular. Different patterns and orders of ministry may develop (and have developed), Christian ministers may function in various ways, in diverse spheres, and with differing levels of responsibility, but there is but a single Christian ministry that, in all its manifestations, is pastoral and priestly, prophetic and apostolic, didactic and evangelistic; a single ministry of Word and Sacrament. This singularity has (in the main) been the consistent witness of Protestantism and, as Robert Jenson notes,

---

[30] Eduard Schweizer, *Church Order in the New Testament*, trans. Frank Clarke (London: SCM Press, 1961).

[31] For a discussion of this possibility see R. Alastair Campbell's *The Elders: Seniority within Earliest Christianity* (Edinburgh: T & T Clark, 1994).

[32] At this point it should perhaps be acknowledged that there is no (and could be no) 'non-episcopal' understanding of local church ministry. Baptist and Congregational churches view local church ministers as exercising 'episcopacy' and, indeed, a proper understanding of diocese is that each diocese is a local church, nurtured by a bishop, with presbyters (priests) and deacons acting on the bishop's behalf.

this essential singularity is affirmed at the second Vatican Council.[33] To affirm such singularity is not necessarily to deny the appropriateness of a junior and preparatory order of ministry (as the office of deacon generally has developed within the Western tradition) or of a junior and limited order of ministry (as the office of deacon may have initially represented and as may now be implied by notions of local licence or local ordination[34]). But to affirm such singularity is necessarily to deny that any ministry is other than a mediation of the single ministry of Christ.

Consequently, the second inference to be drawn (and again as has been assumed throughout this chapter) is that Christian ministry is service and that Christian ministers are servants of Christ and of his Church. This is not necessarily to deny the appropriateness of Christian ministers exercising differing levels of responsibility, nor is it to deny appropriate structures of accountability—such may indeed be the intention of Catholic notions of hierarchy, repeated at Vatican II.[35] But it is necessarily to deny any form of hierarchical authoritarianism, any form of clerical pomposity, any form of arrogant dogmatism that is usually a thin veil for personal insecurity. And it is to affirm the appropriateness of a Baptist and Congregationalist witness to the accountability of Christian ministers to the church as locally gathered as well as to the Church in its connectedness and continuity. We are called to serve one another and to submit to one another. Nowhere are we called to exercise authority over one another—in fact, this is explicitly what Christ tells us we must not do (Matthew 20.25ff.). All Christian ministry is a mediation of the ministry of the Christ who took a towel and washed his disciples' dirty feet.

However, while questions of the nature of ministry and of the orders of ministry are fairly easily resolved, the question of the connectedness and continuity of ministry—specifically the question of the authority to ordain—is more elusive. Though it may be commonplace for Protestant commentators to be dismissive of literal and physical understandings of apostolic succession it should be acknowledged that such literal and

---

[33]   'Roman Catholicism has now clarified its position; according to the second Vatican Council there is a single "divinely instituted ecclesiastical ministry" that is "exercised at different levels by those who from ancient times have been called bishops, priests and deacons." The pastoral office is one office, according to both Catholicism and Protestantism.' Jenson, *Systematic Theology*, vol. 2, pp. 236-37; cf. *LG* III 28.

[34]   For this author, however, language of 'local ordination' is unhelpful: one is either ordained or not ordained, one is either recognised and separated for Christian ministry or one is not so recognised and separated. I am reminded of a quite bizarre proposal brought to the Baptist Union Council (in March 2003) for a national register of accreditation for locally accredited ministers (a national accreditation of local accreditation)—mercifully the proposal was rejected.

[35]   *LG* chapter 3.

physical connectedness would be an eloquent and desirable expression and representation of the continuity of the Church and its ministry.[36] Of course, even such literal and physical connectedness would be no guarantee, in and of itself, of authentic continuity. The rite of ordination, like any other sacrament, is not God's prison: the Spirit can neither be constrained here nor restrained here; the Spirit cannot be manipulated here as though a mere automaton, nor can the Spirit be confined here as one not free to move and act elsewhere. The authentic continuity of the Church and its ministry is a gift of the Spirit—a gift sought humbly, prayerfully, and confidently in the act of ordination, but a gift that cannot simply be guaranteed through a literal succession of ordinations by a series of bishops stretching back to the first apostles. The Spirit is neither constrained nor restrained by any literal chain of succession.

But, in our present circumstance, this claim to a literal and physical apostolic succession has a hollow ring: though the Catholic Church and the Orthodox Churches would profess otherwise, in our present state of visible (physical) disunity no superintendent minister, no bishop, no metropolitan, no pope, has authority to ordain on behalf of the entire Church in its connectedness and continuity (other than with the radically sectarian assumption that defines a part as the whole and implicitly dismisses that which is other as wholly illegitimate). The question of catholicity—of accountability and connectedness to the Church in its wholeness and continuity—appears presently irresolvable. This should be a matter of the deepest grief to any who take Christ's prayer for the oneness of his Church with due weight and seriousness (John 17). This is the cloud if not the contradiction that overhangs the entire effort of this book and that casts a mocking shadow over every attempt at a truly catholic theology and over every manifestation of mission. Appropriately, therefore, this contradiction will be revisited at the conclusion of this book—but without resolution of this contradiction there can be no resolving of the question of appropriate ordination.

Ironically, of course, it is the question of the papacy that represents both the greatest apparent obstacle to visible unity and the greatest potential for achieving that visible unity. *In optimum partem*, just as the notion of papal infallibility (as has already been acknowledged) constitutes a means of acknowledging and affirming doctrinal development, so the title 'Vicar of Christ' identifies the Pope as embodying the unity of the Church and its ministry. For all its

---

[36]   So the documents of Vatican II assume that '[a]mongst those various offices which have been exercised in the Church from the earliest times the chief place, according to the witness of tradition, is held by the function of those who, through their appointment to the dignity and responsibility of bishop, and in virtue consequently of the unbroken succession, going back to the beginning, are regarded as transmitters of the apostolic line.' *LG* III 20.

offensiveness to some, the title can easily be defended if all Christian ministry is recognised as a mediation of Christ's ministry and if the Bishop of Rome can be acknowledged as embodying, symbolising, and enabling the unity of the Church's ministry. In Matthew 18.18 Jesus says to all his disciples that which he had previously said to Peter (Matthew 16.19), that whatever they bind or loose on earth will have been bound or loosed in heaven. But Jesus says things to Peter that he does not say to the others: he promises to build his Church on this rock (and perhaps we should acknowledge that common Protestant attempts to disconnect this promise from Peter have the ring of special pleading); he promises to give to Peter the keys of the kingdom of heaven (which, though enigmatic to us, must imply some specific responsibility); and later he charges Peter with the task of strengthening his brothers (Luke 22.31-32). Moreover (and perhaps most significantly), though Jesus' charge to Peter to feed his sheep is rightly taken as descriptive of all Christian ministry, it is said firstly and definitively to Peter. Peter is an apostle alongside the other apostles—but he is given specific responsibility for them, and he is addressed as representing them.

The question, as acknowledged previously, is not whether these words to Peter provide a blueprint for a papacy but whether a papacy, understood in terms of representation and corresponding responsibility, constitute an appropriate development in the light of these words to Peter. A papacy, thus understood, would not constitute a fourth order of ministry alongside that of bishop, presbyter, and deacon. A papacy, thus understood, would be collegial: the Pope would be a bishop amongst bishops just as Peter was an apostle amongst the apostles.[37] But a papacy, thus understood, would imply a representative embodiment and a foundational responsibility. A papacy, thus understood, would constitute both a symbol and a means of the Church's catholicity—its unity, connectedness, and continuity.[38]

This, at very least, would be one way of reading the significance of the defence of the papacy by Irenaeus: not as a defence of a literal and physical apostolic succession, but as a recognition of exemplary and representative faithfulness in discharging a responsibility.[39] And the Great

---

[37]   '[W]hatever the special prerogatives of the Pope may have been, the papacy is not a fourth or higher order of ministry in addition to the three traditional orders, but is located within the universal episcopate of the church, so that the holder of this office is at the same time in a collegial relation to his fellow bishops, and may not usurp their functions.' Macquarrie, *A Guide to the Sacraments*, p. 210.

[38]   Cf. Macquarrie, *A Guide to the Sacraments*, pp. 205 and 212.

[39]   'Since, however, it would be very tedious, in such a volume as this, to reckon up the successions of all the Churches...[we do this, I say,] by indicating that tradition derived from the apostles, of the very great, the very ancient, and universally known Church founded and organized at Rome by the two most glorious apostles, Peter and Paul;

Schism occurred, and subsequently the Protestant Reformation occurred, because firstly the Eastern Churches and later the Protestant Reformers considered the papacy to have been unfaithful in the fulfilling of that representative responsibility. But that which previously has been deemed unfaithful may yet be renewed in faithfulness. The papacy, through its historical identity if not its biblical rootedness, yet has potential to be the means and the embodiment of the true catholicity of the Church. The encyclical letter of John Paul II, *Ut unum sint*, should be recognised as an extraordinarily humble and gracious first step to act as such a means.[40]

And perhaps a correspondingly humble and gracious step by all engaged in Christian ministry, whether Protestant, Catholic, or Orthodox, would be to acknowledge the partiality of their ordination as denominationally limited and to be prepared to submit to the renewal of that ordination—if not to re-ordination—in a truly catholic context. Re-ordination, like re-baptism, is theologically incoherent—one is either ordained or one isn't ordained—but, unlike baptism which is deemed valid even within this context of disunity, ordination within this context of disunity is not universally deemed valid. Consequently, the mediate uttering of God's calling to ministry in a truly catholic context would not in any way invalidate a previous uttering of that calling within a limited and denominational context: what would be effected through such re-ordination would be a wider recognition of this man or this woman as truly a gift from the ascended Christ as a means of the nurture, maturity, and unity of his Church within the world.

---

as also [by pointing out] the faith preached to men, which comes down to our time by means of the successions of the bishops. For it is a matter of necessity that every Church should agree with this Church, on account of its pre-eminent authority, that is, the faithful everywhere, inasmuch as the apostolical tradition has been preserved continuously by those [faithful men] who exist everywhere.' Irenaeus, *Against Heresies*, III iii 2.

[40]   John Paul II, *Ut unum sint: Encyclical Letter of the Holy Father John Paul II on Commitment to Ecumenism* (London: Catholic Truth Society, 1995). For a discussion of the significance of this encyclical see Carl E. Braaten and Robert W. Jenson (eds.), *Church Unity and the Papal Office: An Ecumenical Dialogue on John Paul II's Encyclical 'Ut Unum Sint' (That they may be one)* (Grand Rapids, MI: Eerdmans, 2001).

CHAPTER 11

The Sacrament of Marriage

Some Pharisees came to him to test him. They asked, 'Is it lawful for a man to divorce his wife for any and every reason?'

'Haven't you read,' he replied, 'that at the beginning the Creator "made them male and female", and said, "For this reason a man will leave his father and mother and be united to his wife, and the two will become one flesh"? So they are no longer two, but one. Therefore what God has joined together, let no-one separate.'

'Why then,' they asked, 'did Moses command that a man give his wife a certificate of divorce and send her away?'

Jesus replied, 'Moses permitted you to divorce your wives because your hearts were hard. But it was not this way from the beginning. I tell you that anyone who divorces his wife, except for marital unfaithfulness, and marries another woman commits adultery.'

The disciples said to him, 'If this is the situation between a husband and wife, it is better not to marry.'

Jesus replied, 'Not everyone can accept this word, but only those to whom it has been given. For some are eunuchs because they were born that way; others have been made eunuchs; and others have renounced marriage because of the kingdom of heaven. The one who can accept this should accept it.' (Matthew 19.3-12).

Vast quantities of paper and print have been expended discussing the significance of the so-called Matthean exception, the meaning of the word πορνεία here translated 'marital unfaithfulness': what precisely is the significance of this word within this context and is Jesus allowing for the possibility of divorce under these particular circumstances (remembering that this 'exception' is omitted from Mark's account of this conversation)? The probable background to the passage was a dispute amongst the rabbis concerning the permitted grounds for divorce in the Torah: what precisely was the significance of the 'something indecent' (ערות דבר) referred to in Deuteronomy 24.1; does the term refer to sexual misdemeanour (and, if so, of what form?) or does the term have a far wider reference?

I must confess to being baffled by this preoccupation with the meaning of words. Are we really supposed to infer that, within the context of a debate concerning the significance of an ambiguous Hebrew word, Jesus contributes a similarly ambiguous Greek word as a means or resolving the argument? If the intention of Jesus within this narrative was to identify a valid ground for divorce why is this 'exception' omitted in Mark's account? And if this really was the intention of Jesus, even as the incident is recorded in Matthew, why do Jesus' disciples apparently react with such extreme perplexity? The manner of the disciples' reaction, as it is recorded both here and in Mark, surely suggests that they did not hear an 'exception' in Jesus' words; their astonishment was a response to Jesus' affirmation of the permanency of marriage, a response to his severe qualification of any apparent provision for divorce within the Torah.

And this, surely, is the focus and impetus of the passage. In response to a dispute over valid grounds for divorce Jesus (as is so often the case) challenges the presuppositions of the question; rather than adjudicating valid grounds for divorce Jesus challenges the assumption that there could be valid (or at least 'commendable') grounds for divorce given God's original covenantal intention for marriage. Jesus reminds his questioners that, according to the Torah, marriage should be defined as a man and a woman becoming 'one flesh' (καὶ ἔσονται οἱ δύο εἰς σάρκα μίαν), which Jesus here interprets as signifying, not just a physical and sexual union, but a being joined together by God—and if God has united a man and a woman in marriage then no human court has authority to dissolve this union. Whatever might or might not be signified by Jesus' use of the word πορνείᾳ (as recorded in Matthew), it was this unequivocal assertion of the permanency of marriage that prompted his disciples' shocked response.

And it is this attestation by Jesus of marriage as a union of a man and woman effected by God that prompts a definition of marriage, not merely as a human covenant (and certainly not merely as a human contract), but as a sacrament; as a visible sign of an invisible grace; as a human event which is to be identified as the means of a divine event. And if this ultimately is the valid definition of marriage, then questions of divorce, of re-marriage, of cohabitation, of same-sex unions, must be considered in the light of this dominical and sacramental definition.

One could, of course, arrive at a sacramental definition of marriage in response to the discussion of marriage within Ephesians, the comparison there made between the union of a husband and wife and the union of Christ and his Church, and the use within the passage of the term μυστήριον (mystery)—given that the term is used so infrequently within the New Testament it might be thought perverse to ignore a passage (and a letter) in which it is used with such theological import (Ephesians 5.32). It must be conceded that the mere use of the term that would later be translated by the Latin term *sacramentum* is insufficient ground, in itself, to confirm a sacramental definition of marriage; it must be conceded that the term as used in Ephesians does not yet have the technical significance it would later acquire.[1] But without prejudice to Jerome's later translation of the term μυστήριον with the term *sacramentum* (the latter, as has already been noted, being etymologically the more problematic), and without prejudice to later ecclesial attempts to define the sacraments with theological precision, it must be valid to explore the significance of this reference to marriage as a mystery (μυστήριον) in the light of the use of the term within the context of this passage and previously within this letter. In chapter three of this letter the term 'mystery' is applied to the gospel, to God's hidden purpose of including the Gentiles with Israel as his covenant people, and specifically to this Church (of Jew and Gentile) as the revelation of this hidden purpose to heavenly (and earthly?) rulers and authorities (Ephesians 3.7ff.). The Church, then, is a 'mystery'; its essence and identity are beyond mere human perception and definition; this apparently human entity is, in fact, the means of a divine dynamic and revelation—and is not such precisely that which the Church would later identify and define as sacramental? And within this specific passage the term 'mystery' is applied both to the union of Christ and his Church and to the union of husband and wife in marriage; the text from Genesis concerning the two becoming one is cited with pertinence to both unions: that Christ is united to his Church is a 'mystery', it is a reality beyond mere human perception and definition; and that a husband and wife are united in marriage is similarly (and analogically) a 'mystery', a reality beyond mere human perception and definition. The human entity which is the Church (as discussed in chapter 3) and the human entity which is marriage (as attested in the words of Jesus) are both significant of other than that which can be directly perceived; they are both significant of a union that is given and effected by God. Moreover, as analogically related to the union of Christ and the Church, marriage is itself a sign of that union, a mystery itself that is significant of this greater and deeper mystery. Perhaps these two sacramental senses should be distinguished (though not separated): marriage is sacramental in the sense that this human joining together signifies a being joined together by God; and marriage is sacramental in the sense that this human joining together, which signifies a being joined together by God, is itself significant of a deeper mystery which is the union of Christ with the Church.

John Calvin freely admits marriage as a 'good and holy ordinance of God', though he rather devalues the insight by comparing it as such to 'farming, building, cobbling, and barbering'. According to Calvin, for marriage to be a sacrament it would need to be 'not only a work of God

---

[1]   'According to Steur, the sacramental character of marriage cannot be deduced from the Pauline word *mysterion* translated by Jerome *sacramentum*, for the term "sacrament" did not then have technical significance.' Berkouwer, *The Sacraments*, p. 35, referring to Steur, *Dogm. Tractaat over het Sacr. v.h. huwelijk* (1947), p. 621.

but an outward ceremony appointed by God to confirm a promise'.[2]
Calvin vehemently denies that marriage could be such (indeed, as is so
often the case in his writings, his argument is little enhanced by the
intemperate language with which he insults those who might conclude
otherwise): marriage may be a sign of Christ's union with the Church, just
as the sight of a vine may remind us that Christ speaks of himself as the
true vine, but marriage is no more a sacrament than a vine is a sacrament.[3]
But surely here Calvin is employing the term 'sign' in too broad a sense:
marriage, according to this passage in Ephesians, is more than a sign in
the sense that a vine (or a shepherd) may remind us of words of Christ;
marriage is more than a metaphor for Christ's union with the Church;
marriage is itself a mystery analogically related to the mystery of Christ's
union with the Church. Farming, building, cobbling, and barbering may
be good and worthy activities but are they truly (and explicitly)
'ordained' by God in the sense that marriage is explicitly ordained by
God? And if marriage is ordained by God (and Calvin would struggle to
find a passage comparable to Genesis 2 or Matthew 19 as an explicit
ordination of farming, building, cobbling, and barbering), to what
purpose and with what significance is marriage thus ordained? The
comparisons Calvin makes here belittle marriage and constitute an
inadequate response to the dignity with which Scripture speaks of the
ordinance.

Moreover, in response to this passage in Matthew 19, and in response
to this passage in Ephesians 5, are we not compelled to interpret marriage
as '...appointed by God to confirm a promise'; or, at least, as appointed
by God to *betoken* a promise? The joining of a man and a woman in
marriage, according to the words of Jesus in Matthew 19, betokens the
promise that this man and woman are joined together by God. The
joining of a man and a woman in marriage, according to this passage in
Ephesians 5, betokens the promise that, albeit in a deeper sense, Christ is
truly joined to the Church. Calvin is surely on far stronger ground when
he repudiates the manner in which a sacramental definition of marriage
has been utilised, both as a means of denying the validity of some
marriages as 'non-sacramental', and as a means of affirming the
indissolubility of some 'sacramental' marriages where credible 'consent'
was lacking.[4]

But can marriage really be considered a 'gospel' sacrament? The
joining of a man and a woman in marriage may not merely betoken, but
may be the means through which their being joined together by God is
effected, but surely the joining of a man and a woman in marriage in no

---

2   *Institutes* IV xix 34.
3   *Institutes* IV xix 34.
4   *Institutes* IV xix 37.

sense is a means through which the union of Christ and the Church is effected? When marriage can validly be contracted without reference to the gospel, can marriage validly be a sign of the gospel, less still a means through which the grace of the gospel is effected? The point is made persuasively by Colin Gunton:

> ...sacraments are what they are by virtue of their enabling of human belonging in the church. That is one reason why it is wrong to call marriage a sacrament. One can be truly married, and 'in the sight of God', without stepping inside a church. Baptism and the Lord's Supper, by contrast, are what they are as sacraments of, respectively, entry into a community formed around the sacrifice of Christ and the maintenance of the community without which the church would not be the embodiment of the image of God.[5]

It is at this point that Calvin's broader theology (expounded both more radically and consistently by Karl Barth), the insistence that there is but one eternal covenant and that this single covenant constitutes the context and basis for all God's ways and works in creation, may be of help and pertinence. Certainly marriage is a provision of God for all creation—its validity is not restricted firstly to Israel and then to the Church—but, since all creation is bounded by a single eternal covenant, might not marriage always betoken that covenant and be a means of the grace which is its outcome? A man and a woman may be ignorant of the gospel, a man and a woman may not acknowledge God in any sense, but their covenantal joining together in marriage nonetheless betokens and foreshadows that deeper union between Christ and the Church which is the goal of creation. A man and a woman may be ignorant of the gospel, a man and a woman may not acknowledge God in any sense, but their covenantal joining together in marriage nonetheless may be a means through which God graciously touches their lives with his love; their covenant love, albeit unconsciously, may yet be a means of God's covenant love. Indeed, may this not be a promise—a promise that cannot be manipulated and a promise that can be rejected or abused—but a promise nonetheless? God's ultimate purpose for creation is that all things should be brought to unity in the Son and by the Spirit, that men and women should participate by grace in the eternal intimacy of the Trinity. Here and now the Church is the supreme anticipation and revelation of this ultimate intimacy, the deepest sacramental mystery of this supreme union. But the intimacy of marriage, even unconsciously, is also an ordained anticipation and echo of this ultimate intimacy. And just as the Church is promised as a means of anticipating this ultimate intimacy, so too, albeit to a lesser degree and perhaps unconsciously, the intimacy of marriage is promised as a means of anticipating this ultimate intimacy. And, if this is the case,

---

[5]   Gunton, *Christ and Creation*, p. 114.

then marriage is not just sacramental in the sense of being a human joining that signifies and is a means of a divine joining, marriage is also a gospel sacrament, a signification and means of anticipating that ultimate gracious intimacy that is the goal of creation. Indeed, precisely as a sacrament beyond the bounds of Israel and the Church, the intimacy of marriage bears witness to the universal graciousness of God, to the covenantal context of all creation.

However, to define marriage sacramentally in these two senses does not of itself resolve the question of the manner of relationship (or the manner of rite by which that relationship is established) that constitutes a true marriage to which this twofold sacramental definition may be applied. When is a marriage validly a marriage? What factors constitute that relationship which can be termed sacramental? In our present context the question is not easily resolved.[6]

It should be admitted that it may appear, albeit superficially, that a valid marriage is easily (and legally) recognisable. A legal marriage (in Western society) is established by valid ceremony and by legal documentation. A marriage is legally contracted. Public vows, duly witnessed and certified, constitute a valid marriage. It was not always so — and too easily we forget that such legal interventions and definitions are quite recent innovations. Are we, for instance, to question the validity of a Quaker marriage simply because, though a man and a woman have publicly expressed a covenantal commitment, for reasons of conscience they decline to conform to legal formalities (such marriages were not legally recognised in Britain until relatively recently)? But, even more seriously, legal and contractual definitions of marriage are deeply problematic. The history of Reformed theology has been plagued in a number of ways by confusion between contract and covenant: a contract is conditional, a covenant is unconditional; a covenant is marked by consequences rather than by conditions; God does not tell his people that he will be their God if they keep his commandments, he rather tells his people that he is their God and that therefore they must keep his commandments. Marriage is not a contract, a conditional relationship; marriage is a covenant, an unconditional relationship albeit carrying consequences. Surely this is the more probable significance of Jesus response to the Pharisees recorded in Matthew 19.1ff. and Mark 10.1ff.: marriage is not a contract that can be terminated when certain conditions have been broken or unfulfilled; marriage is a covenant, it is unconditional but it carries serious consequences.

---

[6]   For a series of discussions relating to contemporary challenges to the marriage relationship (from a variety of standpoints) see Adrian Thatcher (ed.), *Celebrating Christian Marriage* (Edinburgh: T & T Clark, 2001).

When I was married, over thirty years ago, we personalised the vows that we made to one another. At the time this was a radical and unusual feature of a wedding service (and I can remember the unease—if not horror—of some of our more conservative friends). Since then the practice has become quite common in Free Church circles. I cannot express how deeply I regret it. The traditional words of the marriage service are as close to perfection as you can come: '...to have and to hold, from this day forward, for better for worse, for richer for poorer, in sickness and in health, to love and to cherish, until death do us part...'—such promises are comprehensive; to add to them is to dilute and diminish them. But beyond their stylistic merit and their all-encompassing scope, the words are unequivocally covenantal rather than contractual: for better or for worse, for richer or for poorer, in sickness and in health, precisely excludes conditionality; in every condition, foreseeable or unforeseeable, we will love and cherish one another. I have stood on the steps outside a Registry Office while a prospective bridegroom confessed to me that he had learned the lessons from the break-up of his previous marriage, that he would quickly walk away from this one if it started to go wrong—I was hardly surprised when the marriage ended barely more than a year later (and maybe I should have had the courage to declare an impediment).

And I suspect this to be a not uncommon attitude: whether explicitly admitted or not—and making a mockery of the vows to be made whether before a Church or before a Registrar—I suspect that many now come to a marriage ceremony consciously sustaining clear if unexpressed conditions. Whatever promises may be uttered they are qualified by an unspoken conditionality: not '...until death do us part', but rather '...for as long as this works out okay'. Perhaps I'm guilty of cynicism. Would that this were cynicism rather than a sober (albeit anecdotal) reflection on contemporary attitudes to marriage. While I certainly do not rue the passing of an age when many women (and not a few men) were held captive in abusive marriages, an age when a divorce could be obtained only through proof of adultery (often artificially contrived), it is difficult not to conclude that contemporary ease of divorce has introduced an element of conditionality to marriage: if it doesn't work out there is a relatively easy way out. We may not commonly have succumbed to prenuptial agreements—legal contracts determining the division of assets should divorce ensue—though I strongly suspect that a contractual notion of marriage predominates nonetheless.

But is a contractual notion of marriage truly a notion of marriage? In many respects our contemporary ease of divorce resembles the ease of divorce (for men, at least) at the time of Jesus, and consequently our present context corresponds to the context in which Jesus responded to a question concerning valid grounds for divorce with a reaffirmation of the covenantal essence of marriage. A marriage contracted with explicit or implicit conditions is no true marriage. Marriage, by definition, is unconditional. Marriage is covenantal. Marriage is analogous to the unconditional love of Christ for his Church. Marriage anticipates and echoes God's covenantal love for us. Marriage is a reflection—albeit a flickering reflection—of the eternal intimacy of Father, Son, and Spirit. That God declares a hatred of divorce (Malachi 2.16) is simply an outcome of his eternal nature as Father, Son, and Spirit. The changelessness of God is not the immobility of the apathetic but the immutability of the impassable, the faithfulness of the utterly constant (Malachi 3.6).[7] God cannot be faithless; God cannot disown himself (2 Timothy 2.13). The intimate love that binds Father, Son, and Spirit is unchanging, undiminishing, utterly constant. The covenant love which is a reiteration of that eternal intimacy and through which the Father has bound us to himself in the Son and through the Spirit is similarly utterly constant: nothing will ever 'be able to separate us from the love of God that is in Christ Jesus our Lord' (Romans 8.38-39). Consequently the love that binds us to Christ and to one another within the Church, together with the love which binds wife and husband as 'one flesh', ought similarly to be utterly constant, unfailingly faithful. Marriage, like our union with Christ in the Church, is a mysterious intimation of the intimacy of the Triune God. Marriage is covenantal. Marriage is unconditional.[8]

Therefore, though legal contracts of marriage may have some utility in contemporary society, they do not comprise the essence of marriage and, in a context (as apparently in the days of Jesus) where divorce is common and legally straightforward, a legal contract may serve to bolster the notion that marriage is conditional rather than unconditional, a matter of contract rather than a matter of covenant. And if a marriage is not established by a legal contract (in and of itself) then neither is a marriage disestablished or invalidated by the absence of a legal contract (in and of itself). A valid marriage is established as an unconditional covenant commitment of a man and woman to one another for life: in and through this human covenant commitment a man and a woman are joined as one by God. Such covenant commitment is properly public, occurring in a societal context it ought properly to conform to the mores of that particular society, occurring in contemporary Western society it ought properly to conform to the rites of public ceremony and legal certification—but it is not established by such mores; it is established by

---

[7]   For discussion of these crucial distinction see Weinandy, *Does God Suffer?*

[8]   Though—and I am grateful to Dr Jane Craske for this insight—marriage, unlike our union with Christ, is constituted and maintained by the faithfulness of both parties rather than the faithfulness of the one.

God in and through the unconditional covenanting together of a man and a women.

And if the mores of a particular society find expression in the arranging of marriages by families and by the wider community this, of itself, need neither invalidate nor validate a marriage. The issue here as always is the authenticity of an unconditional covenant. Such authenticity is not diminished by the (possible) lack of 'romantic love' (a sometimes destructive fixation of contemporary Western society), but such authenticity would be forfeited by lack of credible consent. A covenant is freely entered. God is not compelled to love us; he would still be the God that he is without us; that God loves us, creates us, and redeems us is unequivocally a matter of grace; God's love for us is entirely gratuitous; it is entirely free. Therefore, though a marriage would not be invalidated by family or community orchestration, nor by the possible lack of 'romantic love', it would be invalidated by lack of consent—and such consent must be credible; those covenanting together must be sufficiently free from external compulsion and of sufficient maturity to be competent for such consent.

Moreover, if an authentic marriage is not established by legal certification, and if an authentic marriage is not invalidated (nor established) by family or community arrangement, then neither is an authentic marriage established by religious rite nor invalidated by the lack of religious rite. As Paul Haffner notes, though the Council of Trent decreed that a priest should be present to officiate at a marriage (thus abolishing 'clandestine' marriages within the Catholic Church),[9] the consent of the man and woman being married remained primary. Indeed, as Haffner later explains, within the Western tradition it is not the officiating priest who ministers this sacrament of marriage to the couple being married but rather the man and the woman being married who minister this sacrament of marriage to one another by expressing their covenant commitment to one another.[10] One danger of affirming the sacramental nature of marriage is the consequent false assumption that only marriages contracted within the sacramental context of an ecclesial ceremony are authentic and valid marriages. That which constitutes the sacramentality (and thereby the authenticity) of a marriage is the consensual covenanting of the man and woman being married, not the ecclesial context in which that covenanting may occur. Wherever and whenever such consensual covenanting occurs there is truly a marriage and there is, thereby, the sacramental promise that these two have been

---

[9]   Haffner, *The Sacramental Mystery*, pp. 208-209.

[10]   'In the Latin Church, it is ordinarily understood that the spouses, as ministers of Christ's grace, mutually confer upon each other the sacrament of Matrimony by expressing their consent before the Church.' Haffner, *The Sacramental Mystery*, p. 210, quoting *CCC*, 1623.

joined by God, that this union, consciously or unconsciously, may be a reflection of the union of Christ and the Church, and that this union, consciously or unconsciously, may be a means of grace, a means through which something of God's love is imparted to this man through this woman and to this woman through this man whether they acknowledge its source or not. A Christian minister may authoritatively declare this sacramental reality, but a Christian minister cannot establish this sacramental reality, it is established by God directly through the mediating consensual covenanting of this man and this woman. Whether such consensual covenanting occurs between two Moslems, two Christians, two Hindus, two atheists, two agnostics, two devotees of any creed, or any combination of such, is entirely irrelevant both to the authenticity of a marriage and to the sacramentality of marriage. Marriage is ordained by God beyond the bounds of the Church.

But if all this be the case then we are confronted by a situation where some legally constituted marriages, by reason of implicit conditionality, may not be authentic marriages, and where some covenantal relationships between men and women, though not confirmed by any religious rite or legal contract, may yet be authentic marriages. Over recent years within British society cohabitation prior to a formal marriage ceremony, or with no expressed intention of submitting to a formal marriage ceremony, has become commonplace. But if a marriage is established by covenantal commitment rather than by formal marriage ceremony one must admit the possibility that some such cohabiting relationships are, in reality, marriages in the full sacramental sense. There are, of course, different forms of cohabitation determined by differing intentions. Some instances of cohabitation represent most radical expressions of conditionality—no covenantal commitment has been made or is intended to be made. Some instances of cohabitation are perceived as trial marriages: a conditional commitment has been made that may (or may not) be followed by an unconditional commitment. One suspects that most instances of cohabitation take this form and there may be a case (as proposed by Adrian Thatcher) for interpreting such as contemporary forms of betrothal.[11] However, some instances of cohabitation represent a deferring of a formal marriage ceremony for entirely economic reasons—a wedding in contemporary British society has become a highly (and unnecessarily) costly affair—yet an unconditional commitment has already been made between this man and this woman. And some

---

[11]   Adrian Thatcher proposes this notion of betrothal as a means of comprehending much that presently occurs as cohabitation and seeks to support the proposal by investigation of the scope of betrothal historically. Adrian Thatcher, 'Living Together before Marriage: The Theological and Pastoral Opportunities', in Thatcher (ed.), *Celebrating Christian Marriage*, pp. 55-70, and *Living Together and Christian Ethics* (Cambridge: Cambridge University Press, 2002).

instances of cohabitation represent a deliberate rejection of a formal marriage rite, perhaps for economic or religious reasons, perhaps as an active refutation of that which the marriage rite has become in contemporary British society.[12] But in this latter case, as in the case of a rite of marriage being delayed merely for economic reasons, an unconditional commitment may have been made between this man and this woman—indeed, it may have been made publicly, in a manner inclusive of their immediate family and community and conforming to the mores of their distinctive sub-culture. And in such cases, even if marriage as a formal rite or institution is explicitly rejected, a marriage nonetheless has occurred: through their mutual unconditional commitment this man and woman have been united by God; their relationship as an unconditional commitment intimates the covenantal union of Christ and the Church; their mutual love, whether consciously or unconsciously, may be a means of God's gracious love to them and through them.

All of which is highly confusing for the Christian minister seeking to encourage coherent and consistent practices of Christian discipleship. We inhabit a post-Christian society where the mores of the Christian community concerning the rite of marriage and a commitment to chastity are no longer commonly understood or accepted. To those already cohabiting who seek a formal rite of marriage within the context of the Church the Christian minister, on behalf of the Church, is called to bear witness to the unconditional covenantal commitment which is the essence of marriage and to its sacramental significance as a being united by God, as a reflection of Christ's union with the Church, and as a means of grace both to and through this man and this woman. But in doing so the Christian minister ought not to be dismissive of the reality of an unconditional commitment that may already exist, any more than the Christian minister should be indulgent of a commitment that is less than unconditional. Any rite of marriage within the context of the Christian Church needs to be conducted with transparent integrity and is dishonoured and devalued by any lack of integrity. In such a confusing context there may be a persuasive case for the clear categorical distinguishing of the covenantal promises that constitute a marriage, the blessing of that marriage, and the legal recognition of that marriage—even if, both within the Christian community and beyond it, all three elements may yet occur simultaneously.

However, it is contemporary society's incomprehension of a commitment to chastity that represents the deepest dissonance between

---

[12]   Note, for instance, the closing scene of the film *Four Weddings and a Funeral*, dir. Mike Newell, wr. Richard Curtis (Working Title Films, 1994) in which the two leading characters parody the traditional marriage vows in the promises they affirm.

the mores of contemporary Western society and any traditional understanding of Christian sexual discipline. The contemporary trivialisation of sex—and a mere cursory analysis of films, of television 'soap operas', of adverts, witnesses to such trivialisation—underlies and undergirds the contemporary phenomenon (or phenomena) of cohabitation.[13] Well over thirty years ago a friend suggested to me in conversation that the availability and efficiency of birth-control would issue inevitably in a change of public sexual morality. I considered this to be an overstatement at the time (the '60s were not as 'swinging' as they are sometime purported to have been) but she has been proved right and I have been proved wrong. In public consciousness, the perceived separation of sexual intercourse from procreation has apparently issued in a consequent separation of sexual intercourse from the context of a relationship that could take responsibility for procreation and the care of children.[14] And, as separated from the context of such a relationship, sexual intercourse ceases to be expressive of such a relationship; it forfeits its previous significance; it acquires a new and more shallow significance: more a matter of receiving than of giving; more a seeking of pleasure than a seeking of intimacy; more a matter of performance than an expression of commitment. A Certificate of Marriage, of course, was never a guarantee against sexual abuse (to the shame of British society it has only relatively recently become possible to charge a husband with the rape of his wife), but unbridled hedonism is inherently (though perhaps unconsciously) abusive. Too easily the Church focuses on the presenting challenge of cohabitation when this underlying trivialisation of sex is potentially far more damaging of human relationships. One does not need to concur with Catholic teaching (for the majority of the Church's history) that procreation is the chief reason for marriage in order to affirm a relationship capable of the responsibility for procreation as the appropriate context for sexual intercourse. An age apparently obsessed with sexual prowess needs to relearn that the quality of sex (in any ultimately meaningful sense) is determined by the quality of the relationship of which it is expressive. It may be worth quoting Colin Gunton at some length at this juncture since he makes the point as well as it could be made:

---

[13]   It is this contemporary trivialisation of sex that, perhaps, is accorded insufficient weight in Adrian Thatcher's discussion.

[14]   For example, the film *Notting Hill*, dir. Roger Michell, wr. Richard Curtis (Working Title Films, 1999), though produced by the same company as *Four Weddings and a Funeral*, conveys a high (if not 'idealised') notion of marriage, yet it conveys precisely the same 'trivial' notion of sex—a trivial notion of sex is not incompatible, in public consciousness, with an idealised notion of marriage.

It can be, and frequently is argued that past generations of Christians have stressed too much the link between sexuality and sin, too little the social and political determinants of human alienation. In so far as such treatment has derived from a generally negative assessment of human sexuality, the current change of emphasis to the social shape of sin would seem to be justified. And yet it can be argued that there is now a danger of over-reaction. If our being made as male and female is at the centre of the way in which we are called to be in the image of God, it may well follow that it is in our sexual relationships—sexual in the broader sense of relations in general between men and women, not only husbands and wives but parents and children, employer and employee, teacher and taught—that will be found the greater opportunities for both good and ill.

The negative side, more than apparent in our society, is that at least as much damage and unhappiness, activity that makes for death rather than life, is to be found in human sexual relations than in economic oppression, political tyranny and ecological disaster. This is because the closer our relatedness to another person, the greater potential there is for both good and ill radiating thence to the wider world.[15]

In the act of sex we give ourselves to another and render ourselves vulnerable to another in a quite unique manner. Such giving and vulnerability are appropriate to a relationship that is utterly mutual, that is accepting and secure, that is unconditional, that is covenantal, that is permanent. Sex without such a relationship is inherently and inevitably abusive, a using of another rather than an honouring of another. Sex other than in the context of such a relationship is not the 'unforgivable sin' but, as the quotation above suggests, its potential for societal damage is incalculable. Sex is properly expressive (and perhaps sacramentally expressive?) of that unconditional covenantal commitment which is marriage—and marriage (I have argued) is established by such unconditional covenantal commitment rather than by legal certification, religious rite, or (implicitly) by mere sexual union.[16] But if this be the case, then Christ's apparent attestation of the indissolubility of marriage is rendered yet more problematic: it is not just a marriage contracted in law or a marriage celebrated by religious rite that is indissoluble; every

---

[15]   Gunton, *Christ and Creation*, pp. 103-104.

[16]   John Macquarrie argues that sexual union itself constitutes a deeper joining and, if this is the case, sexual promiscuity is even more deeply damaging: 'We may repent of what we have done, but we can never undo it. The bearing of this on what I have just been saying about the permanent effects of sexual union is obvious. The identity of each one of us is constituted by a history, including a sexual history. That history I must acknowledge as my own, and willy-nilly it determines to a greater or lesser extent the possibilities open to me now. If that history contains a large number of sexual unions, it must affect what I am able to bring to a marriage today. How can I achieve the self-giving demanded in a truly personal marriage if I am already tangled in bonds that I cannot break?' Macquarrie, *A Guide to the Sacraments*, p. 225.

unconditional covenantal commitment between a man and a woman constitutes a marriage and, thereby, is declared indissoluble.

It would be a grievous mistake in our present context, as in the context within which Jesus responded to the question of the Pharisees, to move too quickly from this apparent impasse (though move from it we must). The danger in a previous generation was that of confining a man or a woman in an abusive and loveless contract, a relationship that was all legality and little or no true intimacy, a relationship that was a sustained denial of all that it was intended to signify and mediate. This is not our contemporary danger, any more than it was the danger in Jesus' context, and we, like Jesus' first hearers, need to hear the full force of this disavowal of divorce. And it is forceful. In response to this disavowal the Catholic Church continues to repudiate divorce and to declare remarriage after divorce to be adulterous. In response to this disavowal, until very recently, the Church of England generally denied the possibility of a rite of marriage in Church following a divorce (though it allowed for the possibility of the blessing of a civil marriage following a divorce). In response to the disavowal not a few Evangelical commentators, while allowing for divorce in the sense of legal separation, have repudiated the possibility of remarriage.[17] There has never been a canonically valid rite of divorce and the mere notion of repeating for a second (or third or fourth) time promises of fidelity and permanency is simply incoherent. Marriage, by definition, is unconditional and indissoluble—this, in context, is plainly Jesus' point. Any provision for divorce within the Torah was a provision for hard-heartedness, it should not be heard as signifying any qualification of the inherent permanency of marriage.

But hard-heartedness is not noticeably on the decline and it would be a strange understanding of the gospel that rendered it more legally rigorous than the Torah. Moreover, where a marriage is not, or is no longer, characterised by covenant faithfulness (and all that this implies), where a marriage is, or has become, the antithesis of the relationship between Christ and the Church, where a marriage is not, or is no longer, in any perceivable sense a means of God's grace both to the husband and wife, and through them to others, can we really maintain that a marriage truly exists? The Catholic Church has always maintained the possibility of annulment, not just on the grounds of sexual non-consummation, but (at least in principle) on the grounds of a lack of credible consent—and, more recently, there has been a trend to interpret such grounds more broadly. John Milton, in the seventeenth century, argued for the recognition of non-compatibility as valid grounds for divorce (though, on examination, his arguments relate more to annulment than to divorce)

---

[17]   See for instance W. A. Heth and G. J. Wenham, *Jesus and Divorce* (London: Hodder & Stoughton, 1988).

alongside the incongruity of an understanding of the gospel as being less merciful in response to human failure than the Law.[18] In the narrative of Genesis 2 God attests that it is not good for Adam to be alone: the subsequent covenantal union and shame-free intimacy of the male and the female must surely signify that covenantal union, in and of itself, is at least as foundational to marriage as the invitation to 'be fruitful and increase in number' (Genesis 1.28). Therefore, following Milton's argument, where such covenantal intimacy simply does not exist there surely must be grounds for annulment as validly as where a union has not been sexually consummated. And, perhaps extending Milton's argument, where such covenantal intimacy no longer exists, where (at least in one sense of the term) there is nothing but hard-heartedness, and certainly where there is abuse, there may yet be valid grounds for divorce. What God has joined together should not be separated—and even contemporary law in Western society recognises that responsibilities have been undertaken in marriage that cannot be entirely abandoned or abdicated—but, as Milton and others have opined, it would be a strange notion of gospel that concluded it to be less merciful than law in response to frailty, failure, and sin; it would be a strange notion of human frailty that affirmed divine mercy and the possibility of new beginnings with respect to any and every human mistake but this one; and it would be a strange notion of divine mercy that restricted its operation to the 'innocent party' (as if divine mercy did not embrace the guilty): '...where sin increased, grace increased all the more' (Romans 5.20).

The temptation to hear Jesus' words concerning divorce as the giving of a new or revised law may seem hard to resist—but resist it we must. Scripture is not given to us primarily as a rule book, as a catalogue of prescriptions and proscriptions. Scripture is given to us primarily as a narrative of God's dealings with us, ultimately in Christ. Scripture primarily is descriptive rather than prescriptive or proscriptive. Its authority, consequently, is more comparable to a series of case studies than to codified legislation. Too easily we gloss over the overwhelmingly patriarchal context of Old Testament legislation concerning marriage: a context in which adultery was a crime against God and against a husband but never explicitly against a wife; a context in which a husband could (under certain circumstances) divorce a wife but a wife apparently could never divorce a husband; a context in which a husband could have more than one wife but a wife could not have more than one husband; a

---

[18]   I am grateful to my former student, Colin Cartwright, for drawing my attention to John Milton's writings on divorce: Colin Cartwright, 'Love, the "Reason" of Marriage and all God's Law: John Milton's Theology of Marriage and Divorce' (Spurgeon's College, the University of Wales: Unpublished MTh dissertation, 1999); cf. *The Complete Prose Works of John Milton*, vols. 1-3, ed. Don M. Wofle, Ernest Sirluck and Merritt Y. Hughes (New Haven, CT: Yale University Press, 1953–62).

context in which a girl who had been raped could be bound in marriage to the rapist. Few (one hopes) would wish to impose this contextually rooted interpretation of Old Testament law on the contemporary Church. And in response to this previous contextual understanding of the laws of marriage and divorce, Jesus subtly but explicitly proffers a radical reinterpretation that challenges such patriarchal assumptions by alluding to a husband committing adultery against his wife (Matthew 19.9) and a wife divorcing her husband (Mark 10.12). But the principal theological significance of Jesus' words lies not in a re-codifying of Old Testament law against a context of patriarchy but in a reaffirmation of the significance of marriage against a context in which, through legalistic observance, it was being devalued. This affirmation of marriage and its permanency is unequivocal but it comes in the form of definition rather than the form of legislation. When Jesus encounters a Samaritan woman who had been set aside in divorce five times, an abused and rejected woman who was now living with one who was not her husband, he did not give her a lecture on the inappropriateness of divorce and re-marriage or on the appropriateness of sex to the marriage relationship; he spoke rather of living water and authentic worship—and without any reference to any change in her circumstances the Fourth Gospel narrates her as the first evangelist. And when Paul the apostle encounters Christian men and women in Corinth whose spouses no longer wished to remain with them in marriage he declared them to be no longer 'bound' (1 Corinthians 7.15).

It is easy for Protestants to mock the blatant special pleading with which Roman Catholicism seeks to extend valid grounds for annulment—it is not difficult to question credible consent with the benefit of hindsight—but underlying such special pleading is a faithful commitment to maintain the indissolubility and sacramentality of the covenant of marriage. It is similarly easy to mock the former Anglican practice of refusing to conduct a service of marriage where one or both parties had previously been divorced, alongside a willingness to bless such a marriage once it had been legally contracted through a registrar—God either blesses such a relationship or God doesn't; such a couple either are validly married or they are not—but underlying this seemingly contradictory stance was a similar commitment to maintain the indissolubility of marriage, a recognition of the incoherence of repeating the same unconditional and exclusive covenantal vows, a faithful acknowledgement that such blessing was a gracious provision in response to failure or rejection, sin or abuse, hard-heartedness or loneliness. If marriage is rightly understood covenantally and sacramentally, then divorce and remarriage are simply incoherent. But if the covenant of marriage is a means of anticipating and reflecting the covenantal intimacy of God's Triune life, then a 'marriage' that militates against such anticipating and reflecting is already incoherent.

The world is not yet as God ultimate determines it to be. We are called to anticipate and reflect divine intimacy in a context of continuing frailty, fallenness, sinfulness, hard-heartedness. It is not good for Adam to be alone and, in this context of the penultimate, remarriage after divorce may be the very best that some can manage as a means of anticipating and reflecting divine intimacy. It may not be appropriate to affirm remarriage after divorce as a sacrament, as corresponding to that which is dominically ordained—and in this respect the former Anglican practice had the merit of maintaining and expressing such distinction—but remarriage after divorce may nonetheless be fully sacramental, a means of anticipating and reflecting divine intimacy, a means of grace both to and through those so joined. Such qualification ought to be expressed as gracious provision rather than begrudging concession—but it ought to be expressed as such lest the inherent indissolubility and sacramentality of marriage be undermined.[19]

This feels an awkward place to conclude the final chapter of a book on sacramental theology—but perhaps its perceived awkwardness is poignant. The underlying theme of this book (in case it has become forgotten in the detail of these last chapters) is that God, in making himself present to us by the Spirit, tends not to bypass the created order he has established; that God mediates his presence to us by the Spirit through human and created instrumentality; that God's presence and action generally are mediatedly immediate rather than unmediatedly immediate. And God promises to mediate his presence to us through creation as it presently is, through humanity as it presently is. Holy baptism is not invalidated by muddy water. Holy Communion is not invalidated by stale bread. And even through human relationships, with all their frailty, sinfulness, and contradictions, God mediates his loving presence. There is nothing automatic about this; nothing to be presumed upon: the presence and action of God by the Spirit is always gracious;

---

[19]   In an earlier draft of this chapter I attempted a discussion of same-sex relationships at this point but, on the advice of friends and readers, I abandoned this attempt for two reasons. Firstly, this has now become a heated and detailed debate and it would not be possible to do justice to the arguments and counter-arguments in a few pages at the end of this chapter. I have discussed this issue elsewhere and will continue to do so (with the luxury of greater space). But secondly and more fundamentally, the theme of this chapter is the sacrament of marriage and however one might view covenantal same-sex relationships, however such relationships might (or might not) be appropriately expressed, and even admitting the possibility that such relationships could prove to be means of grace to the persons involved and to those around them, such a relationship could not be termed a marriage according to the manner in which marriage has been defined dominically, traditionally and within this chapter.

never a 'right'; never manipulable. Even in those instances where God has promised to meet with us, even in the ordained sacraments of the Church, God is not to be presumed upon; his presence is always his gracious presence; not even here is God at our disposal. But God is God, and God may surprise us by his presence, mediating his love in the unforeseen and the unexpected. The sacraments of the Church—and the Church itself—are not God's prison: God mediates his presence in and through creation graciously, freely, extravagantly, and often surprisingly.

CONCLUSION

A Modest Ecumenical Proposal

Accept one another, then, just as Christ accepted you, in order to bring praise to God. (Romans 15.7)

Following centuries of a predominantly Gentile Church it is now quite impossible for us to comprehend the full gravity of the impasse confronted by Paul in his letters to the Romans, the Galatians, and in so many of the churches in which he ministered. Scripture (as it then was) and tradition were unanimous in forbidding table-fellowship—and by implication therefore, we assume, a sharing in the Lord's Supper— between Jews and uncircumcised Gentiles. There was, needless to say, a simple solution to the difficulty: if all Gentile Christians became Jews; if all male Gentile Christians underwent circumcision; if all Gentile Christians, male and female, devoted themselves to live according to the regulations and rites of the Torah and the Jewish tradition; if all Gentile Christians observed Jewish rules of purification and food preparation— then the problem could be resolved. But the apostle Peter had received a vision that had subsequently been interpreted and expressed through the receiving of the Spirit by Cornelius and those with him. And Peter concluded that '...if God gave them the same gift as he gave us, who believed in the Lord Jesus Christ, who was I to think that I could oppose God?' (Acts 11.17).

Since the Reformation and the revolution in Martin Luther's thinking that was prompted by a re-reading of the letter to the Romans, Protestant Churches (and, perhaps as a consequence, the Catholic Church) have focused upon the perceived significance within the letter of 'justification' (δικαιοσύνη), on the relationship between faith and works, and grace and law, and have accordingly assumed that Paul arrives at the climax of his argument in chapter 8 of the letter (leaving chapters 9 to 11 as a somewhat strange excursus, and chapters 12 and following as general—but largely unrelated—ethical instructions). With the so-called 'new perspective on Paul' proposed by Krister Stendahl, E. P. Sanders and more recently (and perhaps more thoroughly) by James Dunn and others,[1] this entire scheme of interpretation has been subjected to severe questioning (at very least one should question a programme of interpretation that so thoroughly divorces the second half of a letter from its first half). Without prejudice to the pertinence of Luther's reading of this text within his own context (in relation to the sale of indulgences and the notion of meritorious penance) this clearly was not Paul's context or the immediate significance of the letter to its first readers. This clichéd opposition of law and grace, works and faith (it is argued), was almost entirely foreign to Jewish self-understanding in the first century (and, indeed, today), and a merely forensic understanding of 'justification' (or better 'righteousness') is simply alien to the use of the term within the New Testament and more widely in Greek literature. The presenting problem in this letter to the Romans (as also in Galatians) is not primarily the question of how Jew and Gentile are 'justified' but rather of how Jew and Gentile can live together within a single Church and how God can be seen to have acted 'justly' towards Israel in this act of mercy towards the Gentiles.[2] Previous chapters of this book already have drawn attention to the rhetorical style of this letter (a rhetoric almost entirely missed by more traditional interpretations), a rhetoric that seems explicitly to link chapter 1 with chapter 11. Indeed, if this letter reaches a climax it surely does so at the conclusion of chapter 11, with Paul's paean of praise. And chapters 12 to 16, therefore, far from being unrelated ethical instructions, represent the entire purpose, context, and conclusion of Paul's argument.

Consequently, if there is a single text that expresses the central message of this letter, it is not that 'there is now no condemnation for those who are in Christ Jesus' (Romans 8.1), compelling though that truth may be; it is rather the text that stands as the summary of this conclusion: '[a]ccept one another, then, just as Christ accepted you...' (Romans 15.7). Paul's rhetorical argument in this letter leads to this simple appeal—a direct repetition of Peter's appeal reflecting upon Cornelius' conversion—God

---

[1]   Krister Stendahl, *Paul Among Jews and Gentiles* (Philadelphia, PA: Fortress Press, 1976); E. P. Sanders, *Paul and Palestinian Judaism: A Comparison of Patterns of Religion* (Minneapolis, MN: Fortress Press, 1985); *Jesus and Judaism* (London: SCM Press, 1985); *Paul, the Law and the Jewish People* (London: SCM Press, 1985); J. D. G. Dunn, 'The New Perspective on Paul', *Bulletin of the John Rylands Library*, 65 (1983) pp. 95-122; *Jesus, Paul and the Law: Studies in Mark and Galatians* (London: SPCK, 1990); *The Theology of Paul's Letter to the Galatians* (Cambridge: Cambridge University Press, 1993); J. D. G. Dunn and Alan M. Suggate, *The Justice of God: A Fresh Look at the Old Doctrine of Justification by Faith* (Carlisle: Paternoster Press, 1993).

[2]   I am grateful to my colleague David Southall for drawing my attention to this latter issue and to the more probable significance of the phrase 'the righteousness of God' (ἡ δικαιοσύνη θεοῦ) in this letter to the Romans: David Southall, 'The Meaning of δικαιοσύνη θεοῦ in Paul's Epistle to the Romans' (Spurgeon's College, the University of Wales: Unpublished MTh dissertation, 2002).

has received both Jew and Gentile by sheer grace and through the faithfulness of Jesus Christ; and in doing so God has proved himself utterly faithful to his promises to Israel (albeit in a surprising manner). And if Jew and Gentile have been accepted by God entirely on the basis of what God has done, then Jew and Gentile simply must accept one another, without qualification, without pre-condition.

It was never the primary purpose of this book to offer a detailed discussion of the sacraments, less still to be an exercise in ecumenism— the primary purpose of this book, as identified in its preface and introduction, is to speak about God and about God's manner of relating to us graciously and mediatedly. But in the course of this discussion, precisely because God's presence and action have been identified as gracious and mediated, the Church has been defined sacramentally— principally by baptism, by Eucharist, and by ministry. In baptism and in the Eucharist God accepts us in Christ by the Spirit—and if God has accepted us, surely we ought to accept one another?

> If there is basic agreement about what constitutes a valid baptism, and if in fact there is already a large measure of agreement whereby the several churches or communions recognize one another's baptisms; and if further there is a modern consensus among theologians that baptism is a sufficient sacrament for fully belonging to the Christian community; then would it not follow, on the basis of baptism so understood, that there should be full intercommunion among the various churches and denominations?[3]

Surprisingly, having posed the question in so positive a manner, John Macquarrie draws back from this ecumenical optimism, suggesting that 'something more is required before there could be intercommunion'.[4] But what more might be required? There would appear to be two lingering obstacles to common communion:[5] the question of common confession and the question of common recognition of ministry.

The question of common confession, a problem principally for Eastern Orthodox Churches,[6] simply does not appear (admittedly to this writer) to

---

[3]   Macquarrie, *A Guide to the Sacraments*, p. 85.

[4]   Macquarrie, *A Guide to the Sacraments*, pp. 86ff.

[5]   Though the phrase 'common communion' might (with some justification) be thought tautologous, I prefer it to 'intercommunion' since the latter seems to imply a preserving of division (and therefore of disunity) in the very place where unity is celebrated and effected.

[6]   'The eucharist has always been received as a sacrament of communion, as a sacrament of the unity of the Church. On these grounds the Orthodox do not accept the practice of ecumenical intercommunion. There may be only communion in the eucharist, and any intercommunion which implies the participation of persons from outside is excluded by virtue of its nature. That is why the participation in the eucharist is preceded by the confession of faith which testifies to the doctrinal unity of thought of the

be as problematic as it is often portrayed. The Church catholic, East and West, is united in confessing the Nicene/Constantinople Creed and, as argued in chapter 1 of this book, the controversial *Filioque* clause cannot really be included or omitted without some qualification. More pertinently, notwithstanding the tensions between East and West, the *Filioque* clause was included by the West from the sixth century onwards yet the final break in communion did not occur until the eleventh century (and although other issues of difference had arisen by that time, they were not expressed in any variation of this catholic creed). Ironically it is the Roman Catholic Church, that has promulgated additional dogmas as 'necessary for salvation', that presently seems willing for inter-communion with the Eastern Churches (a tacit admission, surely, that such additional dogmas are, in fact, *not* necessary for salvation). It must surely be possible, therefore, for the Nicene/Constantinople Creed (with or without the *Filioque* clause) to be affirmed by all truly 'catholic' Churches as sufficient confessional basis for common communion. This would not be to 'paper over cracks', to pretend that remaining matters of difference were unimportant or even secondary—but it would be to affirm a basis of unity that was historically persuasive, real, and realistic; it would be to establish a unity within which such remaining matters of difference could be considered constructively; and it would be to acknowledge that the failure to receive one another in communion, when Christ has received us in baptism, is an offence against Christ and the most grievous sin against one another.

A variation on this demand for confessional unity as the prerequisite for common communion would draw attention to the incongruity of common communion (or even common baptism) when understandings of communion (and of baptism) differ so greatly. But this objection too is plainly disingenuous. In the first place, I hope I have demonstrated in previous chapters that differences of understanding concerning baptism and Eucharist are really not as radical as differences of language might suggest: that an affirmation of a real but mediate presence is common to East and to West, to Catholics and to (most) Protestants; that an affirmation of a reality of God's grace, effected by the Spirit through the sacraments of baptism and Eucharist, and received through faith, is similarly common to East and to West, to Catholics and to (most) Protestants. But more fundamentally, even if I have failed to convince others of this underlying unity of understanding, differences of understanding (like differences of language) exist, and have almost always existed, within the Churches as well as between the Churches. To

---

members of the congregation. There could be no sacrament of the eucharist without unity in faith.' Archbishop Kirill, 'The Significance and Status of BEM in the Ecumenical Movement', pp. 79-95 (p. 87).

deny such is to be historically blinkered. To deny such is to be oblivious to the questionings that exist, and have almost always existed, within the Protestant Churches, but also within the Catholic Church, and (I strongly suspect) within the Orthodox Churches. If we truly believe (as I certainly truly believe) that the sacraments of the Church are means of grace, then surely we should believe that the sacraments of the Church are means of the grace of unity. We grow in faith and unity through our common participation in the sacraments, not as a prerequisite to that common participation. To deny this would be effectively to deny that we truly do believe the sacraments to be means of grace, would be effectively to imply that we anticipate such faith and unity to be mediated by some other means. Or, to put the matter more concisely: we may yet come to a common understanding of the faith through common communion, but we will never come to a common understanding of the faith without common communion—the latter is the means of the former; the former, therefore, can never be the prerequisite of the latter.

However, as acknowledged in chapter 3 and again in chapter 10 of this book, the Church's unity is established and expressed, not just through a common baptism and a common communion, but also through a common ministry. And here, as also acknowledged previously, there would seem to be a far more daunting obstacle to the Church's visible unity. If Christian ministry is a means and expression of the Church's unity then that ministry is undermined by disunity. If Christian ordination is validly enacted on behalf of the Church catholic then the validity of all ordinations is undermined by disunity. At present the ministry of no single Church is unequivocally recognised by the Church universally. At present the ordained ministry of the Churches, like the breach in communion, serves to express the Church's disunity rather than its unity. But, as argued in chapter 10 of this book, re-ordination is not as problematic or as self-contradictory as re-baptism. I have argued for some understanding of the imparting of sacramental character in both baptism and ordination, but whereas the validity of a baptism is generally recognised throughout the Church,[7] the validity of orders of ministry lacks such universal recognition—sacramental character may have been validly imparted through the sacrament of ordination but the impartation of that sacramental character is not affirmed and recognised by the universal Church. Consequently, an act of re-ordination, unlike an act of re-baptism, need not imply an invalidating of previous ordination, but merely the wider affirmation and recognition of that ordination. And if re-ordination is perceived to imply the invalidation of previous ordination

---

[7]   I argued in chapters 5 and 6 that the phenomenon of open-membership or open-communion Baptist churches represents either an implicit acceptance of the validity of infant baptism or an implicit denial of the significance of baptism as defining of the Church or of the Christian.

it is so only inasmuch as any act of ordination on behalf of that which is less than the Church catholic is less than wholly valid.

And if re-ordination is perceived as a means towards the visible unity of the Church, then such re-ordination ought not just to be accepted, it ought to be eagerly sought. The apostle Paul could wish himself 'cursed and cut off from Christ' for the sake of Israel (Romans 9.3), and no minister of Christ worthy of that name should flinch from the humility of re-ordination if, through that re-ordination, the visible unity of the church might be furthered. Jesus prays that we may be one 'so that the world may believe' (John 17.21)—it is difficult to perceive how an invisible unity of the Church could ever satisfy the hope of that prayer: how might the world recognise a unity that is invisible (not least when what is actually recognised is an all too visible disunity)? To be joined by the Spirit to Christ in his praying must imply a preparedness to take a humble path as a means of that prayer's fulfilment.

All the above, of course, is little more than a response (albeit a personal response) to the statement of the World Council of Churches on *Baptism, Eucharist, and Ministry*.[8] Since that statement was issued discussions have continued, denominational responses have been offered, and perhaps some genuine progress (at least in mutual understanding) has been achieved—and such achievements should not be belittled. However, over the last thirty years or so—since the first issuing of that statement on *Baptism, Eucharist, and Ministry*—something entirely informal but at least as significant has occurred.

To define the phenomenon of post-denominationalism as a form of 'bottom-up' ecumenism is probably misleading: the phenomenon is more an outcome and outworking of post-modernity than any conscious pursuit of formal ecumenical union; the unity of Christians is an assumption underlying the phenomenon rather than a goal explaining the phenomenon. As such, of course, the phenomenon can easily be dismissed as theologically indifferent if not theologically illiterate, merely a manifestation of the general distrust of authority, lack of commitment, and refusal to be categorised that are among the outcomes of the perceived collapse of the certainties of modernity. And, to a degree (at least initially), such dismissals are not without justification. Whereas thirty to forty years ago those attending a particular local church did so out of some theological conviction and denominational allegiance, it would not be at all uncommon in Britain today for someone (at least someone aged

---

[8]   World Council of Churches, Faith and Order Commission, *One Baptism, One Eucharist and a Mutually Recognized Ministry: Three Agreed Statements* (Geneva: World Council of Churches, 1975); cf. *Baptism, Eucharist and Ministry* (Geneva: World Council of Churches, 1982); cf. *Baptism, Eucharist and Ministry 1892–1990: Report on the Process and Responses* (Geneva: World Council of Churches, 1990); for a discussion of Baptists' responses to these initiatives see Cross, *Baptism and the Baptists*, pp. 244ff.

forty or younger) to attend a local church simply because it had an effective children's work, a competent and contemporary music group, comfortable seats, or a welcoming atmosphere; whether that local church is Anglican, Methodist, URC, Baptist, or a new and 'independent' church grouping is at best a secondary consideration; there may be some concern for the quality and pertinence of the preaching, but there is little or no concern for underlying ecclesiology. Nor, I suspect, are the Catholic and Orthodox Churches entirely immune from the phenomenon (though here certainly there remains a far stronger sense of denominational identity). I am aware of Protestants who have 'migrated' to the Catholic or Orthodox Church without entirely abandoning their Protestant instincts and roots. I similarly know of Catholics (if not Orthodox) who worship regularly in Protestant churches without apparently any awareness of denying their Catholic identity. To previous generations this rootless phenomenon could only appear bizarre and confusing—and maybe it should be regretted (I teach Christian doctrine and am hardly likely to applaud a phenomenon that is so doctrinally careless). But the phenomenon is real and is growing whether it is approved of or not and, for the purposes of this present discussion, I am more interested in its outcomes than in either its causes or its demerits.

For whatever reasons people may begin to attend a particular local church they only remain there, and certainly they only flourish there, because there they receive that which they expect to receive through a local church. Certainly they may expect to receive a welcome, the warmth of friendship, a competent crèche, children's work and youth work, comfortable seating, engaging preaching—but even the most theologically unaware and undiscerning (and I have no desire to be cynical at this point) expect something more profound from or through a church: they expect to be encountered by God. And that people remain within a local church that is other than their denominational background (if they have a discernible denominational background) surely suggests that alongside these more immediate but tangential expectations, the expectation of being encountered by God is fulfilled. The phenomenon of post-denominationalism, for all its possible triviality, is testimony to the 'felt' reality of the gracious presence of God mediated through local churches almost regardless of their denominational status and affiliation; mediated through their ministry; mediated through their celebration of the sacraments; mediated simply through their existence as communities of faith, hope, and love. Of course many (though by no means all) of those who participate in this post-denominational phenomenon may have little or no conscious sacramental theology—but they recognise grace when they are encountered by grace. And encountering grace similarly in an Orthodox church, a Catholic church, an Anglican church, a Methodist church, a United Reformed church, a Baptist church, or a new and 'independent' church (and I hope I haven't missed anybody out), denominational distinctiveness becomes less important or perhaps entirely unimportant.

And this phenomenon has been more officially and formally accompanied in Britain by the various initiatives sponsored by 'Churches Together': again through worshipping together and simply being together God's gracious presence is mediated and distinctions previously held to be primary come to be perceived as secondary if not superfluous. If the sacraments of the Church are not God's prison then the sacramental and sacerdotal boundaries that have been developed over centuries most certainly cannot hem him in or restrict him; he graciously mediates his presence in surprising ways and in surprising places.

And in this context of popular denominational transmigration, trans-illumination, and transmutation, beyond the debates of ecumenical conclaves, a sacramental unity of the Church is assumed. One can perhaps foresee a time when denominational hierarchies will finally become aware of their popular irrelevance—a practical unity will have been achieved despite their best efforts.

I would not have attempted to write this book had I not believed theological precision to be important, had I not believed a sacramental theology to require careful definition. But beyond our denominational definitions, for all their significance, it is the Holy Spirit who freely effects the gracious sacramental presence of God. He does so in response to prayer. He does so as an outcome of promise. But he does so freely and graciously. He cannot be manipulated by sacerdotal presumption. He cannot be imprisoned by denominational distinction. Ultimately it is the Spirit who defines the Church sacramentally, and he does so far more inclusively, far more surprisingly, far more graciously, than we would dare venture. And if the Spirit so acts, is it really so hard for us to accept one another as we have been accepted?

Bibliography

Abraham, William J., *Canon and Criterion in Christian Theology: From the Fathers to Feminism* (Oxford: Clarendon Press, 1998).

Achtemeier, Paul J., *A Commentary on First Peter* (Minneapolis, MN: Fortress Press, 1996).

Alison, James, *The Joy of Being Wrong: Original Sin through Easter Eyes* (New York: Crossroad, 1998).

—, *Faith beyond Resentment: Fragments Catholic and Gay* (London: Darton, Longman and Todd, 2001).

Athanasius, *On the Incarnation*, trans. A Religious (London: Mowbray, 1953).

Augustine, *Letters*, in *NPNF* 1, vol. 1, pp. 219-593.

—, *The City of God*, in *NPNF* 1, vol. 2, pp. 1-511.

—, *On the Holy Trinity*, in *NPNF* 1, vol. 3, pp. 17-228.

—, *In answer to the letters of Petilian, the Donatist*, III 43, in *NPNF* 1, vol. 4, pp. 519-628.

—, *Anti-Pelagian Writings*, in *NPNF* 1, vol. 5.

—, *Homilies on the Gospel of John* (Tr. 80 3), in *NPNF* 1, vol. 7, pp 7-452.

Aulén, Gustav, *Christus Victor: An Historical Study of the Three Main Types of the Idea of the Atonement*, trans. A. G. Herbert (London: SPCK, 1931).

Austin, J. L., *How to do Things with Words* (Oxford: Oxford University Press, 2nd edn, 1976).

Baillie, D. M., *The Theology of the Sacraments* (London: Faber and Faber, 1957).

Balz, Horst. U. und Wolfgang Schrage, *Das Neue Testament Deutsch* 10, *Die "Katholischen" Briefe* (Göttingen: Vandenhoeck & Ruprecht, 1980).

Baillie, John, *Our Knowledge of God* (London: Oxford University Press, 1939).

Barr, James, *The Semantics of Biblical Language* (Oxford: Oxford University Press, 1961).

Barth, Karl, *The Epistle to the Romans*, trans. Edwyn C. Hoskyns from 6th edition (London, Oxford and New York: Oxford University Press, 1933).

—, *The Word of God and the Word of Man*, trans. Douglas Horton (London: Hodder & Stoughton, 1928).

—, *The Teaching of the Church Regarding Baptism*, trans. Ernest A. Payne (London: SCM Press, 1948).

—, *Church Dogmatics*, vols. I–IV, trans. and eds. G.W. Bromiley and T.F. Torrance (Edinburgh: T & T Clark, 1956–75).

—, *The Humanity of God*, trans. John Newton Thomas and Thomas Wieser, Fontana Library of Theology and Philosophy (London and Glasgow: Collins, 1961).

—, *The Christian Life: Church Dogmatics IV.4 Lecture Fragments*, trans. Geoffrey W. Bromiley (Edinburgh: T & T Clark, 1981).

Bartholomew, C., C. Greene and K. Möller, (eds.), *After Pentecost: Language and Biblical Interpretation* (Carlisle: Paternoster Press/Grand Rapids, MI: Zondervan, 2001).

Basil the Great, *Letters*, NPNF 2, vol. 8, pp. 109-327.

Baum, Gregory, *De Ecclesia: The Constitution on the Church of Vatican Council II with commentary* (London: Darton, Longman & Todd, 1965).

Beasley-Murray, G. R., 'The Church and the Child', *The Fraternal* (April 1943), pp. 9-13.

—, *Baptism in the New Testament* (London: Macmillan, 1962).

—, *Baptism Today and Tomorrow* (London: Macmillan/New York: St Martin's Press, 1966).

—, *John*, Word Biblical Commentary 36 (Waco, TX: Word Books, 1987).

Beasley-Murray, Paul, 'The Ministry of All and the Leadership of Some: A Baptist perspective', in P. Beasley-Murray (ed.), *Anyone for Ordination?* (Tunbridge Wells: Marc, 1993), pp. 157-74.

Bebbington, D. W., *Evangelicalism in Modern Britain: A History from the 1730s to the 1980s* (London: Unwin Hyman, 1989).

Begbie, Jeremy, *Voicing Creation's Praise: Towards a Theology of the Arts* (Edinburgh: T & T Clark, 1991).

Béguerie, Philippe, and Claude Duchesneau, *How to Understand the Sacraments*, trans. John Bowden and Margaret Lydamore (London: SCM Press, 1991).

Berkouwer, G. C., *The Sacraments* (Grand Rapids, MI: Eerdmans, 1969).

Betz, J., *Die Eucharistie in der Zeit der Griechischen Väter* (Freiburg: Herder, 1955).

Boff, Leonardo, *The Sacraments of Life, Life of the Sacraments*, trans. John Drury (Washington: Pastoral Press, 1987)

Braaten, Carl E., and Robert W. Jenson (eds.), *Church Unity and the Papal Office: An Ecumenical Dialogue on John Paul II's Encyclical 'Ut Unum Sint' (That they may be one)* (Grand Rapids, MI: Eerdmans, 2001)

Briggs, Richard, *Words in Action: Speech Act Theory and Biblical Interpretation: Toward a Hermeneutic of Self-involvement* (Edinburgh: T. & T. Clark, 2001).

Brox, Norbert, *Der erste Petrusbrief: Evangelisch-Katholischer Kommentar zum Neuen Tetament* (Zürich: Benziger Verlag; Neukirchen-Vluyn: Neukirchener Verlag, 1979).

Buchanan, Colin, *Adult Baptisms: Grove Worship Series* 91 (Bramcote: Grove Books, 1985).

Bunyan, John, *The Whole Works of John Bunyan*, vol. II, ed. George Offor (London: Blackie & Son, 1862)

Buttrick, David, *Homiletic: Moves and Structures* (London: SCM Press, 1987).

Calvin, John, *Institutes of the Christian Religion* (ed. J. T. McNeill, trans. F. L. Battles; Philadelphia, PA: Westminster Press, 1960).

—, *Treatises against the Anabaptists and against the Libertines*, ed. and trans. Benjamin Wirt Farley (Grand Rapids, MI: Baker Book House, 1982).

Catechism of the Catholic Church (London: Geoffrey Chapman, 1994).

Campbell, John McLeod, *The Nature of the Atonement and its Relation to Remission of Sins and Eternal Life* (London: James Clarke, 1959).

Campbell, R. A., *The Elders: Seniority within Earliest Christianity* (Edinburgh: T & T Clark, 1994).

Cavanaugh, William T., *Torture and Eucharist: Theology, Politics, and the Body of Christ* (Oxford: Blackwell, 1998).

Chase, Frederic Henry, *Confirmation in the Apostolic Age* (London: Macmillan, 1909).

Christ, Carol P., *Laughter of Aphrodite: Reflections on a Journey to the Goddess* (San Franscisco: Harper, 1987).

Church of England, General Synond, *A Time to Heal: A Report for the House of Bishops on the Healing Ministry* (London: Church House Publications, 2000).

Clark, Gordon H., *Religion, Reason and Revelation* (Phillipsburg, NJ: Presbyterian and Reformed Publications, 1961).

Clark, Neville, *An Approach to the Theology of the Sacraments* (London: SCM Press, 1956).

Coakley, Sarah, '"Femininity" and the Holy Spirit', in *Mirror to the Church: Reflections on Sexism*, ed. Monica Furlong (London: SPCK, 1988), pp. 124-135.

—, *Powers and Submissions: Spirituality, Philosophy and Gender* (Oxford: Blackwell, 2002).

Colish, Marcia L., 'Peter Lombard', in *The Medieval Theologians*, ed. G. R. Evans (Oxford: Blackwell, 2001), pp. 168-183.

Colwell, John E., 'A Radical Church? A Reappraisal of Anabaptist Ecclesiology', *Tyndale Bulletin*, 38 (1987), pp. 119-141.

—, *Actuality and Provisionality: Eternity and Election in the Theology of Karl Barth* (Edinburgh: Rutherford House, 1989).

—, 'Alternative Approaches to Believer's Baptism (from the Anabaptists to Barth)', *The Scottish Bulletin of Evangelical Theology*, 7 (1989), pp. 3-20.

—, 'Baptism, Conscience and the Resurrection: A Reappraisal of 1 Peter 3:21', in *Baptism, the New Testament and the Church: Historical and Contemporary Studies in Honour of R. E. O. White*, eds. S. E. Porter and A. R. Cross (Sheffield: Sheffield Academic Press, 1999), pp. 210-227.

—, 'The Glory of God's Justice and the Glory of God's Grace: Contemporary Reflections on the Doctrine of Hell in the Teaching of Jonathan Edwards', in *Called to One Hope: Perspectives on Life to Come*, John E. Colwell (ed.), (Carlisle: Paternoster Press, 2000), pp. 113-129.

—, *Living the Christian Story: The Distinctiveness of Christian Ethics* (Edinburgh & New York: T & T Clark, 2001).

—, 'The Sacramental Nature of Ordination: An Attempt to Re-engage a Catholic Understanding and Practice', in *Baptist Sacramentalism*, ed. Anthony R. Cross and Philip E. Thompson (Carlisle: Paternoster Press, 2003), pp. 228-246.

Cotterell, P., and M. Turner, *Linguistics and Biblical Interpretation* (London: SPCK, 1989).

Craddock, Fred B., *Preaching* (Nashville, TN: Abingdon Press, 1985).

Cross, Anthony R., *Baptism and the Baptists: Theology and Practice in Twentieth-Century Britain* (Carlisle: Paternoster Press, 2000).

—, 'Dispelling the Myth of English Baptist Sacramentalism', *Baptist Quarterly* 38 (2000), pp. 367-391.

—, 'Faith-Baptism: The Key to an Evangelical Baptismal Sacramentalism', *Journal of European Baptist Studies* 4.3 (2004), pp. 5-21.

Dalton, W. J., *Christ's Proclamation to the Spirits: A Study of 1 Peter 3:18-4:6*, Analecta Biblica, 23 (Rome: Editrice Pontificio Istituto Biblico, 2nd 1989).

Davids, Peter H., *The First Epistle of Peter*, The New International Commentary on the New Testament (Grand Rapids, MI: Eerdmans, 1990).

D'Costa, Gavin, *Sexing the Trinity: Gender, Culture and the Divine* (London: SCM Press, 2000).

de Lubac, Henri, *Catholicism, Christ and the Common Destiny of Man* (London: Burns and Oates, 1950).

Denzinger, Henricus, *Enchiridion Symbolorum: Definitionum et Declarationum de Rebus Fidei et Morum* (Barcelona: Herder, 24th edn, 1946).

Dillistone, *Christianity and Symbolism* (London: Collins, 1955).

Dix, Gregory, *Confirmation or the Laying On of Hands*, Occasional Paper, (London: SPCK, 1936).

—, *The Shape of the Liturgy* (London: Dacre Press, 1945).

—, *The Theology of Confirmation* (London: Dacre Press, 1946).

Dudley, Martin, and Rowell, Geoffrey (eds.), *The Oil of Gladness: Anointing in the Christian Tradition* (London: SPCK, 1993).

Dulles, Avery, *Models of the Church* (Dublin: Gill and Macmillan, 1976).

Dunkley, Anne. *Seen and Heard: Reflections on Children and Baptist Tradition* (Oxford: Whitley Publications, 1999).

Dunn, J. D. G., *Baptism in the Holy Spirit: A Re-examination of the New Testament Teaching on the Gift of the Spirit in Relation to Pentecostalism Today* (London: SCM Press, 1970).

—, 'The New Perspective on Paul', *Bulletin of the John Rylands Library*, 65 (1983), pp. 95-122.

—, *Jesus, Paul and the Law: Studies in Mark and Galatians* (London: SPCK. 1990).

—, *The Theology of Paul's Letter to the Galatians* (Cambridge: Cambridge University Press, 1993).

Dunn, J. D. G., with Alan M. Suggate, *The Justice of God: A Fresh Look at the Old Doctrine of Justification by Faith* (Carlisle: Paternoster Press, 1993).

Edwards, Jonathan, *Freedom of the Will*, in *Works of Jonathan Edwards*, general. ed. Perry Miller, vol. 1, ed. Paul Ramsey (New Haven and London: Yale University Press, 1957).

—, *Religious Affections*, in *Works of Jonathan Edwards*, general. ed. Perry Miller, vol. 2, ed. John E. Smith (New Haven and London: Yale University Press, 1959).

—, *Original Sin*, in *Works of Jonathan Edwards*, general. ed. John E. Smith, vol. 3, ed. Clyde A. Holbrook (New Haven and London: Yale University Press, 1980)

—, *The Great Awakening*, in *Works of Jonathan Edwards*, general. ed. Perry Miller, vol. 4, ed. C. C. Goen (New Haven and London: Yale University Press, 1972).

—, 'The Mind', in *Scientific and Philosophical Writings*, in *Works of Jonathan Edwards*, general. ed. John E. Smith, vol. 6, ed. Wallace E. Anderson (New Haven and London: Yale University Press, 1980), pp. 332-393.

—, 'Diary', in *Works of Jonathan Edwards*, general. ed. Perry Miller, vol. 16, *Letters and Personal Writings*, ed. George S. Claghorn (New Haven and London: Yale University Press, 1998), pp. 759-789.

—, 'A Divine and Supernatural Light' (1733), in *Sermons and Discourses 1730-1733*, in *Works of Jonathan Edwards*, general. ed. Harry S. Stout, vol. 17, ed. Mark Valeri (New Haven and London: Yale University Press, 1999), pp. 408-426.

Estep, W. R., *The Anabaptist Story* (Grand Rapids, MI: Eerdmans, 1975);

Evans, G. R., (ed.), *The Medieval Theologians* (Oxford: Blackwell, 2001).

Farrow, Douglas, 'St. Irenaeus of Lyons: The Church and the World', *Pro Ecclesia*, IV/3 (1995), pp. 333-355.

—, *Ascension and Ecclesia: On the Significance of the Doctrine of the Ascension for Ecclesiology and Christian Cosmology* (Edinburgh: T & T Clark, 1999).

Fiddes, Paul S., *The Creative Suffering of God* (Oxford: Clarendon Press, 1988).

—, (ed.), *Reflections on the Water: Understanding God and the World through the Baptism of Believers* (Oxford: Regent's Park College, 1996).

—, *Participating in God: A Pastoral Doctrine of the Trinity* (London: Darton Longman and Todd, 2000).

—, *Tracks and Traces: Baptist Identity in Church and Theology* (Carlisle: Paternoster Press, 2003).

Fiorenza, Elisabeth Schüssler, *In Memory of Her: A Feminist Theological Reconstruction of Christian Origins* (New York: Crossroad, 1984).

Fish, Stanley, *Is There a Text in This Class? The Authority of Interpretive Communities* (Cambridge, MA: Harvard University Press, 1980).

Flannery, Austin (ed.), *Vatican Council II: The Conciliar and Post Conciliar Documents*, (Dublin: Dominican Publications, 1975).

Flew, Antony, *An Introduction to Western Philosophy: Ideas and Argument from Plato to Popper* (London: Thames and Hudson, 2nd edn, 1989).

Forsyth, P. T., *The Church and the Sacraments* (London: Independent Press, 2nd edn, 1947).

Fowler, Stanley K., *More Than a Symbol: The British Baptist Recovery of Baptismal Sacramentalism* (Carlisle: Paternoster Press, 2002).

Gerrish, B. A., *Grace and Gratitude: The Eucharistic Theology of John Calvin* (Edinburgh: T & T Clark, 1993).

Goldingay, John, 'Old Testament Sacrifice and the Death of Christ', in John Goldingay, (ed.), *Atonement Today: A Symposium at St John's College, Nottingham* (London: SPCK, 1995), pp. 3-20.

Gorringe, T. J., *God's Just Vengeance: Crime, Violence and the Rhetoric of Salvation* (Cambridge: Cambridge University Press, 1996).

Grebel, Conrad, and Friends, 'Letters to Thomas Müntzer', in *Spiritual and Anabaptist Writers*, ed. George Huntston Williams and Angel M. Mergal (Philadelphia, PA: Westminster Press, 1957).

Gregory Nazianzen, *The Third Theological Oration on the Son* (Oration 29 2), trans. Charles Gordon Browne and James Edward Swallow, in *NPNF* 2, vol. 7, pp. 301-309.

Gregory of Nyssa, *Dogmatic Treatise on 'Not Three Gods' to Ablabius*, trans. William Moore and Henry Austin Wilson, in *NPNF* 2, vol. 5, pp. 331-336.

—, *On the Baptism of Christ*, in *NPNF* 2, vol. 5, pp. 518-524.

Grudem, Wayne A., *The First Epistle of Peter*, Tyndale New Testament Commentaries (Leicester: IVP, 1988).

Gunton, Colin E., *Becoming and Being: The Doctrine of God in Charles Hartshorne and Karl Barth* (Oxford: Oxford University Press, 1978).

—, *The Actuality of Atonement: A Study of Metaphor, Rationality and the Christian Tradition* (Edinburgh: T & T Clark, 1988).

—, 'Proteus and Procrustes: A Study in the Dialectic of Language in Disagreement with Sallie McFague', in Alvin F. Kimel Jr. (ed.), *Speaking the Christian God: The Holy Trinity and the Challenge of Feminism* (Grand Rapids, MI: Eerdmans, 1992), pp. 65-80.

—, *Christ and Creation: The Didsbury Lectures 1990* (Carlisle: Paternoster Press/Grand Rapids, MI: Eerdmans, 1992).

—, *The One, The Three and the Many: God, Creation and the Culture of Modernity*, The Bampton Lectures 1992 (Cambridge: Cambridge University Press, 1993).

—, 'God, Grace and Freedom', in *God and Freedom: Essays in Historical and Systematic Theology*, ed. Colin E. Gunton (Edinburgh: T & T Clark, 1995), pp. 119-133

—, *A Brief Theology of Revelation* (Edinburgh: T & T Clark, 1995).

—, *The Triune Creator: A Historical and Systematic Study* (Edinburgh: Edinburgh University Press, 1998).

—, 'Salvation', in John Webster (ed.) *The Cambridge Companion to Karl Barth* (Cambridge: Cambridge University Press, 2000), pp. 143-158.

—, 'The Church as a School of Virtue? Human Formation in Trinitarian Framework', in *Faithfulness and Fortitude: In Conversation with the Theological Ethics of Stanley Hauerwas*, ed. Mark Thiessen Nation and Samuel Wells (Edinburgh: T & T Clark, 2000), pp. 211-231.

Haffner, Paul, *The Sacramental Mystery* (Leominster: Gracewing, 1999).

Harris, Harriet Anne, *Fundamentalism and Evangelicals* (Oxford: Clarendon Press, 1998).

Hartshorne, Charles, *Man's Vision of God and the Logic of Theism* (New York: Harper, 1941).

—, *A Natural Theology for our Time* (La Salle: Open Court, 1967).

Hauerwas, Stanley, *Character and the Christian Life: A Study in Theological Ethics* (Notre Dame and London: University of Notre Dame Press, 1994 [1975]).

—, *Vision and Virtue: Essays in Christian Ethical Reflection* (Notre Dame and London: University of Notre Dame Press, 1981).

—, *Suffering Presence: Theological Reflections on Medicine, the Mentally Handicapped, and the Church* (Edinburgh: T & T Clark, Edinburgh: 1988).

—, *Christian Existence Today: Essays on Church, World, and Living in Between* (Durham, NC: Labyrinth, 1988).

—, *A Better Hope: Resources for a Church Confronting Capitalism, Democracy, and Postmodernity* (Grand Rapids, MI: Brazos Press, 2000).

—, *With the Grain of the Universe: The Church's Witness and Natural* Theology, Gifford Lectures 2001 (London: SCM Press, 2002).

Haykin, Michael A. G., *Kiffin, Knollys and Keach: Rediscovering the English Baptist Heritage* (Darlington: Carey, 1996).

Helm, Paul, *Faith and Understanding* (Edinburgh: Edinburgh University Press, 1997).

Hendriksen, William, *The Gospel of John* (Edinburgh: Banner of Truth Trust, 1954).

Heth, W. A., and Wenham, G. J., *Jesus and Divorce* (London: Hodder & Stoughton, 1988).

Hippolytus, *The Apostolic Tradition*, trans. Burton Scott Easton (Cambridge: Cambridge University Press, 1934).

Holmes, Stephen R., *God of Grace and God of Glory: An Account of the Theology of Jonathan Edwards* (Edinburgh: T & T Clark, 2000).

—, 'The Upholding of Beauty: A Reading of Anselm's *Cur Deus Homo*', *SJT* 54 (2001), pp. 189-203.

—, *Listening to the Past: The Place of Tradition in Theology* (Carlisle: Paternoster Press, 2002).

—, *Tradition and Renewal in Baptist Life* (Oxford: Whitley Publications, 2003).

—, 'Towards a Baptist Theology of Ordained Ministry', in *Baptist Sacramentalism*, eds Anthony R. Cross and Philip E. Thompson (Carlisle: Paternoster Press, 2003), pp. 247-262.

Hoskyns, Edwyn Clement, *The Fourth Gospel*, ed. Francis Noel Davey (London: Faber and Faber, 2nd edn, 1947)

Hubmaier, Balthasar, 'A Form of the Supper of Christ' (1527), in *Balthasar Hubmaier: Theologian of Anabaptism*, trans. and ed., H. W. Pipkin, and J. H. Yoder (Scottdale, PA: Herald Press, 1989), pp. 393-408.

Irenaeus, *Against Heresies*, in *ANF*, vol. 1, pp. 315-567.

Irving, Edward, *Christ's Holiness in Flesh, The Form, Fountain Head, and Assurance to Us of Holiness in Flesh* (Edinburgh: John Lindsay, 1831).

—, *The Day of Pentecost or The Baptism with the Holy Ghost* (Edinburgh: John Lindsay, 1831).

—, *The Collected Writings of Edward Irving in Five Volumes*, ed. Carlyle, G. (London: Alexander Strahan, 1864).

Israel, Martin, *Healing as Sacrament: The Sanctification of the World* (London: Darton, Longman and Todd, 1984).

Jenkins, Jonathan L., 'Newman, Luther and Justification', *Pro Ecclesia* 7 (1998), pp. 10-16.

Jenson, Robert W., *America's Theologian: A Recommendation of Jonathan Edwards* (Oxford and New York: Oxford University Press, 1988)

—, 'The Father, he...', in Alvin F. Kimel Jr. (ed.), *Speaking the Christian God: The Holy Trinity and the Challenge of Feminism* (Grand Rapids, MI: Eerdmans, 1992), pp. 95-109.

—, 'What is the Point of Trinitarian Theology?', in Christoph Schwöbel (ed.), *Trinitarian Theology Today: Essays on Divine Being and Act* (Edinburgh: T & T Clark, 1995), pp. 31–43.

—, 'Hermeneutics and the Life of the Church', in *Reclaiming the Bible for the Church*, ed. Carl E. Braaten and Robert W. Jenson (Edinburgh: T & T Clark, 1995), pp. 89-105.

—, 'The Church and the Sacraments', in *The Cambridge Companion to Christian Doctrine*, ed. Colin E. Gunton (Cambridge: Cambridge University Press, 1997), pp. 207-225.

—, *Systematic Theology*, vol. 1, *The Triune God* (Oxford and New York: Oxford University Press, 1997).

—, *Systematic Theology*, vol. 2, *The Works of God* (Oxford and New York: Oxford University Press, 1999).

Jeremias, Joachim, *The Eucharistic Words of Jesus*, trans. Norman Perrin (London: SCM Press, 1966).

Pope John Paul II, *The Splendor of Truth* (*Veritatis Splendor*), Encyclical Letter 6 August 1993.

—, *Ut unum sint: Encyclical Letter of the Holy Father John Paul II on Commitment to Ecumenism* (London: Catholic Truth Society, 1995).

Johnson, William Stacy, *The Mystery of God: Karl Barth and the Postmodern Foundations of Theology* (Louisville, KY: Westminster John Knox Press, 1997).

Jüngel, Eberhard, *The Doctrine of the Trinity: God's Being is in Becoming*, trans. Horton Harris (Edinburgh and London: Scottish Academic Press, 1976).

Kelly, J. N. D., *A Commentary on the Epistles of Peter and of Jude* (London: Adam and Charles Black, 1969).

Kendall, R. T., *Once Saved, Always Saved: Biblical Assurance for Every True Believer* (London: Hodder and Stoughton, 1983).

Klaassen, Walter (ed.), *Anabaptism in Outline: Selected Primary Sources*, (Scottdale, PA: Herald Press, 1981).

Kreider, Alan, *The Change of Conversion and the Origin of Christendom* (Harrisburg, PA: Trinity, 1999).

Lathrop, Gordon W., *Holy Things: A Liturgical Theology* (Minneapolis, MN: Fortress Press, 1993)

—, *Holy People: A Liturgical Ecclesiology* (Minneapolis, MN: Fortress Press, 1999)

Lawson, A. B., *John Wesley and the Christian Ministry: The Sources and Development of His Opinions and Practice* (London: SPCK, 1963).

Leeming, B., *Principles of Sacramental Theology* (London: Longmans, Green, 1956).

Leenhardt, F. J., *Ceci est mon corps* (Neuchâtel: Delachaux and Niestle, 1955).

Lewis, C. S., *The Great Divorce* (London: G. Bles, 1952).

Limouris, Gennadios, and Vaporis, Nomikos Michael (eds.), *Orthodox Perspectives on Baptism, Eucharist, and Ministry*, Faith and Order Papers 128 (Brookline, MA: Holy Cross Orthodox Press, 1985).

Lindars, Barnabas, *The Theology of the Letter to the Hebrews* (Cambridge: Cambridge University Press, 1991).

Lloyd-Jones, D. M., 'John Bunyan: Church Union', in *Light from John Bunyan and other Puritans* (London: Westminster Conference, 1978), pp. 86-102.

Lodge, David, *Working with Structuralism: Essays and Reviews on Nineteenth- and Twentieth-Century Literature* (London and New York: Routledge, 2nd edn, 1991).

—, *Small World: An Academic Romance* (1984), in *A David Lodge Trilogy* (London: Penguin, 1993)

Long, Thomas G., *The Witness of Preaching* (Louisville, KY: Westminster John Knox, 1989).

Lucas, Ernest (ed.), *Christian Healing: What can we Believe?* (London: Lynx, 1997).

Luther, Martin, *Luther's Works*, vols. 1–55, gen. ed. (vols. 1–30) Jaroslav Pelikan, gen. ed. (vols. 31–55) Helmut T. Lehmann (Philadelphia, PA: Muhlenberg Press, 1955–75).

Macquarrie, John, 'Baptism, Confirmation, Eucharist', in *Signs of Faith, Hope and Love: The Christian Sacraments Today*, eds. John Greenhalgh and Elizabeth Russell (London: St Mary's Bourne Street, 1987), pp. 57-70.

—, *A Guide to the Sacraments* (London: SCM Press, 1997).

Marpeck, Pilgram, *The Writings of Pilgram Marpeck*, trans. and ed. William Klassen and Walter Klaassen (Scottdale, PA: Herald Press, 1978).

Marsden, George M., *Fundamentalism and American Culture: The Shaping of Twentieth-Century Evangelicalism, 1870–1925* (New York and Oxford: Oxford University Press, 1982).

Marshall, I. Howard, *1 Peter*, IVP New Testament Commentary Series (Leicester: IVP, 1991).

Martos, J., *Doors to the Sacred: A Historical Introduction to Sacraments in the Christian Church* (Ligouri, MO: Triumph Books, 1991).

Matzko, David McCarthy, 'The Performance of the Good: Ritual Action and the Moral Life', *Pro Ecclesia* 7 (1998), pp. 199-215.

Meyendorff, Paul, *The Sacrament of Healing in the Orthodox Church* (Crestwood, NY: St. Vladimir's Seminary Press, 2003).

McFadyen, Alistair, *Bound to Sin: Abuse, Holocaust and the Christian Doctrine of Sin* (Cambridge: Cambridge University Press, 2000).

McFarlane, Graham, *Christ and the Spirit: The Doctrine of the Incarnation According to Edward Irving* (Carlisle: Paternoster Press, 1996).

McGrath, Alister E., (ed.), *The Christian Theology Reader* (Oxford: Blackwell, 2nd edn, 2001).

Milbank, John, *Theology and Social Theory* (Oxford: Blackwell, 1990).

Milbank, John, *et al* (eds.), *Radical Orthodoxy: A New Theology* (London: Routledge, 1999).

Milton, John, *Milton: Poetical Works*, ed. Douglas Bush (Oxford: Oxford University Press, 1966)

—, *The Complete Prose Works of John Milton*, vols. 1-3, ed. Don M. Wofle, Ernest Sirluck and Merritt Y. Hughes (New Haven, CT: Yale University Press, 1953-1962)

Molnar, Paul D., *Karl Barth and the Theology of the Lord's Supper* (New York: Peter Lang, 1996)

Moltmann, Jürgen, *The Crucified God: The Cross of Christ as the Foundation and Criticism of Christian Theology*, trans. R. A. Wilson and J. Bowden (London: SCM Press, 1974).

—, *The Church in the Power of the Holy Spirit: A Contribution to Messianic Ecclesiology*, trans. Margaret Kohl (London: SCM Press, 1977).

—, *The Trinity and the Kingdom of God: The Doctrine of God*, trans. Margaret Kohl (London: SCM Press, 1981).

—, *The Spirit of Life: A Universal Affirmation*, trans. Margaret Kohl (London: SCM Press, 1992).

Mühlen, Heribert, *Una Mystica Persona: die Kirche als das Mysterium der Identität des Heiligen Geistes in Christus und den Christen—eine Person in vielen Personen* (München: F. Schöning, 1964).

Newton, Isaac, *Philosophiae Naturalis Principia Mathematica* (1687), trans. I. B. Cohen and A. Whitman (Los Angeles, CA: University of California Press, 1997).

Noll, Mark A., (ed.), *The Princeton Theology, 1812–1921: Scripture, Science, and the Theological Method from Archibald Alexander to Benjamin Breckinridge Warfield* (Grand Rapids, MI: Baker Book House, 1983).

Owen, John, *A Discourse Concerning the Holy Spirit* (1674), in *The Works of John Owen*, vol. 3, ed. W. H. Goold (London: Banner of Truth Trust, 1965).

—, *The Death of Death in the Death of Christ*, in *The Works of John Owen*, vol. 10, ed. W.H. Goold, (London: Banner of Truth Trust, 1967), pp. 140-421.

Paley, William, *Natural Theology, or Evidences of the Existence and Attributes of the Deity Collected from the Appearances of Nature* (London: R. Faulder, 1802)

Pannenberg, Wolfhart, *Systematic Theology*, vol. 2, trans. Geoffrey W. Bromiley (Edinburgh: T & T Clark, 1994)

Payne, Ernest A., *The Fellowship of Believers: Baptist Thought and Practice Yesterday and Today* (London: Carey Kingsgate Press, 2nd edn, 1952).

Perkins, Pheme, *Interpretation: A Bible Commentary for Teaching and Preaching: First and Second Peter, James, and Jude*, New Testament ed. Paul J. Achtemeier (Louisville, KY: John Knox Press, 1995).

Pickstock, Catherine, *After Writing: On the Liturgical Consummation of Philosophy* (Oxford: Blackwell, 1998).

Pinnock, Clark H., *Most Moved Mover: A Theology of God's Openness* (Carlisle: Paternoster Press, 2001).

Powers, Joseph, *Eucharistic Theology* (London: Burns and Oates, 1968).

Pusey, Edward B., *The Doctrine of the Real Presence, as Contained in the Fathers from the Death of St. John the Evangelist to the Fourth General Council* (Oxford and London: J. H. Parker, 1855).

Quick, O. C., *The Christian Sacraments* (London: Nisbet, 2nd edn, 1932).

Rahner, K., *The Church and the Sacraments* (Tunbridge Wells: Burns & Oates, 1963).

Reicke, Bo, *The Disobedient Spirits and Christian Baptism: A Study of 1 Pet. III.19 and its Context* (København: Ejnar Munksgaard, 1946).

Robinson, H. Wheeler, *The Life and Faith of the Baptists* (London: Methuen, 1927).

Rogers, Eugene F., Jr., *Sexuality and the Christian Body* (Oxford: Blackwell, 1999).

Ruether, Rosemary Radford, 'The Female Nature of God: A Problem in Contemporary Religious Life', in J. B. Metz and E. Schillebeeckx (eds.), *'God as Father?'*, *Concilium* 143 (New York and Edinburgh: Seabury Press and T & T Clark, 1981), pp. 61-66.

Russell, Bertrand, *History of Western Philosophy and its Connection with Political and Social Circumstances from the Earliest Times to the Present Day* (London: Unwin, 2nd edn, 1979).

Sanders, E. P., *Paul and Palestinian Judaism: A Comparison of Patterns of Religion* (Minneapolis, MN: Fortress Press, 1985).

—, *Jesus and Judaism* (London: SCM Press, 1985).

—, *Paul, the Law and the Jewish People* (London: SCM Press, 1985)

Schelkle, Karl Hermann, *Herders Theologischer Kommentar zum Neuen Testament* XIII, 2, *Die Petrusbriefe der Judasbrief* (Freiburg, Basel & Wien: Herder, 1980).

Schillebeeckx, Edward, *Christ the Sacrament* (London: Sheed and Ward, 1963).

—, *The Eucharist* (London: Sheed & Ward, 1968).

Schmemann, Alexander, *The World as Sacrament* (London: Darton, Longman and Todd, 1965).

Schweizer, Eduard, *Church Order in the New Testament*, trans. Frank Clarke (London: SCM Press, 1961).

Scott, David A., 'Creation as Christ: A Problematic Theme in Some Feminist Theology', in Alvin F. Kimel Jr. (ed.), *Speaking the Christian God: The Holy Trinity and the Challenge of Feminism* (Grand Rapids, MI: Eerdmans, 1992), pp. 237-257.

Searle, John R., *Expression and Meaning: Studies in the Theory of Speech Acts* (Cambridge: Cambridge University Press, 1985).

Sibbes, Richard, *A Description of Christ* (1639), in *Works of Richard Sibbes*, vol. 1, ed. Alexander B. Grosart (Edinburgh: Banner of Truth Trust, 1973), pp. 1-31.

Smail, Tom, *The Giving Gift: The Holy Spirit in Person* (London: Hodder and Stoughton, 1988).

Snyder, C. A., *The Life and Thought of Michael Sattler* (Scottdale, PA: Herald Press, 1984).

Souter, Alexander, *Tertullian's Treatises: Concerning Prayer, Concerning Baptism* (London: SPCK, 1919).

Spurgeon, C. H., *Till He Come: Communion Meditations and Addresses* (London: Passmore & Alabaster, 1896).

—, *Lectures to My Students* (London: Marshall, Morgan & Scott, 1954).

Stendahl, Krister, *Paul Among Jews and Gentiles* (Philadelphia, PA: Fortress Press, 1976)

Stevenson, Kenneth W., *Gregory Dix 25 Years On*, Grove Liturgical Study 10 (Bramcote: Grove Books, 1977).

Strachan, Gordon, *The Pentecostal Theology of Edward Irving* (London: Darton, Longman & Todd, 1973).

Temple, William, *Nature, Man and God* (London: Macmillan, 1940).

Tertullian, *On the Resurrection of the Flesh*, in *ANF*, vol. 3, pp. 545-594.

—, *Against Praxeas*, in *ANF*, vol. 3, pp. 597-627.

—, *On Baptism*, in *ANF*, vol. 3, pp. 669-679.

—, *Against Hermogenes*, in *ANF*, vol. 3, pp. 477-502.

Thatcher, Adrian (ed.), *Celebrating Christian Marriage* (Edinburgh: T & T Clark, 2001).

Thiselton, Anthony C., *New Horizons in Hermeneutics* (London: HarperCollins, 1992).

Thomas Aquinas, *Summa Theologica*, trans. by Fathers of the English Dominican Province (Westminster, MD: Christian Classics, 1981).

—, *Philosophical Texts*, selected and trans. Thomas Gilby (Oxford: Oxford University Press, 1951).

Thornton, L. S., *Confirmation: Its Place in the Baptismal Mystery* (London: Dacre Press, 1954).

Tillard, Jean-Marie Roger, O.P., *Église d'églises: L'ecclésiologie de communion* (Paris: Cerf, 1987)

Torrance, T. F., *The Ground and Grammar of Theology* (Belfast: Christian Journals, 1980).

—, *Karl Barth: Biblical and Evangelical Theologian* (Edinburgh: T & T Clark, 1990).

Vanhoozer, Kevin J., *Is There a Meaning in this Text? The Bible, the Reader, and the Morality of Literary Knowledge* (Leicester: Apollos, 1998).

Verduin, Leonard, *The Reformers and their Stepchildren* (Grand Rapids, MI: Eerdmans, 1964).

Vos, Arvin, *Aquinas, Calvin, and Contemporary Protestant Thought: A Critique of Protestant Views on the Thought of Thomas Aquinas* (Grand Rapids, MI: Eerdmans, 1985).

Walker, Michael J., *Baptists at the Table: the Theology of the Lord's Supper amongst English Baptists in the Nineteenth Century* (Didcot: Baptist Historical Society, 1992).

Warfield, B. B., *The Works of Benjamin B. Warfield*, vol. 1, *Revelation and Inspiration* (Grand Rapids, MI: Baker Book House, 1981).

Watson, Francis, *Text, Church and World: Biblical Interpretation in Theological Perspective* (Edinburgh: T. & T. Clark, 1994).

—, *Text and Truth: Redefining Biblical Theology* (Edinburgh: T & T Clark, 1997).

Webster, John, *Barth's Ethics of Reconciliation* (Cambridge: Cambridge University Press, 1995).

—, *Barth's Moral Theology: Human Action in Barth's Thought* (Edinburgh: T & T Clark, 1998).

—, 'The Self-Organizing Power of the Gospel of Christ: Episcopacy and Community Formation', *IJST* 3 (2001), pp. 69-82.

Weinandy, Thomas G., *Does God Suffer?* (Edinburgh: T & T Clark, 2000).

West, W. M. S., 'The Child and the Church: A Baptist Perspective', in W. H. Brackney, P. S. Fiddes and J. H. Y. Briggs (eds), *Pilgrim Pathways: Essays in Honour of B. R. White* (Macon, GA: Mercer University Press, 1999), pp. 88-92.

White, B. R., *The English Baptists of the Seventeenth Century* (London: Baptist Historical Society, 1983).

White, Keith J., *A Place for Us* (London: Mill Grove, 1981).

White, R. E. O., *The Biblical Doctrine of Initiation* (London: Hodder & Stoughton, 1960).

Williams, G. H., *The Radical Reformation* (Philadelphia, PA: Westminster Press, 1962).

Williams, Rowan, 'The Nature of a Sacrament', in *Signs of Faith, Hope and Love: The Christian Sacraments Today*, eds. John Greenhalgh and Elizabeth Russell (London: St Mary's Bourne Street, 1987), pp. 32-44.

On Christian Theology (Oxford: Blackwell, 1999).

Wolterstorff, Nicholas, *Divine Discourse: Philosophical Reflections on the Claim that God Speaks* (Cambridge: Cambridge University Press, 1995).

World Council of Churches, Faith and Order Commission, *One Baptism, One Eucharist and a Mutually Recognized Ministry: Three Agreed Statements* (Geneva: World Council of Churches, 1975).

—, *Baptism, Eucharist and Ministry* (Geneva: World Council of Churches, 1982).

—, *Baptism, Eucharist and Ministry 1892–1990: Report on the Process and Responses* (Geneva: World Council of Churches, 1990).

Yoder, J. H., (trans. and ed.) *The Legacy of Michael Sattler* (Scottdale, PA: Herald Press, 1973).

Young, Frances, '"Creatio ex Nihilo": A Context for the Emergence of the Christian Doctrine of Creation', *SJT* 44 (1991), pp. 139-151.

Zizioulas, John, *Being as Communion: Studies in Personhood and the Church* (London: Darton Longman and Todd, 1985).

Zwingli, Ulrich, *Selected Works*, ed. Samuel Macauley Jackson (Philadelphia, PA: University of Pennsylvannia, 1972).

Scripture Index

Name Index

Subject Index

Lord's Supper Ch. 7 *passim*
and 'communion' 74, 160-
161, 176-177
and Church unity 74-75,
176-178
and human agency 171-174
and pagan sacrifice 155-156
and Passover meal 156-159
and physical presence of
Christ 166-169, 175-176
and prayer 159, 161, 173,
175
as eschatologically oriented
74, 159
as means of grace 74, 149,
171
as sign/symbol 156, 161-162
common communion 253-
255
exclusion from partaking
188-189
mediate-ness 169-176
participation in Christ 158-
163, 174-177
sacrificial nature 155-162
transubstantiation 163-166,
170-171
veneration of reserved
sacrament 175-176
Lumen Gentium 80, 83-84, 126
nn.54-55, 127 nn.56 and 58

Marburg Colloquy 166 n.30
marriage Ch. 11 *passim*
and grace 236-237, 248
and mystery 233-234
and sexuality 242-244
as covenantal 236-242
as sacramental 233-237,
240-241
mechanistic worldview 48-51

ordained ministry – see
'Christian ministry',
'apostolic succession'

paedo-baptism – see 'baptism,
and children'

Pelagianism 141 n.23
penance 76-77, Ch. 8 *passim*
and confession 184-190
and grace 184-186, 194
and participation in Christ
193-194
and satisfaction or penalty
190-195
as sacramental 194
as virtue 192-193
Pentecostalism 145-148, 206
priesthood of all believers 213-
214
promise 29-30
See also under 'Christian
ministry', 'sacraments'

redemption – see 'creation'
repentance 183-185, 189-190

Sabellianism 31-32
sacraments
and belief/discernment 58
and grace 6-11, 29-30,
172,184, 255
and human action 115-118
and mystery 4-5, 58-59
and promise 57-59, 111
and the 'sacramental' 3-4
as sign/symbol 5-7, 10-11,
59-61
eschatological orientation
61
See also 'baptism',
'Christian ministry',
'church', 'creation',
'healing', 'Holy Spirit',
'marriage', 'penance'
sacrifice – see under 'Jesus
Christ' and 'Lord's Supper'
salvation 126-130
Schleitheim Confession 67-70,
212 n.2
and the 'ban' 75
Scripture
and meaning 88-94, 102
and the Holy Spirit 89-90,
95-100, 103-105